CLASSIC KNITS OF THE 1980s

CLASSIC KNITS OF THE 1980s

SANDY BLACK

THE CROWOOD PRESS

First published in 2021 by
The Crowood Press Ltd
Ramsbury, Marlborough
Wiltshire SN8 2HR

enquiries@crowood.com

www.crowood.com

© Sandy Black 2021

All rights reserved. No part of this publication may be reproduced or transmitted in any form or by any means, electronic or mechanical, including photocopy, recording, or any information storage and retrieval system, without permission in writing from the publishers.

British Library Cataloguing-in-Publication Data
A catalogue record for this book is available from the British Library.

ISBN 978 1 78500 802 3

Dedication
This book is for Kevin, who shared all the twists and turns of the fantastic knitwear journey.

Photo credits
The modelled Sandy Black knitwear images have been taken by different photographers over time; see the individual captions. Jo Teasdale created the brand new photographs; original 1980s photographs were taken by David McIntyre, Barbara Bellingham, and Paul Dennison. Barbara Bellingham and Paul Dennison also provided a few of the close-up photographs as indicated. All other knitting close-up and documentary images are by Morris Baker; early knitwear and inspiration photographs are my own. I am grateful to Rowan Yarns for permission to reproduce their 1980s images of Sandy Black designs plus designs by Artwork, Susan Duckworth and Martin Kidman. Thanks also to designers Kaffe Fassett, Sasha Kagan and Patricia Roberts for providing images. Historical knitting images were supplied by V&A Images, and *Visionary Knitwear* exhibition images by the Fashion and Textile Museum London. Thanks go to Nolan Simon and 47 Canal for permission to reproduce his Sweater painting of my landscape design.

Frontispiece
Original 1985 image of the Lion and Unicorn sweater – part of the Sandy Black Original Knits Heraldic collection. (Photo: David McIntyre)

Disclaimer
Every effort has been made to trace the original copyright holders of the images in this book.
Please contact the publisher in case of queries.

Typeset by Kelly-Anne Levey
Printed and bound in India by Parksons Graphics

CONTENTS

Preface 7

Introduction 13

Part 1: Knitwear Design, Techniques and Inspiration

1	Knitwear in Fashion, and the 1980s Knitwear Revolution	19
2	Design and Inspiration	29
3	Knitting-Pattern Fundamentals	49
4	Working with Colour and Imagery	63
5	Designing Knitwear	71

Part 2: The Knitting Patterns

	Introduction	89
6	Textural	95
7	Graphic	117
8	Floral	151
9	Heraldic	175
10	Ornamental	195
11	Accessories	231

Appendix 261

Endnotes 266

Acknowledgements 268

Index 269

PREFACE

Long before beginning my own knitwear business, I would regularly collect haberdashery- and knitting-related items that interested me – old knitting patterns from the 1930s to the 1960s; large quantities of buttons, in all shapes and sizes that were like sweets in their varied colours, purchased from wholesalers; patterns and materials (with no clear purpose for them at the time); wonderful beehive-shaped yarn holders, produced by Patons Yarns to promote their Beehive brand of yarns and now collectors' pieces, made of colourful Bakelite; and knitting needles and accessories made of Bakelite, metal, wood, plastic and bone.

From the late 1970s, through the 1980s and into the 1990s, I ran my Sandy Black Original Knits designer-knitwear label as one of a distinctive and influential group of British knitwear designers producing one-off pieces and fashion collections that were sold internationally in prestigious fashion stores worldwide. This style of handmade, colourful and fun fashion knitwear became highly popular, and designs and patterns were featured regularly in the fashion and craft press. Having regularly designed knitting patterns for magazines and books, I took the bold step of producing some of my ready-to-wear designs as colourful knitting kits and published patterns for home knitters. In 1982, my partner and I developed Sandy Black: our own brand of knitting yarns and colours in wool, mohair, cotton and luxurious 100-per-cent angora, for home knitting.

My career has followed an unconventional path in both the fashion industry and academia. With a great love of knitting and its potential, but without any formal training, I became a knitwear designer and created an international fashion-knitwear business. At school, I was equally interested in both the sciences and the arts and decided to specialize in mathematics in an attempt to bridge the two fields. Having learnt to knit and crochet as a child, taught by my mother and grandmother, I loved making things for myself. My interest in hand knitting was revived whilst studying mathematics at university, as a practical way to make interesting and unusual clothes, and I was regularly to be seen knitting in public and around the campus – much to the amusement of everyone. 'My gran knits!' was a regular comment, as knitting was thought to be so old-fashioned then.

Knitting was for me a perfect combination of mathematics and creative arts. I was inspired by the infinite potential of

OPPOSITE PAGE: The Swanscape sweater, one of my signature range of landscape and skyscape sweaters, here in a dramatic colour palette. Worked in machine-knitted intarsia with wool, angora and rayon yarns. The range included a statement dress with a similar design over the entire front. (Photo: Barbara Bellingham)

Early examples of knitwear that I made by machine and by hand, including a Fair Isle-patterned man's sweater and a lacy woman's sweater, inspired by knitting traditions from the 1930s and 1940s. Note the green sweater with children's characters Noddy and Big Ears (from Enid Blyton books). This was my first foray into hand-worked intarsia knitting and design.

The Alpaca Fields landscape sweater with embroidered flying ducks, worked in machine-knitted intarsia with alpaca–wool-blend yarns. (Photo: Barbara Bellingham)

A variety of machine-knitted cushions, created in sets of three to make a continuous picture.

yarns and the knitted stitch as a unit of pattern design and began to draw all kinds of images on my graph paper, from stylized characters to landscapes, for translation to hand knitting. A breakthrough came when I was still at university, when I bought a simple knitting machine. Using this machine, I could more rapidly explore the visual and textural possibilities of knitting as a medium for design. I was able to manipulate and 'interfere' with the basic knitting by using manual techniques, such as making bobbles, to create textural patterns, and to incorporate textured yarns into the surface of the fabric. But, my favourite technique became intarsia, which is a specialized manual process historically made on the simplest types of machine. The intarsia technique is similar to tapestry weaving on a loom, where it is possible to introduce an endless array of colours in each row. With this technique, I could create knitted imagery and pictures inspired by the paint-by-numbers kits that I had as a child – and the concept of the landscape sweater was born! I knew immediately that these endless possibilities were to become my full-time occupation, and I decided to be a knitwear designer, even though I wasn't sure how! I had hoped to go on to more formal study of knitted textiles; however, funding was difficult, and the link between mathematics and knitting was little understood at the time, so I forged my own independent career path, becoming a self-taught designer and entrepreneur running my own business.

As a self-taught designer, I had the benefit of not being constrained by any existing rules, so, in my view, anything can be translated into knitting. It was simply a question of visualizing an idea (based on inspirational sources) and then working out the logic of how to make it! This clearly owes something to my mathematics background – knitting is for me the perfect combination of creative, mathematical and technical skills. Supporting myself initially by teaching numeracy to adults[1], I set up my first small studio in a riverside warehouse in Rotherhithe, in the abandoned London docklands, making one-off commissions, and built up my business with a handful of skilled outworkers, selling my own range of designs for knitwear and soft furnishings. My key specialty was the invention of the landscape sweater – machine knitted in extremely fine yarns and using the intarsia technique; landscapes and skyscapes became part of my design signature. (*See* Chapters 2 and 4 for more information about the machine-knitted landscape sweaters and working the hand-knitted version of intarsia, respectively, and for examples of several landscape sweaters.)

The cover of the Wild Knitting *book, with quirky knitting patterns, first published by Mitchell Beazley in 1979.*

Fun Knitting, *a special edition of* Wild Knitting *that was published for Marks & Spencer in 1983, featuring the Sandy Black Winged Traveller design on the cover.*

At the same time, I worked as a freelance knitwear designer on special commissions for theatre, television, magazines and books. One notable commission in 1981 was to create three of the early costumes for the long-running London musical *Cats*. Another was from Courtaulds, to knit an 8-metre (26-foot)-long wall frieze with their Courtelle hand-knitting yarns for their 1980 trade-exhibition stand (*see* Chapter 2). I published many designs in women's and fashion magazines and in craft books, including *Wild Knitting*, one of the earliest books to celebrate a new wave of creativity in knitting (first published in 1979 by Mitchell Beazley), for which I designed a fun armadillo wrap and a more sophisticated batwing cardigan, featured on the cover of a second, special edition. This book was way ahead of its time and is still inspiring and relevant to new knitters now.

My work was featured widely in the press, and I made several appearances on national television and radio, including for BBC radio's *Woman's Hour* and BBC TV's

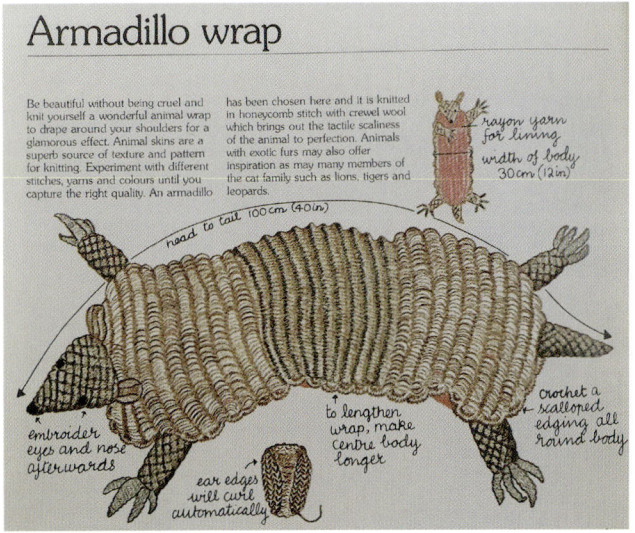

A sketch of my Armadillo wrap, featured in Wild Knitting *(1979).*

The Knitting Fashion *book published by BBC Television to accompany the 1976 television series, showing the popularity of knitting and crochet at the time.*

A Vogue *press cutting, October 1980, featuring the Sandy Black Midnight Mohair hand-knitted cardigan and Daytime Clouds machine-knitted sweater, both with bobbles.*

A Vogue *press cutting, January 1981, featuring the Sandy Black Five-Colour Clouds sweater, machine knitted in wool–angora-blend yarns.*

Nationwide, and two BBC television series, *Knitting Fashion* and *Bazaar,* where I was resident knitwear designer for two years, all testament to the popularity of knitting at the time.

By the start of the 1980s, my Sandy Black Original Knits collections of sweaters, cardigans and glamorous evening coats were selling in prestigious outlets in the UK and USA, and the business had expanded considerably. I was joined by my business partner Kevin Bolger, and we continued to show seasonal knitwear collections at the biannual international fashion fairs in Milan, London, New York and Tokyo for the following six years and sold to major fashion stores throughout the world, especially in the USA and Japan. Our customers included Saks Fifth Avenue, Bloomingdales and Bendel in New York; Takashimaya and Isetan in Tokyo; and Harrods, Harvey Nichols and Browns in London, plus key stores in Italy, Germany, Australia and Canada.

FAR LEFT: The Jigsaw pattern, one of a range of summer designs made in cotton, for the Georges Picaud yarn brand.

LEFT: The Fairisle Fun knitting-kit special offer in Woman *magazine, January 1983, launched our range of colourful kits for designs made in Sandy Black Mohair.*

As a complement to our ready-to-wear fashion knitwear, after publishing many designs and patterns in women's magazines, fashion magazines and books, we continued to develop the hand-knitting side of the business. In 1981, I designed and published two ranges of hand-knitting leaflets for Georges Picaud yarns in France.

One year later, we launched our range of unique Sandy Black branded yarns and hand-knitting kits for the UK and international fashion and craft retail markets.

My work was part of a British 'knitwear revolution', a craft-led design movement that repositioned knitwear as fashion and went on to influence the wider fashion industry, helping to inspire developments in industrial knitting technology (*see* Chapter 1).

Running a small fashion business was then, and still is, a challenging task. After fifteen years in business, including supporting textile-design students with work placements, I decided to continue my career teaching fashion knitwear design in the university sector. I became a lecturer in knitwear at the University of Brighton, where I directed the undergraduate programme in textiles and fashion, and was proud of the exciting work created by the students, including Julien Macdonald, who went on to make a key contribution to high-fashion knitwear under his own name and in French fashion houses. I later moved to the London College of Fashion (LCF), University of the Arts London, to set up and lead their new postgraduate Master's programme in Fashion Studies.

To celebrate a new wave of creativity in knitting, in 1997 I curated a touring exhibition, *The New Knitting*, and from this developed my book *Knitwear in Fashion*, on twentieth-century knitwear design. After leading the MA Fashion Studies programme for eight years at LCF, I became a Research Professor in Fashion and Textile Design and Technology. In this broader role, I have supervised many design-led PhD research students, led several funded research projects and published key books on knitting design and technology, the history of knitwear[2], and fashion design and sustainability (*see* Further Reading).

As a designer, businesswoman, lecturer, academic researcher and author, I have championed the study and creative practice of knitted textiles and knitwear and celebrated the unique design capabilities of knitted structures, whether made by hand or machine. I think of knitting as a form of soft engineering, with endless possibilities for shape, texture and form, and enjoy inventing textural stitches as much as working with imagery and graphic designs – and not forgetting the mathematics of working out the patterns!

The first Sandy Black Mohair knitting kit, packaged in a transparent shoulder bag including the colourful knitting yarns and full-colour pattern charts for the Fairisle Fun sweater. (V&A: T.64 & 65 -1999 © Victoria and Albert Museum, London)

Knitting continues to be for me the perfect blend of creative, mathematical and technical skills, which my education seemed to want to separate. Knitting used to be a poor relation of the textile crafts but has now grown to be recognized for its importance and flexibility for fashion, design and manufacturing – no longer old-fashioned but at the forefront of creative design and advanced technology.

INTRODUCTION

Inventive, handmade, colourful, fun and often generously oversized fashion knitwear was at the height of popularity from the late 1970s and throughout the 1980s. My own designs covered a wide range of inspirational themes, from bold and graphic to stylized imagery and florals. Several designs, including the Fairisle Fun sweater (Chapter 7) and Vase of Flowers coat (Chapter 8) became Sandy Black classics, and many inspired a new generation to learn to knit for themselves or at least to find a relative or friend to teach them to knit or to knit for them!

For this book, it has been a great pleasure to revisit my Sandy Black Original Knits designs, many of which are published for the first time here, and to make several patterns available to contemporary knitters after their being long out of print. The book offers the knitter insights into my approach to the development of these original and fashionable designs from the 1980s. A selection of popular designs, updated for currently available yarns, are included here to inspire knitters across a range of abilities, with a special focus on working with multiple colours and imagery, using clear charts. The designs are grouped into my signature themes – Textural, Graphic, Floral, Heraldic and Ornamental.

This book is for anyone and everyone who loves to knit – whether a novice or a more experienced knitter. Each will find plenty of inspiration and scope to extend their practice.

I have written the book to suit any knitter with some basic skills and knitting knowledge and to inspire and challenge those who are a little more experienced. You will need to be comfortable with the fundamental processes of knitting – casting on and off, knitting stitches, purling stitches, cabling, increasing and decreasing; for absolute beginners, there are now many resources available online to teach these skills, complemented by an extensive network of local knitting groups. The designs are not graded in degree of difficulty, but clear descriptions are given in the introduction to each pattern of the techniques and methods involved in the design, plus hints on achieving the best results. You will be carefully guided through each pattern, so don't be put off, as many designs – such as patchwork ones – are not as difficult as they may seem. Why not be bold and try something different?

The designs in this book use the basic stitches of stocking stitch (US term: stockinette), reverse stocking stitch, garter stitch and moss stitch, plus bobbles, twisted rib and a variety of cable stitches. Each pattern includes explanation of the

OPPOSITE PAGE: *Designs to knit for each of the six themes featured in Part 2: Textural – Travelling Vine tunic; Graphic – Triangles sweater; Floral – Persian Flower tunic; Heraldic – Lion and Unicorn sweater; Ornamental – Rosette tunic; Accessories – Leopard scarf and mittens. Photos: Jo Teasdale.*

specific bobbles or cable stitches used. The majority of the patterns – multicoloured designs in stocking stitch, designs using textural stitches, or a combination – are to be knitted from clear charts together with step-by-step instructions for shaping. This is a method that I championed in my 1980s knitting kits and published patterns. I strongly believe that visual pattern methods are excellent for communicating the design and helping the knitter to keep their place, and visually presented patterns are ultimately easier to follow than are purely written instructions, including for stitch-based designs. If you are new to charted-colourwork knitting, there is a range of options to suit your level of skill and experience. Some designs (such as the Dogtooth sweater and jacket) utilize smaller repeating motifs but others, such as the Shield sweater and cardigan, follow a non-repeating design chart for the entire piece and are a little more challenging. The Lion and Unicorn sweater is the most complex of the charted designs, because of the detail and intensity of the design. The Shawl cardigan, in contrast, is fully charted but has a limited amount of colourwork in each pattern row and is therefore easier than it may appear. All the charts give a clear picture of the knitting as it progresses and are not difficult to follow by using simple rules, as explained in Chapter 3. Also included are two designs – the Zig-Zag Cable sweater and Bobbly Grid cardigan – that are to be knitted from step-by-step written instructions, without the use of any charts. Today, due to the growth in popularity of lace knitting, knitters are more familiar with working from stitch charts and also working in the round with circular needles. This was not the case in the 1980s, when the majority of patterns were knitted flat, from the bottom up, on two straight needles. The original patterns in this book therefore reflect this method of working.

Chapter Structure and Overview

The book is divided into two main parts. In Part 1 of the book, I have shared my approach to designing, with ideas for gathering inspiration, and the design process for translating ideas into knitting designs, plus techniques for working with multiple colours and using charts. Finishing touches are also covered, including making up and embroidery.

Part 2 comprises the knitting patterns: twenty-four designs for sweaters, cardigans, jackets and longer-length tunics, plus accessories – my fun cat scarves and mittens, and a colourful set of beret and mittens. Most designs feature graphic patterning or imagery, some simple, others more intricate; three designs – Zig-Zag Cable sweater, Travelling Vine tunic and Bobbly Grid cardigan – rely mainly on textural stitches for their visual effect.

Throughout the book and especially in Part 2, original photographs of a wider range of design ideas around each theme are featured to give you further inspiration, as well as insights into design variations.

The first chapter sets the fashion context of the knitwear revolution of the late 1970s to early 1980s that came out of the crafts revival of the 1970s and the fashions of the 1980s. The second chapter, Design and Inspiration, looks at sources of inspiration and includes detailed examples of two commissioned (non-fashion) projects that I developed at that time. Chapter 3 covers the knitting-pattern fundamentals of getting to grips with the basic mechanics of knitwear design and understanding knitting patterns, such as tension and stitch calculations, plus working from charts. Chapter 4 focuses on working with colour and imagery, including the design of imagery by using charts, plus working with multiple colours and with different colour combinations. Chapter 5 guides you through the process of designing knitwear from your own inspiration, giving examples of heraldic-patterned sweaters and a patchwork design. It is not essential to read all chapters before starting a pattern, but I do suggest working through Chapter 3, to understand the importance of checking your tension.

Part 2 comprises twenty-four knitwear designs selected from my collections from 1980 to 1990, including fun animal accessories. These have full knitting instructions and are grouped into the design themes of Textural, Graphic, Floral, Heraldic and Ornamental. Many designs have been reknitted using contemporary yarns, mainly pure wools and mohair blends, and re-photographed, but the proportions and styling are true to the 1980s originals, with their oversized, generous silhouettes. These are complemented by the original photographs from the 1980s, together with photos of companion designs, to show variations on themes, including several designed for Rowan Yarns' early booklets.

Overview of the Designs and Patterns

Part 2 starts with an overview of the basic stitches and abbreviations used throughout the following patterns. Each pattern is self-contained and guides the knitter through all of the relevant steps for checking tension and explains any special stitches used for that particular pattern. More detailed explanations of techniques can be found in Chapter 3, if required.

Chapter 6 features two Textural designs knitted in pure wool: the casual Zig-Zag Cable sweater, which is worked in moss stitch and simple cables, from written instructions, and the more complex Travelling Vine tunic, which is worked from stitch-pattern charts featuring three original motifs created with different types of cable stitches and bobbles.

Covering the Graphic theme, Chapter 7 includes patterns that were all designed for mohair-blend yarns and featuring different methods of combining colours: the Bobbly Grid cardigan features a simple all-over grid pattern made with bobbles of several colours and is worked from written instructions; the classic Dogtooth sweater and jacket are worked in two-colour stranded-colourwork (Fair Isle) knitting from a simple, small chart to achieve a dramatic effect; the Triangles sweater features a repeated triangle shape knitted with the intarsia (colour-block) technique by using multiple colours, randomly placed, and has a separately knitted yoke; and the popular Fairisle Fun sweater design features a simple patchwork technique, with colourful Fair Isle panels cleverly knitted in different directions.

The first two designs in the Floral-theme Chapter 8 are knitted in mohair yarns and take a naturalistic approach: the all-over-patterned Trailing Roses sweater is worked from a full chart in a repeating pattern and the batwing Iris sweater, knitted in one piece from cuff to cuff, features an elegant iris spray on the front, worked from a chart. The third design, the Persian Flower tunic, is knitted in pure wool, with an intricate stylized floral-border design that is worked from a chart, and knitted flower motifs scattered over the body and sleeves, positioned according to the body and sleeve charts.

The designs in the next two chapters are worked by following colour charts for the entire design.

Heraldic-theme Chapter 9 includes two designs: the boldly-patterned designs of the Shield sweater and cardigan feature large and small coloured shield motifs that change texture between stocking stitch and reverse stocking stitch; the more challenging Lion and Unicorn sweater design has the same intricate heraldic patterns on the back and the front and complementary plain sleeves with a bobble trefoil motif.

The Ornamental-theme Chapter 10 comprises three intricate-looking designs, knitted with different approaches: the impactful Azulejos tunic and jacket are made up of a patchwork of separate small 'tiles' (azulejos means 'tiles' in Portuguese) that are knitted in three colours and sewn together, with knitted-on edgings; the Rosette tunic design is based on a simple repeating circle motif formed into larger rosettes by changing colours according to the chart; and the *trompe l'œil* effect Shawl cardigan features simple cabled or plain-knit areas around an intricate border design worked from the chart, with flower motifs embroidered over the shawl part.

The final Accessories in Chapter 11 include fun designs featuring animals – the Leopard, Tiger and Siamese Cat scarves, with matching Leopard and Tiger mittens, plus the Striped beret and mittens to use up your leftover colours. The three animal scarves are worked from charts, with the simpler Siamese Cat scarf requiring a colourwork chart only for the face, as the rest is knitted plain. The Striped beret and mittens patterns are presented here for circular knitting but can of course be knitted flat, if preferred.

I hope that you will find something amongst the designs to suit your taste and provide a little challenge and that you will enjoy knitting the pieces as much as I enjoyed designing them. Once you have tried out some of the ideas, I also hope you will gain more confidence to adopt the methods for your own creations. So, surprise yourself, get knitting and have fun!

PART 1

KNITWEAR DESIGN, TECHNIQUES AND INSPIRATION

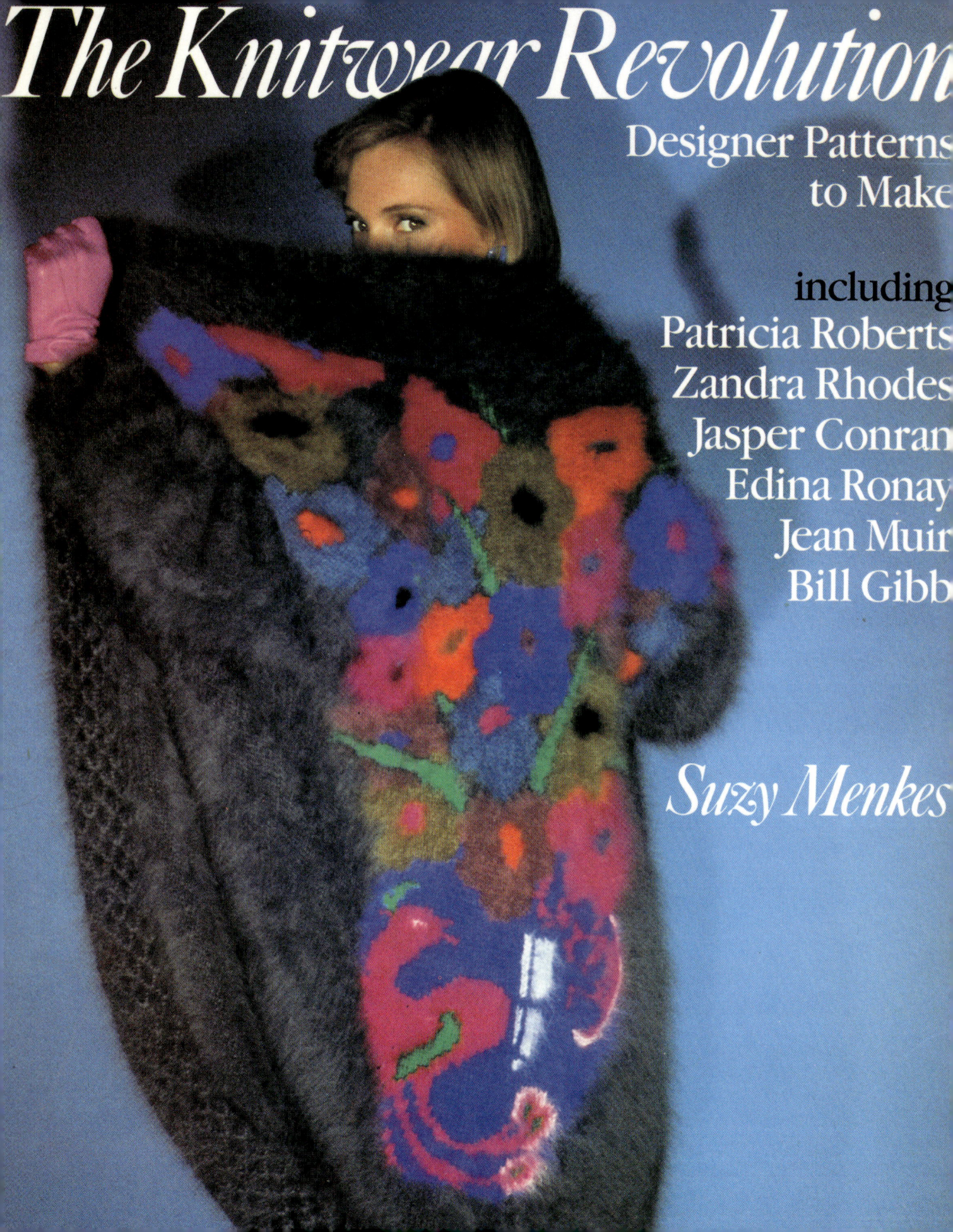

CHAPTER 1

KNITWEAR IN FASHION, AND THE 1980s KNITWEAR REVOLUTION

Some Knitting History

Knitting is an ancient, distinctive and versatile method of constructing textiles, with a long but relatively uncertain history – its origins and evolution may never be definitively proven. The historical record is very patchy, and there is no reliable existing evidence of truly knitted artefacts before the twelfth to thirteenth centuries. Several foot coverings (toe socks) dated to the third to fifth centuries can be found in museums; these appear to have been knitted but were actually made with a sewing-needle technique[1]. True knitted caps, gloves and stockings dating from the sixteenth century are preserved in museums, but fashionable body garments known variously as vests, shirts or waistcoats did not start to appear until the seventeenth century.

Made from a wide range of materials including wool, linen, silk, cotton and man-made fibres, knitted items can be created by hand on knitting needles or by utilizing knitting machines of domestic to industrial scales. Following the very early invention of the knitting machine at the end of the sixteenth century, industrial-scale manufacturing and mass production developed strongly throughout the Industrial Revolution of the eighteenth and nineteenth centuries and largely displaced commercial hand knitting, especially for making stockings, caps and undergarments. As industrial technology developed, so did the capacity for patterning in both woven and knitted textiles, enabling complex motifs and all-over designs to be created. The invention of jacquard

Toe socks, dating from the fourth to fifth centuries, found in Egypt. Made in red wool using a single-needle looping technique (naalbinding) and constructed without sewn seams. (V&A: 2085&a-1900. © Victoria and Albert Museum, London)

OPPOSITE PAGE: The Knitwear Revolution book of designer knitting patterns compiled by fashion writer Suzy Menkes, published in 1983, featuring Sandy Black's Vase of Flowers coat knitted in 100-per-cent-angora yarns on the cover.

A brocade knitted waistcoat, dating from the seventeenth century, British or Italian. Coral pink and green silk with metal-wrapped silk, probably hand knitted. (V&A: 807-1904. © Victoria and Albert Museum, London)

Frame-knitted stockings with seams, dating from the seventeenth century, Spanish. Intarsia knitted in green and pink silk with embroidered decoration. (V&A: T.156/A-1971. © Victoria and Albert Museum, London)

techniques in weaving (including the production of brocade fabrics) was especially significant, and a similar technique was applied to industrially knitted fabrics.

With the advent of printed books and the increasing availability of cheaper magazines and pamphlets, hand knitting regained popularity as a leisure pursuit and for charitable causes, especially during the two World Wars of the twentieth century. Knitwear has had brief periods of great popularity in fashion, such as during the 1930s jazz era or for early sportswear, but otherwise remained somewhat unremarkable until the late twentieth century. Despite a wonderfully creative flowering of hand-knitting ingenuity and design in the wartime austerity years of the 1940s and 1950s, by the 1970s, handmade knitwear was considered dowdy and decidedly old-fashioned. The knitwear industry was a parallel industry to that of fashion, a Cinderella of fashion, which had arisen out of the important, but essentially practical, hosiery and underwear trade, and which only occasionally intersected with fashionability. For more information on this history, see *Knitting: Fashion, Industry, Craft; Knitwear in Fashion; A History of Hand Knitting*, plus other titles listed in Further Reading.

During the 1960s youthquake in both music and fashion, pioneering fashion designers emerged in London, such as Mary Quant, Barbara Hulanicki of Biba, Foale and Tuffin, and Ossie Clark, but this innovative spirit seemed to pass knitwear by. Apart from some very chunky 'kwik knits', hand knitting remained a largely utilitarian and somewhat staid element of basic clothing, and commercial knitwear consisted mainly of mass-produced classic sweaters, cardigans and hosiery.

At that time, knitting as a handcraft was usually associated with children's home-made clothes or well-meaning gifts. However, the advent of miniskirts in the mid-1960s stimulated a demand for designer stockings and tights (designed, for

Two liturgical gloves, dating from the sixteenth century, Spanish. The gloves, each from a different pair, are knitted in red silk and metal-wrapped yellow silk; both are colour-patterned using stranded or weaving-in techniques. The left glove is partly cut and sewn, mimicking the construction of a glove made from woven cloth.
(V&A: 437-1892 and 876-1897. © Victoria and Albert Museum, London)

Knitting patterns and booklets from the 1960s and 1970s, including Supersonics (quick multi-strand knitting patterns by Patons) and Coats Knitting in Synthetics: at that time synthetics were a new phenomenon.
(© Victoria and Albert Museum, London)

example, by Mary Quant), and Vogue began to feature new knitted fashions from companies such as Women's Home Industries, Jaeger and Susan Small[2].

During the 1970s and early 1980s, a great British burst of creativity occurred, fuelled in part by the creative freedom of UK art-college education at that time. Responding to the zeitgeist, individual designers brought a fresh approach to handmade knitwear, focused on colour, texture and often quirky graphic design, inspired by decorative arts of all kinds. Some had studied textiles or fine art, occasionally even fashion; others such as myself were completely self-taught – whatever the origins, a new genre of designer knitwear was born. From the early 1970s – in tandem with a resurgence of interest in crafts and the handmade, and a backlash to uninteresting mass production and synthetic materials – this new wave of British designers (mostly women) rediscovered the delights of knitting, reinterpreting old techniques and inventively working with colour and natural materials in a true renaissance of the art. My work was part of this craft-led design movement that repositioned knitwear as fashion, rather than just boring basics; British designer knitwear went on to influence the wider fashion industry, helping to create a new market for creative and colourful statement knitwear and inspiring new developments in industrial knitting technology.

As a reaction to the blandness of much commercial knitwear design, the designer knitwear of the 1980s focused on the blending of colour, texture, pattern and scale to create each individual design, whether a bold geometric design or a pretty floral, or from any other inspiration. Several key names emerged, each with their distinctive design repertoire and colourful yarn palettes, including Patricia Roberts, Kaffe Fassett (initially working with Bill Gibb and with Missoni, then under his own name and with Rowan Yarns) and my contemporaries Susan Duckworth, Artwork by Jane and Patrick Gottelier, Jamie and Jessie Seaton, Vanessa Keegan, Sasha Kagan, and Martin Kidman for Joseph Tricot.

As I learnt from personal experience, our type of designer knitwear was initially considered too crafty for serious fashion and too fashion-orientated for the crafts community – perhaps the mark of an original production. However, designer knitwear quickly found its own niche and, in the

Examples of distinctive 1980s designer knitwear from Patricia Roberts, Kaffe Fassett, Susan Duckworth, Martin Kidman, Artwork, Vanessa Keegan and Sasha Kagan. All garments are knitted in natural yarns and by hand, except for Vanessa Keegan's machine-knitted intarsia designs. (Photos: courtesy of the designers and of Rowan Yarns)

early 1980s, gained a fantastic following in many countries around the world; overseas buyers, especially from prestigious department stores in the USA and Japan (such as Saks Fifth Avenue, Bloomingdales, Bullock's and Isetan), rushed to snap up original knitwear designed and made in the UK. Saks Fifth Avenue even set up a new line called 'Sweaters as Art'!

The respected and influential fashion writer Suzy Menkes captured the importance of this movement for fashion, calling it 'The Knitwear Revolution' in her book of the same name published in 1983, a rare accolade for knitwear to have been dealt with seriously in terms of fashion. Contained within this book are patterns from twenty fashion and knitwear designers, including Bill Gibb, Kaffe Fassett, Zandra Rhodes, Jasper Conran, Patricia Roberts, Artwork and myself. As shown at the beginning of this chapter, my own 100-per-cent-angora Vase of Flowers coat design featured on the cover of this book – although not my name!

British designer knitwear owed its distinctiveness to the fact that the complex multicoloured and multi-textured designs using many yarns could only be made manually (on needles or by manual work on hand-operated domestic knitting machines) and could not at the time be replicated by mass-production methods, and certainly not in the UK. In Italy, of course, the exceptional Missoni company translated their unique creative vision into colourful fabrics and complex knitwear made on industrial knitting machines (often by using older warp-knitting machinery formerly used for making shawls), but these garments were made up in the same way as garments made of woven fabrics, by cut-and-sew methods,

A selection of labels from US department stores and boutiques that purchased Sandy Black and other British designer-knitwear brands – being 'Made in England/Made in Great Britain' was a key selling point. Note the Saks Fifth Avenue 'Sweaters as Art' label.

New York European Fashion Fair trade-show catalogues for Fall/Winter 1981/2 and Spring/Summer 1982, where our group of British knitwear designers sold to American store buyers.

The Design Studio was a group of thirty-five fashion and knitwear designers exhibiting within the British Designers Show fashion trade fair in London, Autumn/Winter 1985, including Sandy Black Original Knits.

Knitting Exhibitions

People everywhere were greatly inspired by the fresh approach of designer hand knitting, and the 1980s saw a burgeoning of designer knitting-pattern books and knitting kits (including my own) and the holding of three key exhibitions in the UK, *The Knitwear Revue* in 1983, featuring twenty-eight contemporary British knitwear designers, *Knit One Purl One* in 1985, a historical exhibition, and *Knitting a Common Art* in 1986[4], a historical and contemporary exhibition celebrating knitters of all eras. The first and last exhibitions featured work by a large group of British knitwear designers including Patricia Roberts, Susan Duckworth, Kaffe Fassett, Sasha Kagan, Carrie White, Susie Freeman, myself and many other designer–makers. In addition, in 1984, Kaffe Fassett had a solo exhibition of his work in the Victoria and Albert Museum (V&A) in London. It was at that time unprecedented for a knitwear designer to be featured in a museum such as the V&A in this way.

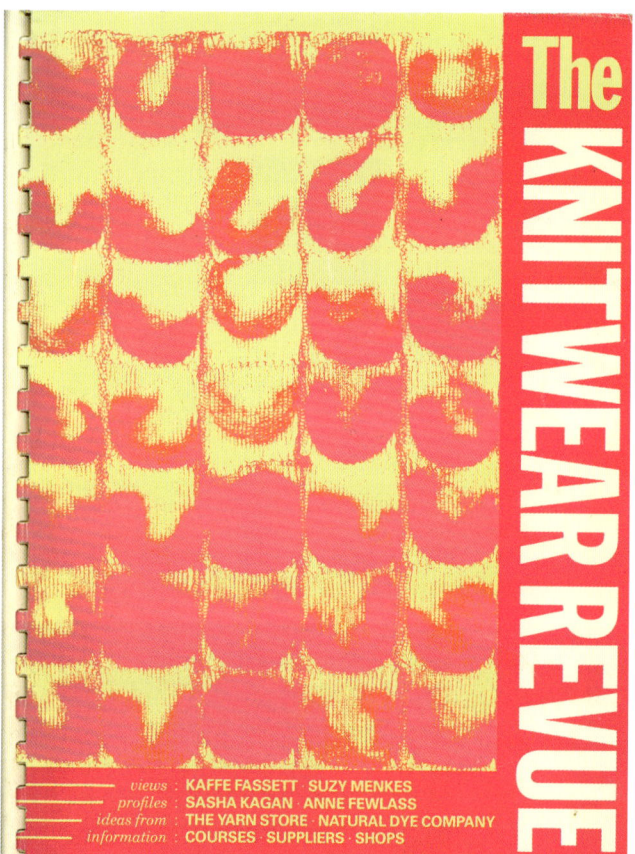

The Knitwear Revue, *1983, British Crafts Centre London. The exhibition and catalogue celebrated work from twenty-eight British knitwear designers including Sandy Black. It toured eleven UK venues throughout 1983 and 1984, reflecting the popularity for hand knitting in export markets. Several designers offered home knitting kits.*

Knitting: A Common Art *exhibition catalogue, 1986. Devised by historian June Freeman, the exhibition featured both historical and contemporary knitted objects and knitwear, contextualizing the knitting boom of the 1980s within centuries of knitting practice, celebrating the artistry of knitters past and present. The cover shows the Hoover machine-knitted sweaters by Vanessa Keegan, making social comment on 'women's work' through humour.*

rather than being knitted to shape. In contrast, the British approach to designer knitwear, coupled with the legacy of hand-knitting skills, which had continued to be passed down through many generations, provided a ready-made workforce for our group of fledgling designer-knitwear businesses, and we rose to the challenge of successfully trading in the international fashion markets. The USA was a key market, as summed up in this quote from *The Washington Post* in 1987: 'The most varied and imaginative sweaters have always come from English designers, perhaps because of the accessibility of a variety of wools and the cool weather. But the design freedom given in art schools – compared with the emphasis on technical training in many [US] design centers – has also helped produce a remarkable range of knits'[3].

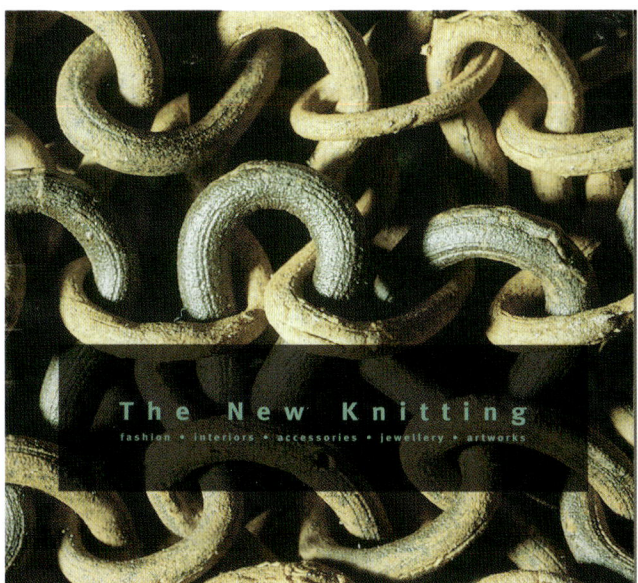

The New Knitting exhibition catalogue, 2000, showed innovative knitting in fashion, interiors, accessories, jewellery and artworks by twenty-nine diverse designers and artists. Curated by Sandy Black, the exhibition was staged in London, Leicestershire and Scotland from 2000 to 2002.

The New Knitting exhibition installation in Hawick Museum, Scotland, including Vivienne Westwood hand-knitted dresses from the mid-1990s.

The 'City of Stitches' knitted installation by Isabel Berglund, 2005, reinstalled in the Breien! (Knitting!) exhibition, Fries Museum, the Netherlands, 2016. The show included both historical and contemporary knitwear, knitted artworks and installations. (Photo: courtesy of Isabel Berglund)

However, for over ten years, there were no further knitting exhibitions held in the UK[5], until in 1998 I curated *The New Knitting*[6], an exhibition highlighting contemporary design (for knitwear, furnishings, jewellery and artworks) that utilized knitting as a fundamental element. Exhibits included cutting-edge designer fashions from Julien Macdonald, Vivienne Westwood and Issey Miyake, inventive fashion knitwear from Clements Ribeiro and Delphine Wilson, innovative knitted artworks by Freddie Robins, Frances Geesin and Emily Bates, dramatic jewellery by Nora Fok and Jan Truman, and idiosyncratic furnishings by Hikaru other works. The work of recent graduates in knitted textiles was also included, to show the vitality of new textile thinking, taking knitting in groundbreaking new directions and demonstrating its versatility as an expressive medium. Two years later, in 2000, another exhibition, *Slipstitch*, curated by John Allen, took place in the Netherlands, showcasing both UK and Dutch knitting designers and emerging graduates[7]. More recently, reflecting the renewed interest in knitting as a craft, there have been further exhibitions devoted to knitting, including two taking place in the Netherlands – *Unravel: Knitwear in Fashion*, in 2011, and *Breien!* (Knitting!), in 2016[8].

In London in 2014, the Fashion and Textile Museum staged *Knitwear: Chanel to Westwood*, a key historical exhibition of fashionable knitwear throughout the twentieth century. This included 1980s designs from Sonia Rykiel, Zandra Rhodes, Body Map, Vivienne Westwood, Comme des Garçons, Patricia Roberts, Katharine Hamnett and Kaffe Fassett, as well as my own Vase of Flowers coat.

Knitwear: Chanel to Westwood, 2014–2015, an exhibit of 1980s knitwear, with pieces by Patricia Roberts, Sonia Rykiel, Zandra Rhodes, Sandy Black and Body Map. (Photo: Fashion and Textile Museum, London)

The Visionary Knitwear *exhibition of twenty-first-century knitwear, selected by Sandy Black to complement the* Knitwear: Chanel to Westwood *exhibition, Fashion and Textile Museum, London, 2014–2015. The image features experimental work by Craig Lawrence, for AnOther Magazine, 2009, worn by Tilda Swinton. (Photo: Craig McDean)*

As a complement to this twentieth-century exhibition, I curated the *Visionary Knitwear* exhibition[9] of knitwear of the twenty-first century that brought into public view the innovation nurtured over the past two decades through UK textile and fashion higher-education courses at both undergraduate and postgraduate levels. Some of the irreverence and humour applied to classic forms is evident in the image shown here, featuring exciting and extreme knitted outfits by Sibling and Yang Du.

Visionary Knitwear 2014/15 *exhibition installation featuring animal-themed intarsia-machine-knitted knitwear by Yang Du and two extreme knitwear outfits by Sibling. (Photo: Fashion and Textile Museum, London)*

Dresses displayed at the Visionary Knitwear *exhibition by award-winning graduate Rory Longdon and high-fashion designer Julien Macdonald. (Photo: Fashion and Textile Museum, London)*

Since the turn of the millennium, a contemporary hand-knitting revival has emerged, capturing a new participative and social mood, where knitting is experienced in social groups once more, returning to a community-based practice. Online communities in particular have fuelled the resurgence of popularity in knitting and other make-it-yourself activities, with patterns, information, tutorials and images of personal creations being avidly shared, both online and offline. This has enabled knitting to be mobilized for activism through craft (known as 'craftivism'), to draw attention to political issues and subvert expectations of knitting (and crochet) as merely being a benign craft. The practice of yarn-bombing grew up as a humorous and mildly subversive activity, where objects such as bicycles, tanks, statues in public spaces and even entire buildings are tagged with knitted or crocheted coverings. Another more political example is the phenomenon of pink 'Pussyhats', knitted by thousands of women and worn on the women's marches that took place across the USA and Europe in January 2017. These became a symbol of women's empowerment and solidarity in the face of sexism. All these diverse activities are testament to the enduring and quietly powerful nature of the amazing and versatile craft of knitting.

An example of yarn-bombing: a tree with knitted branch covers. (Photo: Denise Litchfield, pixabay.com)

CHAPTER 2

DESIGN AND INSPIRATION

Knitting to Shape – Knitting as Soft Engineering

The technique of hand knitting has been practised for many centuries, to make essential protective coverings first for the head, hands and feet and later the body. Importantly, the construction process of knitting enables both a fabric and its form to be created simultaneously – either as flat pieces made to specific shapes, for later assembly, or as knitting made 'in the round', for creating seamless garments, with no further construction required. Many of the oldest surviving historic knitted items are hand knitted in the round, such as sixteenth-century Tudor caps and liturgical gloves, and eighteenth and nineteenth-century stockings and purses. Fine hand-knitted silk stockings, knitted in the round, fitted and flattered the shape of the (male) leg much more successfully than earlier stockings made from woven fabric and were in high demand. Inspired by such fashions amongst the European nobility, the sixteenth-century period saw great innovation in knitting, including the invention of the first mechanical knitting frame in 1589.

This ability to easily make complete, wearable, three-dimensional items without seams is a fantastic property of knitting, and it also applies to the technique of crochet, made by hand with a single hooked needle. However, in my opinion, knitting is unrivalled amongst the needlecrafts as an accessible form of soft engineering, whether made by hand or by machine. Seamless garments knitted in the round

A man's cap, dating from the sixteenth century, found and probably made in London. Hand knitted to shape in the round in wool, then felted and slashed to form four lappets. Randomly placed decreases (where two lines of stitches merge) can be seen shaping the piece towards the centre of the crown. (V&A: 741-1904. © Victoria and Albert Museum, London)

OPPOSITE PAGE: *A mosaic floor with a complex pattern of fan shapes and outlined fleur-de-lys motifs, from the porch of a former medical college, dated 1895, in Newcastle, England.*

Detail of shaping of the fingers of sixteenth-century liturgical gloves, hand knitted in the round in red silk. (V&A: 876-1897. © Victoria and Albert Museum, London)

and seamed garments sewn from two-dimensional pieces knitted to precise shapes both make the most efficient use of materials (and labour) without any waste. Take, for example, the ingenious construction of historical seamless stockings and contemporary socks; these items contain an incredibly efficient angular bend in a tubular form. The change of direction, forming a pouch to accommodate the heel, is achieved by creating extra knitted fabric precisely where it is needed, by changing the direction of work and knitting only parts of certain rows. The standard contemporary sock heel is knitted across approximately half of the leg tube's stitches, first by symmetrically decreasing over several rows the number of stitches being worked and then increasing to the same number of stitches again symmetrically over the same number of rows to correspond, and so creating the heel pouch. In this way, the integrity of the fabric is maintained throughout the change in direction. Without

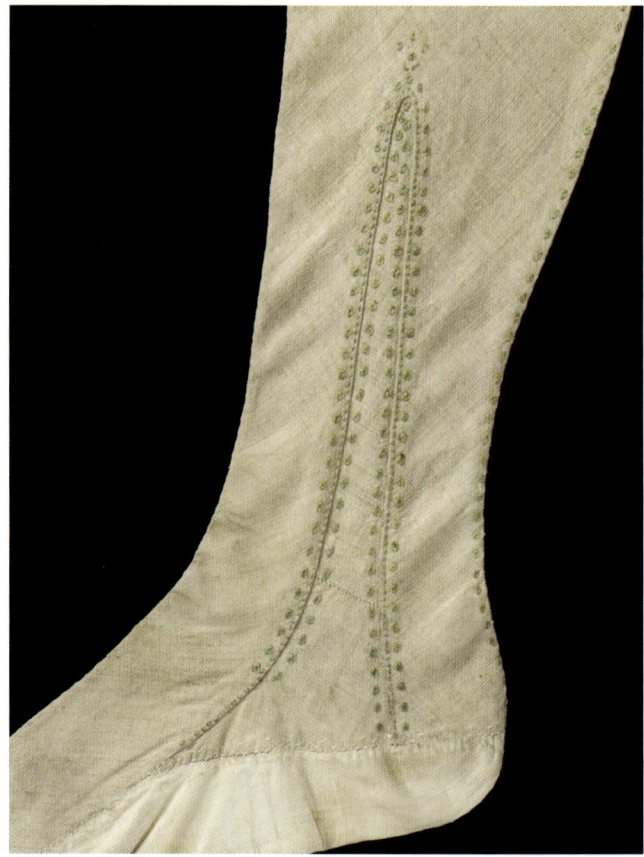

A pair of hand-knitted seamless boot hose, dating to the 1640s, English. Knitted in the round in wool, starting from the top and w rking down and made to be worn inside fashionable Cavalier boots, popular in the reign of Charles I. (V&A: T.63&A-1910. © Victoria and Albert Museum, London)

Detail of woven linen stocking, showing the seamed construction of the heel and foot, with a shaped gore, dating from 1590 to 1615, English. (V&A: T.126&A-1938. © Victoria and Albert Museum, London)

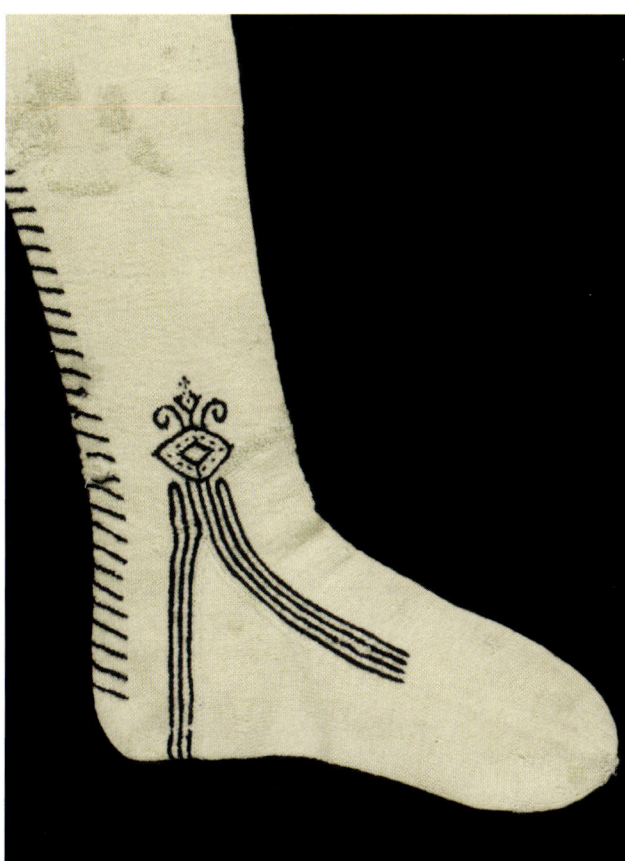

Detail of the foot and heel construction of knitted boot hose, seamlessly shaped by dividing the knitting for the foot and knitting on stitches for the gore in a new direction and decreasing for the toe. Blue embroidery outlines the knitted gore structure. (V&A: T.63&A-1910. © Victoria and Albert Museum, London)

Hand-frame machine-knitted fully fashioned silk stocking by manufacturer I&R Morley, 1923, British. The knitting is divided for the foot, and stitches are knitted on to the heel in a new direction to shape the foot. Hand embroidery was still undertaken by home workers at this time. (V&A: T.147&A-1975. © Victoria and Albert Museum, London)

A contemporary children's standard sock showing the angle formed by narrowing and widening the rows of stitches being worked, to create both the heel and toe pouch. The same technique also creates the three-dimensional flower shapes.

such engineered construction, in order to create a bend in any given tube, its material would buckle at the inside and be stretched on the outside[1].

Although hand-knitted stockings had always been made in the round without seams, the groundbreaking invention of the mechanical knitting frame at the end of the sixteenth century meant that frame-knitted garments had to be made in flat pieces, because of the constraints of its fixed needle bed. Increased speed of production was the new goal, in order to meet demand. Stockings and other items were therefore knitted flat to the exact shapes required (a technique known as 'fashioning', to create 'fully fashioned' knitting), and early frame-knitted stockings always have seams. The term 'fully fashioned' is today associated with fine, high-quality, industrially made knitwear and with women's nylon stockings from the mid-twentieth century, and it also applies to hand-knitted garments.

DESIGN AND INSPIRATION 31

By the 1980s, the great majority of hand knitters and knitwear designers created knitwear from flat, shaped pieces, as knitting in the round had fallen away in common practice, partly due to the increasing popularity of printed patterns from the mid-nineteenth century onward. The designs in this book reflect the practice of knitting flat on two needles, which was the way that knitting was handed down to my generation. Today, there has been a resurgence of interest in hand knitting in the round, and the knitting of socks and stockings using double-pointed or circular needles has become a regular activity amongst contemporary knitters, but it was hardly seen in the 1980s.

Designing with Knitting and Personal Inspiration

When I began to experiment with creating my own ideas, I was excited by the infinite range of possibilities that knitting opened up and the flexibility to create both two- and three-dimensional shapes and highly textural surfaces from nothing but a length of yarn and a few basic stitches.

Patricia Roberts' 1978 Fruit Machine sweater, featuring knitted bunches of grapes and cherries, made with bobbles. From Patricia Roberts Knitting Book, 1981. (Photo: Rolph Gobits)

Everything is within the knitter's control – from the choice of yarn, stitches and fabric quality, to give the desired handle, weight and structure, to their combination with colour, pattern and design – and limited only by imagination. However, such wide choices can be daunting, so it is important to have some initial visual ideas to inspire and guide the creative process. I always carried a camera (today replaced by the ubiquitous mobile phone) and took lots of photographs of patterns and surface textures that caught my eye, without necessarily having a specific design idea in mind, but these would fuel my imagination and inspire ideas for stitches and patterns when needed. I often worked on a number of different visual ideas at the same time, for example, studying tiles of many kinds and finely patterned Chinese vases from museum sources and reference books, alongside the bold colours and graphic designs of Henri Matisse.

Whatever the inspiration, an essential part of creating knitwear designs is to constantly experiment and test out ideas for stitch textures and colour patterns through sampling with small swatches, until a pleasing balance between structure, pattern and scale on the body is achieved. There are now many stitch dictionaries and online sources that can give initial inspiration for stitch structures, but in the 1980s it was key books by American Barbara Walker, collector of knitting patterns, that provided a rich source of stitch patterns and techniques for many knitwear designers (see Further Reading).

The designer knitwear of the 1980s reinvented knitting traditions, with a focus on the blending of colour, texture, pattern and scale to create each individual design. Designs for sweaters, cardigans and jackets featured a riot of colour and texture, inspired by all manner of things, including antique rugs and kilims, historical fabrics, ceramics and other decorative arts, and the natural world. Several designers also injected a touch of humour with quirky motifs and imagery, for example, Patricia Roberts' bunches-of-grapes designs, Sasha Kagan's Scottie-dogs designs, Warm and Wonderful's black-sheep sweater (as worn by Princess Diana) and my own animal wraps (see Chapter 11) – including an armadillo, leopard and snake!

My work of this period encompassed a wide range of themes, from bold geometric, floral or textural patterns to complex imagery, and included garment styles from casual sweaters to glamorous angora evening coats. I viewed the body as a canvas to be decorated and adorned with beautiful patterns, sometimes subtle, sometimes bold. I enjoyed working in a great variety of ways – inspired by anything that caught my eye or simply the pleasure of combining wonderful materials and textures with new imagery and stitches.

The Flower Garland jacket, machine knitted in a wool–angora-blend yarn, with flowers created from bobbles worked individually by manually knitting over three needles for a few rows. (Photo: Barbara Bellingham)

Intarsia machine knitting in industry, worked with high-quality cashmere, which is a former traditional manufacturing technique in Scotland. The knitter reads from a coloured graph and lays the yarns across the machine needles by hand to correspond. (Photo: courtesy of Caerlee Mills)

Intarsia machine knitting and the landscape sweater

Whilst at college, I began to hand knit and crochet things for myself and later bought a simple knitting machine. This enabled me to produce items more quickly than by hand and explore the visual and textural possibilities of knitting as a medium for design, beyond simple repeating patterns. I experimented with manual techniques such as making bobbles to create textures, which became a signature technique for me.

From the beginning, I specialized in working with the intarsia technique, a highly labour-intensive manual process, historically knitted on the simplest knitting machines and similar in concept to tapestry weaving on a loom. This made it possible to introduce an endless array of colours and yarn textures at will and therefore had the potential to create pictorial imagery, an idea inspired by the paint-by-numbers kits that I used to love as a child. This was the origin of my signature landscape sweaters. I developed my own method of working from a full-sized drawing, which I fed

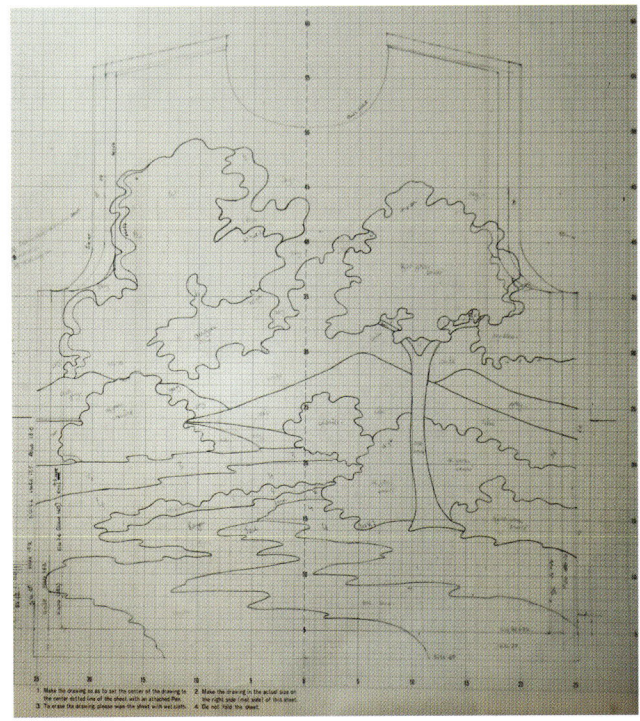

My own design drawing for intarsia knitting for the Knitleader attachment of a domestic knitting machine that facilitated the reading of the pattern.

through an attachment originally designed for knitting shaped pattern pieces. In this way, I could create knitted imagery at a large scale over the blank canvas of the garment's, body to create my pictures and landscape sweaters.

DESIGN AND INSPIRATION 33

The ever-changing sky provides endless fascination: here is a skyscape over a beach in New Zealand.

A tranquil landscape scene dramatically framed by trees and bushes.

The Five-Colour Clouds sweater with an abstract cloud design, intarsia machine knitted. Colours are matched over the entire body and across all the seams and edgings throughout. (Photo: Barbara Bellingham)

My first pictorial sweater design was inspired by an old tin I discovered in a flea market that depicted a Peter Pan character. I thought to myself 'I'd like to knit that' and set about doing it by using the machine-knitted intarsia method.

Inspired by the idealized landscapes of the American illustrator Maxfield Parrish and the classical romanticism of paintings by Lawrence Alma-Tadema, I developed several more designs depicting rural landscapes and skyscapes that would fill the fronts of close-fitting sweaters and spill over the sleeves, transitioning over the seams. I greatly enjoyed the challenge of working out how to match up the imagery at the top of the sleeves. Due to the time required to make each landscape sweater (even using a manual machine), and hence the cost, the back was simply an echo of the image in stripes of the colours and yarns used for the image on the front.

In my view, anything can be an inspiration for knitting – it is simply a question of visualizing an idea (based on sources) and then working out the logic of how to make it! Here are

Themes of landscape and skyscape became central to my early work, as both imagery and more abstract patterns, interpreted through the application of both hand-knitted and machine-knitted intarsia techniques. One design series was based on day and night-time skyscapes – one garment, the Night and Day sweater, featured a half-night and half-day design!

The Night and Day sweater combines two versions of the same design – daytime and midnight. Machine-knitted intarsia, with the clouds being made three-dimensional by using manual bobble techniques. The front is daytime, with an appliqué rainbow and embroidered rain worked in metallic yarn, and the sleeves are made in two halves.

The Night and Day sweater back view, with darker clouds and an embroidered moon and stars worked in silver metallic yarn. The sleeves are half day and half night.

A vintage metal tin, possibly for sweets, with an image of Peter Pan and the pirate ship that inspired the creation of my first landscape sweater.

RIGHT: The Peter Pan sweater, worked in fine wool yarns, interpreted into a picture suitable for intarsia machine knitting, with the design spilling over on to one sleeve.

DESIGN AND INSPIRATION 35

LEFT: The Flying Duck sweater landscape and skyscape captures a favourite theme of billowing clouds and birds overhead, knitted in wool and angora-blend yarns and metallic thread. (Photo: Barbara Bellingham)

RIGHT: The Wandering Path sweater, a less complex design based on perspective, with a tree worked in bouclé wool over the entire left shoulder, and simplified embroidered birds.

Inspirational photographs of monumental stonework, a stained-glass window in Scotland, and tiles and mosaic floors in Spain and Portugal.

The Cobweb sweater knitted in two-colour stranded-colourwork knitting, inspired by an intriguing fan-shaped mosaic pattern from a cobbled street in Nottingham. Creating the repeat was an enjoyable challenge. This design featured in The Rowan Knitting Book No 2 *in 1987. See also the featured mosaic at the start of this chapter. (Photo: courtesy of Rowan Yarns)*

LEFT: The Architextural bolero inspired by relief patterns in architecture and tiled floors, featuring patterned diamonds within cabled borders, knitted in wool yarn with chenille motifs. (Photo: Paul Dennison)

BELOW: Detail of the Architextural bolero, with diamonds of travelling cables embedded in a double-moss-stitch ground. The cabled border is worked in twisted rib to give extra definition. (Photo: Paul Dennison)

LEFT: A stained-glass-inspired, geometric-patterned mohair sweater – intarsia knitted and embroidered with chain-stitch borders in black to contrast and to unify the design; hexagons and diamonds combine with a motif on the sleeve. (Photo: Barbara Bellingham)

BELOW: Detail of a Stained Glass design with intarsia-knitted diamonds and borders in black travelling cables, to create relief window leading for the knitted stained glass. This is a pattern typical of old cottage windows. (See Chapter 7 for an image of a cardigan using this pattern.)

The Fields sweater and jacket, an early outfit featuring both machine-knitted (sweater) and hand-knitted (jacket) intarsia methods, aiming to capture the essence of the rural landscape. Made in two different weights of heathery Shetland wools and finished with embroidery worked in green bouclé yarn for the hedges. (Photo: Barbara Bellingham)

Green rolling fields and hedgerows of England.

Detail of the Fields jacket, worked in hand-knitted intarsia in chunky-weight Shetland yarns and with different stitches, including reverse stocking stitch, moss-stitch variations and garter stitch. Embroidered bouclé-yarn hedges help mask any imperfections!

examples of my own typical sources, from architectural details to stained glass and decorative arts, and some knitted pieces that they inspired.

In the landscapes and many other designs, I liked to think of painting with yarns, to decorate the body with imagery or pattern. I was recently surprised and delighted to come across an actual painting of one of my earliest landscape sweaters that was featured in a book published in 1978, romantically photographed in a river landscape to resonate with my knitted picture[2]. The painting, produced in 2012, is by American artist Nolan Simon and poetically echoes my idea of the body as a canvas. The artist says of his motivation:

I was attracted to the simple presentation of this garment which, worn in this particular context, reiterated the body into the landscape imperfectly. At the time I had a latent idea, still being formulated, about the boundaries between bodies and images, and this image felt like it did a good job pointing (metaphorically) at that permeable boundary.

It was wonderful to hear about one of my designs inspiring another creative output in a different medium.

DESIGN AND INSPIRATION

Finding your own Visual Inspiration

On observing

Inspiration can be gathered from anywhere, when travelling at home and abroad or by collecting imagery for pattern and texture ideas – always being vigilant and open to any sort of stimulus. Architecture and the decorative arts are a very rich source of inspiration, including entire buildings or fine details, and clean modernist lines or rococo embellishments and sculpted surfaces, whether found on your travels, in museums or in books. Keep a notebook or tablet handy to jot down ideas; take photographs and/or sketch to record any visually inspiring or intriguing imagery or patterns from your own physical surroundings. Engaging physically with sources of inspiration is a most rewarding activity, as looking closely at real objects, surfaces and textures and recording details gives depth to your observations and often leads to the development of new ideas.

Historical textiles can be a wonderful source of visual and structural inspiration, especially elaborate woven, embroidered, printed and knitted textiles from the seventeenth to nineteenth centuries. The intricate combinations of patterns, colours and stitches used by many knitwear designers of the 1970s and 1980s are reminiscent of some of the finest colour-patterned knitting from the seventeenth and eighteenth centuries, such as the silk brocade jackets and masterpiece knitted carpets that can be seen in museum collections in several countries.

The natural environment of landscape and nature – plants, rocks, flowers, shells and animal markings, for example – provides an infinite variety of colours, patterns and forms, and cycles of growth and decay can be endlessly inspiring; dereliction and the many neglected places in cities or the countryside can spark great ideas too. Of course, museums and galleries provide countless riches of historical and contemporary decorative arts and the fine arts: paintings, artworks and photographs. Colour inspiration can be found in all of these places and more. Look at not just the colours themselves but also the proportions and balance of colours that can be translated into an overall design – this can be inspiration for simple stripe sequences (regular or irregular) or for combinations of colours in a Fair Isle-style pattern or graphic intarsia design.

Inspiration for abstract patterns can be found at both macro and micro scales – in landscape photography and from microscopic images on the cellular scale, for example.

This early River Landscape sweater features sheep grazing in the foreground and distance, worked in chenille yarn, and a rather delicate tree over the shoulder. Designed for The Marshall Cavendish Complete Book of Needlecraft, 1978.

Sweater Painting 2012, by American artist Nolan Simon, with inspiration taken from the detail photograph of the River Landscape sweater. Oil on canvas, 41cm × 51cm (16in × 20in). Image courtesy of the artist and 47 Canal, New York. (Photo: Joerg Lohse)

Detail of a seventeenth-century silk-brocade hand-knitted Italian jacket, showing a basket-weave-stitch border and intricate floral pattern knitted in three colours with a purl-stitch filling. The gold ground yarn is yellow silk wrapped with silver metallic strip, See also Chapter 1. (V&A: 473-1893. © Victoria and Albert Museum, London)

A masterpiece carpet, made in order to qualify as a master knitter in a knitting guild in Alsace, dated 1781. Knitted in many coloured wools, the intricate patterning is achieved to a very high standard. These pieces would also be used as wall hangings or table coverings and often featured religious imagery. (V&A: T.375-1977. © Victoria and Albert Museum, London)

The seeming uniformity of a pebble beach can uncover a surprising range of colours for inspiration.

Considering another perspective, observing the earth from above can be fascinating. Serendipitously, as a schoolgirl, I was given a stack of old *National Geographic* magazines, and the awe-inspiring photography of landscapes, wildlife and peoples from around the world provided endless fascination and inspiration when researching ideas. These covered such diverse examples as terraced fields, the Rocky Mountains, flocks of flamingoes, Persian temples and folk costumes. I also made use of all kinds of specialist reference books, from children's encyclopedias and books on birds and animals to a wonderful volume of images, *The Earth from Above*, produced by Yann Arthus-Bertrand. Today, there are many extraordinary collections of images available in photography books and online, featuring the natural world and aerial photography of landscapes and cityscapes.

DESIGN AND INSPIRATION 41

Aerial view over Ireland, from an original cutting from National Geographic *magazine.*

Two contemporary designers, Anna Murray and Grace Winteringham, who founded the Patternity image archive and consultancy[3], created a reference sourcebook to inspire everyone to observe and connect with pattern from our everyday surroundings, whether in cities or the natural landscape. Looking beyond the mundane to see the underlying patterns that we may otherwise miss also becomes a mindful activity of connecting ourselves to the environment and to others.

Another useful book, *Visual Research Methods in Fashion* by Julia Gaimster, is aimed at fashion students and provides some helpful strategies on undertaking systematic and productive visual research.

On collecting

Noticing interesting items and collecting things is just part of the response of a designer to their environment, in just the same way as recording interesting visual surroundings in snapshots whilst travelling. Design students and practitioners often have small groups or displays of assorted objects that they might not call a 'collection'; however, multiples of things kept for their aesthetic qualities deserve close attention, in order to analyse what is interesting about them – so check what your own obsession might be! Multiples can assist with putting together colours and variations on a theme but also emphasize what the objects have in common and start to suggest broad design ideas for form, colour or pattern.

I don't think of myself as a collector, but I have amassed all sorts of things that interest me, almost subconsciously, as a regular activity; the constant gathering of interesting objects, printed ephemera and general jumble has been part of my life. I have collections of old cigarette cards, match boxes and swallow-patterned vases (which inspired my logo and skyscape designs), but mostly items associated with knitting – accessories made from Bakelite (including the wonderful beehive-shaped yarn holders made by Patons Yarns in the 1950s to promote their Beehive-brand yarns – now collectors' pieces), knitting needles in many materials and colours (Bakelite, metal, wood, plastic and bone), knitting patterns from the 1920s to the 1970s, a vast collection of buttons, and extraordinary finely knitted patterned hats from Bolivia and Peru.

Whilst a student, I began to collect buttons in all shapes and sizes that were like sweets in their varied colours: this was long before I knew I would be using them in knitwear designs. This was not an insignificant hobby – I would buy up the entire stock of a shop closing down, or I would root around in the dank basement of warehouse premises in the East End of London and be so excited about the diversity and multiple magnificence of everything, from mother-of-pearl, glass and jet to early plastic hand-painted buttons and metal fastenings.

Part of my collection of early coloured-plastic beehives made in Bakelite, these yarn-holders were produced by Patons & Baldwins knitting-yarn manufacturers in the 1950s, to promote their Beehive yarn brand and prevent your ball of yarn rolling around.

A collection of very finely knitted cotton conical hats from Bolivia and Peru, amassed when I travelled to South America. They are knitted in the round, with the decreases worked whilst the integrity of the patterns is also maintained. Amazing! (Image courtesy Selvedge *magazine)*

A cabinet of personal and household items with appealing graphics, including sewing kits, toothpaste, soap and tea.

A tiny fraction of my button collection, showing buttons made of mother-of-pearl, plastics, wood and horn, in wonderful shapes including abstract layers and ladybirds.

The quantities I had amassed also meant that my enjoyment of the buttons could later be shared with the customers who bought my knitwear and knitting kits, as a unique touch.

A sense of the past, of recording and celebrating things unrepeatable, the product of their own age, is still the driving force behind this form of collecting.

Of course, many knitters are inspired simply by the yarns alone and have a collection of yarns referred to, sometimes rather guiltily, as a stash – and I am no exception. I sought out the most interesting and unusual textured yarns that I could find – discontinued lines; rare, fine, 3ply wools; bouclé hand-knitting yarns; fancy knopped yarns; fluffy angora or mohair yarns; and fine chenille yarns designed for industrial weaving, to use in my landscape designs. Yarns with exciting and broad colour ranges are in themselves an inspiration, and I was especially drawn to Shetland yarns that have been consistently created from the start of the twentieth century to the present day. Today, the variety of multicoloured, dyed and printed yarns available is adding a totally new colour dimension to even the simplest of knitting.

Researching and developing visual concepts for designs is a constant delight, and being receptive to many kinds of stimulus becomes a way of life, with a little practice. Anyone can develop original ideas for knitwear – all that is needed is an open mind, a little inspiration and the excitement provided by the potential of a visual motif, a new yarn or a stitch pattern. This book gives an insight into the thinking behind some of the presented designs across a range of themes, and the next section works through two (non-fashion) projects in detail, to identify the stages involved.

DESIGN AND INSPIRATION 43

Example Projects – Combining Colour, Texture, Pattern and Scale

As well as designing my own knitwear collections, I undertook many one-off commissions for television, theatre, events and publications, some with a very open brief where I had free rein to devise my own ideas. Here are two such designs that illustrate an open-ended creative design process in which there is an overall concept and starting point but the details are worked out as the project progresses.

A Sandy Black sweater design for a Courtelle Technological Chic promotional pattern with Wendy yarns.

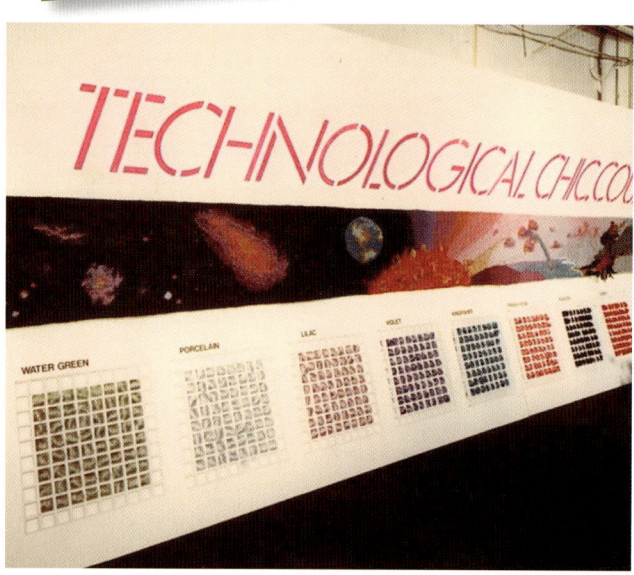

A view of the entire History of the Universe Frieze in situ at the Courtelle trade stand, 1980, promoting the concept of technological chic.

History of the Universe Frieze

Over several years, at the end of the 1970s and in the early 1980s, I designed many garments for the new Courtelle hand-knitting yarns that featured in magazine editorials and promotional shows, under the strapline 'Technological Chic' – a testament to different times, when easy-care synthetics were desirable and popular in mainstream markets.

When I was commissioned to design a display for the Courtelle trade stand at a major yarn fair, I decided to celebrate their new yarns and colours by knitting the history of the universe in a frieze stretching the length of the stand – 8 metres (26 feet)! I had just three weeks to complete the project and began with a full-sized drawing, roughly mapping out the sections, starting with the darkness of outer space and its galaxies, through the evolution of the earth and its inhabitants, from dinosaurs to man, including industrialization and the space age – with a rocket launching into space at the end.

Working from some wonderful images in a children's book that I had read as a child, I ambitiously started off by hand

An inspirational image of galaxies from the children's book The World We Live In[1].

An image of dinosaurs and mountains from the children's book The World We Live In[2].

From galaxies and darkness to life on earth via the magnificent sun.

From dinosaurs to civilization and industry – and back out into space.

knitting on large needles, knitting the galaxies and planets from these pictures by eye as I went along. However, the clock was ticking, and I soon realized I would not meet the deadline unless I could work faster, so I transferred everything to a simple coarse-gauge knitting machine and knitted separate pieces by machine or hand to appliqué on to the background. These pieces included the earth and the sun (complete with flames made from the fibres), fiery volcanoes, dinosaurs and a power station. This became the ultimate landscape and skyscape in my complete design repertoire.

RIGHT: The galaxy was hand knitted by using a picture and a brief sketch as a guide and by mixing colours around a central elliptical shape with spiralling strands. Beads and sequins were then sewn on to represent stars.

DESIGN AND INSPIRATION

Volcanoes were knitted sideways using a partial knitting technique and then sewn on to the base fabric, which consisted of two sections, sky and ground. The dinosaurs, trees and bushes were knitted separately and sewn on.

A Garden Rug

In 1978, I was commissioned by the publishers of a regular series of craft publications, for a compendium book, *The Complete Book of Needlecraft*[4], to design an inspirational child's play rug to illustrate many stitch techniques. I decided to make it a small garden complete with vegetable plot, lawn and pond. I used the same sturdy rug wool as used for popular tufted rugs, which was then available in knitting-yarn form. This was the thickest wool I had ever used and was wonderful for showing textured purl effects such as used for the mowed lawn. The rug was intended to be approximately 92cm × 122cm (3ft × 4ft) in size; I had needles that were 61cm (2ft) long specially made from wooden dowelling by a woodturner friend in order to knit it. I first tested my knitting tension over stocking stitch to determine the estimated stitches and rows required and then made a life-sized sketch of the basic idea on graph-paper sheets taped together. I then just started knitting, working directly from this plan and making notes as I went along, developing the ideas into three-dimensional effects. A mix of stitches is used to convey the texture of the paths and garden: moss-stitch variations, purl stitches on plain knitting for the contrast between rough and smooth, a stone path in plain knitting embedded in a region of purl knitting, and loop stitches for plants and grasses. Other techniques included ridges, mini sock heels for the representation of rocks, and bobbles of varying sizes to represent vegetables, flowers and

The development of civilization is shown in agriculture. All landscape pieces were knitted to shape, padded and sewn on to the base fabric. Industry is represented by non-knitted shapes made of card, depicting factories and power stations.

A contemporary image showing the design of the entire rug and the three-dimensional effects achieved in a variety of ways. The formal lawn has purl ridges on a knitted background and is surrounded by a bobble-flower border and larger bobble shrubs, merging into a rockery of random bumps created by knitting extra rows shaped rather like a sock heel. The conical bushes are knitted to shape separately and sewn on. The pond, with an appliqué lily, is surrounded by densely spaced loops representing reeds and foliage.

small shrubs. I started knitting the rug from the vegetable-patch end and had hoped to complete it all in one piece, but it would have been too unwieldy and heavy, so I split the rug along the line of the curving path and divided the knitting into two main pieces. The vegetable patch consists of ridges, bobbles, blackberry stitch and loop stitches forming plants in ribbed furrows. Beyond the hedge (a ridge) is a wilder patch with small bobble flowers. Everything was knitted into the fabric except for the groups of shrubs that were sewn on: larger shrubs were made as separate flat wedge-shaped pieces and sewn into a conical shape; smaller shrubs were made from small, flat squares that were gathered around their outside edges. The brown fence was made in French knitting (or I-cord) and appliqué pyramids created hen huts. I was particularly pleased with the rhododendron bushes made from squares of reverse stocking stitch with small coloured bobbles. Recognizing that this piece would be a challenge for many knitters to replicate, *Woman's Own* magazine commissioned me to create a simplified version of the play rug that was published with the knitting pattern a year later.

The play rug featured in Woman's Own *magazine in February 1979. This simplified rug is made from separate pieces that are then sewn together in patchwork fashion. Hedges are made by a crochet technique, and the shrubs are knitted*

CHAPTER 3

KNITTING-PATTERN FUNDAMENTALS

The essential attributes of a knitted fabric – flexibility, stretch and drape – derive from its fundamental structure. The loop structure of the basic knitted fabric (known as stocking stitch, or stockinette) creates an undulating wave in the yarn across the width of the knitted piece, allowing the fabric to easily stretch. In contrast to the construction of woven fabric, based on straight and taut threads, there is inherent extensibility in basic knitted fabric. This means that successful garments can be created from simple shapes that either mould to the body or drape over it, and the overall garment construction can be simplified, compared to that of other types of tailored garments made from woven fabrics. Hence, many designs for handmade knitwear feature simple square and rectangular garment-body shapes, as can be seen in some of the knitting patterns in Part 2.

In working with knitting design, it is important to gain an understanding of the basic properties and structures of knitted fabric in order to create designs that utilize the inherent nature of the knit construction and exploit its creative possibilities in tandem with individual visual inspiration.

You may have noticed that a piece of plain knitted fabric (that is, of stocking stitch, or stockinette), without any edgings, has an inbuilt tendency to curl – whether the fabric is a fine-weight, industrially produced jersey (think of tee shirts) or a heavier-weight hand-knitted fabric. The curl is always towards the purl side at the vertical edges and towards the knit side at the top and bottom. This is evidence of the small-scale but significant forces at work within the basic, plain knit structure, because of the unique interconnected loop formation and undulating yarn path. This is utilized to advantage with textural stitch patterns to create really three-dimensional surface effects, from knit–purl ribs and cables to surface textures using purl-stitch patterns on a knitted background, basket-weave patterns and many more. The approach that I like to take when designing, and always use when teaching about knitting design, is to emphasize what can be achieved because it's knitting – not in spite of the fabric being knitted – and therefore to experiment with the unique stitch structures and often surprising properties that can result from playing with stitch combinations. The wide range of patterns available is testament to the versatility of the technique of hand knitting, and developing your own design ideas or variations is not difficult once the fundamentals are understood.

Knowledge of how various stitch structures affect the basic knitted fabric is quickly gained by experimenting and testing using trial and error. For example, garter stitch (where every row is knitted, for back-and-forth knitting on two needles)

OPPOSITE PAGE: The Cameo cardigan, a 1980 design, machine knitted in alpaca, with flower motifs, formed of angora bobbles, and embroidered baskets.
(Photo: Barbara Bellingham)

The interlocking-loop structure of stocking stitch, as seen from the technical front of the fabric, with the knit loops facing.

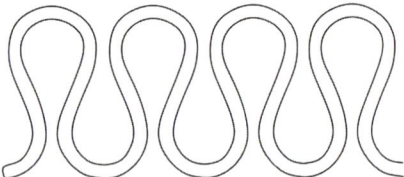

The fundamental interlocking-loop structure of knitting creates an undulating yarn path across the width of the fabric and allows the resulting fabric to stretch.

The interlocking-loop structure of stocking stitch, seen from the technical back of the fabric, with the purl loops facing.

Stocking-stitch fabric, with the knit side facing, curls to the knit side at the top and bottom and to the purl side at the left and right.

creates a stable fabric that is wider than stocking stitch worked over the same number of stitches; ribbing often narrows and elongates the fabric compared to stocking stitch[1]. A garment loosely knitted on medium to large needles, to form open stitches within the fabric, will drape from the shoulders when worn; alternatively, a garment knitted on fine needles gives a more solid fabric, which still has flexibility and stretch, and can be made to hug the body. Recently, there has been a popular revival in lace knitting in very fine cobweb-weight yarns, ideal for softly draping shawls, where the yarn quality comes fully into focus.

Knitted fabric can be precisely shaped through decreasing and increasing (or full fashioning in the industry, to produce fully fashioned garments) to create pattern pieces with no raw edges that can be neatly sewn together, a technique associated with high-quality, fine-weight knitwear. But, most significantly, knitted fabric and garments can easily be created in the round without seams, as found in socks, stockings, berets and gloves – both handmade and machine-knitted. The well-known fisherman's ganseys and many original Fair Isle sweaters worn by seafarers in the nineteenth century were also made without seams.

With knitted fabrics being so flexible, many knitwear designs rely on creating simple shapes, such as sweaters based on rectangles with drop shoulders and simplified sleeve shaping, as the fabric takes on the form of the body beneath, giving a relaxed feel when worn in contrast to tailored garments made from non-stretch woven fabrics. The simple shape is also an ideal canvas upon which to focus on the colour, pattern and stitch textures of the design. An oversized silhouette was particularly popular in the 1980s, often with emphasis on the shoulders, and is reflected in the designs in this book.

Understanding Tension (Gauge) and Sizing

Although the word 'tension' can have different general meanings, the terms 'tension' and 'gauge' in a knitting context are equivalent and refer to the number of stitches and rows of knitting, made by using needles of a recommended size, within a standard measurement, usually 10cm/4in, measured in both the horizontal (when counting stitches) and vertical (when counting rows) directions. Note that in stocking stitch there are more rows than stitches in a given measurement, as the plain knitted stitch is not square. Guidance found on a yarn ball band often suggests a tension or tension range recommended for the particular yarn when the knitter uses a particular size or size range of needles, and this can be helpful when selecting yarns to use for a particular project. Be careful to check your chosen needles before you start work on a new project, as the needle size referred to in the pattern may be given as a metric, US or old-UK needle size, or a combination of several of these sizes (*see* the Appendix needle-size-equivalents chart). A physical needle gauge is a useful tool for checking any odd needles that you may have, especially where it might not be possible to tell which system a number on the needle refers to and when there is no number present.

Checking your tension

Time invested in this early step of a knitting project is well rewarded, as the size and success of the finished piece is dependent on knitting as close to the designer's recommended tension as possible. In my own patterns, I stress that the needle sizes given are only recommended sizes and the correct needles to use are dependent on the individual knitter.

To check your own tension, always knit a swatch bigger in both directions than the target measurement given, to enable you to measure the tension more accurately from the

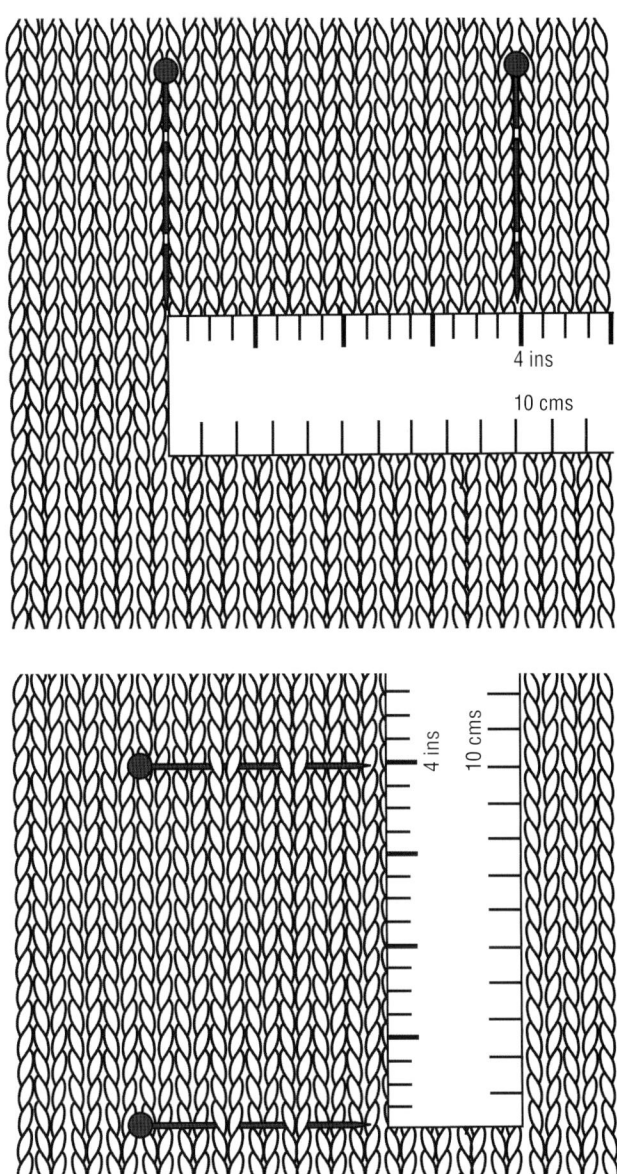

Measuring tension over 10cm/4in. In this example, there are 10sts and 14 rows between the pairs of pins marking the distance of 10cm/4in.

centre of the swatch, as the edges can be a little distorted. For example, for a recommended tension of 16sts and 24 rows to 10cm/4in, knit a swatch of 24 stitches in width by 30 rows in length. Pin or lay the swatch flat without stretching it, put a pin between two stitches near the left-hand side of the fabric and count across to the right the number of stitches given, that is, 16, then put in another pin between the sixteenth and seventeenth stitches. Mark out the given number of rows in the same way, then measure between the pins. This measurement should be 10cm/4in in each direction. If the distance is larger than this measurement, your knitting is too loose in tension and the garment will be too big: try knitting the swatch again with a smaller needle size; if the distance is less that this measurement, your knitting is too tight in tension and the garment will be too small: try again with a larger needle size. This process is repeated until the correct measurements are achieved. However, if you cannot match both the recommended stitch and row tensions together in one swatch, then it is usually best to match the stitch tension and to adjust the length at key points in the pattern, which are often indicated by a measurement within the pattern instructions. It is also important to change the sizes of any other needles used accordingly, for example, for ribbing, to keep the tension difference between different parts of the garment as the designer intended. I also recommend using larger needles if in any doubt, as a garment a little too large is usually preferable to one a little small.

Tension and garment size

The basic tension is normally measured over stocking stitch. Patterns of course vary, and some require tension to be tested over fabric worked with a specific stitch pattern or colourwork pattern, for greater accuracy. This is the case with many patterns in this book, and detailed instructions for creating an appropriate fabric swatch and measuring its tension are given. Working such a swatch is also a great way to try out the pattern, whilst also checking your tension.

It is important to note that even a small error in your tension can lead to a significant difference in sizing of the finished garment, so do not be tempted to skip this stage of checking and preparing for knitting. For example, if a sweater pattern specified 16sts to 10cm/4in, but you knitted it at 17sts to 10cm, if the width of the sweater back piece was 80sts then your piece would be 3cm/1¼in too narrow, and, when repeated across the front, would make an overall difference of 6cm/2½in to the garment's circumference: a whole size smaller! So fractions of stitches do matter – especially with thicker yarns worked with fairly large needles, as in many of the patterns in Part 2. Although several of the designs in this book are generously sized to fit loosely and comfortably, checking tension is still important for the overall success of the garment's fabric, patterning and proportions, as the designer has determined a good balance between the scale of the pattern and the handle of fabric. Typically, to optimize a design, several swatches are knitted by using different needle sizes, to provide the designer with different tension measurements.

For example, for the Triangles sweater, when the tension is looser, the fabric texture and graphic quality are less satisfactory, and the tighter tension achieved by working with smaller-sized needles was selected for this design, giving the fabric a firm handle that is suitable for outdoor wear and giving the design a clear graphic quality.

Two swatches of Triangles pattern knitted to different tensions, with needles that were one size different. The top swatch is of a tension of 13sts and 20 rows to 10cm/4in; the bottom swatch is of 14sts and 22 rows to 10cm/4in.

The Triangles-pattern final tension swatch, knitted at a gauge of 17sts and 24 rows to 10cm/4in.

Sometimes, tension differences can be used intentionally and positively to make a difference in the sizing of a design, for example, when pattern matching is key. This has been applied in the first pattern in the book, the Zig-Zag Cable sweater, which has a detailed stitch pattern repeated exactly across the width of the sweater welts, yoke and sleeves. To maintain the integrity of this pattern across two sizes, the sizing-by-tension method is used, so that only one set of instructions is required. However, confirming your desired result by knitting to the correct tension is even more important here!

Casting on and casting off

A major point to note is that care must be taken with casting on and off, whichever technique you choose, and whether for a swatch or the actual project, to ensure that the beginning and ending rows of knitting have sufficient elasticity to stretch with the rest of the knitted fabric, as, in my experience, knitters often hold the yarn more tightly when casting on or off and may not allow it to slip through sufficiently to form stitches that match the main tension of the fabric. This can create problems with shoulders and certain close-fitting necklines, such as crew necks, that must fit over the head and rely on the elasticity of the knitting to do so (*see* the Triangles and Fairisle Fun designs in Chapter 7). With ribbed collars and edgings, casting off in rib rather than plain knitting is recommended.

Working from Charts – for Colour and Structure

For a designer, the knitting chart is the key to developing the detailed design, once the building blocks of stitches, overall design layout and tension have all been determined. This is the stage where all details are worked out, including a complete picture of the shaping. The chart becomes both a visually and a technically accurate representation of the design. Most of the designs in this book are knitted by using charts – for example, the charts may show the whole of a garment in full detail or a motif that is repeated in areas throughout the design.

How to read the charts

Most of the charts in Part 2 are for colourwork, but one, for the Travelling Vine tunic, uses motif charts for stitch textures where symbols have specific technical meanings and indicate specific actions, worked according to the instructions. However, both types of chart are interpreted in the same manner. The chart is an exact picture of the work, with one square representing one stitch and each line representing one row, seen from the right side of the fabric, whether for a colour or stitch design. It can also be an exact picture of the garment shaping, although written instructions are also given. Once understood, the charts are easy to follow and allow you to keep your place. When working from a visual chart, most knitters find that it helps to follow the row they are currently knitting by positioning a ruler at the relevant place on the chart – a magnetic board and ruler are particularly good for this, or, alternatively, removable highlighting tape can be used.

The standard way to read a knitting chart for designs worked flat on two needles, as presented in this book, is starting from the bottom right and reading row by row in alternate directions, that is, from right to left and then from left to right. Each row of the chart is numbered, starting where the knitting commences. In general, odd-numbered rows are right-side rows and are therefore read from right to left; this in turn means that even-numbered rows are wrong-side rows and are therefore read from left to right. Many of the colour charts in this book represent designs worked in stocking stitch, so the odd-numbered rows are usually of knit stitches and the even-numbered rows usually of purl stitches. The Shield designs, however, are knitted in reverse stocking stitch, with stocking-stitch motifs, so, in this case, the

An example of a colourwork chart with shaping, for the Fairisle Fun sweater (see Chapter 6).

background is of purl stitches on the right side of the fabric (odd-numbered rows) and of knit stitches on the wrong side (even-numbered rows). An accompanying key gives the instructions to interpret each specific chart.

Working from charts can also be flexible, for example, in order to reverse a pattern. In the Shawl-cardigan design, the sleeve chart is worked as normal for one sleeve, and then, for the second sleeve, the pattern is knitted in reverse from the same chart, by working odd-numbered rows as wrong-side rows (of purl stitches, and reading right to left) and even-numbered rows as right-side rows (of knit stitches, and reading left to right). It is not as difficult as it might sound!

Reading stitch-pattern charts

Stitch-pattern charts are read in a similar way to colourwork charts, again with the right side of the fabric being represented. Every stitch-pattern chart has a key explaining the symbols used within the chart; these symbols each stand for a specific stitch or structure and sequence of actions, which may be different on right-side and wrong-side rows. There is also another important convention to note for these charts: with textural designs including cable and bobble patterns, additional stitches may be created and then lost within a specific stitch sequence. These are therefore not part of the overall stitch count and are represented by greyed-out squares on the chart, initially for stitches that do not yet exist and later for stitches that no longer exist. For example, in the motifs of the Travelling Vine design, the same number of stitches is created as is later lost, but the corresponding grey no-stitch squares may be represented in different positions within a pattern repeat, as appropriate. Nevertheless, this does not affect the overall result.

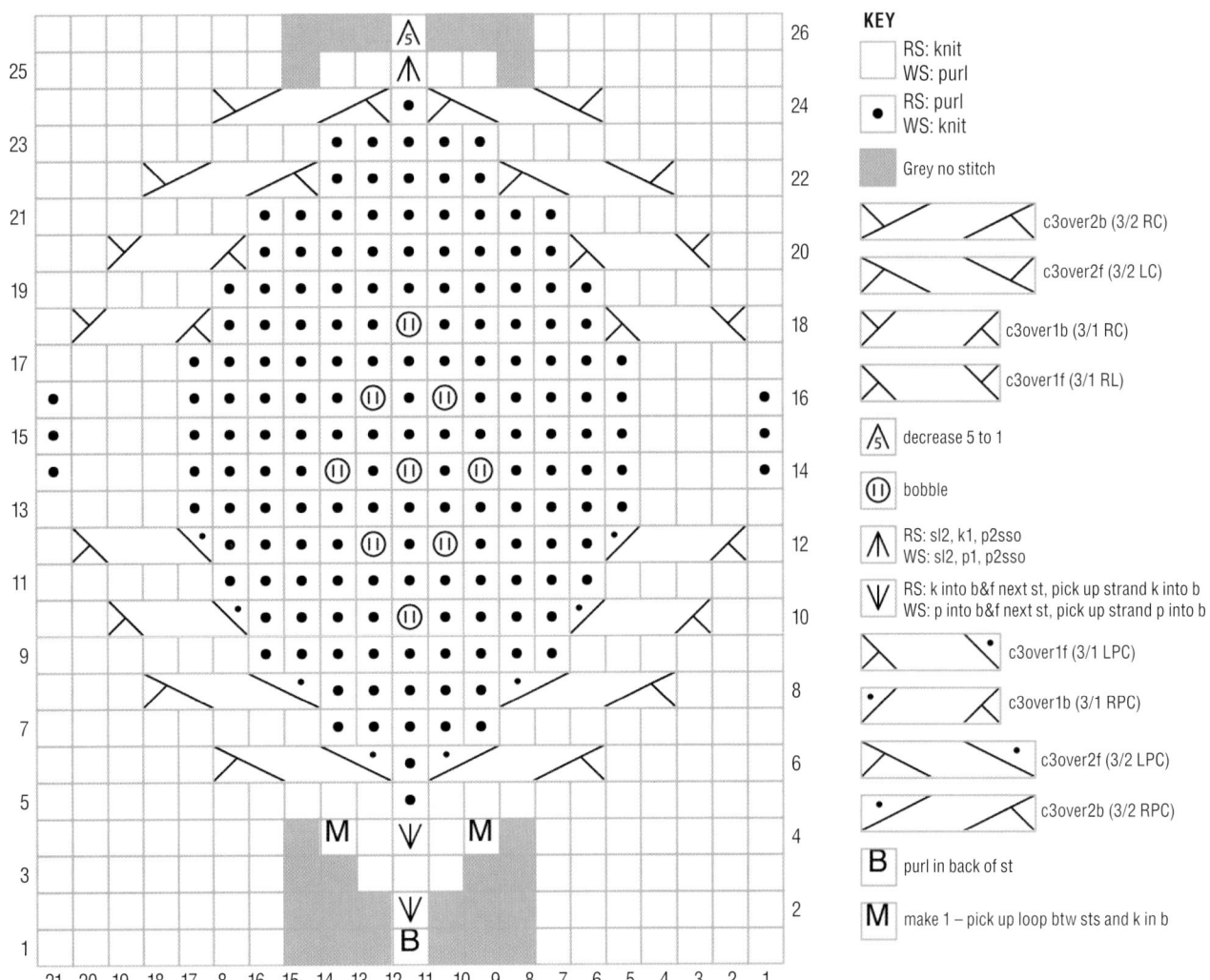

Oval Window-motif chart for the Travelling Vine design (see Chapter 10).

Reading shaping from charts

Some charts show the complete shape of a garment piece, in addition to the graphic or stitch-texture pattern of the design. Shaping is followed from the outline of the graph, guided by the numbered rows. Steps of single squares at the beginning or end of the row represent ordinary increasing, by working twice into the edge stitch, or decreasing, by working the first two or last two stitches of the row together. Where the step line moves in horizontally over more than one square at the beginning of a row, these stitches are to be cast off at the beginning of this row; if the step line moves out horizontally over more than one square at the beginning of a row, these stitches are to be cast on at the beginning of the row. (For example, *see* the Tiger-scarf head chart in Chapter 11). However, to avoid any doubt, the patterns also describe the shaping required within the written instructions.

Detail of the Shawl-cardigan design showing embroidered flowers and the paisley border with Swiss-darned details.

Finishing Touches

Embroidery

Impressive effects can be achieved with simple embroidery stitches to add highlights and finishing touches to a design. For example, the Shawl-cardigan design features embroidered flowers scattered across the shoulders, worked in stem stitch, lazy-daisy stitch and French knots. The featured details from a design called Posy Trellis include embroidered flowers worked with French knots on top of a knitted-in spray of leaves.

To work a French knot, first secure the yarn with a small backstitch on the inside of the work, insert the needle from the back and bring the yarn to the right side. Prepare to make a small backstitch and, before pulling the needle through, wrap the yarn two or three times around the point of the needle, pull the needle through the wraps whilst holding them in place and then reinsert the needle close to where the yarn came through, taking the yarn to the back to complete the knot. Continue making knots individually or in clusters, and finish off with a small backstitch on the wrong side. Experiment with the number of wraps of yarn made around the needle shaft to give the desired effect: many turns give a long caterpillar-like knot; fewer turns create a rounder knot.

To work a lazy-daisy stitch, first secure the yarn on the inside of the piece and bring the needle through to the right side, from back to front, make a small loop of yarn for the flower petal and insert the needle back into the fabric in the same place that the yarn came through, pulling the loop to the desired size, then bring the needle up through the fabric again just inside the curve of the yarn loop and secure the loop with a small stitch made over the yarn, to give a petal or leaf effect.

To work stem stitch, simply make short, overlapping, adjacent, straight stitches in a slight diagonal direction, to create an overall straight or curved line, for example, to represent a flower or leaf stem.

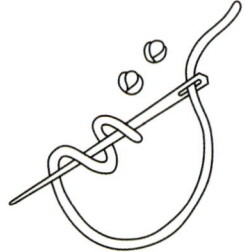

French-knot embroidery method.

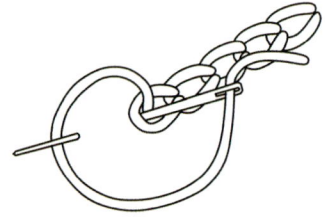

Method of working chain-stitch embroidery.

The Posy Trellis cardigan featuring flowers embroidered with French knots. (Photo: David McIntyre)

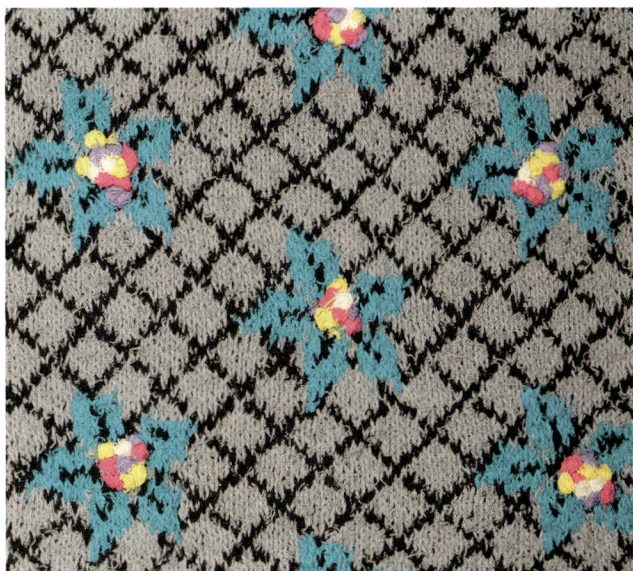

The Posy Trellis pattern knitted in textured cotton yarn with French-knots embroidery.

The Posy Trellis pattern knitted in cotton gimp with embroidery of longer French knots.

To work chain stitch, first secure the yarn on the inside of the piece and bring the needle through to the right side, from back to front, make a small loop of yarn on the surface and, holding the loop with your thumb, insert the needle back into the same place that the yarn came through, then bring the needle up a small distance ahead, ensuring that the yarn is underneath the point of the needle. Now, pull the needle and yarn fully through the fabric, drawing up the yarn (not too tightly) to make the first chain stitch. Insert the needle back into the fabric, inside the chain loop in the same place the yarn came through, and take a stitch forward, bringing the needle up through the fabric and passing the yarn underneath the point of the needle to form the next chain-stitch loop (*see* accompanying diagram). Pull the needle and yarn fully through the fabric to complete the second chain stitch, drawing up the yarn to the appropriate tension. Repeat the process, taking the needle down into the last-completed chain stitch, and working along the intended stitching line, in either straight or curved lines. Finish by securing the last chain-stitch loop with a small stitch over the yarn loop, taking the needle and yarn to the back of the work.

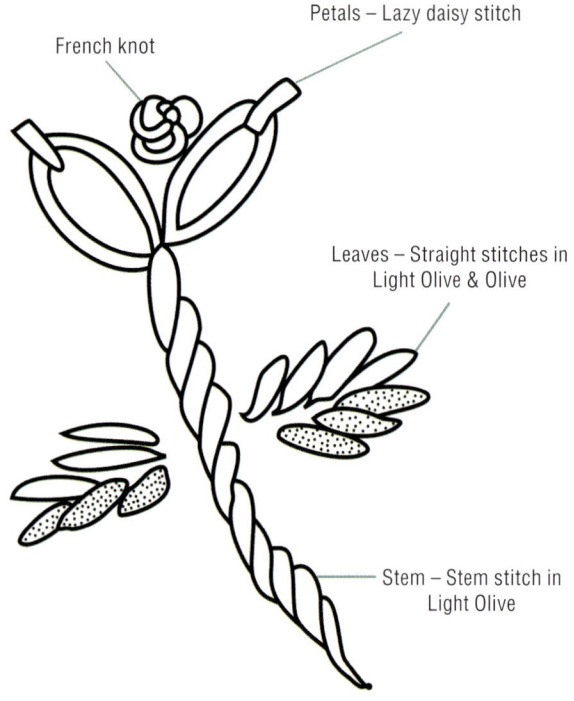

Techniques used in the Shawl-cardigan flower motif.

Embroidered Shawl-cardigan flower motif.

Embroidered flying ducks in an aerial-landscape design precisely worked in straight stitches.

In my collections, I would often embellish the knitting with embroidered motifs to bring the design into a third dimension: a cabled lattice would be transformed into a trellis with climbing roses made from crocheted leaves and flowers with embroidered chain-stitch stems; embroidered ducks would fly across a landscape, created with straight stitches.

Swiss darning

The Swiss-darning technique (also known as 'duplicate stitch') is specific to knitted fabric, particularly stocking stitch. It is also very versatile and can be used to add small details (even a single stitch) in graphic designs, instead of knitting them in whilst the fabric is being worked, or to work larger motifs, instead of intarsia knitting them, although over a larger area the effect is not as neat as knitting in the colour with intarsia. Swiss darning is also a very effective way to correct any colourwork errors, as the technique mimics the knitted stitch precisely, in terms of its size, shape and placement.

To work this technique, use a yarn of the same thickness as that used for the knitted fabric or one slightly thicker.

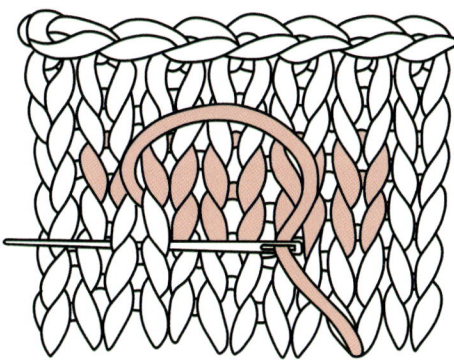

Swiss darning exactly replicates the knitted yarn path and can be used to add decoration or make corrections. (This technique is also known as duplicate stitch.)

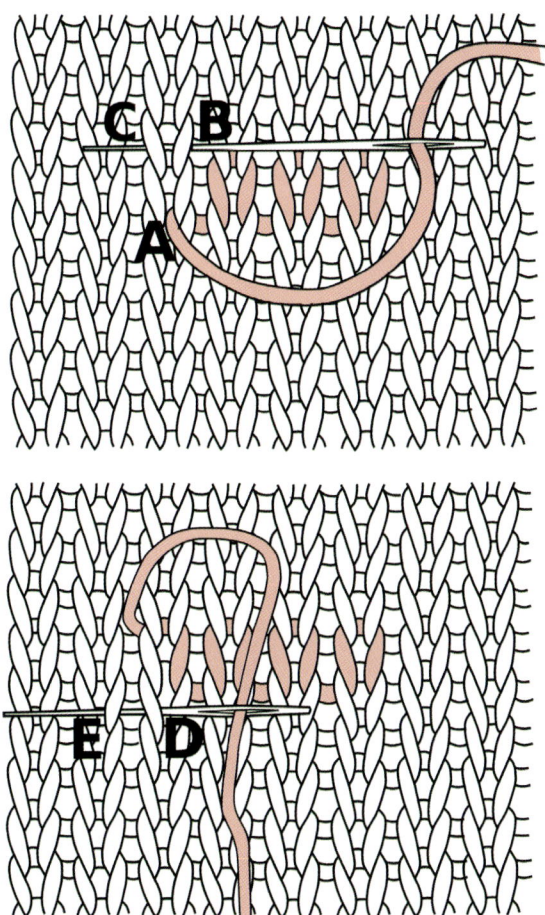

Method of working Swiss darning. Any motif or shape can be easily created.

If a thinner yarn is used, the background colour will show through. Secure the Swiss-darning, contrast-colour yarn at the back of the work, and bring the needle threaded with this yarn through to the front of the fabric at the base of the first knit stitch to be duplicated, or covered (A). Pass the needle from right to left through the base (that is, behind both the right leg and the left leg) of the stitch above the stitch to be duplicated (B–C), then take the needle back into the base of the stitch to be duplicated (D, that is, where the needle was originally brought up at A) and also bring the needle up at the base of the next stitch to be covered (D–E). Do not pull the yarn too tight but try to match the size and tension of the existing stitches. Repeat this process to cover stitches in a row, or bring the needle up at the base of a stitch on a different row, as necessary, to create the desired coloured shape. If working over a larger area, it is best to start at the top and work down in rows. Note that the yarn of the new, contrast colour follows the exact yarn path of the yarn of the stitches in the underlying knitted fabric.

In some designs, such as the Leopard scarf and mittens, I use a variation on this technique that I call elongated Swiss darning, which is quicker to work but does not cover the knitting so densely. This variation on the technique is worked in exactly the same manner, but, instead of covering every stitch, two or more stitches in the vertical direction are covered with one duplicate stitch, as can be seen in the accompanying photo.

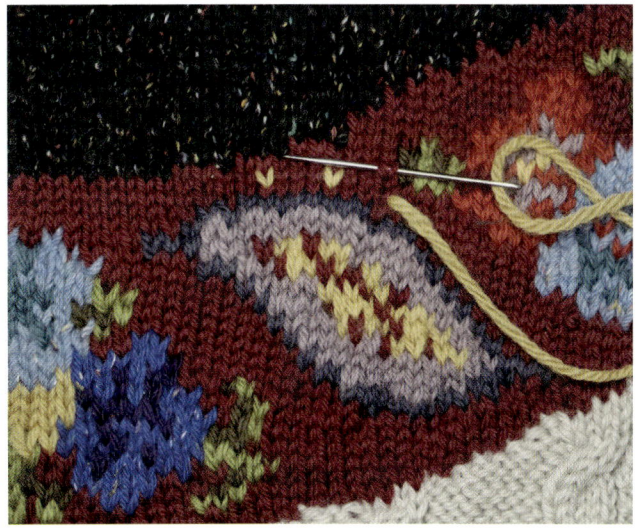

Swiss darning of individual stitches in the Shawl-cardigan paisley border.

KNITTING-PATTERN FUNDAMENTALS 59

The elongated Swiss-darning technique has been used here to cover two to four stitches at a time when adding a third colour to the Leopard-scarf upper-side spot pattern. This technique is quicker to work over a large piece and works well with a textured yarn such as mohair.

The inside of the Triangles sweater, with loose ends darned through the joins between yarn colours.

Making Up

Finishing and blocking

Having invested much time and care in knitting the pieces for a particular design, equal care should be taken when finishing these pieces. If knitting a coloured intarsia design, there will be loose ends to be dealt with in the body of the pieces. I recommend carefully darning in the ends along the colour joins on the back of the work, using a sufficient amount of this yarn so that the ends do not easily pull out when the fabric stretches during dressing and wearing. Take care to neaten up any loose stitches at the start or end of each colour section, and close up any gaps by taking the yarn through the adjacent stitch on the back of the work before darning the yarn end in. This process can be a very satisfying and therapeutic exercise! However, it is up to you – some knitters believe in just leaving the ends, others simply tie knots (which may come loose). I prefer to have my designs looking as good on the inside as the outside. Where yarn ends are at the edges of a piece, when seaming, use some of the loose ends matching the yarn colours on each side of the seam to sew that part of the seam, and darn the rest of the ends into the seams after making up.

The designs in the book are made from either 100-per-cent-wool yarns or mohair–wool-blend yarns. Follow the instructions on the manufacturer's ball band, but, as a general guide, pieces made from wool yarns or majority-wool blends can be steam pressed, but sweaters made from the 75-per-cent-mohair yarns do not need to be pressed, although steaming (without the iron or steamer making contact with the fabric) may sometimes be helpful, for example, for Fair Isle-type designs. If you are pressing, block the knitted pieces to size before making up to achieve an excellent finish. Using the measurement diagrams as a guide, pin out each piece to shape and size, ideally on a padded board, placing pins closely and regularly around the edge, but inside any edgings. Using a steam iron, or a dry iron together with a damp cloth, lightly steam press, but excluding ribbed or cabled edgings, in order to preserve their elasticity. Allow the pieces to dry fully before removing the pins. Never press too heavily, as this results in a lifeless garment, and most pieces require no more than a light passing over of the iron.

Seaming

Three different methods of seaming are recommended here to make up the knitted pieces, as per the instructions for a particular pattern.

Most body seams are worked by using backstitch, by putting the right sides of the pieces together and sewing close to their edges, giving structure to the garment and a neat appearance; backstitch seams also have the advantage that they mask any imperfect edges.

Most edging and collar seams are oversewn to minimize bulk and because they may be seen from both sides.

The patchwork-tile designs are assembled using an edge-to-edge seam that is worked from the right side, taking one loop of the fabric from each side alternately and drawing the pieces together; this is also known as mattress stitch or ladder stitch[2]. This seam is used where a backstitch seam would be too bulky and the edges of the pieces to be joined are neat.

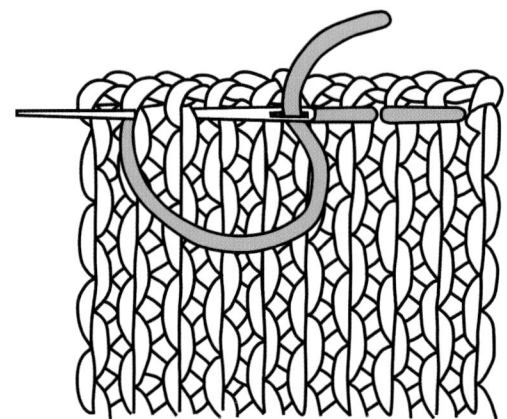

Backstitch seam.

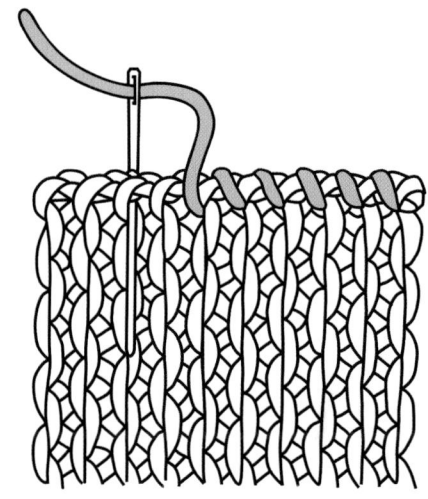

Oversewn seam.

Aftercare

Looking after your knitwear once it has been worn is also important for ensuring that your work lasts for a long time. Do not machine wash your knitwear as this may cause felting. Follow instructions on the yarn's ball band in relation to washing or dry cleaning your finished knitwear. With care, wool and natural-fibre yarns can be hand washed using a very mild detergent or soap especially designed for delicate fabrics and low temperatures or even cold-water hand washing (maximum 30°C). Squeeze the garment gently in the soapy water, but do not rub the fabric. Rinse the garment several times in clean water and then squeeze the fabric to remove excess water. Last, roll the still-wet garment in a towel to remove any remaining water or, briefly, spin it in a washing machine. Reshape the garment to the required measurements, and allow it to air-dry flat, preferable on a drying rack. Do not tumble-dry or spin the garment for longer than a few seconds, because extended tumble-drying or spinning could also cause felting of the fabric.

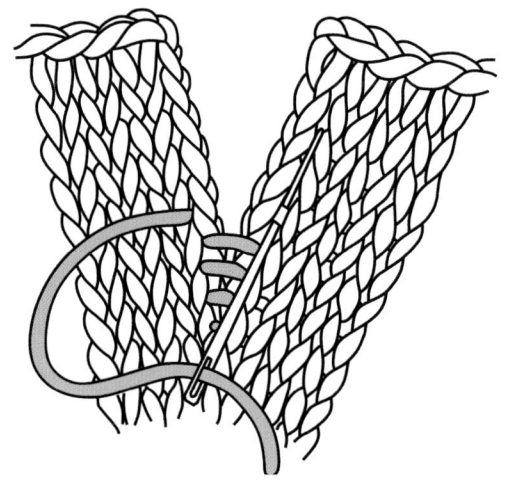

Edge-to-edge, mattress- or ladder-stitch seam.

CHAPTER 4

WORKING WITH COLOUR AND IMAGERY

Most designs throughout this book feature combinations of colour, geometric motifs and imagery that utilize one of two main methods of working – either the intarsia (colour-block) technique or the stranded-colourwork technique (also referred to as Fair Isle). One design, the Rosette tunic, combines the use of both methods. Further details on working with several colours are given here, together with tips on designing with colour and imagery.

Intarsia or Colour-Block Knitting

As mentioned in Chapter 2, intarsia is a machine-knitting industry term to describe a free-form manual method of creating imagery or patterns of any scale within a knitted garment, using as many colours as desired in any one row. This term has now been adopted by hand knitters, although the term 'colour-block knitting' is also used to describe designs that are often non-repeating and pictorial in nature and that are worked in a similar manner to that of hand-woven tapestry; hence, this process is sometimes known as 'picture knitting'. The basis of the technique is that each coloured area is worked from a separate small ball or length of yarn and that there are no floats on the back of the work. Therefore, unlike Fair Isle, or two-colour, stranded-colourwork knitting, intarsia knitting (often of stocking stitch) remains of single-stitch thickness throughout. The colours are used in turn along the row, and there is no limit to the number of colours that can be incorporated or the size of each area of colour – except for your patience!

When working an intarsia design and changing from one yarn colour to the next, always ensure that the yarns cross over each other on the wrong side of the fabric, to link the two yarn lengths together and prevent gaps appearing between the two adjacent areas of colour. To do this, simply drop the first colour that was is use and pick up the new colour to be used from underneath the first colour, so that the yarns cross and link together. This is especially important where there is a vertical join between blocks of colour, as otherwise a gap will appear. There will be loose ends at the beginning and end of each colour section, which can be darned in along the joins between the two adjacent colours after the knitting has been completed. Alternatively, carefully darn into the back surface of the stitches on the wrong side of the fabric, working upwards and then downwards so that each loose end does not pull out when the garment is stretched.

OPPOSITE PAGE: The Tranquil Vale landscape sweater, 1979, worked in machine-knitted intarsia in a variety of yarns – rayon (river), acrylic bouclé (tree), Shetland wool (hills and foreground), merino wool (sky), an angora blend (clouds) and cotton chenille (bushes). (Photo: Barbara Bellingham)

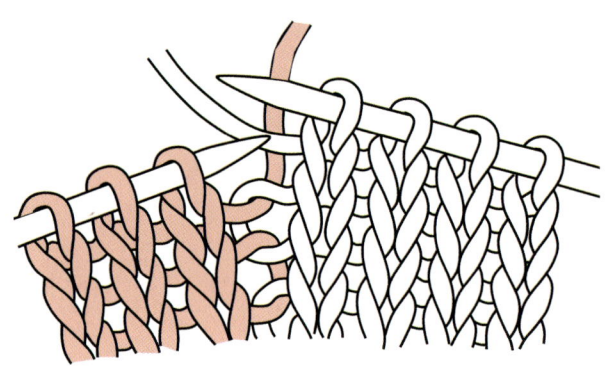

Crossing yarns on a knit row – pick up the new yarn colour from under the yarn being dropped.

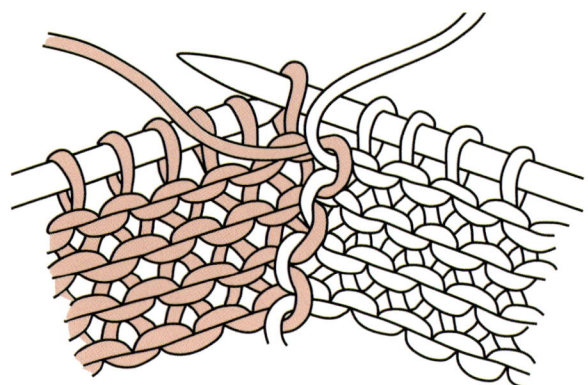

Crossing yarns on a purl row – pick up the new yarn colour from under the yarn being dropped.

Handling many colours

When working the intarsia (colour-block) designs in this book, such as the Shield sweater and cardigan, Triangles sweater, and Lion and Unicorn sweater, many colours are used within each row. This requires some preliminary organization in order to manage all of the yarns and avoid too much frustrating tangling of the yarns. Two methods can be used: either winding small amounts of each yarn colour on to bobbins (commercially bought or home-made from stiff card) or making 'butterfly twists', also called simply 'butterflies' or mini skeins, of smaller amounts of yarn.

Card bobbins can be cut in the shape of a letter H, with a slit to hold the end of the yarn firmly. Wind several bobbins, at least one for each yarn colour, according to the design, as working each area of colour requires a separate bobbin. These bobbins are kept close to the needle whilst the knitting is being worked, with the knitter unravelling just small amounts of the bobbin yarn as required.

The butterfly twists are, in my opinion, easier to work with when there are a lot of colours in use. To make a butterfly twist, start with one end of the yarn in the palm of your hand, then wind the yarn in a figure-of-eight path around your thumb and little finger. Wrap the end of the yarn around the centre and secure this end. Work from the loose yarn end left at the start of the butterfly twist, so that the yarn feeds out from the centre of this mini skein and does not unravel during knitting. When working with very small areas of colours, such as for the Shawl or Persian Flower designs, it is easiest to use just a length of yarn to reduce tangling, and then this length can be easily pulled free from any other yarn in use. More guidance on yarn colours and their management is given in the individual patterns.

The inside of the Lion and Unicorn sweater after meticulous finishing. (See also Chapter 9.)

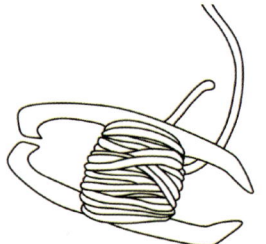

Bobbins in the general shape of an H can be purchased or made from stiff card.

Make a butterfly twist for working a small area of colour, and pull the yarn from the beginning strand from winding the butterfly twist.

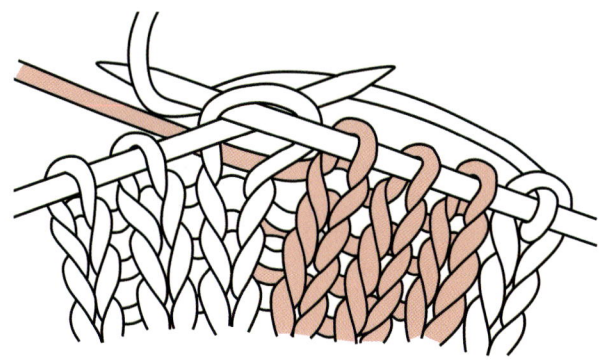

Stranding the second yarn colour across three stitches on a knit row.

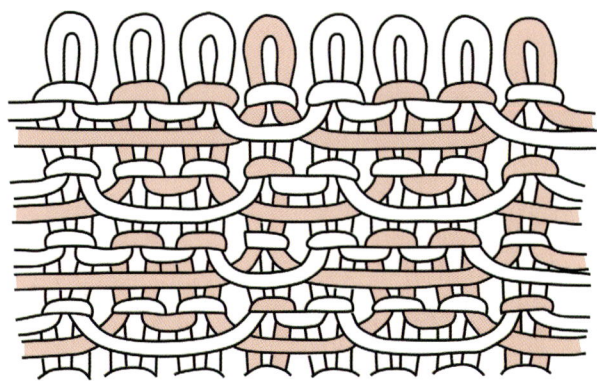

The result of two-colour stranded-colourwork knitting when working over one stitch, two stitches and three stitches, as seen from the back of the work.

Fair Isle or Stranded-colourwork Knitting

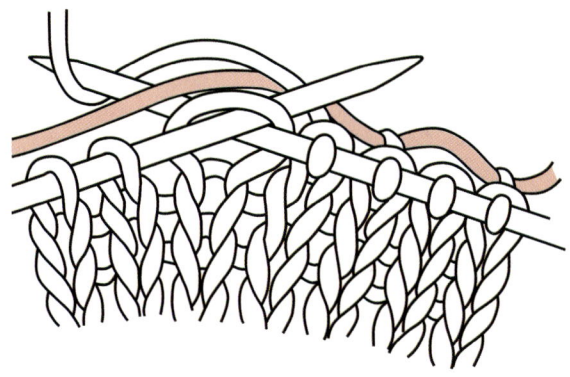

Weaving in a yarn colour at the back of the work on alternate stitches so that it is caught by the working yarn.

Much of the colourwork featured in this book is knitted with the intarsia technique, as described above, but some designs, including Dogtooth, Fairisle Fun and Azulejos, are knitted with the two-colour stranded-colourwork technique, often referred to generically as Fair Isle knitting, even when the patterns are nothing like classic Fair Isle. Note that the Azulejos tile pattern also involves some three-colour stranded-colourwork knitting for the rows at the centre and top of each tile. To work the stranded-colourwork technique, float the yarn (or yarns) not currently in use loosely across at the back of the work until it is next required, but over not more than three or four stitches. If more stitches need to be spanned by the yarn not in use then weave in this floating yarn by taking it under and over the yarn being used, so the floating strand is regularly caught in at the back of the work at every second or third stitch, as preferred. Take great care not to pull the yarn not in use too tight, whether creating floats or weaving it in, because this

Two-colour stranded-colourwork knitting in the Scroll-gilet tile.

The reverse of the Scroll-gilet tile, demonstrating the floats of the stranded-colourwork technique.

WORKING WITH COLOUR AND IMAGERY 65

The Vase of Flowers coat, worked in 100-per-cent-angora yarn, features a full-body-sized motif on the back, with the flowers spilling over the shoulders on to the front and sleeves. The motif colours are close in tone to the grey ground, giving a rich but relatively subtle effect. (Photo: David McIntyre)

A second colourway of the 100-per-cent-angora Vase of Flowers coat creates more drama, with purple, red and lilac motifs on a white background. (Photo: Barbara Bellingham)

will pucker the knitting, and the knitted fabric will not lie flat or have enough stretch, and the garment is therefore likely to be too small. The resulting fabric is always thicker than that worked in stocking stitch, because of the multiple strands of the yarn floats at the back. The stranded-colourwork technique also has an effect on the resulting stitch and row tension, as the floating threads change the overall proportion of the stitch from rectangular to square (as can be seen, for example, in the Fairisle Fun and Dogtooth designs).

Colour and Texture

One of the joys of knitting is in combining yarn colours and textures with a design concept. The exciting challenge is to achieve an aesthetic balance between colour, texture, pattern and scale on the body. Some designs feature small motifs in repeated patterns and others large-scale imagery and patterns spread over the entire garment-body canvas. In my hand-knitting designs, I favoured yarns such as mohair and angora[1] that created a surface texture and also blurred and softened the lines between shapes. Wool and cotton yarns of my own brand were not smooth but highly textured, to give additional surface interest and visual depth to enhance the patterns in which they were used.

In my early landscape-sweater designs, I liked to 'paint' with yarns to decorate the body with colour, texture and imagery (*see* Chapter 2). To enhance the effects, I sought out varied types of yarns that could be added in with the plain wool yarns in use, mixing in rayon and silver thread for the depiction of sparkling water, using textured bouclé and fine chenille yarns for foliage and trees, and utilizing angora mixes for fluffy clouds, as can be seen in the image at the beginning of this chapter and here.

Within my collections, several designs such as the Rosette tunic and Tapestry Flower coat (*see* Chapter 10) combined wool with long-haired 100-per-cent-angora yarns.

Experimenting with colourways

Developing a colour palette and grouping colours together is a real pleasure. A very different mood can be obtained from the same design simply by changing the colour palette, as can be seen in the examples shown throughout this book. Many of the designs use six or more colours,

The cotton Posy Trellis cardigan features a simple diamond grid and a single motif repeated over the entire garment. (Photo: Barbara Bellingham)

Detail of the Flying Duck landscape sweater, showing a mix of yarns – merino wool with silver metallic thread (water), acrylic bouclé (tree), merino wool (hills and foreground) and a wool–angora blend (clouds).

and some, such as the Triangles and Shawl designs, can combine ten to twelve colours together. For multicoloured designs to work well, it is helpful for most of the colours to have a similar intensity and depth of tone, but bright or dark highlight colours can also be important to accentuate a design, for example, purple used with pastel colours, or black with brights. Multiple colours are also effective when used together in several shades of the same colour group, say, purples to blues and blue/greens, or tones of reds, oranges, pinks and plums, giving a more subtle effect than achievable with highly contrasting colours. Creating a specific colour palette is best done with the actual yarns you will use, so wind little balls of yarn from the colours that you have available and play around with samples. Weavers traditionally wind stripes of colour around a thin strip of card to test the colour balance. Once a palette has been created, finalized designs can be worked out on paper by quickly trying out variations by using coloured pens or crayons. If your design is in a software programme, most have a facility to create custom colourways and change the colours around at will, although colour compatibility between screen colour, printed colour and yarn colour can be tricky. However, a good general impression of a colour combination is easily obtained.

After many years of sourcing yarns in commercial collections, it was a delight to be able to produce my own (limited) range of colours in mohair, wool and cotton yarns. To create variety, I approached creating my wool colour palette with two distinctive design possibilities within a range of twelve shades –a group of brights and a group of pastels, together with dark and light neutrals – ecru, dark grey and mid grey – to offset the other colours. As an example of the design possibilities of such a colour palette, the Shield sweater is shown in two different colourways that give a very different feel to the same design – ecru with brights and ecru with pastels (*see* Chapter 9).

Yarn samples of the Sandy Black Mohair and Wool Twist ranges of twelve colours each.

WORKING WITH COLOUR AND IMAGERY 67

The Shield design is shown here knitted in mohair yarn on a natural-cream background and in wool yarn on a dark-grey background.

Two colourways from the mohair range for the Rectangles design are shown here, one featuring six bright colours and another a subtler palette omitting gold and red and instead including lilac and pinks.

In the 1980s, a key supplier of yarns to knitwear designers was Rowan Yarns, with their distinctive and wide ranges of natural fibres and colours, many developed with colourist Kaffe Fassett. Today, there are many more small suppliers of knitting yarns, producing a variety of original blends and textures, especially in natural fibres, including alpaca and llama fibres blended with wools. Many of these producers also hand dye yarns and create spectacular colour-imprinted yarns that require little more than plain knitting to show off their qualities – a very different scenario compared with the 1980s!

Charting Graphic Imagery

Tension (gauge) becomes especially important when planning knitted imagery, to ensure that the visual effects are to be as desired. To realize my early graphic motifs or pictorial designs, I first sketched my visual ideas on standard graph paper using one square to represent one knitted stitch. Although accurate in numbers of stitches and rows, it could be only approximately visually correct for imagery to be knitted in stocking stitch. This is because the basic proportion of a stitch in stocking-stitch fabric is not square but rectangular – the stitch is squashed vertically so that, in any given measurement, there will normally be more rows than stitches, as seen in a typical sample tension of 24sts and 30 rows per 10cm/4in. This proportion is in the ratio of 4 to 5 (width to length), other stitch patterns and tensions in the book are closer to a 3 to 4 ratio. Therefore, a design drawn on standard graph paper would not be created in the exact proportions of the drawing when knitted. For example, a circle would appear compressed top to bottom into an ellipse in the knitting. Because of this effect, I used to draw my own graph paper in order to get the exact proportions for the design I was working on and to perfect my imagery down to the last detail. (*See*, for example, the Lion and Unicorn design first explained in Chapter 5 and presented as a pattern in Chapter 9.) In the late 1980s, knitting author Montse Stanley pioneered the commercial production of her True Knit proportional graph paper, especially created for knitting design, with rectangular cells shaped such that there are more 'rows' present vertically than 'stitches' horizontally per cm/in. Today, proportional graph paper is readily available to knitters, either in paper form or downloadable online, corresponding to different tension ratios. Using this proportional graph paper as a basis, graphical or pictorial designs drawn directly will be more accurately proportioned when knitted, as extra rows have been automatically taken into the design.

The Shield cardigan, with a bold design, knitted in mohair yarns, to soften the imagery. (Photo: David McIntyre)

Detail of the Shield design, knitted in wool in bright colours on a dark-grey ground.

RIGHT: The Rectangles design, worked in six bright colours of mohair yarn. (Photo: David McIntyre)

FAR RIGHT: The Rectangles design, worked in blue, green, lilac and pink mohair yarns. (Photo: David McIntyre)

Charting Graphic Garment Designs

First, the size of the main garment piece must be worked out, based on the tension measurement for your selected yarn (*see* Chapter 3), to reveal the space available for the design. This shape can be simplified to a basic rectangle, as are many designs in this book.

Draw out the frame corresponding to the number of stitches and rows required for the garment piece or motif on to a large piece of proportional graph paper. In pencil, roughly sketch your design on to the graph paper in the position that you want. For best results, keep the design fairly clean and simple, avoiding too much fussy detail, as small details and thin lines can be added later by using Swiss darning or other embroidery techniques. Think in blocks of colour, and always be aware that the design will be built up from horizontal rows. Laying a ruler across the outline design clearly indicates that, every time a line crosses the ruler, a change of colour is required. The next stage is to translate the outlines of the drawing into stepped outlines following the lines of the rectangular cells of the graph paper, whilst also ensuring that the design 'reads' well. Once you are satisfied with the general outlines, the design can be finalized with clear outlines and filled in with colour.

Several software programmes are now available specifically for creating design charts for knitting, and some produce proportional grids. They are particularly suitable for working on small-scale colourwork motifs and stitch patterns such as lace, and many programmes can also generate written instructions. Pattern charts are created stitch by stitch, by filling in each square on the grid with colours or stitch symbols, although there is limited facility for freehand drawing for intarsia patterns. It is therefore advisable to have a clear idea and a rough sketch of what you want to achieve, before starting to create a digital version of the design with such a programme. Some programmes allow you to upload an image or photo and translate that into a knitting chart in the correct proportions. However, the best test of a chart is to knit a sample of the design to check whether the translation from chart to knitting is as you want. The finer the gauge of the knitted fabric, the more detailed your graphic imagery will be. The flexibility of knitting design based on the graphing of individual stitches in this way is limitless.

The initial stylized leaf design sketched on graph paper according to a calculated scale, and squared up to create a workable knitting chart.

CHAPTER 5

DESIGNING KNITWEAR

This chapter looks at the design and development process for creating knitwear, which inevitably involves some calculations, in addition to the creative design-development process.

Basic Pattern Calculations

When designing garments, knitting up test samples is fundamental to understanding the behaviour of the yarns and the effect of stitch patterns on the size of the finished piece, compared to plain stocking-stitch fabric. Much of the design-concept work is completed during this stage of practical experimentation, and, following this, the pattern calculations have to be completed.

OPPOSITE PAGE: The Tapestry Flower jacket, constructed from a patchwork of individual tile modules, with a stylized-flower and asymmetric-border design.
(Photo: David McIntyre)

The tension square is the basic building block for planning a design and calculating the precise numbers of stitches and rows required for the pattern. Calculations are based on simple arithmetic (using a calculator), although they do sometimes require the use of decimal fractions in order to be accurate. To ensure accuracy, rounding up is done only at the end of the calculation.

Although it is more reliable to measure overall tension based on the 10cm/4in swatch square, when making calculations, the basic building block is the number of stitches per cm/in. Choose one measurement system to work with, centimetres or inches, as this also ensures accuracy: the precise equivalence of inches to centimetres is that 1in = 2.54cm, to 2 decimal places, but it is usual to use the slightly less accurate measurement equivalence of 1in = 2.5cm, rounded to 1 decimal place.

The key measurements to be determined for a simple sweater with drop shoulders made to a rectangular proportion, such as the Trailing Roses, Triangles or Dogtooth sweater, are simply the required length from the shoulder point to the bottom edge and the width of the underarm. The other key measurements are then the armhole depth and sleeve length (taking into account the drop shoulder, which simplifies the shape of the sleeve). The width and style of the neckline are important elements of the design decisions – the sweaters mentioned above all have crew necks but with different collar treatments.

Example: Dogtooth sweater

The Dogtooth sweater is based on a rectangular shape, with drop shoulders and a crew neck, with simple, tapered sleeves. The tension given for this design in two-colour stranded-colourwork knitting is in a square proportion – 18sts and 18 rows to 10cm/4in.

Basic Garment Calculations

Desired measurements for the first-size sweater are a width of 54cm/21½in and a length of 58.5cm/23in, including the ribbing. The tension of 18sts and 18 rows to 10cm/4in equates to 1.8sts per 1cm or 4.5sts per 1in. In this case, it also equates to 1.8 rows per 1cm or 4.5 rows per 1in. Therefore, using the centimetre measurement, the number of stitches required is 54 × 1.8 = 97.2, which translates to 97sts. Similarly, using the inch measurement, the number of stitches required is 21½ × 4.5 = 96.75 or 97sts again. Although there is a very slight difference, in reality, the two systems are compatible, when rounded up at only the very end of the calculation.

Sometimes a designer may slightly adjust the number of stitches to take into account the fitting of a pattern repeat into the available stitches of a pattern piece and the seams. Here, the pattern repeat is 10sts in width, and the pattern has been laid out in such a way as to centre the design, taking into account a 1-stitch seam allowance at each side of the body pieces. The size difference for this design between the first and second sizes is only 5cm/2in all round, which equates to a 5-stitch difference in width, when rounded up, so accuracy is important here.

The Dogtooth-sweater design, based on a simple rectangular shape. (Photo: Jo Teasdale)

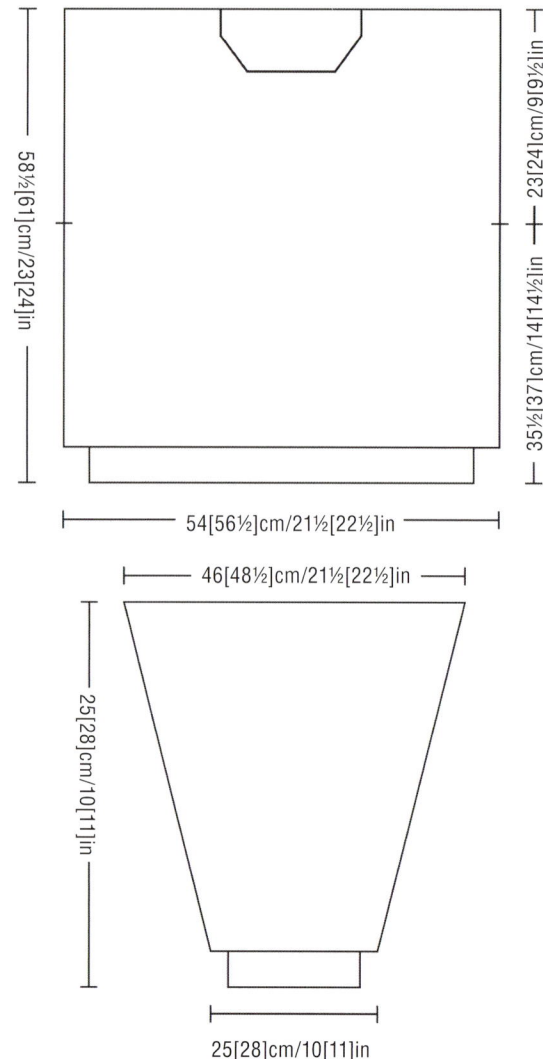

Dogtooth-sweater measurement diagram.

Sleeve-shaping Calculations

The desired sleeve length including ribbing is 49.5cm/19½in. The comfortable wrist width of 25cm/10in of the knitted-flat sleeve is drawn in by the cuff ribbing, and the sleeve width at the wrist is increased to 46cm/18½in at the top. This translates to 25 × 1.8 = 45sts (exactly) at the wrist (or, for inches, 10 × 4.5 = 45sts), increasing to 46 × 1.8 = 82.8 or 83sts (or, for inches, 18.5 × 4.5 = 83.25 or 83sts). To work out the increases required from the wrist to the sleeve top, there is a difference of 38sts, meaning that 19sts must be increased on each side of the sleeve over a length of 44.5cm/17½in (excluding the 5cm/2in cuff), that is, 44.5 × 1.8 = 80.1 or 80 rows. There are 80 rows in which to increase 19 times (at each side), so the basic calculation is 80 divided by 19 = 4.2. This suggests increasing on every fourth row, which will require 76 rows, leaving 4 rows, or around 2cm, or just over ¾in, to be worked straight at the top of the sleeve. It was decided to increase this straight section at the top of the sleeve a little by starting the sleeve shaping on the second row of the sleeve pattern; this left 6 rows (3.3cm, or around 1¼in) to be worked straight at the top of the sleeve at full width.

Designing a Garment

The next sections look at the general principles and stages that apply to developing all knitwear designs, from initial inspiration to planning the detailed patterns. Two examples are given here from my own process, both using charted design motifs. The first example, here focusing on the development of the precise graphic patterns and subtle textural details, is of a group of intarsia sweaters with strong visual impact, based on a heraldic theme. These two heraldic patterns are included in Chapter 9, the Shield sweater and cardigan, and the Lion and Unicorn sweater. The second example, of the Scroll gilet, is based on a patchwork (or modular) design, created by the joining together of repeating units or tiles. This patchwork technique is a favourite of mine, enabling the creation of intricately patterned designs by changing the orientation of just one knitted element, and has many potential variations. The example given below illustrates the manner in which modular tile designs can be developed, and further patchwork designs using a single repeated unit are shown in the accompanying photographs. Two complete patchwork patterns are given in Part 2: the Fairisle Fun design (*see* Chapter 7) features a simple two-piece construction for the back and front, and the more complex Azulejos tunic and jacket (*see* Chapter 10) illustrate a patchwork design created from two mirror-image tiles.

The Medieval Tile sweaters, constructed from one main tile used in different orientations, shown in light and dark colourways and two different lengths. (Photo: Paul Dennison)

A tile pattern and border from the Alhambra, Spain, a direct inspiration for the Medieval Tile sweater design.

Back view of the Shield cardigan, demonstrating the design layout. (Photo: David McIntyre)

The Lion and Unicorn sweater, in a gold colourway. (Photo: David McIntyre)

LEFT: Inspirational imagery from classic heraldry, with lions and eagles being prominent.

RIGHT: A preliminary sketch of a lion rampant and plumes (see the start of Chapter 9 for a photograph of the Coat of Arms coat that features these motifs).

Example: The Heraldic Collection

These sweaters are from an award-winning knitwear collection first shown in 1984, inspired by the theme of heraldry. My interest in the subject was sparked when an artist friend took on work hand painting small heraldic shields in brightly coloured enamels for a company that researched people's ancestry. I explored the topic further through reference books and was immediately inspired by the rich imagery and bold colours associated with heraldry, in particular the stylized animal motifs such as the lion rampant – a lion rising up on its hind legs.

I set about sketching ideas to be used as graphic patterns in the designs, based on a classic oversized sweater with drop shoulders – a simple rectangular shape that provided ample scope for designing the colourwork patterns. I fixed on the basic proportions and devised a series of ideas including a sweater with a large shield incorporating my bird logo and complete with an embroidered Latin motto: Arte et Labore – art and work.

The large scale of the main shield worked well as a dramatic focal point on either the front (as in the sweater version) or the back (as in the cardigan) of the body. To give dimension to the larger motifs, the shield and banner are knitted in stocking stitch in colours on a reverse-stocking-stitch ground.

Lion and Unicorn-design rough sketch for design layout.

Lion and Unicorn-design colour-arrangement testing.

The small shield shapes are defined by a subtle texture change and colour stripe, evolved during knitting trials from the initial pattern chart. Then came the process of translating the sketches on to the precisely calculated graph-paper pattern-piece shapes, including the exact number of stitches and rows available based on the width and length that I had decided upon and the tension swatches I had knitted.

Other designs in the heraldic range incorporated simpler all-over repeat patterning of small shields or fleur-de-lys motifs on a diamond ground (*see* Chapter 9). However, the Lion and Unicorn design is the pièce de résistance – the most complex graphically and the most challenging to knit, with its all-over colourwork-pattern motifs worked on both the front and the back. In this design, I wanted to use all of the fabulous heraldic creatures – lion rampant, spread eagle, unicorn and griffin – and positioned them in rectangles around a central shield (inspired by several of the historical heraldry images).

I then spent considerable time developing the individual motifs based on the tension (gauge) already established for the yarn (Sandy Black Wool Twist) by trial knitting the detailed shapes. For this, I drew out my own graph paper to the correct proportions of the yarn's tension determined from a tension swatch, in order to ensure that the drawn motifs looked as accurate as possible when knitted. Happily, today, we can buy proportional graph paper especially designed for knitting charts.

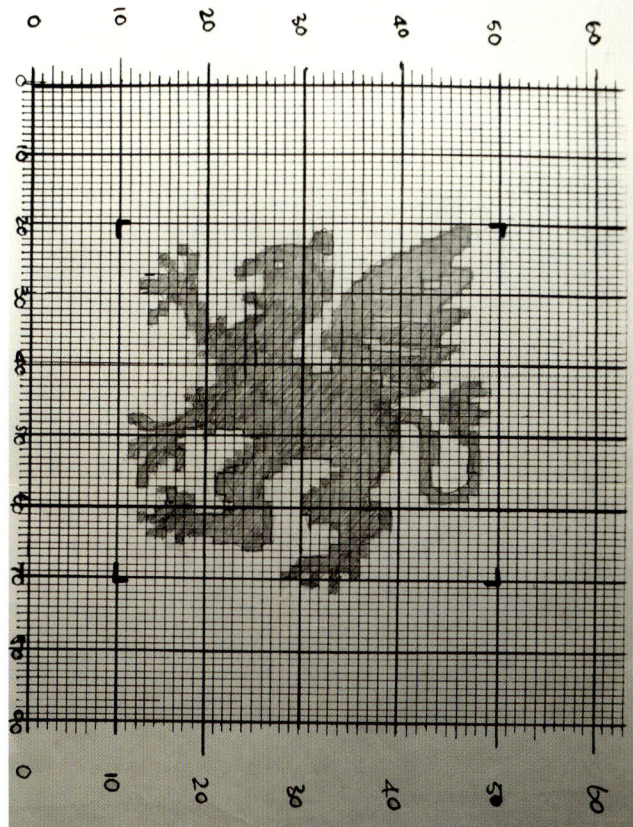

Griffin sketch on hand-drawn proportional graph paper.

DESIGNING KNITWEAR 75

Eagle sketch on hand-drawn proportional graph paper.

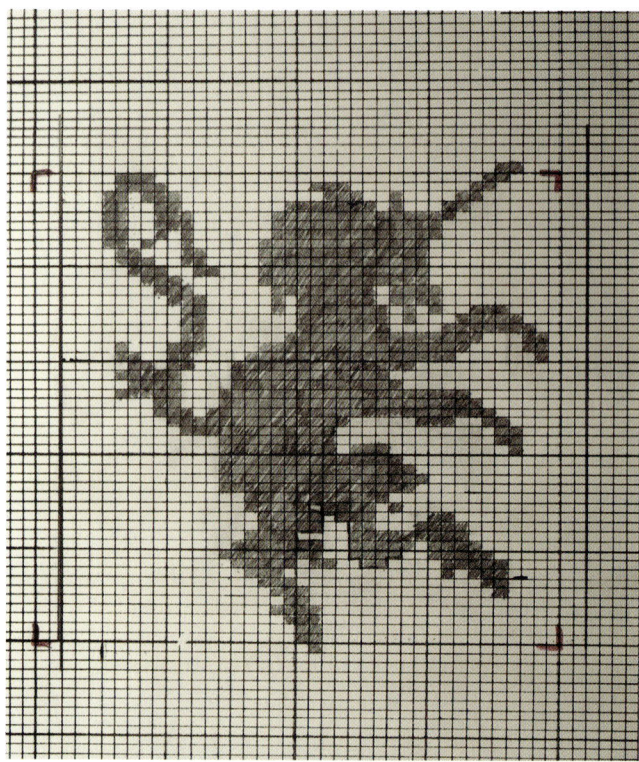
Unicorn sketch on hand-drawn proportional graph paper.

Once I had one of the creatures working well, I could develop the others with confidence, paying careful attention to every stitch, especially the placement of the stitch representing the eye of each creature. Once all of the decisions about the design of elements and colours had been made and trialled to satisfaction, and the garment proportions had been confirmed, the final design chart was developed and instructions written, with the chart providing the key information for the design.

To offset the intense patterning of the graphic design, I added some textural detail to the plain sleeves by creating a contrast-colour trefoil motif from three bobbles and for which

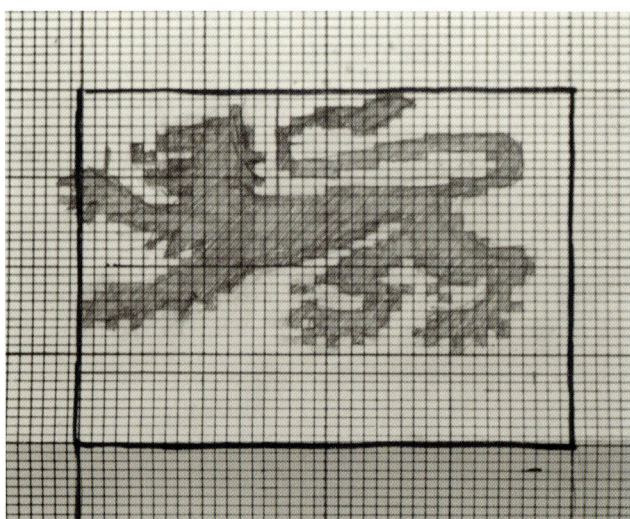
Lion sketch on hand-drawn proportional graph paper.

A test swatch worked from the Lion chart.

76 DESIGNING KNITWEAR

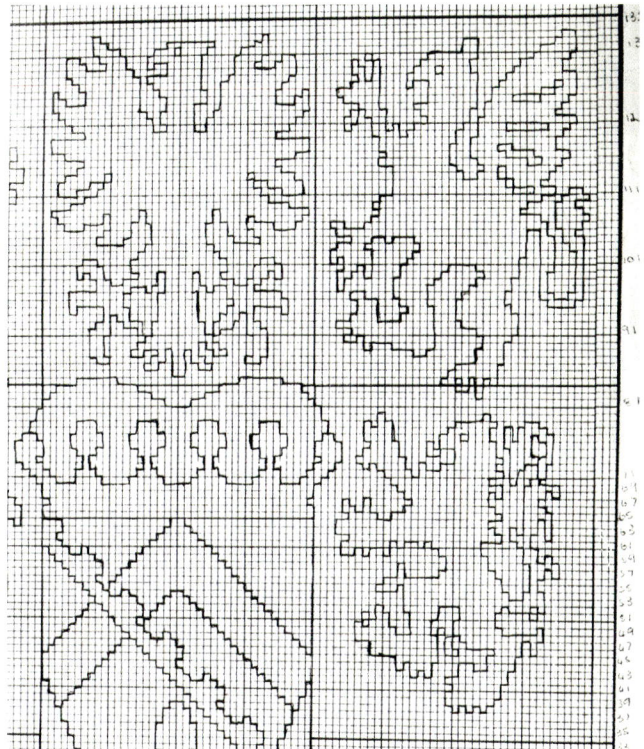

Detail of the hand-drawn chart for the Lion and Unicorn design.

Tiles of Seville, Spain. The rhythms created through repetitions are fascinating in their endless variety.

Back view of the Scroll gilet, constructed from tiles. (Photo: courtesy of Rowan Yarns)

the tail ends of the contrast-colour yarn are brought to the front of the work, to complete these decorative details (and neatly avoiding the need for darning in these yarn ends). The heraldic sweaters were each finished with cables or diagonal rib at top and bottom, to give structure, texture and stability, and two designs, Shield and Lion and Unicorn, were finished off with a dramatic cabled cowl collar. This process of finding inspiration, researching, design drawing, graphing, knitting trials and finalizing the charts and details is fundamentally the same for all types of knitwear design.

Example: Patchwork or Modular Knitting Design

In the next example, we look at the inspiration and design process behind a patchwork garment constructed from modular knitted 'tiles': the Scroll gilet. Abundant visual inspiration for tile designs and patterning is readily available and is especially evident in Spain, Portugal, the Netherlands and countries with an Islamic tradition. Both abstract and figurative decorative tiles are used prolifically on the inside and outside of buildings, from palaces to more modest dwellings. However, the source of inspiration behind this Scroll gilet design was rather more mundane!

This design was commissioned by Rowan Yarns for a book of patterns by several designers, and as such the brief was completely open – the only firm information was that there would be both summer and winter garments included[1].

Stage 1: Initial inspiration

The starting point for this design was some decorative tiles that I observed in the ladies' toilets at St Pancras Station in London! I made a quick sketch at the time. (Sadly, these tiles were long since removed in renovation work.)

A series of tile sketches, made from material in reference books.

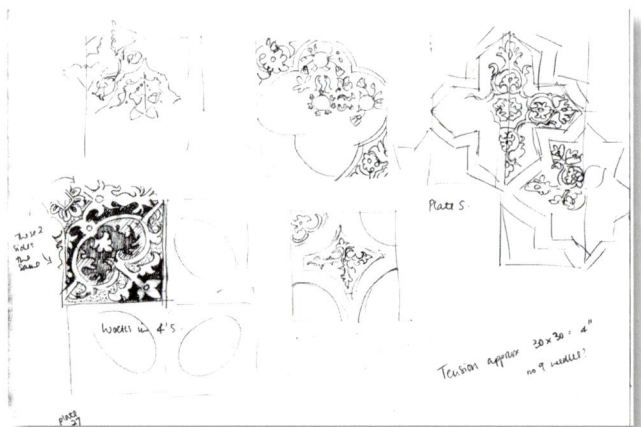

Further sketches analysing different repeating rhythms in tiles.

Stage 2: Further research

The idea of tiles led me to research Dutch tiles via reference books.

Stage 3: Design drawings

From this research, I made pencil sketches of all of the patterns that interested me, and I started to think about suitable yarn. Colours were to be as in the tiles – basically traditional blue and white – and therefore the garment would be for summer wear and made with a fine cotton yarn.

Stage 4: Selection

I sketched different variations of design elements to understand how they worked, refining and simplifying the patterns so that they would be suitable for knitting. I did not copy any particular tile, but I devised my own combination of the pattern elements I had found that would create a definite rhythm when repeated.

The final tile design at actual size 14.5cm/5/5in square, photocopied to test out the design layout as full scale.

RIGHT: The tile design in one version of the repeat pattern.

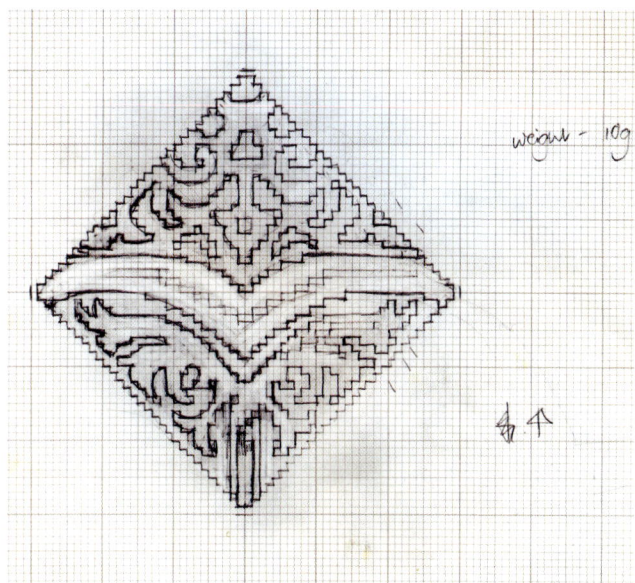

The initial working chart for the tile design.

Stage 5: Charting the design

The first step towards creating a garment with a patchwork construction is to finalize the building block of the tile unit. I wanted the design to use just one basic piece, but for it to be arranged in clever ways to form an overall pattern. This idea referred back to my mathematics days when I had been very interested in the theory of repeating patterns, which is fundamental to much textile design – here was a knitted application!

On graph paper, I drew a pencil chart with two strong elements, to be worked in different colours, as the initial working chart.

Stage 6: Yarn selection and knitting trials

With the help of this working chart, I tested various cotton yarns – both smooth and textured – and selected one with a subtle matt texture when worked into a knitted fabric. After the first knitting trial, I amended the chart to get the best effect and reknitted the swatch. I then decided to

The initial concept for different layouts of the modular garment and colour effects.

give the tile some further textural interest by introducing a garter-stitch section in its centre. This would enhance the decorative overall effect by giving definite textural variation to the graphic pattern.

The initial test swatch, testing both colour and texture in the centre of the tile.

Testing colours, demonstrating a change of knitting direction and the finalized garter-stitch section.

A swatch for trying out a different colourway, which turned out to have insufficient contrast.

The final tile sample worked in two shades of blue with white.

Stage 7: Colour finalization

After further experiments on paper and with the yarn colours, I decided on the final colouring and worked the final swatch. At the same time, I noted down other potential colourways that I wanted to try.

Stage 8: Garment finalization

To create the final garment shape and size, I experimented with full-sized photocopies of the tile and decided on a simple gilet with no sleeves, to avoid any complicated shaping. To finish the garment off, I developed a simple straight band to

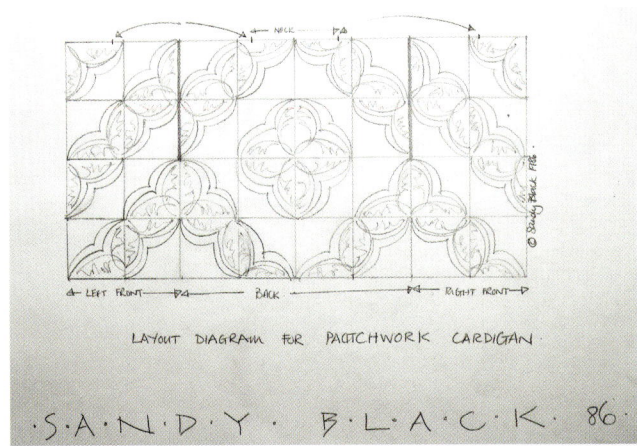

A sketch of final tile layout.

Design-concept sketch of the sleeveless gilet.

A sample of the chosen edging stitch, showing a slight bias, because of the one-way direction of the stitch structure, which is very helpful for edging curves and turning corners.

edge the entire shape, to be knitted in a textured stitch that echoed the diagonal feel of the pattern. Here, the stretch and flexibility of knitted fabric enables corners to be turned without any problems, unlike for a woven-cloth edging.

Stage 9: Pattern writing and test knitting

I wrote the first instructions as notes during design development and finalized them for test knitting by one of my sample knitters. These initial instructions would then be revised if necessary for clarity and to correct any errors. The final design decision was to create two half tiles to be used as a facing for the front neck opening to give the finishing touch.

A knitting pattern for production or publication needs to be logically written so that anyone can understand it, and every detail must be accurately recorded, so a further stage of professional pattern checking would always be carried out.

A contemporary version of the Scroll-gilet tile chart.

DESIGNING KNITWEAR

Diagram of the alternative layout for the second colourway.

Stage 10: Variations

To give the gilet a completely different look and appeal, and to show the versatility of patchwork knitting, I knitted a more subtle colourway and put the tiles together in a different formation.

Working with the patchwork technique

The most successful way that I found of knitting the patterned tiles is to work them as a diamond shape, starting and finishing with one stitch, by increasing and then decreasing stitches.

The tiles feature the stranded-colourwork knitting technique, with colours not in use woven in at every third stitch on the back of the work. With this technique, the gauge of the knitting becomes closer to a square proportion, rather than rectangular as in stocking stitch. In this way, the resulting squares all have sides of similar lengths, making for a firm edge all round, and can be used together in different orientations.

This technique is infinitely variable, as seen in patchwork quilts, depending on the tile design. As shown in the accompanying photographs, tiles can be made into different patterns or garments styles or simply be used to create a blanket or throw.

Experiment with squares or diamonds to see what garment ideas you could create. Using photocopies of your sample tiles allows you to create a paper version of your ideas without any difficulty and stimulates the creation of variations. However, the delight of this technique is making use of the flexibility of knitted pieces to create wearable dimensions even from geometric elements. In order to create more subtle shaping for necklines, for example, half tiles or specially shaped tiles can be created. The Scroll gilet described above is based on one tile that is used in different orientations, with just two half tiles to create a facing for the top neck opening, whereas the Azulejos design in Chapter 10 is based on two tiles that are a reflection of each other, plus four specially shaped tiles to create the neckline.

A taupe-and-cream colourway and alternative layout, showing the full pattern module created by four tiles and the effect of the garter-stitch texture.

A taupe-and-cream colourway, modelled and demurely styled.

A Medieval Tile light colourway, showing half motifs on each side of the tile that will match with the half motifs on adjacent tiles.

The Medieval Tile sweater featured earlier in this chapter is based on the single tile, shown here made with either a light or a dark colourway. *See* Chapter 10, following the Azulejos design, for further details and a chart for this pattern.

The patchwork-jacket design illustrated at the very start of this chapter is based on larger tiles that are knitted with intarsia and incorporates half tiles at the edges, but the design also relies on the stretch and drape of stocking-stitch knitting for the garment to create a flattering shape around the body. The coat version of this Tapestry Flower design is pictured in Chapter 10 in a pale colourway.

Exercise: Designing a Knitted Garment

Stage 1: Initial inspiration

Find a source of inspiration to spark your own ideas. This is easier if the inspiration source is based on something tangible, as described in the section 'Finding your own visual inspiration' in Chapter 2, but it can also be an abstract idea or concept found, for example, whilst reading. Try looking again at photos you have already taken, or go out and take new pictures around a theme; engage closely with objects, observing from the natural world or in a museum, for example.

Stage 2: Further research

Delve deeper into your subject by further visual and information research – from books and images found in physical libraries or from online searches. Look closely at image details for sources of texture, colour and pattern that might inspire the selection of yarn colours and stitch structures.

Stage 3: Design drawings

From this research, make rough sketches of details and elements plus any overall garment ideas you may have, however vague, using any medium you prefer – on paper using coloured crayons, felt pens, and so on, or drawing on a tablet or computer. Sketching is a wonderful way to think through ideas without worrying about having totally finished designs – it is more important to get a flow of ideas going at this stage, and do not reject anything as yet. Start to think about colours that you would like to use, based on your inspiration and potential yarns – make use of your own stash of yarns if you have one.

Stage 4: Selection and garment ideas

Step back and look at your work – pinning physical sketches up on a wall or laying them all out flat is very helpful. Begin to select and refine your ideas, and think more about how they would be suitable for knitting. Devise your own combination of pattern elements for your initial garment designs. Knitwear works well based on very simple shapes – refer to the garment-shape diagrams of the designs in this book, or work with an existing favourite garment shape, to check the proportions and measurements that you would like to use.

Stage 5: Knitting trials and charting the design

The first steps towards a complete garment are to finalize the building blocks of design elements such as graphic motifs, cables or stitch structures. Plan out the overall design on paper, and create detailed knitting charts of the design elements either on graph paper or by utilizing specialist knitting software. Test out the stitches or patterns by using your preferred yarns and a range of needle sizes until the feel of the knitted swatch is to your liking, and especially ensuring that the fabric is not too tight or too loose.

Stage 6: Yarn selection and final design

After the first knitting trials, make any amendments to the charted design elements to get the best effect, and create the final swatch(es). Use this final swatch to confirm the final tension you are working to, and as a basis for calculating the number of stitches across the maximum width and number of rows for the required length of the garment.

Stage 7: Colour finalization

If the design features several colours, try a number of variations and then decide on the final colourway, noting other potential colourways.

Stage 8: Garment finalization

Decide on the final garment style, shape and proportions to be used, and create an overall diagram with key measurements. Consider all of the final details of the design, such as how edgings and the neckline will be finished off. Work samples of knitted-on edgings by using earlier swatches for testing out ideas.

Stage 9: Pattern writing and test knitting

If using specialist knitting software to graph your design, a draft text pattern may be automatically generated, but this should be carefully checked by test knitting. If not using software, manually draw a graph chart for each element of the garment, showing any shaping for the neckline and armholes. If this pattern is for only your own use, the charts with some annotations and notes may be all that you require, as the charts are an exact picture of the knitting, stitch by stitch. However, a knitting pattern for production or publication must be logically written so anyone can understand it, and every detail must be accurately recorded and presented so that there are no ambiguities.

Stage 10: Variations

You may wish to apply the same fundamental design in a complementary shape or style (for example, *see* the Shield sweater and cardigan designs in Chapter 9). Variations in colour can also give the same design a completely new look (*see*, for example, the Shield and Rosette designs).

BELOW: The Lion and Unicorn design was, like the Shield design, adapted as a cardigan, here worn by a man.

PART 2

THE KNITTING PATTERNS

INTRODUCTION

This section features twenty-four knitting patterns for sweaters, tunics, cardigans and fun animal accessories, selected from Sandy Black collections from 1980 to 1990. These are grouped into five design themes with a chapter each: Textural, Graphic, Floral, Heraldic and Ornamental, plus Accessories. Many designs have been reknitted and re-photographed. These new garments have been made using contemporary yarns, mainly pure-wool and mohair-blend yarns, but the proportions and styling of these reknitted garments are true to the 1980s originals, with their oversized, generous silhouettes. These are complemented by original photographs from the 1980s, together with photos of other designs from my collections, showing variations on design themes. These include designs published in Rowan Yarns' first few pattern booklets.

The designs in this section utilize several basic stitches: stocking stitch, reverse stocking stitch, garter stitch and moss stitch. In addition, different types of ribbing including twisted rib, different types of bobbles and a variety of cable stitches are used. Many of the patterns are multicoloured and knitted from clear charts by using the intarsia method, mainly worked with stocking stitch. More detailed explanations of some techniques, such as working in intarsia, can be found in Chapters 3 and 4.

The introductions for each pattern explain the stitches and techniques used, so you can understand the level of experience required. Each pattern guides the knitter through all of the relevant techniques and the specific method for checking tension for that pattern, plus how to work any special stitches used. Less commonly used abbreviations are also defined within the pattern (as well as in the following sections 'Basic stitches' and 'Standard abbreviations'). Read through the pattern first to understand it fully, before commencing knitting.

For best results, it is really important to check your tension and use needles of the appropriate size – these needles may differ from the recommended needles, as each individual knitter knits differently.

OPPOSITE PAGE: Designs to knit from the six themes: Textural – ZigZag sweater; Graphic – Fairisle Fun sweater; Floral – Trailing Roses sweater; Heraldic – Shield sweater; Ornamental – Shawl cardigan; Accessories – Tiger scarf and mittens. (Photos: Paul Dennison, Jo Teasdale and David McIntyre)

BASIC STITCHES

Note that the following explanations are for working the basic stitches in rows, being worked flat, back and forth, with two needles (not in the round).

Stocking stitch

US: stockinette
Worked as 1 row knit, 1 row purl, repeated throughout; the knit side of the fabric is the right side.

Reverse stocking stitch

US: reverse stockinette
Worked as 1 row purl, 1 row knit, repeated throughout; the purl side of the fabric is the right side.

Garter stitch

Worked as every row knit; the fabric appears the same on both sides.

Moss stitch

Worked as a first row of k1, p1, repeated to the end of the row, then, for the next and every following row, for each stitch, work the opposite stitch to that of the previous row each time, so purl one stitch where the stitch of the previous row presents as a knit stitch, and knit one stitch where the stitch of the previous row presents as a purl stitch; the fabric appears the same on both sides.

Cables

Worked by utilizing a short cable needle (or double-pointed needle), to help the knitter to exchange the positions of the two groups of cable stitches. If the first group of stitches for the cable is slipped on to the cable needle and this cable needle is then held at the back of the work, a right cross (RC) is produced; this stitch manipulation is referred to as 'cable stitches to the back', or 'cable back' for short. If the first group of stitches for the cable is slipped on to the cable needle and this cable needle is then held at the front of the work, a left cross (LC) is produced; this stitch manipulation is referred to as 'cable stitches to the front, or 'cable front' for short.

Cables can be worked as knit stitches crossing knit stitches, knit stitches crossing a background of purl stitches, and several other variations. When knit stitches cross a purl-stitch background, these are known as 'travelling cables', and the stitch manipulations used to create these cables are often referred to as 'right purl cross' (RPC) and 'left purl cross' (LPC). Travelling cables are used in the Travelling Vine design (*see* Chapter 6), where detailed explanations for working them are given.

Where knit stitches cross over knit stitches, this creates a standard cable, for example:

c4b = cable 4 knit stitches to the back: slip the next 2 stitches purlwise on to the cable needle and leave it at the back of work, knit 2 stitches, then knit 2 stitches from the cable needle. This is also known as a **2/2 RC**: 2-over-2 right cross.

Where knit stitches cross over purl stitches, this is sometimes known as a purl cable and can be written with a different notation, for example:

c2over2b purl = cable 2 knit stitches over 2 purl stitches to the back: slip the next 2 stitches purlwise on to the cable needle and leave it at the back of work, knit 2 stitches, then purl 2 stitches from the cable needle.
This is also known as a **2/2 RPC**: 2-over-2 right purl cross.

Both styles of notation are included for the Travelling Vine pattern: the process of knitting is identical and the cables are the same, and knitters can work with the notation that they most easily relate to.

Twisted stitches

Two stitches are crossed over each other without the use of a cable needle, often worked within a rib section of knitting, such as at a cuff or hem, to give a mini-cable effect – *see* the following abbreviation for tw2.

Twisted rib

This is a variation on either k1, p1 rib or k2, p2 rib, where each of the knit stitches is worked into the back loop of the stitch of the previous row every time, causing that stitch to be twisted, to give a firmer structure to the rib.

Bobbles

These are made by typically creating 3 or 4 stitches from 1 stitch of the previous row, by increasing 3 or 4 times, then returning to the original number of stitches by decreasing the newly made stitches; some bobbles also include extra rows, by turning the work, and knitting over only the newly made bobble stitches.

Special instructions are given in each pattern, as required.

STANDARD ABBREVIATIONS

alt = alternate
approx = approximately
B = work into the back loop of the next stitch – RS: knit into the back loop of the next stitch; WS: purl into the back loop of the next stitch
b&f = back and front; often used for 'k b&f next st' or 'inc by k b&f', or the purl equivalents, meaning to knit (or purl) into the back loop of the next stitch on the LH needle, knit (or purl) into the front loop of the same stitch and to then allow the knitted-into (or purled-into) stitch to slip off the LH needle, to make 2 stitches from 1 stitch
beg = begin(ning)
btw = between
central double decrease = RS: sl2, k1, p2sso; WS: sl2, p1, p2sso
central double increase = RS: knit into the back and then the front of the next stitch (1 new st), with LH needle pick up vertical strand just formed between the 2 stitches just knitted (on RH needle), and knit into the back of this strand (1 new stitch) (3 stitches total)
cm = centimetre(s)
col(s) = colour(s)
cont = continue; continuing
dec = decrease; decreasing
dec 5 to 1 = decrease 5 stitches to 1 stitch (multiple-slip-stitch method) – slip 3 stitches purlwise to RH needle, * pass 2nd st on the RH needle over the first st (closest to the RH-needle point, to be the centre stitch of decrease), slip the centre stitch purlwise to the LH needle, pass the 2nd stitch on the LH needle over the centre st, slip the centre st purlwise to the RH needle, rep from * until 1 st is left of the original 5sts, knit or purl into the back loop of this stitch, as appropriate for the background
f&b = front and back; often used for 'k f&b next st' or 'inc by k f&b', or the purl equivalents, meaning to knit (or purl) into the front loop of the next stitch on the LH needle, knit (or purl) into the back loop of the same stitch and to then allow the knitted-into (or purled-into) stitch to slip off the LH needle, to make 2 stitches from 1 stitch
foll = following
folls = follows
g = gramme(s)
g st = garter stitch (every row knit)
in = inch(es)
inc = increase; increasing
inc 1 k = knit into the front loop of the next stitch on the LH needle, knit into the back loop of the same stitch and then allow the knitted-into stitch to slip off the LH needle, to make 2 stitches from 1 stitch knitwise
inc 1 p = purl into the front loop of the next stitch on the LH needle, purl into the back loop of the same stitch and then allow the purled-into stitch to slip off the LH needle, to make 2 stitches from 1 stitch purlwise
inc 1 to 3 = increase 1 stitch to 3 stitches – RS: (k1, yo, k1) in the next stitch; WS: (p1, yo, p1) in the next stitch (3 stitches total)
inc 1 to 5 = increase 1 stitch to 5 stitches – RS: (k1, yo, k1, yo, k1) in the next stitch, turn, p5, turn, k5 (5 stitches total)
k = knit
k2tog = knit the next 2 stitches together
k2tog-tbl = knit the next 2 stitches together through the back loops
LH = left-hand (often used for 'LH needle')
M or m1 = make 1 stitch (knitwise or purlwise): pick up the strand of yarn running between the stitch closest to the LH-needle point and the stitch closest to the RH-needle point so that the yarn passes over the LH-needle point from front to back and then knit (or purl) into the back of the strand (also known as 'pk1'). See also the abbreviations for 'm1k' and 'm1p' m = metre(s)
m1k = make 1 stitch knitwise – pick up the strand of yarn

running between the stitch closest to the LH-needle point and the stitch closest to the RH-needle point so that the strand passes over the LH-needle point from front to back, then knit into the back of this strand

m1p = make 1 stitch purlwise – pick up the strand of yarn running between the stitch closest to the LH-needle point and the stitch closest to the RH-needle point so that the strand passes over the LH-needle point from front to back, then purl into the back of this strand

MC = main colour
mm = millimetre(s)
p = purl
p2sso = pass 2 slipped stitches over
p2tog = purl the next 2 stitches together
p2tog-tbl = purl the next 2 stitches together through the back loops
patt = pattern(ing)
patts = patterns
pk1 = see the abbreviation for 'M' or 'm1'
prev = previous
psso = pass slipped stitch over
rem = remain(s); remaining
rep = repeat(ing)
reps = repeats
rev st st = reverse stocking stitch (RS: purl; WS: knit)
RH = right-hand (often used for 'RH needle')
RS = right side
sl = slip next stitch (or stitches) purlwise from the LH needle to the RH needle; a stitch that has been transferred in this way is known as a 'slipped stitch', sometimes 'ss' for short (for example, see the abbreviation for 'psso')
sl1k = slip 1 st knitwise from LH needle to RH needle
st(s) = stitch(es)
st st = stocking stitch (RS: knit; WS: purl)
tbl = through the back loop(s)
tog = together
tw2 = twist 2 stitches: knit into the front of the second stitch on the LH needle, knit into the front of the first stitch on the LH needle, then allow both knitted-into stitches to slip off the LH needle together
WS = wrong side
yo or yrn = yarn over needle or yarn round needle: pass yarn over/round RH-needle point from front to back, to make 1 new stitch

CABLE ABBREVIATIONS

LC = left cross (for cable)
LPC = left purl cross (for travelling cable)
RC = right cross (for cable)
RPC = right purl cross (for travelling cable)
2/2 RC = 2-over-2 right cross; see the abbreviation for 'c4b'
2/2 RPC = 2-over-2 right purl cross; see the abbreviation for 'c2over2b purl'
c1over1b purl (1/1 RPC) = cable 1 knit stitch over 1 purl stitch to the back: slip the next stitch purlwise on to the cable needle and leave it at the back of the work, k1, then p1 from the cable needle
c2b (1/1 RC) = cable 2 knit stitches to the back: slip the next stitch purlwise on to the cable needle and leave it at the back of the work, k1, then k1 from the cable needle
c2f (1/1 LC) = cable 2 knit stitches to the front: slip the next stitch purlwise on to the cable needle and leave it at the front of the work, k1, then k1 from the cable needle
c2over1b purl (2/1 RPC) = cable 2 knit stitches over 1 purl stitch to the back: slip the next 2 stitches purlwise on to the cable needle and leave it at the back of the work, k2, then p1 from the cable needle
c2over1f purl (2/1 LPC) = cable 2 knit stitches over 1 purl stitch to the front: slip the next 2 stitches purlwise on to the cable needle and leave it at the front of the work, p1, then k2 from the cable needle
c2over2b purl (2/2 RPC) = cable 2 knit stitches over 2 purl stitches to the back: slip the next 2 stitches purlwise on to the cable needle and leave it at the back of the work, k2, then p2 from the cable needle
c2over2f purl (2/2 LPC) = cable 2 knit stitches over 2 purl stitches to the front: slip the next 2 stitches purlwise on to the cable needle and leave it at the front of the work, p2, then k2 from the cable needle
c2over3b purl (2/3 RPC) = cable 2 knit stitches over 3 purl stitches to the back: slip the next 3 stitches purlwise on to the cable needle and leave it at the back of the work, k2, then p3 from the cable needle
c2over3f purl (2/3 LPC) = cable 2 knit stitches over 3 purl stitches to the front: slip the next 2 stitches purlwise on to the cable needle and leave it at the front of the work, p3, then k2 from the cable needle

c3over1b (3/1 RC) = cable 3 knit stitches over 1 knit stitch to the back: slip the next stitch purlwise on to the cable needle and leave it at the back of the work, k3, then k1 from the cable needle

c3over1b purl (3/1 RPC) = cable 3 knit stitches over 1 purl stitch to the back: slip the next stitch purlwise on to the cable needle and leave it at the back of the work, k3, then p1 from the cable needle

c3over1f (3/1 LC) = cable 3 knit stitches over 1 knit stitch to the front: slip the next 3 stitches purlwise on to the cable needle and leave it at the front of the work, k1, then k3 from the cable needle

c3over1f purl (3/1 LPC) = cable 3 knit stitches over 1 purl stitch to the front: slip the next 3 stitches purlwise on to the cable needle and leave it at the front of the work, p1, then k3 from the cable needle

c3over2b (3/2 RC) = cable 3 knit stitches over 2 knit stitches to the back: slip the next 2 stitches purlwise on to the cable needle and leave it at the back of the work, k3, then k2 from the cable needle

c3over2b purl (3/2 RPC) = cable 3 knit stitches over 2 purl stitches to the back: slip the next 2 stitches purlwise on to the cable needle and leave it at the back of the work, k3, then p2 from the cable needle

c3over2f (3/2 LC) = cable 3 knit stitches over 2 knit stitches to the front: slip the next 3 stitches purlwise on to the cable needle and leave it at the front of the work, k2, then k3 from the cable needle

c3over2f purl (3/2 LPC) = cable 3 knit stitches over 2 purl stitches to the front: slip the next 3 stitches purlwise on to the cable needle and leave it at the front of the work, p2, then k3 from the cable needle

c4b (2/2 RC) = cable 4 knit stitches to the back: slip the next 2 knit stitches purlwise on to the cable needle and leave it at the back of the work, k2, then k2 from the cable needle

c4f (2/2 LC) = cable 4 knit stitches to the front: slip the next 2 knit stitches purlwise on to the cable needle and leave it at the front of the work, k2, then k2 from the cable needle

c6b (3/3 RC) = cable 6 knit stitches to the back: slip the next 3 stitches purlwise on to the cable needle and leave it at the back of the work, k3, then k3 from the cable needle

c8b (4/4 RC) = cable 8 knit stitches to the back: slip the next 4 stitches purlwise on to the cable needle and leave it at the back of the work, k4, then k4 from the cable needle

The cubist sweater, an original 1989 design, intricately blends bright mohair colours in vibrant brushstrokes, highlighted with black embroidery.

CHAPTER 6

TEXTURAL

The versatility of knitting as a construction technique is evident in the way that intricate surface textures can be created based on just the two basic stitches, knit and purl, plus simple manipulations such as cables. The flexibility inherent in the structure of knitting means that stitches can be made to change places, creating three-dimensional surface effects, as found in classic fisherman's jerseys and Aran-style designs.

The Zig-Zag Cable-sweater design illustrates the use of both purl-stitch patterning and cables that are worked in an unusual zigzag formation, whereas the Travelling Vine tunic exhibits more sculptural surface textures, created from new combinations of travelling cables – where stitches travel in relief across a purl background – together with three-dimensional bobbles.

Architectural ornamentation and historical relief carvings provided the initial inspiration for the Travelling Vine design, and the tunic is photographed at the Royal Pavilion in Brighton, against the extraordinary sculptural stucco columns of this exotic building. The new photography restages the original shoot, echoing the timelessness of the design. With its cream colour and three-dimensional effects, this design is also reminiscent of traditional Aran patterns. One challenge that I set myself when creating this design was to create a circle with cabled stitches; however, an oval shape proved to be more feasible, resulting in the design pictured. I was delighted to find and adapt techniques from the wonderful Barbara Walker book *Charted Knitting Designs* to create my own original motifs.

OPPOSITE PAGE: The Travelling Vine tunic, knitted in an aran-weight 100-per-cent-wool yarn and shown being worn with a relaxed style. (Photo: Jo Teasdale)

Zig-Zag Cable Sweater

The smaller version of the Zig-Zag Cable sweater, knitted in a wool yarn. (Photo: Jo Teasdale)

The Sandy Black for Rowan Zig-Zag Cable sweater, knitted in a tweed double-knitting yarn; this is the original 1986 image. (Photo: courtesy of Rowan Yarns)

The cover of The Rowan Knitting Book No 1, *published in 1986, which includes the Zig-Zag Cable sweater as the first pattern.*

This texture-patterned sweater featured as the first design in the first ever issue of *The Rowan Knitting Book*, published in 1986, a pattern magazine that presented designs from a range of knitwear designers. *The Rowan Knitting Book* continues to be published by Rowan Yarns. Within the Sandy Black Original Knits fashion collections, we created a smaller version of this design in our Wool Twist yarn, either worked in a single bold colour or with colourful fans intarsia-knitted across the body (for the Fans sweater).

The sweater is generously sized, with a zigzag design of cables on a moss-stitch background for the body and moss stitch on a stocking-stitch background for the sleeves, plus a large cabled collar, either closed as a cowl or open at one side. Striped contrast edgings are optional. Two size variations are shown, both knitted from the same instructions, with the sizing difference achieved by a change of tension (and therefore needles being used). This variation in size works using either the same or a similar yarn – here, one yarn is tweed and the other is plain.

The Zig-Zag Cable sweater, shown in red and a variation in blue with intarsia-knitted fan motifs over the body and sleeves. (Photo: Paul Dennison)

Sizes and measurements

Two sizes to fit up to a 96(107)cm/38(42)in bust circumference

Two size variations (small and large) can be knitted by using the same pattern instructions but knitted to different tension measurements – that is, sizing by tension. This tension difference creates the difference in overall body width and length; however, length can be adjusted to suit the intended wearer by working to the necessary measurements, as guided by the pattern instructions.

Knitted measurements
All-round circumference at underarms: 116(134) cm/45(53)in
Length: 58(71)cm/23(28)in
Sleeve length: 48(51)cm/19(20)in

Materials

Yarn
Small size shown is knitted in a light-aran-weight 100-per-cent-wool yarn with approx 95–110m/50g. Large size shown is knitted in a tweed 100-per-cent-wool yarn with approx 85–110m/50g.
The original was knitted in Rowan Classic Tweed yarn, and the closest currently produced Rowan yarns are Valley Tweed and Cashmere Tweed.
Main colour (A): 14(15) × 50g balls
Optional contrast colour (B): 1 × 50g ball

Recommended needles and accessories
Small size:
  1 pair 5.5mm (UK 5, US 9) needles for body
  1 pair 4mm (UK 8, US 6) needles for edgings
Large size:
  1 pair 6mm (UK 4, US 10) needles for body
  1 pair 4.5mm (UK 7, US 7) needles for edgings
Cable needle
Optional: Circular needle of the larger size for cowl collar

A promotional image of the Zig-Zag Cable sweater for the Fashion Trade Fair in New York, 1983.

Tension

It is important to check your tension and use the needles that give you the correct tension, as stated below; note that these needles may not be of the recommended needle size. If in doubt about which needles to use, match the stitch tension and knit to the correct length as given in the pattern.

Small size: 19sts and 30 rows to 10cm/4in, measured over moss stitch, using 5.5mm (UK 5, US 9) needles or the size required to give the correct tension and therefore measurements.

Large size: 16sts and 26 rows to 10cm/4in, measured over moss stitch, using 6mm (UK 4, US 10) needles or the size required to give you the correct tension and therefore measurements.

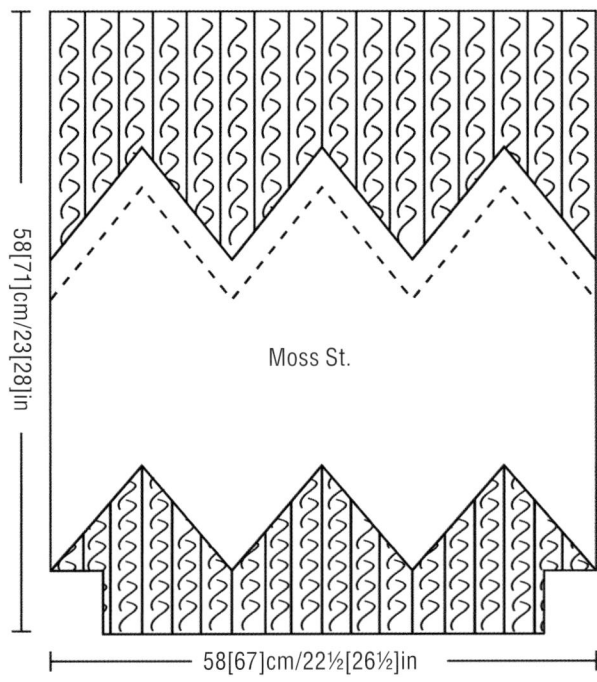

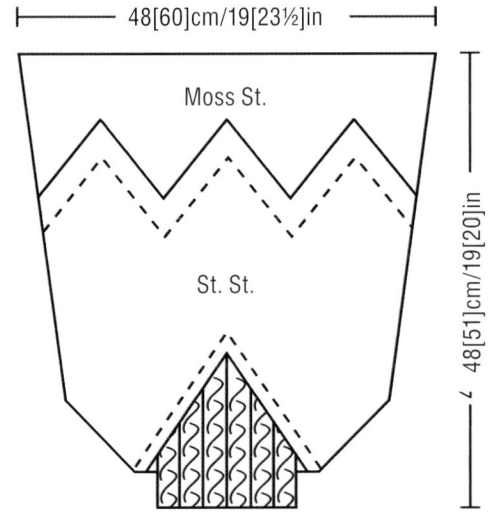

Measurement and stitch-pattern positioning diagram.

Abbreviations and special stitches

c4b = cable 4sts back: slip next 2sts purlwise on to cable needle and leave it at back of work, k2, then k2 from cable needle

inc 1 k = knit into front loop of next st on LH needle, knit into back loop of same st and then allow knitted-into st to slip off LH needle

inc 1 p = purl into front loop of next st on LH needle, purl into back loop of same st and then allow purled-into st to slip off LH needle

tw2 = twist 2sts: knit into front of 2nd st on LH needle, knit into front of 1st st on LH needle, then allow both knitted-into sts to slip off LH needle

Pattern

Back

Cast on 108sts using the smaller needles and yarn B (if being used) or yarn A.

Work in cable rib as folls:
Row 1 (RS): P1, k2, (p2, k2) to last st, p1.
If using yarn B as a contrast col, now change to yarn A.
Row 2: K1, p2, (k2, p2) to last st, k1.
Row 3: As row 1.
If using yarn B as a contrast col, now change to yarn B.
Row 4: As row 2.

Note: If using yarn B as a contrast col, now change to yarn A; cont with this yarn for the rest of this piece.

Row 5: P1, tw2, (p2, tw2) to last st, p1.
Rows 6–13: Rep rows 2–5 twice, thus ending with a tw2 row.

Change to the larger needles, and work Zig-Zag patt as folls:
Note: For each row below, work instructions given 3 times across the row.
Row 14: P3, (k2, p2) 8 times, k1.
Row 15: K1, p1, k1, p2, (k2, p2) 7 times, k2, p1.
Row 16: P1, k1, p1, k2, (p2, k2) 7 times, k1, p1, k1.
Row 17: (K1, p1) twice, p1, tw2, (p2, tw2) 6 times, (p1, k1) twice, p1.
Row 18: (P1, k1) twice, p3, (k2, p2) 6 times, k1, (p1, k1) twice.

Row 19: (K1, p1) 3 times, k1, (p2, k2) 6 times.
Row 20: (P1, p1) 3 times, p1, k2, (p2, k2) 5 times, k1, (p1, k1) 3 times.
Row 21: (K1, p1) 4 times, p1, tw2, (p2, tw2) 4 times, p1, (k1, p1) 4 times.
Row 22: (P1, k1) 4 times, p3, (k2, p2) 4 times, k1, (p1, k1) 4 times.
Row 23: K1, (k1, p1) 5 times, k1, p2, (k2, p2) 3 times, k1, (k1, p1) 5 times.
Row 24: (P1, k1) 5 times, p1, k2, (p2, k2) 3 times, k1, (p1, k1) 5 times.
Row 25: (K1, p1) 6 times, p1, tw2, (p2, tw2) twice, p1, (k1, p1) 6 times.
Row 26: (P1, k1) 6 times, p3, (k2, p2) twice, k1, (p1, k1) 6 times.
Row 27: (K1, p1) 7 times, k1, (p2, k2) twice, p1, (k1, p1) 6 times.
Row 28: (P1, k1) 7 times, p1, k2, p2, k3, (p1, k1) 7 times.
Row 29: (K1, p1) 8 times, p1, tw2, p1, (k1, p1) 8 times.
Row 30: (P1, k1) 8 times, p2, (p1, k1) 9 times.
Row 31: (K1, p1) to end. *

Cont in moss st until work measures 41(50)cm/16(19¾)in from beg, ending with a WS row.

Work Zig-Zag patt for yoke as folls:
Note: For each row below, work instructions given 3 times across the row.
Row 1 (RS): (K1, p1) to end.
Row 2: (P1, k1) 17 times, p2.
Row 3: K3, (p1, k1) 15 times, p1, k2.
Row 4: P3, (k1, p1) 14 times, k1, p3, k1.
Row 5: K1, p1, k3, (p1, k1) 13 times, p1, k3, p1.
Row 6: P1, k1, p3, (k1, p1) 12 times, k1, p3, k1, p1, k1, k1, p1, k1.
Row 7: P2, k1, p1, k3, (p1, k1) 11 times, p1, k3, p1, k1, p1.
Row 8: K2, p1, k1, p3, (k1, p1) 10 times, k1, p3, (k1, p1) twice, k1.
Row 9: P1, k2, p1, k1, p1, k3, (p1, k1) 9 times, p1, k3, (p1, k1) twice, p1.
Row 10: K1, p2, k1, p1, k1, p3, (k1, p1) 8 times, k1, p3, k1, p1, k1, p3, k1.
Row 11: P1, k4, p1, 1, p1, k3, (p1, k1) 7 times, p1, k3, p1, k1, p1, k3, p1.
Row 12: K1, p4, k1, p1, k1, p3, (k1, p1) 6 times, k1, p3, k1, p1, k2, p4, k1.
Row 13: P1, c4b, p3, k1, p1, k3, (p1, k1) 5 times, p1, k3, p1, k1, p2, c4b, p1.
Row 14: K1, p4, k3, p1, k1, p3, (k1, p1) 4 times, k1, p3, (k1, p1) twice, k2, p4, k1.
Row 15: P1, k4, p2, k2, p1, k1, p1, k3, (p1, k1) 3 times, p1, k3, (p1, k1) twice, p2, k4, p1.
Row 16: K1, p4, k2, p2, k1, p1, k1, p3, (k1, p1) twice, k1, p3, k1, p1, k1, p3, k2, p4, k1.
Row 17: P1, k4, p2, k4, p1, k1, p1, k3, p1, k1, p1, k3, p1, k1, p1, k3, p2, k4, p1.
Row 18: K1, p4, k2, p4, k1, p1, k1, p3, k1, p3, k1, p1, k2, p4, k2, p4, k1.
Row 19: P1, (c4b, p2) twice, p1, k1, p1, k5, p1, p1, (p2, c4b) twice, p1.
Row 20: K1, (p4, k2) twice, k1, p1, k1, p3, (k1, p1) twice, (k2, p4) twice, k1.
Row 21: P1, (k4, p2) twice, k2, (p1, k1) 4 times, (p2, k4) twice, p1.
Row 22: K1, (p4, k2) twice, p2, (k1, p1) twice, k1, p3, (k2, p4) twice, k1.
Row 23: P1, (k4, p2) twice, k4, p1, k1, p1, k3, (p2, k4) twice, p1.
Row 24: K1, (p4, k2) to end, ending last rep with k1.

Cont cables as set, by cabling on next and every foll 6th row until work measures 58(71)cm/23(28)in.

Cast off loosely in rib.

Place markers at each side at 24(30)cm/9½(12)in below top edge for underarm positions of armholes.

Front

Work as for back to *.
Cont in moss st until work measures 44(53)cm/17(21)in from beg, ending with a WS row.
Work Zig-Zag patt for yoke as for back.

Sleeves

Both sleeves are worked alike.
Cast on 50sts using the smaller needles and yarn B (if being used) or yarn A.

Work in cable rib as folls:

Row 1 (RS): (K2, p2) to last 2sts, k2.
If using yarn B as a contrast col, now change to yarn A.
Row 2: (P2, k2) to last 2sts, p2.
Row 3: As row 1.
If using yarn B as a contrast col, now change to yarn B.
Row 4: As row 2.

Note: If using yarn B as a contrast col, now change to yarn A; cont with this yarn for the rest of this piece.

Row 5: (Tw2, p2) to last 2sts, tw2.
Rows 6–17: Rep rows 2–5 3 times.

Change to the larger needles, and work in patt as folls:
Row 18: Inc 1 p, p1, (k2, p2) to last 4sts, k2, p1, inc 1 p.
Row 19: Inc 1 k, k1, p3, (k2, p2) 11 times, p1, k1, inc 1 k.
Row 20: Inc 1 p, p3, k2, (p2, k2) 11 times, p3, inc 1 p.
Row 21: Inc 1 k, p1, k4, p1, tw2, (p2, tw2) 10 times, p1, k4, p1, inc 1 k.
Row 22: Inc 1 p, p2, k1, p6, (k2, p2) 10 times, p4, k1, p2, inc 1 p.
Row 23: Inc 1 k, k4, p1, k4, p3, (k2, p2) 9 times, p1, k4, p1, k4, inc 1 k.
Row 24: Inc 1 p, p6, k1, p4, k2, (p2, k2) 9 times, p4, k1, p6, inc 1 p.
Row 25: Inc 1 k, k8, p1, k4, p1, tw2, (p2, tw2) 8 times, p1, k4, p1, k8, inc 1 k.
Row 26: Inc 1 p, p10, k1, p6, (k2, p2) 8 times, p4, k1, p10, inc 1 p.
Row 27: Inc 1 k, k12, p1, k4, p3, (k2, p2) 7 times, p1, k4, p1, k12, inc 1 k.
Row 28: Inc 1 p, p14, k1, k4, k2, (p2, k2) 7 times, p4, k1, p14, inc 1 p.
Row 29: Inc 1 k, k16, p1, k4, p1, tw2, (p2, tw2) 6 times, p1, k4, p1, k16, inc 1 k.
Row 30: P19, k1, p6, (k2, p2) 6 times, p4, k1, p19.
Row 31: K20, p1, k4, p3, (k2, p2) 5 times, p1, k4, p1, k20.
Row 32: P21, k1, p4, k2, (p2, k2) 5 times, p4, k1, p21.
Row 33: K22, p1, k4, p1, tw2, (p2, tw2) 4 times, p1, k4, p1, k22.
Row 34: Inc 1 p, p22, k1, p6, (k2, p2) 4 times, p4, k1, p22, inc 1 p.
Row 35: K25, p1, k4, p3, (k2, p2) 3 times, p1, k4, p1, k25.
Row 36: P26, k1, p4, k2, (p2, k2) 3 times, p4, k1, p26.
Row 37: K27, p1, k4, p1, tw2, (p2, tw2) twice, p1, k4, p1, k27.
Row 38: P28, K1, p6, (k2, p2) twice, p4, k1, p28.
Row 39: Inc 1 k, k28, p1, k4, p3, k2, p3, k4, p1, k28, inc 1 k.
Row 40: P31, k1, p4, k2, p2, k2, p4, k1, p31.
Row 41: K32, p1, k4, p1, tw2, p1, k4, p1, k32.
Row 42: P33, k1, p10, k1, p33.
Row 43: K34, p1, k8, p1, k34.
Row 44: Inc 1 p, p34, k1, p6, k1, p34, inc 1 p. (80sts)
Row 45: K37, p1, k4, p1, k37.
Row 46: P38, k1, p2, k1, p38.
Row 47: K39, p2, k39.
Row 48: P across row.

Cont in st st and, *at the same time*, inc 1 st at each end of next row and every foll 5th row until there are 96sts.

Work 4 rows more in st st, ending with a WS row, and, *at the same time*, inc 1 st at end of last row. (97sts)

Work Zig-Zag patt for sleeve top as folls:
Row 1 (RS): (P1, k31) 3 times, p1.
Row 2: P1, (k1, p29, k1, p1) 3 times.
Row 3: (K2, p1, k27, p1, k1) 3 times, k1.
Row 4: P1, (p2, k1, p25, k1, p3) 3 times.
Row 5: (K4, p1, k23, p1, k3) 3 times, k1.
Row 6: K1, (p4, k1, p21, k1, p4, k1) 3 times.
Row 7: (K1, p1, k4, p1, k19, p1, k4, p1) 3 times, k1.
Row 8: K1, (p1, k1, p4, k1, p17, k1, p4, k1, p1, k1) 3 times.
Row 9: ([K1, p1], twice, k4, p1, k15, p1, k4, p1, k1, p1) 3 times, k1.
Row 10: K1, ([p1, k1] twice, p4, k1, p13, p4, k1, [p1, k1] twice) 3 times.
Row 11: ([K1, p1] 3 times, k4, p1, k11, p1, k4, [p1, k1] twice, p1) 3 times, k1.
Row 12: K1, ([p1, k1] 3 times, p4, k1, p9, k1, p4, k1, [p1, k1] 3 times) 3 times.
Row 13: ([K1, p1] 4 times, k4, p1, k7, p1, k4, [p1, k1] 3 times, p1) 3 times, k1.
Row 14: K1, ([p1, k1] 4 times, p4, k1, p5, k1, p4, k1, [p1, k1] 4 times) 3 times.
Row 15: ([K1, p1] 5 times, k4, p1, k3, p1, k4, [p1, k1] 4 times, p1) 3 times, k1.
Row 16: K1, ([p1, k1] 5 times, p4, k1, p1, k1, p4, k1, [p1, k1] 5 times) 3 times.
Row 17: ([K1, p1] 6 times, k4, p1, k4, [p1, k1] 5 times, p1) 3 times, k1.
Row 18: K1, ([p1, k1] 6 times, p7, k1, [p1, k1] 6 times) 3 times.
Row 19: ([K1, p1] 7 times, k5, [p1, k1] 6 times, p1) 3 times, k1.

Row 20: K1, ([p1, k1] 7 times, p3, k1, [p1, k1] 7 times) 3 times.
Rows 21–22: K1, (p1, k1) to end.
Cont in moss st until work measures 48(51)cm/19(20)in from beg. Cast off loosely.

Collars

Open collar
Cast on 162sts using the larger needles and yarn A.
Row 1 (RS): (P1, k4, p1) to end.
Row 2: (K1, p4, k1) to end.
Rows 3–4: Rep rows 1–2.
Row 5: (P1, c4b, p1) to end.
Row 6: As row 2.
Rep rows 1–6 four times, then rep rows 1–4 once.

If using yarn B as a contrast col, now change to yarn B, and work as given for row 5.

If using yarn B as a contrast col, now change to yarn A, and work row 6, row 1 and row 2.

If using yarn B as a contrast col, now change to yarn B, and work as given for row 3.

Cast off loosely in rib.

Closed cowl collar
Alternatively, to work this collar variation, work the collar in the round by using a circular needle.

Cast on 162sts using the larger needles and yarn A. Arrange cast-on sts and needle points to work in the round, taking care not to twist the sts. All rounds are RS rounds.

Rounds 1–4: (P1, k4, p1) to end.
Round 5: (P1, c4b, p1) to end.
Round 6: As round 1.
Rep rounds 1–6 4 times, then rep rounds 1–4 once.
Cast off loosely in rib.

Making up and finishing

Do not press pieces.
Mark 4(5) cables in from side edge at top of both back and front for shoulder width.
Join both shoulders using backstitch, referring to the position of the just-placed markers.
Backstitch sleeves into position, referring to the position of the markers placed for underarm positions of armholes.
Join body sides and sleeve sides using backstitch.
For the open collar: With cable side of collar to WS of neck edge, oversew collar to neck edge, starting and finishing at left shoulder seam.
For the closed cowl collar: If required, with the RS of collar facing itself, first join short ends of collar to form circle. With cable side of collar to WS of neck edge, oversew collar to neck edge.

Travelling Vine Tunic

A re-creation of the original Travelling Vine shoot at Brighton Pavilion, with the tunic being worn in a smart style. (Photo: Jo Teasdale)

An original 1989 photograph, smartly styled at Brighton Pavilion. (Photo: David McIntyre)

This long-line tunic echoes the tradition of Aran textural motifs. Inspired by architectural ornamentation, three original stitch motifs have been created to give really three-dimensional sculpted surface effects by using variations on classic cables. The Grape Vine pattern forms the central panel, the Scroll motif alternates with cables for the borders and collar, and the Oval Window motifs have coloured bobbles in the middle and are scattered over the side panels and sleeves. All motifs are worked from the stitch charts using combinations of knit, purl and cable stitches, together with special increases and decreases.

Tension

20sts and 29 rows to 10cm/4in, measured over st st, using 4mm (UK 8, US 6) needles or the size required to give the correct tension and therefore measurements.

How to check tension
Using the recommended needles, cast on 28sts, and work in st st for 40 rows. Cast off. Pin the knitted swatch square down flat, without stretching the fabric. Place a pin between 2sts near the left side of the swatch, count 20sts across to the right, and place another pin between the 20th and 21st sts. Mark out 29 rows in the same manner, starting from 2sts near the top of the swatch. Measure the distance between each pair of pins. The measurements should both be 10cm/4in. If a measurements is less than 10cm/4in, your knitting is too tight – try using needles of one size larger to reknit the swatch, and again check the tension. If a measurement is more than 10cm/4in, your knitting is too loose – try using needles of one size smaller to reknit the swatch, and again check the tension. Repeat the process until the correct tension is achieved. Do not be afraid to go up or down by more than one size of the recommended needles to achieve the required tension. Adjust the size of the smaller pair of needles for the edgings accordingly.

Size and measurements

One size to generously fit up to a 102cm/40in bust circumference

Knitted measurements
All-round circumference at underarms: 119cm/47in
Length: 79cm/31in
Sleeve length: 66cm/26in

Materials

Yarn
Knitted with an aran-weight 100-per-cent-wool yarn with approx 170–200m/100g. The featured example was knitted in ecru Bluefaced Leicester Aran by West Yorkshire Spinners.
Main colour (MC): 23 × 50g balls or 12 × 100g hanks
Contrast colours: 1 × 25g ball (or oddments) each of 6 contrast colours in two groups – reds and blues:
Reds group: claret, red, mulberry, gold
Blues group: teal, mulberry, purple, claret
Alternatively, select any colours of your choice.

Recommended needles and accessories

Two pairs of needles are required: one pair of the size to give the correct tension, for main parts, and one pair of one size smaller, for edgings.
1 pair 4mm (UK 8, US 6) needles for main parts
1 pair 3.75mm (UK 9, US 5) needles for edgings
Cable needle
Stitch holder

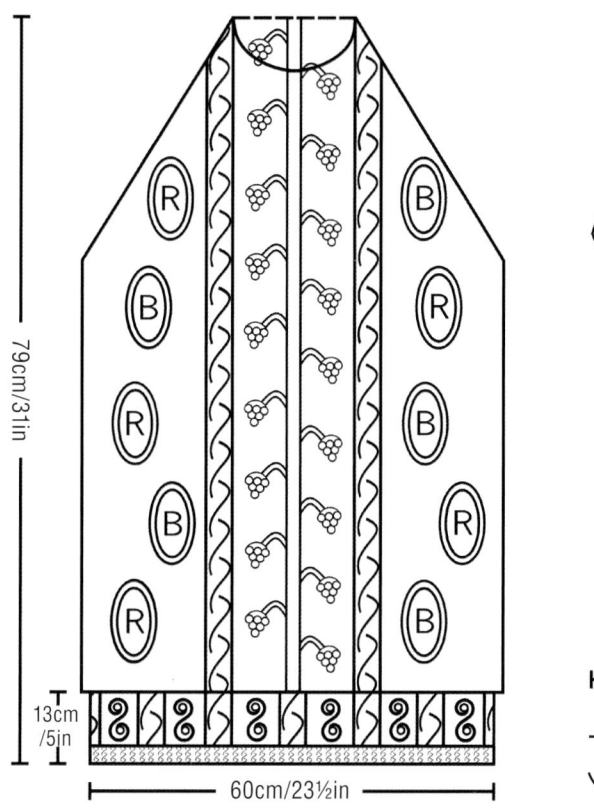
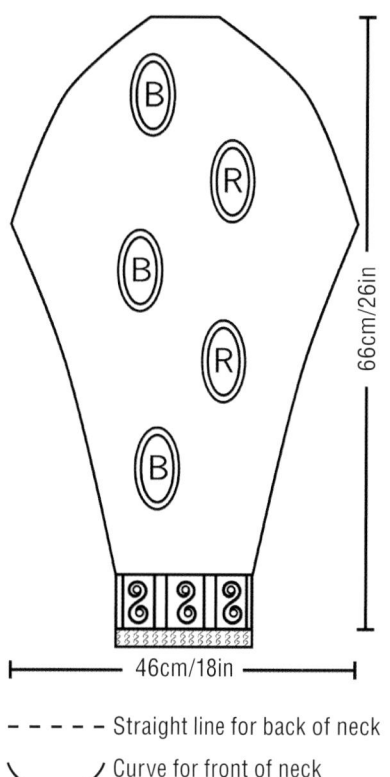

Measurement and stitch-pattern positioning diagram.

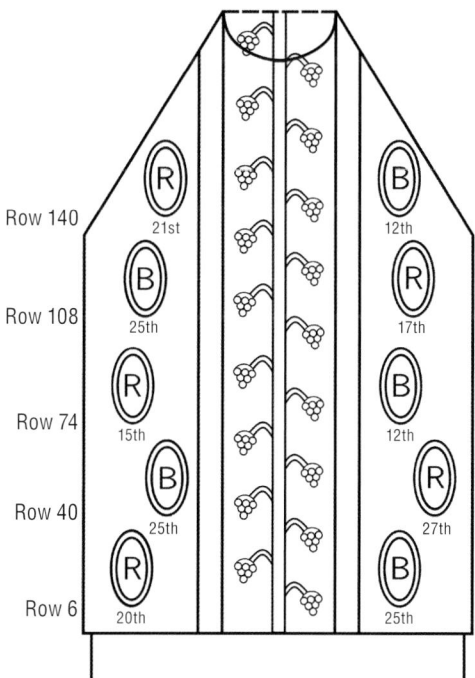
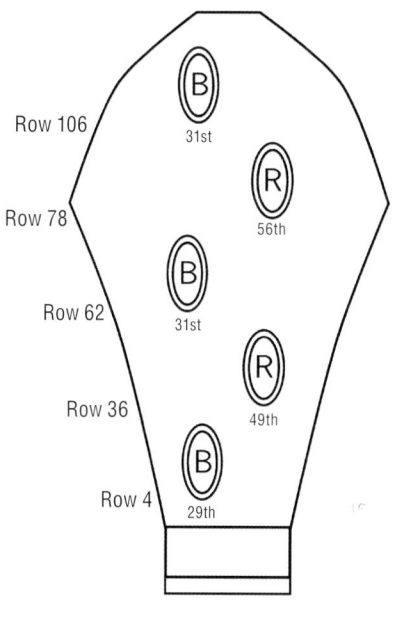

Diagram demonstrating the stitch and row positioning of each Oval Window motif.

Abbreviations and special stitches

Below are definitions for abbreviations and symbols included in both the text and the charts.

B = WS: purl into back loop of st
central double decrease ⒶA = RS: sl2, k1, p2sso; WS: sl2, p1, p2sso
central double increase Ⓥ = RS: knit into back and then front of next st (1 new st), with LH needle pick up vertical strand just formed between 2sts just knitted (on RH needle), and knit into back of this strand (1 new st) (3sts total)
dec 5 to 1 (multiple-slip-stitch method) Ⓐ = decrease 5sts to 1 st, to finish bobble – slip 3sts purlwise to RH needle, * pass 2nd st on RH needle over 1st st (closest to RH-needle point, to be centre st of decrease), slip centre st purlwise to LH needle, pass 2nd st on LH needle over centre st, slip centre st purlwise to RH needle, rep from * until 1 st left of original 5sts, knit or purl into back loop of this st, as appropriate for background
inc 1 to 3 Ⓥ = increase 1 st to 3sts – RS: (k1, yo, k1) in next st; WS: (p1, yo, p1) in next st (3sts total)
inc 1 to 5 Ⓥ = increase 1 st to 5sts, to start bobble – RS: (k1, yo, k1, yo, k1) in next st, turn, p5, turn, k5 (5sts total)
M = make 1 st – on a purl row, m1p (see 'm1p'); on a knit row, m1k (see 'm1k')
m1k = make 1 st knitwise – pick up strand of yarn running between st closest to LH-needle point and st closest to RH-needle point so that strand passes over LH-needle point from front to back, then knit into back of this strand
m1p = make 1 st purlwise – pick up strand of yarn running between st closest to LH-needle point and st closest to RH-needle point so that strand passes over LH-needle point from front to back, then purl into back of this strand
MC = main colour
p2sso = pass 2 slipped sts over
psso = pass slipped st over
tw2 = twist 2sts – knit into front of 2nd st on LH needle, knit into front of 1st st on LH needle, then allow both knitted-into sts to slip off LH needle together
yo = yarn over needle – pass yarn over RH-needle point from front to back, to make 1 st

Cables

c1over1b purl (1/1 RPC) = slip 1 st purlwise on to cable needle and leave it at back of work, k1, then p1 from cable needle
c2over1b purl (2/1 RPC) = slip 1 st purlwise on to cable needle and leave it at back of work, k2, then p1 from cable needle
c2over1f purl (2/1 LPC) = slip 2sts purlwise on to cable needle and leave it at front of work, p1, then k2 from cable needle
c2over2b purl (2/2 RPC) = slip 2sts purlwise on to cable needle and leave it at back of work, k2, then p2 from cable needle
c2over2f purl (2/2 LPC) = slip 2sts purlwise on to cable needle and leave it at front of work, p2, then k2 from cable needle
c2over3b purl (2/3 RPC) = slip 3sts purlwise on to cable needle and leave it at back of work, k2, then p3 from cable needle
c2over3f purl (2/3 LPC) = slip 2sts purlwise on to cable needle and leave it at front of work, p3, then k2 from cable needle
c3over1b (3/1 RC) = slip 1 st purlwise on to cable needle and leave it at back of work, k3, then k1 from cable needle
c3over1b purl (3/1 RPC) = slip 1 st purlwise on to cable needle and leave it at back of work, k3, then p1 from cable needle
c3over1f (3/1 LC) = slip 3sts purlwise on to cable needle and leave it at front of work, k1, then k3 from cable needle
c3over1f purl (3/1 LPC) = slip 3sts purlwise on to cable needle and leave it at front of work, p1, then k3 from cable needle
c3over2b (3/2 RC) = slip 2sts purlwise on to cable needle and leave it at back of work, k3, then k2 from cable needle
c3over2b purl (3/2 RPC) = slip 2sts purlwise on to cable needle and leave it at back of work, k3, then p2 from cable needle
c3over2f (3/2 LC) = slip 3sts purlwise on to cable needle and leave it at front of work, k2, then k3 from cable needle
c3over2f purl (3/2 LPC) = slip 3sts purlwise on to cable needle and leave it at front of work, p2, then k3 from cable needle

c6b (3/3 RC) = cable 6 knit sts back: slip next 3sts purlwise on to cable needle and leave it at back of work, k3, then k3 from cable needle

c8b (4/4 RC) = cable 8 knit sts back: slip next 4sts purlwise on to cable needle and leave it at back of work, k4, then k4 from cable needle

LC = left-cross
LPC = left purl cross
RC = right cross
RPC = right purl cross

Bobbles

Oval Window and Grape Vine bobbles: Use a contrast colour yarn for bobbles within the Oval Window motifs, and use the MC yarn for the Grape Vine bobbles.

⊙ = make bobble – knit into front, back, front, back and front of next st (5sts), turn, p5, turn, dec 5 to 1 (using multiple-slip-stitch method: see 'dec 5 to 1' in 'Abbreviations and special stitches'), and knit rem 1 st in MC

Scroll bobbles: The bobbles for the Scroll motif are larger and made over 3 rows of the chart.
First row: ⓥ = inc 1 to 5 – (k1, yo, k1, yo, k1) into st, turn, p5, turn, k5
Second row: ⑤ = purl 5sts of bobble
Third row: △ = dec 5 to 1 (using multiple-slip-stitch method: see 'dec 5 to 1' in 'Abbreviations and special stitches')

- One square of the chart represents one knitted stitch, but, in order to demonstrate how the pattern develops, it is necessary to leave some squares blank (greyed out) at appropriate places in the chart, to allow for the increase stitches made as part of the pattern motif. These stitches are decreased again later in the pattern and are therefore not included in the number of stitches cast on or required for working the first row of the chart. The symbols represent stitches as seen on the RS of the work: *see also* the key for each chart and the abbreviations and definitions provided earlier.

Scroll-motif chart

The Scroll motif is worked in st st on a rev-st-st background, with one large bobble within each curve. In each 14-stitch Scroll motif, an extra 4sts are created to start the scroll and then lost again at the end. Scroll and cable columns are worked alternately with a repeat of 22sts, not including the extra sts. Note that only the centre 6sts of the 8-stitch cable panel are crossed (with c6b, not c8b).

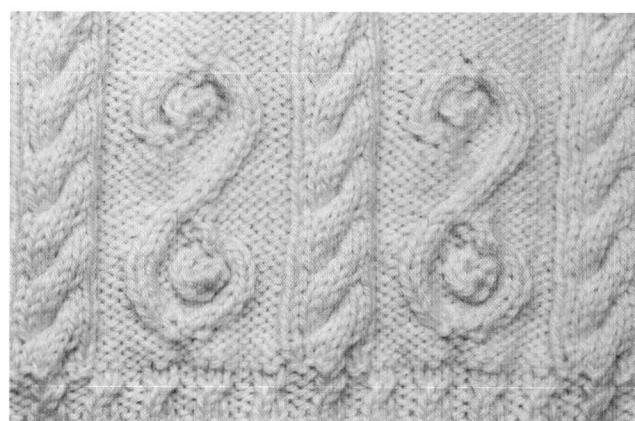

Knitted Scroll motif and cable border.

Pattern

Notes on working the pattern

- The three motifs are worked from their individual pattern charts and placed as shown in the measurement and positioning diagrams for the body and sleeves that show the overall shape of the garment pieces and where each Oval Window motif begins. RS rows are to be read from right to left; WS rows are to be read from left to right. For the Scroll motif and Grape Vine pattern, odd-numbered rows are RS rows and even-numbered rows are WS rows, but, for the Oval Window chart, exceptionally, odd-numbered rows are for WS rows and even-numbered rows are for RS rows.

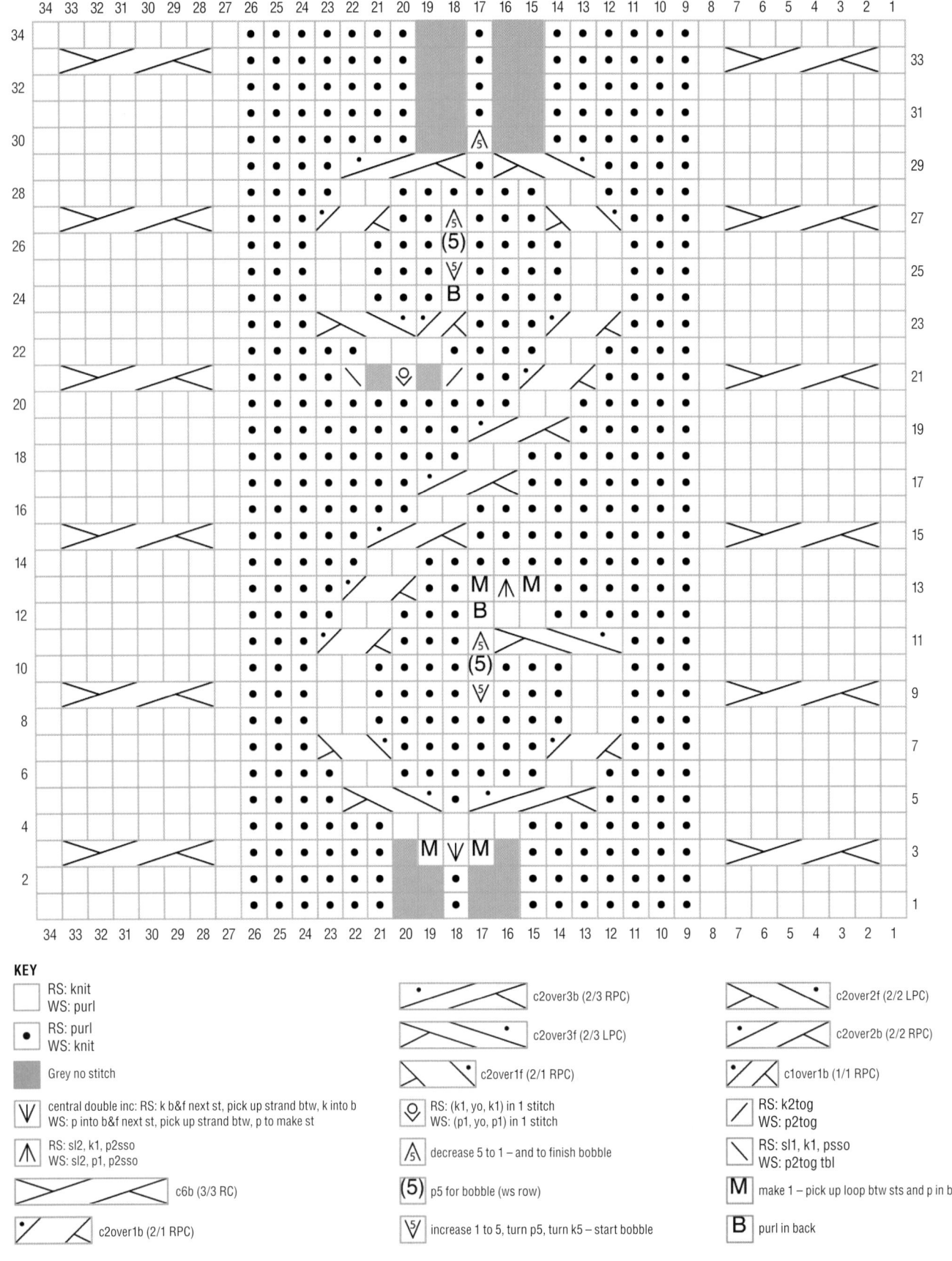

Scroll-motif chart.

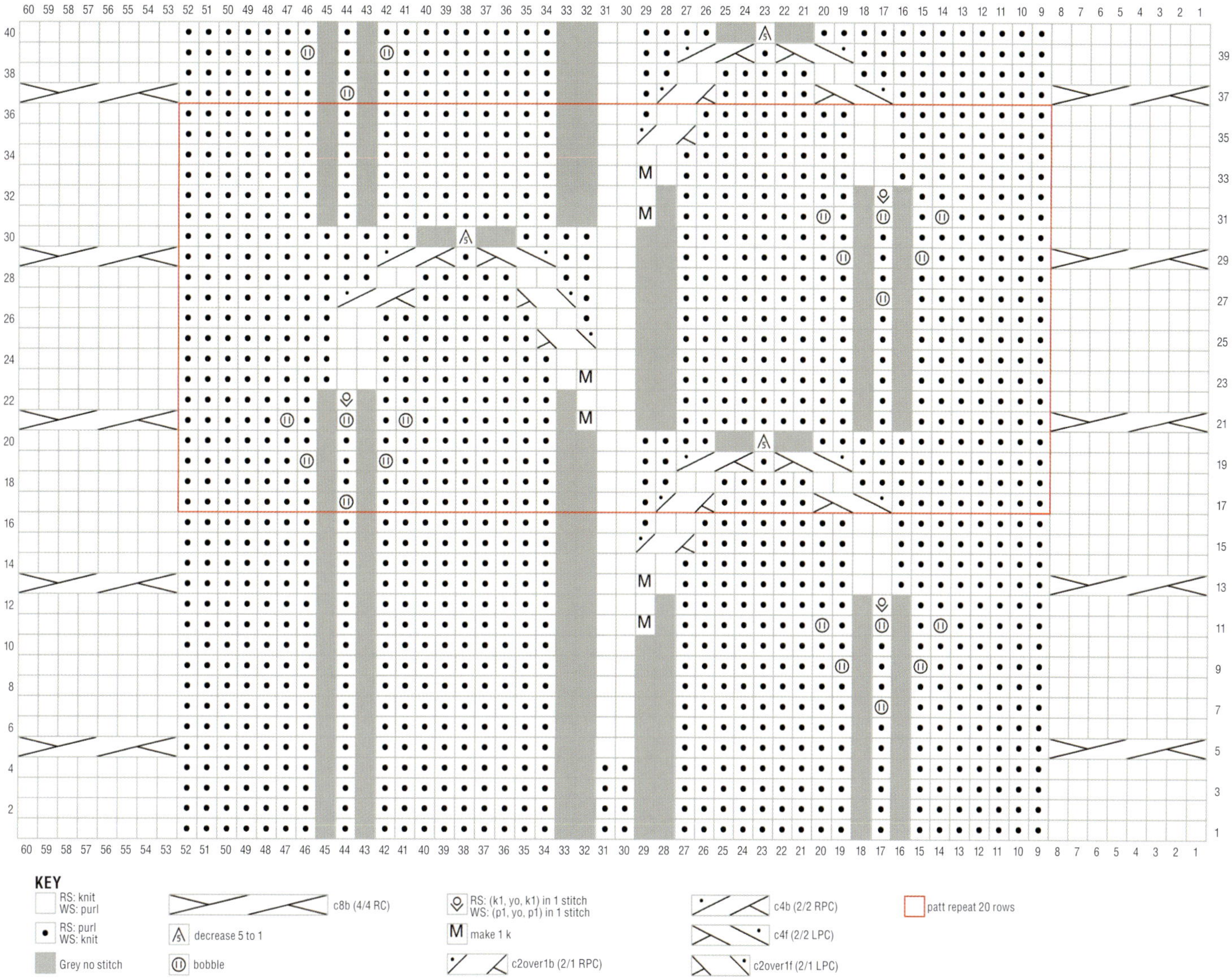

Grape Vine-pattern chart.

Grape Vine-pattern chart

The Grape Vine pattern of 56sts is also worked in st st on a rev-st-st background, with bobbles worked in the main colour to represent grapes. For each branch, 4sts are created and then lost as shown by grey squares on the chart. A cable panel in st st is worked on each side of the central Grape Vine panel, creating a sculptural effect. The 20 pattern rows for the central Grape Vine pattern and the 8 rows of the cable pattern are repeated throughout the front and back garment pieces, each in their own sequence. Be sure to start a new bunch of grapes on the 11th row of each repeat sequence as shown on the chart, before the current branch is finished.

Knitted Grape Vine-pattern central panel with cables.

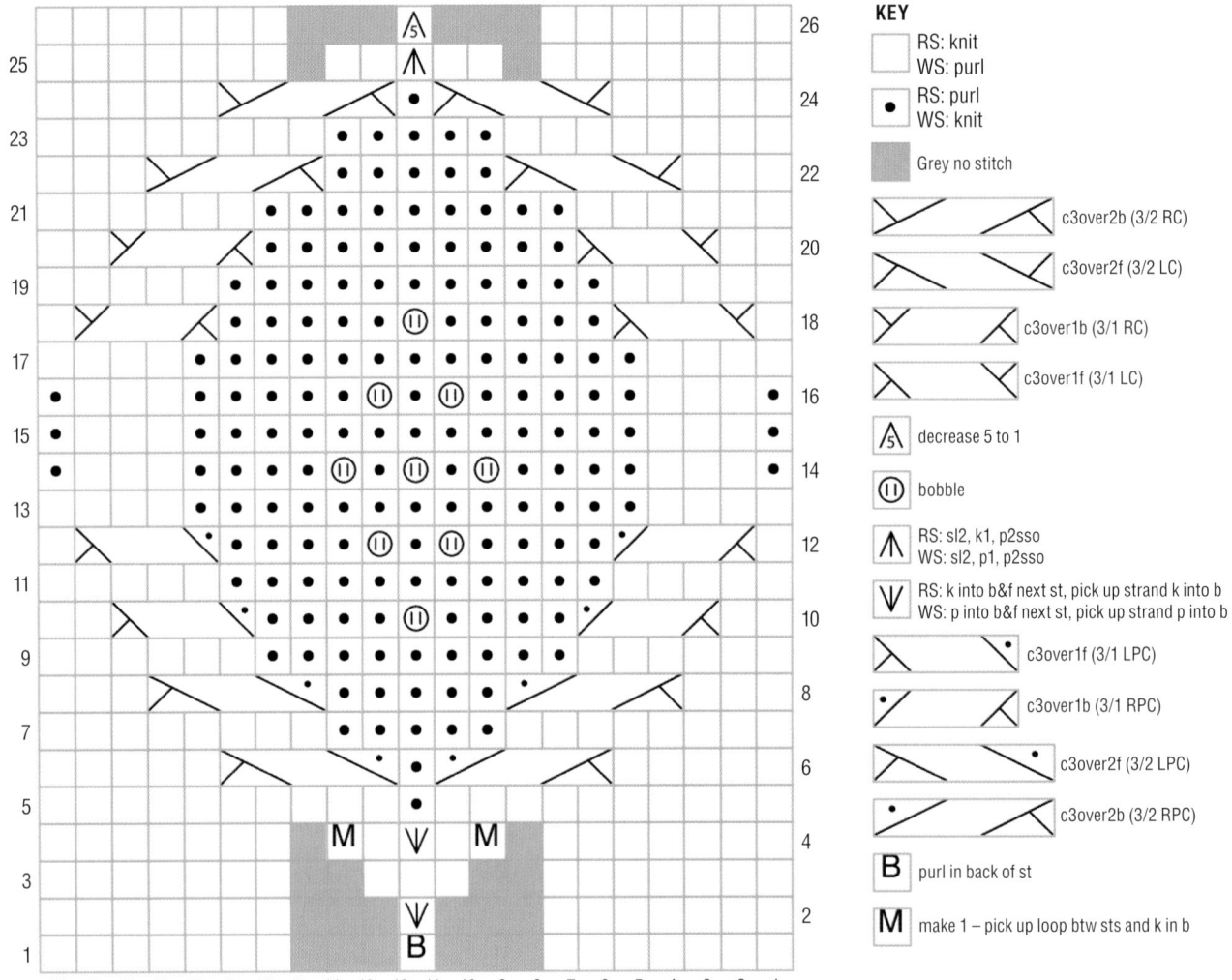

Oval Window-motif chart.

Oval Window-motif chart

The Oval Window motifs are worked in st st with a rev-st-st centre, on a st-st background, over a panel of 15sts and 26 rows. Each Oval Window motif starts with a twisted purl stitch ('B' on the chart) on the WS, and note that 6sts are created at the start of each motif and then lost at the end. A group of nine coloured bobbles is worked into the centre of each oval, alternating between the red and blue colour groups each time (denoted by 'R' and 'B', respectively, on the measurement and positioning diagrams for the body and sleeves). For the bobbles, use one length of each of the four colours of the relevant colour group, positioning these four colours at random within each bobble. The positions of the Oval Window motifs on each side of the central Grape Vine panel and on the sleeves are given in the instructions as indicated on the Oval Window positioning diagram, based on the rows worked and the position of the starting twisted purl stitch.

To familiarize yourself with working from the stitch charts, try working a practice swatch of the Scroll motif. Using the smaller needles, cast on 26sts, and work twisted rib as folls:

Row 1 (RS): K2, (p2, k2) to end.
Row 2: P2, (k2, p2) to end.
Row 3: Tw2, (p2, tw2) to end.
Row 4: As row 2.

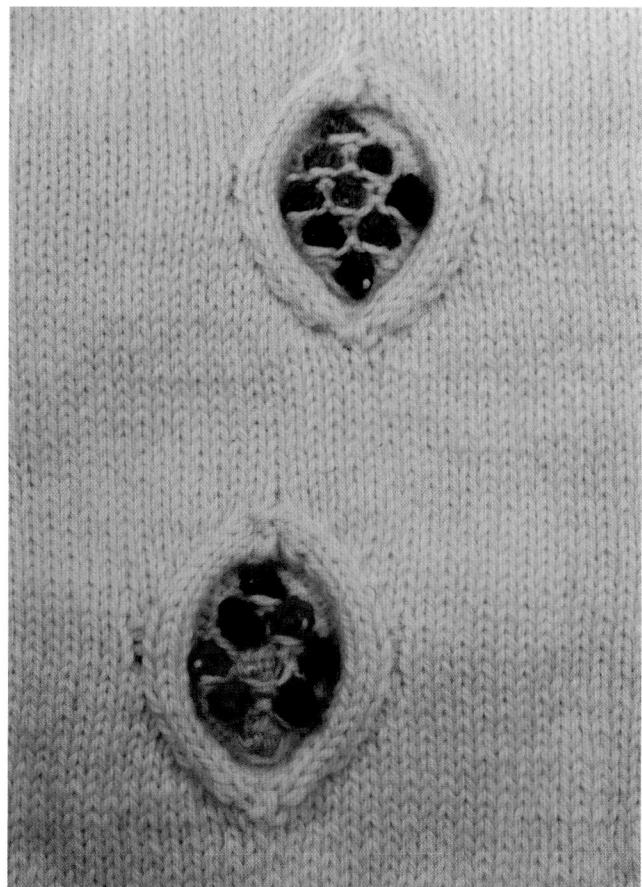

Knitted Oval Window motifs including bobbles made with yarns from the two colour groups.

Row 5: As row 1.
Preparation row for cables (WS): K2, p2, m1p, p2, m1p, p2, k14, p2, m1p, p2, m1p, p2, k2. (34sts)
Note: At each end of every row, 2 edge sts are worked that are not shown on the Scroll-motif chart.
Cont working from row 1 of the Scroll-motif chart to row 34, then cast off. The scroll should measure 4cm/1½in wide and 8cm/3in long; if not, recheck your tension swatch, and, if necessary, reknit a new swatch with smaller or larger needles, as appropriate.

Back and front

Back and front are knitted alike until neck shaping, as detailed in the following instructions.

Scroll border
Using the smaller needles, cast on 130sts, and work in twisted rib as folls:
Row 1 (RS): K2, (p2, k2) to end.
Row 2: P2, (k2, p2) to end.
Row 3: Tw2, (p2, tw2) to end.
Row 4: As row 2.
Row 5: As row 1.
Preparation row for cables (WS): K2, (p2, m1p, p2, m1p, p2, k14) 6 times, p2, m1p, p2, m1p, p2, k2. (144sts)
Note: At each end of every row, 2 edge sts are worked that are not shown on the Scroll-motif chart.
Start working from row 1 of Scroll-motif chart as folls (6 patt reps + 1 cable panel + 2 edge sts each side): K2, (k8, p14) 6 times, k8, k2.
Cont by working rows 2–34, until Scroll-motif chart is completed.
Next row (RS): Work to end of row, and, *at the same time*, dec 2sts at each cable panel as folls: K2, ([k2, k2tog] twice, k14) 6 times, (k2, k2tog) twice, k2. (130sts)
Knit 3 more rows in g st (to create 2 g-st ridges).

Body

Change to the larger needles, and establish patt layout for body as folls, with side panels of 41sts in st st and central Grape Vine panel of 52sts (36sts in rev st st with 8-st st-st cable panels at each side), and, *at the same time*, inc 4sts across row for new cables, as folls:
Row 1 (RS): K40, k2tog, k2, m1k, k2, m1k, k2, p14, m1p, p6, m1p, p14, k2, m1k, k2, m1k, k2, k2tog, k40. (134sts)
Row 2: P49, k36, p49.
Row 3: K49, p36, k49.
Row 4: As row 2.

Cont working from Grape Vine-patt chart over central 52sts from row 5:
Row 5: K41, c8b, p17, k2, p17, c8b, k41.
Position first two Oval Window motifs on a WS row with B sts as folls:

Row 6: P19, p into back of next st (B st), p29, k17, p2, k17, p24, p into back of next st (B st), p24.
Cont with motifs as set, without shaping, and work from Oval Window-motif chart (starting at RS row 2) in side panels and from Grape Vine-patt chart in centre, cont with row 7 (start of bobbles).

Note: Alternate the colour group of each Oval Window panel, with the red group on one side of the garment and the blue on the other side, then reverse the group colour, as indicated on the positioning diagram.

Keeping continuity of Grape Vine patt correct throughout, cont in patt without shaping, positioning six more Oval Window motifs, two at a time, starting on a WS row, with B sts, as folls:
Row 40: B st at 25th st from beg and 27th st after second cable.
Row 74: B st at 15th st from beg and 12th st after second cable.
Row 108: B st at 25th st from beg and 17th st after second cable.
Shape raglan, starting on **next row:**
Row 109: Keeping continuity of Grape Vine patt and Oval Window motifs correct, cast off 2sts at beg of next 2 rows. Dec 1 st at each end of foll 6th, 11th and 16th rows. (Row 126 is completed).
Dec 1 st each end of every foll 3rd row 6 times, to row 144, but, *at the same time*, start the final two Oval Window motifs on row 140 as folls:
Row 140: B st at 21st st from beg and 12th st after second cable.
Row 145: Cont in patt, and, *at the same time*, dec 1 st each end of every 2nd row until Oval Window motifs are completed, there are 84sts and row 172 is completed.
Row 173: Cont in Grape Vine patt.

Back only: Shape neck as folls:
Row 174: Cont in patt, and, *at the same time*, dec 1 st each end of next and every row to 52sts. Cast off.

Front only: Divide and shape neck as folls:
Row 174: With WS facing, cont in patt and divide for neckline as folls: dec 1 st, patt 28sts, leave rem sts on st holder for left side of front.
Turn, and patt to last 2sts, then dec 1 st. Dec 1 st at beg of next row. Cont to dec 1 st on every row at raglan edge and, *at the same time*, shape neck edge as folls:
Cast off 4sts at beg of next (RS) row and 3sts at beg of foll RS row. Dec 1 st at beg of next 5 rows at neck edge and then every 2nd row until no sts rem.
Return to sts on st holder for left side of front, and, with WS facing, cast of 24sts in centre of front, patt to last 2sts, then dec 1 st. Cont in patt and dec 1 st on every row at raglan edge and complete neck shaping to mirror that of first side.

Sleeves

Both sleeves are worked alike, but note the reversal of the colour groups for the Oval Window motifs.

Scroll border
Using the smaller needles, cast on 62sts, and work in twisted rib as folls:
Row 1 (RS): P1, k2, (p2, k2) to last 3sts, p3.
Row 2: K3, (p2, k2) to last 3sts, p2, k1.
Row 3: P1, tw2, (p2, tw2) to last 3sts, p3.
Row 4: As row 2.
Row 5: As row 1.
Preparation row for cables (WS): K1, (p2, m1p, p2, m1p, p2, k14) 3 times, k1. (68sts)
Start working from row 1 of Scroll-motif chart as folls (3 patt reps + 1 edge st at each side).
Cont by working rows 2–34, until Scroll-motif chart is completed.
Next row (RS): Work to end of row, and, *at the same time*, dec 2sts at each cable panel as folls: K1, ([k2, k2tog] twice, k14) 3 times, k1. (62sts)
Knit 3 more rows in g st (to create 2 g-st ridges).

Sleeve body
Change to larger needles, and start working in st st, positioning five Oval Window motifs up the centre of the sleeve, alternating colour groups, as indicated on the positioning diagram.
Position first Oval Window motif on a WS row with a B st as folls:
Row 4 (WS): B st at 29th st from beg.
Cont straight in patt for rows 5–19.
Shape sleeve: Work as folls:
Row 20: Keeping continuity of patt correct, inc 1 st at each end of this and every foll 4th row 11 times, then every 3rd row 3 times, to 96sts overall (Note: this is 90sts for sleeve +

an extra 6sts for an Oval Window motif). *At the same time*, position second Oval Window motif at 49th st of Row 36 (that is, the 7th row after the first Oval Window motif is completed), and position third Oval Window motif at 31st st of Row 62 (on the next row after the second Oval Window motif is completed).

Patt 3 rows (Row 69 is completed).

Shape raglan and complete Oval Window motifs:
Work as folls:

Rows 70–71: Keeping continuity of patt correct, cast of 2sts at beg of these 2 rows, then dec 1 st at each end of every foll 5th row 3 times (Row 86 is completed). *At the same time*, position fourth Oval Window motif at 56th st of Row 78, whilst also completing third Oval Window motif.

Row 87: Keeping continuity of patt correct, dec 1 st each end of every foll 3rd row 6 times (Row 104 and fourth Oval Window are completed).

Row 105: Patt 1 row.

Row 106: Dec 1 st at each end of this row and every foll 2nd row, and, *at the same time*, position fifth Oval Window motif at 31st st of Row 106 (3rd row after fourth Oval Window is completed).

Keeping continuity of patt correct, dec 1 st each end of every foll 2nd row 14 times to 38sts (fifth Oval Window is completed). Finish raglan shaping by dec 1 st each end of every foll row to 10sts, then cast off.

Make second sleeve to match, but reverse the colour group used for each Oval Window motif.

Collar

Using the larger needles, cast on 142sts, and work 4 rows of g st (to create 2 g-st ridges).

Preparation row for cables (WS): K2, (p2, m1p, p2, m1p, p2, k14) 7 times (156sts).

Start working from row 1 of Scroll-motif chart as folls (7 patt reps + 2 edge sts at the end of RS and beg of WS rows): (K8, p14) 7 times, k2.

Cont by working rows 2–34, until Scroll-motif chart is completed, and cont in cable patt for a further 6 rows. Then, work 5 rows of twisted rib as given for back and front, and, *at the same time*, dec 2sts at each cable panel on first row, by working (k2, k2tog) twice across the 8sts of each cable (142sts). Cast off in rib.

Alternatively, the collar can be knitted seamlessly by using a circular needle and substituting RS rows for WS rows for the twisted rib and the Scroll-motif chart.

Making up and finishing

Using backstitch, sew raglan, side and sleeve seams. Steam press all seams. Oversew collar seam with WS facing to make a circle, if required. With WS of collar to RS of neckline, pin collar in position, with collar seam at centre back. Working from WS, neatly oversew cast-off edge of collar to neck edge.

Detail of the Travelling Vine tunic showing all three stitch motifs and edgings.

The Scroll-cardigan design for Rowan, worked in KidSilk mohair/silk-blend yarn. (Photo: courtesy of Rowan Yarns)

The Arches-tunic design for Rowan, worked in KidSilk mohair/silk-blend yarn. (Photo: courtesy of Rowan Yarns)

RIGHT: Rowan's Designs in Kaffe's Kid/Silk knitting book, featuring the Scroll cardigan and Arches tunic.

Design Variations

The two featured designs, published in the 1986 booklet *Designs in Kaffe's Kid/Silk* by Rowan Yarns, demonstrate more variations on the idea of creating ornamental shapes through travelling cables. The Scroll-cardigan pattern was inspired not by architecture but by some highly textural wallpaper of a kind known as Anaglypta, which is a 120-year-old brand of embossed papers, that I observed on a domestic staircase. I set out to translate the observed motif, shaped rather like a lyre, into a knitted texture, developing my own variations to bend the travelling stitches into the correct shape, using similar techniques to those used for the Travelling Vine and Scroll motifs. The Arches tunic incorporates the same Scroll-motif borders as used for the Travelling Vine tunic but in a more classically inspired design, with arches on a pedestal rather than ovals to contain the bobbles.

This Chevron Rib cardigan, knitted in pure silk, featured in the magazine *The Rowan Knitting Book No 3* (published in 1988) and highlighted the twisted-rib technique. The design is simple, with the main interest being chevrons in the border created by increases and decreases.

The Textural bolero, part of the 1990 Sandy Black range, illustrates a different interpretation of texture through the use of honeycomb stitch, which is based on slipped stitches, to create a ruched effect. The plaited border is directly translated from a pattern found in the arch of a church doorway and was highlighted with attached metallic buttons from my collection. A long-sleeved version was given a more glamorous treatment with the addition of jet-black beads, sewn on after the knitting was completed.

The ribbed Chevron cardigan knitted in mulberry-silk yarn, featured in *The Rowan Knitting Book No 3*. (Photo: courtesy of Rowan Yarns)

A textural sleeveless cotton bolero from the 1990 collection, knitted in a honeycomb slip-stitch pattern with a cabled-rib border and button decoration. (Photo: Paul Dennison)

CHAPTER 7

GRAPHIC

The designs in this chapter were all created to rejoice in multiple colours, by using graphic lines and geometric shapes, and are knitted in mohair-rich textural yarns that have the effect of blurring the sharpness of the graphic lines because of the natural hairiness of the mohair fibre, giving depth to the design. Simple geometric motifs, such as various types of crosses or stars, can be traced throughout history and across different cultures and can be found in many forms of textiles worldwide.

The well-known Fair Isle patterns developed their own mythology over time and became highly fashionable in the early twentieth century, when popularized by the then Prince of Wales[1]. They are relatively simple to knit, as Fair Isle patterns use no more than two colours in any row. The Fairisle Fun sweater translates the technique into a larger scale and simple patterns, knitted with mohair-rich yarns, with added visual interest created from the change in direction of the pattern bands, achieved by joining together two separately knitted pieces. The Fairisle Fun sweater became a bestselling design and kick-started the Sandy Black range of mohair knitting kits, the patterns for four of which are included here.

'We'll send you the yarn – you do the knitting': Fairisle Fun as originally photographed for an exclusive Sandy Black Mohair knitting-kit special offer in Woman *magazine, 1983.*

OPPOSITE PAGE: *The Triangles sweater is colourful, sporty and cosy, knitted in mohair-rich yarns. (Photo: Jo Teasdale)*

The classic dogtooth sweater design is so versatile, and can be worn by anyone.

A good introduction to two-colour stranded-colourwork knitting is the Dogtooth sweater or jacket, as each design features a small but classic pattern motif in all-over repeat that is easily memorized. Working the back of the jacket does though require handling a large number of stitches, as the sleeves and body are knitted in one piece, which is achieved by using a long circular needle.

The Triangles sweater features a simple graphic pattern in repeat but is given a lively visual quality by the use of a fairly large group of colours completely at random. The colour-block technique (also known as intarsia – *see* Chapter 4) is worked by using separate small balls or butterfly twists of each yarn colour. This random choice may be unusual for some knitters, but, with just a little care in selecting the colours initially (avoiding colours that are very similar), be assured that there cannot really be any 'wrong' choices, and each resulting garment is unique.

The final pattern in this group is the Bobbly Grid cardigan, where the colour pattern is created entirely from bobbles (made on right-side rows), in colours selected randomly from a group of around seven colours. As well as variations in colours to suit your tastes – and your available yarns – the graphic lines can be varied with just a little planning to create other geometric configurations, such as diagonal lines, diamonds or squares.

Other graphical designs in the Sandy Black range featured all-over geometric patterns such as rectangles or hexagons (as in the Stained Glass sweater) or, alternatively, utilized scattered geometric motifs, such as for the Curves cardigan and Fans sweater (*see* Chapter 6). These designs are illustrated with the original 1980s styled photographs and may provide further inspiration for your own ideas.

Fairisle Fun Sweater

Fairisle Fun's crazy colour pattern brings a smile to the model's face. (Photo: Jo Teasdale)

Detail of the Fairisle Fun design.

This sweater is worked completely from the charts using seven colours of mohair-rich yarn knitted in two-colour Fair Isle-style bands of stocking stitch, with garter-stitch ridges in between. To create the unusual patterning, the front and back are each knitted as two triangles and later sewn together, in a simple patchwork style. Ribbed edgings and garter-stitch ridges are in main colour throughout.

Tension

16sts and 16 rows to 10cm/4in, measured over Fairisle Check patt (*see* the tension section), using 6.5mm (US 10.5, UK 3) needles or the required size to give the correct tension and therefore measurements.

To avoid disappointment, it is essential to check your tension carefully before commencing the knitting of the garment and to use the needles that give you the correct tension. These needles may not be of the needle size quoted in the standard tension information, as each knitter knits differently.

Size and measurements

One size to fit up to a 97cm/38in bust circumference

Knitted measurements
Width at underarms: 53cm/21in
Length: 57cm/22½in
Sleeve length: 51cm/20in
Note: For a longer sweater, simply knit an extra pattern band (without shaping) on back section 1 and front section 1 after the rib has been worked.

Materials

Yarn
Knitted with a mohair–wool-blend yarn with approx 75-per-cent mohair content and 100m/50g in 7 colours as folls:
Main colour (MC): 3 × 50g balls in grey or black
Contrast colours:
2 × 50g balls each in pink, red, gold and blue
1 × 50g ball each in blue/green and forest green

The sample is knitted in Wool and the Gang's Take Care Mohair in Deep Grey for MC and Hot Punk Pink, Lipstick Red, Tangerine Dream, Midnight Blue, Blue Steel and Powder Green for contrast colours. Many alternative colourways can be devised, for example, grey with shades of blues, plums and greens: deep pink, lilac, turquoise, mulberry and blue and sea green.

Recommended needles and accessories
Two pairs of needles are required: one pair of the size to give the correct tension, for main parts, and one pair four sizes smaller, for ribbing.
1 pair 6.5mm (US 10.5, UK 3) needles for main parts
1 pair 4.5mm (US 7, UK 7) needles for ribbing
Stitch holder or spare needle

How to check tension

Using the recommended needles and 2 colours, A and B, cast on 24sts, and work in Fairisle Check patt in st st for 24 rows as folls:
Work 2sts A, 2sts B for 2 rows, then swap colour positions for next 2 rows; repeat these 4 rows 5 times. Cast off. Pin the knitted swatch square down flat, without stretching the fabric.

A black/brights colourway.

A blue/pink colourway.

Place a pin between 2sts near the left side of the swatch, count 16sts across to the right, and place another pin between the 16th and 17th sts. Mark out 16 rows in the same manner, starting from 2sts near the top of the swatch. Measure the distance between each pair of pins. The measurements should both be 10cm/4in. If a measurement is less than 10cm/4in, your knitting is too tight – try using needles of one size larger to reknit the swatch, and again check the tension. If a measurement is more than 10cm/4in, your knitting is too loose – try using needles of one size smaller to reknit the swatch, and again check the tension. Repeat the process until the correct tension is achieved. Do not be afraid to go up or down by more than one size from the recommended needles to achieve the required tension. Adjust the size of the smaller pair of needles for the ribbing accordingly.

A note of caution: due to the fairly loose tension of this design, even a small mismatch in tension will result in a garment of the wrong size. For example, if the tension is 0.5cm/¼in too tight, that is, 16sts measure 9.5cm/3¾in, this results in a garment about 6cm/2½in smaller all round than the given measurements; similarly, 1cm/½in too tight, that is, 16sts measure only 9cm/3½in, will result in a garment that is approximately 12cm/4¾in smaller all round and correspondingly shorter.

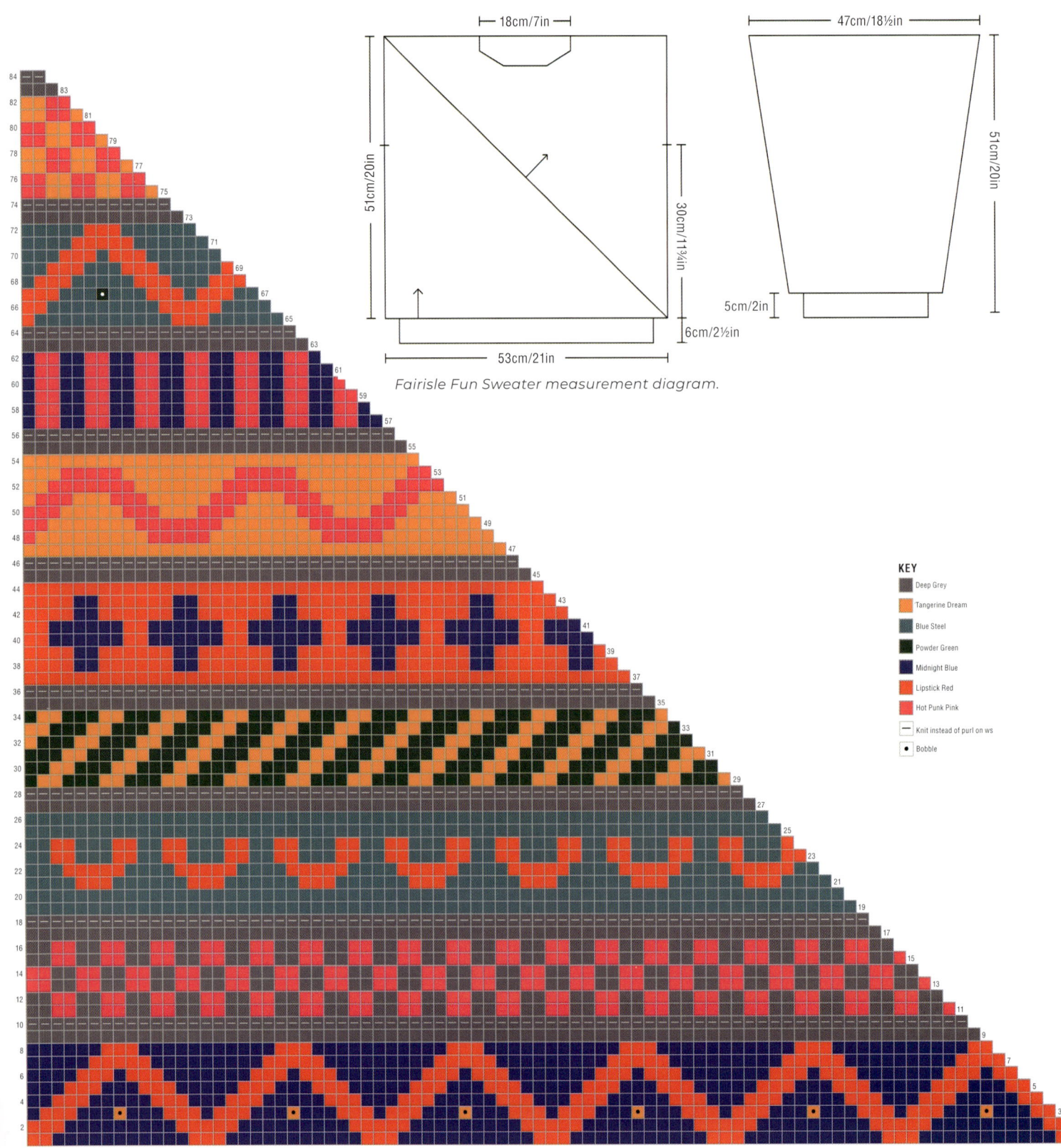

Fairisle Fun Sweater measurement diagram.

Chart A back and front section 1.

Chart B back section 2.

Chart C front section 2.

GRAPHIC 123

Chart D left sleeve.

124 GRAPHIC

Chart E right sleeve.

Abbreviation and special stitch

k b&f = knit back and front: knit into back loop of next stitch on LH needle, knit into front loop of same stitch and then allow knitted-into st to slip off LH needle

Pattern

Notes on working the pattern
- One square of the chart represents one knitted stitch. Odd-numbered rows (RS) are read from right to left and the corresponding stitches are to be knitted; even-numbered rows (WS) are read from left to right and the corresponding stitches are to be purled except where marked as knit stitches on the chart, for the creation of g-st ridges.
- Strand the yarn colour not in use loosely across the back of the work, and weave it in evenly every 3rd or 4th st where necessary.
- Ensure that all cast-on and cast-off edges are loose enough to stretch with the rest of the knitted fabric.

Shaping
The charts represent an exact picture of the knitting, including its shaping – where the chart outline moves in or out by 1 square on a particular row, this represents a simple decrease or increase, respectively, of 1 st at the relevant edge of the knitting.

Ribbing
All ribbing is worked in k2, p2 twisted rib, that is, k2, p2 rib with every knit st worked into the back loop of the stitch of the previous row, using needles 4 sizes smaller than used for knitting the main parts of the garment.

Bobbles
Where a large dot symbol is marked on a square of the chart, make a bobble on this st as folls:
With the appropriate colour, knit into the front and back loops (or 'k f&b') of this stitch twice (4sts total). Turn, k4, turn, p4, pass the 3sts furthest from the LH-needle point over the stitch closest to the RH-needle point (1 st total), slip single bobble st purlwise on to the LH needle, and knit this slipped st in background colour.

Back section 1

Using the smaller needles and MC, cast on 64sts, and work in k2, p2 twisted rib for 5cm/2in, ending with a RS row. Change to the larger needles.

Inc row (WS): Knit across and, *at the same time*, inc by k b&f into 5th and every foll 3rd st. (84sts)

Starting with row 1 of chart A, commence working Fairisle patt in cols as stated on the chart, with odd-numbered rows being knitted and even-numbered rows being purled, except where marked for knit stitches, for g-st ridge between Fairisle bands (note that the g-st ridges are of MC throughout). Shape piece as shown on the chart by working 2sts tog at beg of RS rows and end of WS rows on every row from row 3 onwards. Place a marker at straight edge on row 49 for position of underarm for armhole. After chart is completed, fasten off rem 2sts.

Back section 2

Using the larger needles and MC, cast on 115sts (not tightly), and knit 2 rows for g-st ridge. Starting with row 3 of chart B, commence working Fairisle patt in cols as stated on chart, and, *at the same time*, dec 1 st at each end of every row until 1 st rem and chart is completed. Fasten off rem st. Place one marker each at the LH side of row 21 and row 41 for position of sides of neck, and place one marker at RH side of row 35 for position of underarm for armhole.

Front section 1

Work as for back section 1.

Front section 2

Using the larger needles and MC, cast on 115sts (not tightly), and knit 2 rows for g-st ridge. Starting with row 3 of chart C, work as for back section 2 until row 17 of chart is completed.

Divide for neck: Work as folls:
Row 18: P2tog, patt next 6sts and leave rem sts on holder. Turn.

Shape right side of neck: Work as folls:
Row 19: Cast off 3sts, patt to last 2sts, k2tog.
Row 20: Sl1, k2tog, psso, and fasten off.

Shape left side of neck: With WS facing, return to sts on st holder, and work from chart as folls:
Cast off 11sts, patt to last 2sts, k2tog.
Row 19: K2tog, k to last 2sts, k2tog.
Row 20: K2tog, k to last 2sts, k2tog.
Row 21: K2tog, patt to last 2sts, k2tog.
Cont working from chart C for Fairisle patt, and, *at the same time*, dec 1 st at each end of every row until row 26 is completed, then work without shaping at neck edge until row 35 is completed. (40sts)

Row 36: Inc in 1st st, patt to last 2sts, p2tog.
Row 37: K2tog, k to end.
Row 38: Inc in 1st st, k to last 2sts, k2tog.
Row 39: K2tog, patt to end.
Row 40: Inc in 1st st, patt to last 2sts, p2tog.
Row 41: K2tog, patt to end.
Cont working from chart C for Fairisle patt, and, *at the same time*, dec 1 st at each end of every row until 1 st rem and chart is completed. Fasten off.

Sleeves

Each sleeve is worked from the appropriate chart, D or E; the sleeve shaping is identical, but the Fairisle pattern is different. Using the smaller needles and MC, cast on 32sts, and work in k2, p2 twisted rib for 5cm/2in, ending with a RS row. Change to the larger needles.
Inc row (WS): Knit across and, *at the same time*, inc by k b&f into 5th and every foll alt st. (46sts)

Starting with row 1 of the appropriate chart, commence working Fairisle patt in cols as stated on the chart, and, *at the same time*, inc as shown at each end of every 5th row to 74sts. When chart is completed, cast off loosely.

Making up and finishing

Joining body pieces

Join section 1 and section 2 of back and front along the diagonal as follows, taking care not to sew too tightly, to allow for stretch of the fabric: slightly overlap section 2 on to section 1 and backstitch through the cast-on edge of section 2. Sew left shoulder seam with backstitch, using the left neck-side marker as a guide.

Neckband

Using the smaller needles and MC, with RS facing, pick up and knit 28sts across back neck and 44sts around front neck (72sts). Knit 1 row, work in k2, p2 twisted rib for 7.5cm/3in, then cast off very loosely in rib.

Assembly and seams

Do not press pieces. Join right shoulders with backstitch. Oversew or backstitch the sides of the neckband together. Set in sleeves to armholes, using the underarm markers as a guide. Sew side and sleeve seams. Darn in all loose ends neatly, working into the seams.
Fold neckband in half around its circumference, turn it to the inside of the garment, and slip stitch the cast-off edge loosely in place, taking care that the neckband will fit over the intended wearer's head.

Dogtooth Designs

The Dogtooth sweater and jacket create impact with this classic pattern worked in bold and bright colours with black. (Photo: Jo Teasdale)

The dog-tooth check is a classic pattern originally found in woven fabrics, and it works extremely well when scaled up and knitted in a mohair-rich yarn. The choice of colour is entirely yours – use either strong contrasts, such as in the featured black-and-gold jacket, or a more subtle combination, such as black and grey. Both jacket and sweater are knitted with two-colour stranded-colourwork (Fair Isle) knitting and have ribbed edgings. The sweater is of a classic rectangular shape with drop shoulders and a crew neck. The jacket is worked in three main pieces, plus the collar pieces: the sleeves and body are knitted all in one, which requires the use of a circular needle. Vertical pockets are knitted into the jacket fronts.

Dogtooth Jacket

The original Dogtooth-jacket image, with a touch of 1950s cool. (Photo: David McIntyre)

Sizes and measurements

Two sizes to fit up to a 91[97]cm/36[38]in bust circumference

Knitted measurements

All-round circumference at underarms: 100[112] cm/39½[44]in
Length: 61[62]cm/24[24½]in
Sleeve length: 50cm/19¾in

Materials

Yarn
Knitted in a mohair–wool-blend yarn with approx 75-per-cent-mohair content and 100m/50g (for example, Wool and the Gang's Take Care Mohair) in 2 colours:
Main colour (A): 7[8] × 50g balls
Contrast colour (B): 5[5] × 50g balls
3 large buttons

Recommended needles and accessories
Two pairs of needles are required: one pair of the size to give the correct tension, for patterned st-st parts, and one pair of two sizes smaller, for ribbing and collar.
1 pair 6mm (US 10, UK 4) needles for patterned st-st parts
1 pair 5mm (US 8, UK 6) needles for ribbing
1 circular needle in the larger size
2 stitch holders
Medium-sized crochet hook

Tension

18sts and 18 rows to 10cm/4in, measured over Dogtooth patt, using 6mm (US 10, UK 4) needles or the size required to give the correct tension and therefore measurements.

To avoid disappointment, it is essential to check your tension carefully before commencing the knitting of the garment and to use the needles that give you the correct tension. These needles may not be of the needle size quoted in the standard tension information, as each knitter knits differently.

How to check tension
Using the recommended needles and the 2 colours, A and B, work Dogtooth patt (note: weave in col not in use loosely at the back of every 3rd or 4th st, and take care not to pull strands of yarn floats too tight) as folls:
Cast on 30sts, and work as indicated by Dogtooth-patt chart (patt rep: 10sts and 10 rows):
Row 1 (RS): Knit *5A, 2B, 2A, 1B; rep from * to end.
Row 2 (WS): Purl *2B, 2A, 1B, 5A; rep from * to end.
Row 3: Knit *7A, 2B, 1A; rep from * to end.

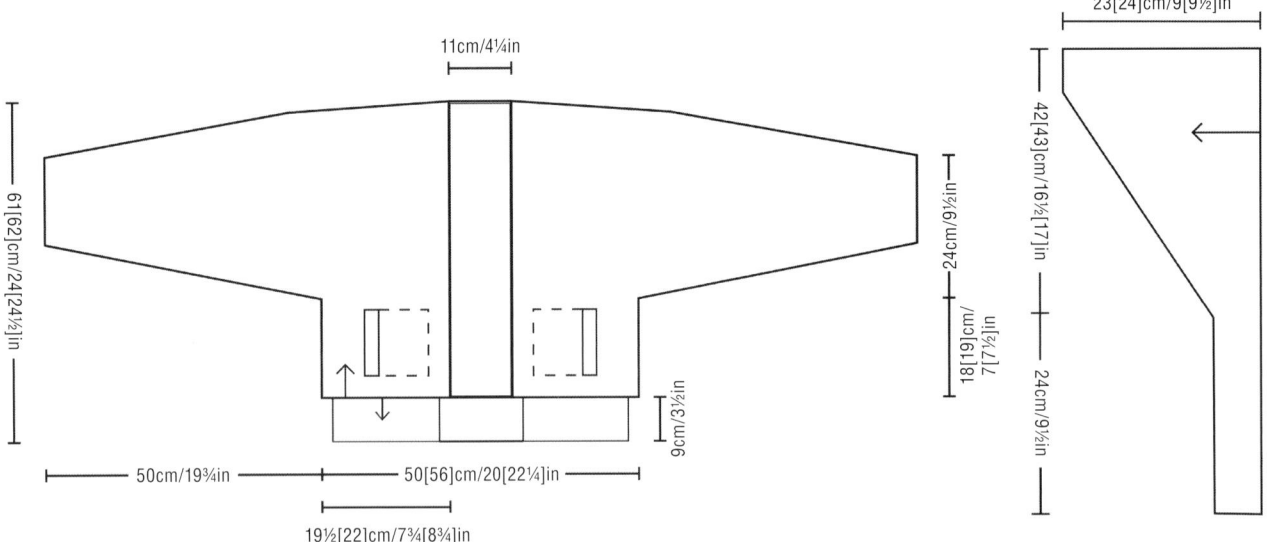

Dogtooth-jacket measurement diagram.

Dogtooth-jacket collar diagram.

Row 4: Purl *1A, 3B, 6A; rep from * to end.
Row 5: Knit *5A, 3B, 2A; rep from * to end.
Row 6: Purl *5B, 1A, 2B; 2A, rep from * to end.
Row 7: Knit *1A, 2B, 2A; 5B, rep from * to end.
Row 8: Purl *6B, 2A, 2B; rep from * to end.
Row 9: Knit * 1B, 3A, 6B; rep from * to end.
Row 10: Purl *7B, 3A; rep from * to end.

Rep rows 1–10 twice. Cast off loosely. Pin the knitted swatch square down flat, without stretching the fabric. Place a pin between 2sts near the left side of the swatch, count 18sts across to the right, and place another pin between the 18th and 19th sts. Mark out 18 rows in the same manner, starting from 2sts near the top of the swatch. Measure the distance between each pair of pins. The measurements should both be 10cm/4in. If a measurement is less than 10cm/4in, your knitting is too tight – try using needles of one size larger to reknit the swatch, and again check the tension. If a measurement is more than 10cm/4in, your knitting is too loose – try using needles of one size smaller to reknit the swatch, and again check the tension. Repeat the process until the correct tension is achieved. Do not be afraid to go up or down by more than one size from the recommended needles to achieve the required tension. Adjust the size of the smaller pair of needles for the ribbing accordingly.

Pattern

Notes on working the pattern

- A small chart of the colourwork Dogtooth patt in repeat is given for guidance – the repeat is of 10sts and 10 rows and is easily learnt. Strand the yarn colour not in use loosely across the back of the work, and weave it in evenly at the back of every 3rd or 4th st. Take great care not to pull the yarn strands at the back of the work too tight, as too-tight strands will distort the knitting.
- One square of the chart represents one knitted stitch. Odd-numbered rows (RS) are read from right to left and the corresponding stitches are to be knitted; even-numbered rows (WS) are read from left to right and the corresponding stitches are to be purled.

Back

Using the larger needles and A, cast on 90[100]sts. Join in B, and work in Dogtooth patt, starting from row 1 of the chart, for 18[19]cm/7[7½]in (*see* measurement diagram for guidance).

Shape sleeve lower edges: Keeping continuity of patt correct, cast on 10sts at beg of next 18 rows, changing to using the circular needle when desired, as number of sts increase (270[280]sts). Cont working in rows back and forth without shaping until work measures 42[43]cm/16½[17]in from beg.

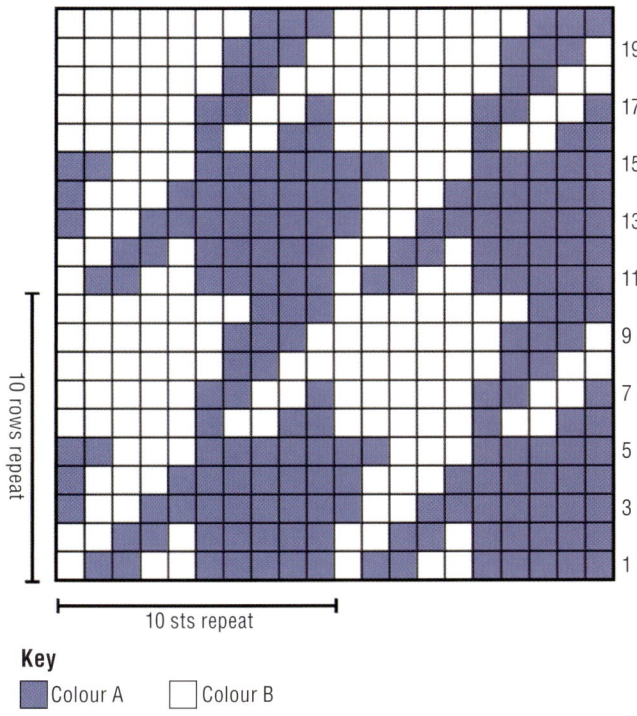

Key
■ Colour A   □ Colour B

Dogtooth-pattern chart.

A hot-pink/grey colourway.

Shape sleeve upper edges and shoulders: Cast off 10sts at beg of next 16 rows. Cast off 20sts at beg of next 2 rows. Cast off 25[30]sts at beg of next 2 rows. Cast off rem 20sts.

Right front

Using the larger needles and A, cast on 35[40]sts. Join in B, and work 8[10] rows in Dogtooth patt, starting at row 1 of chart, working a half patt rep (for smaller size only) at beg of all RS knit rows and end of WS purl rows.

Divide for pocket (RS facing): Patt 15sts, turn, and leave rem 20[25]sts on a st holder for rest of front. Work in Dogtooth patt for 17 rows, starting at row 10[2] and thus ending on row 6[8] of patt. Break yarn. Leave these 15sts on a st holder, for outer side of pocket. Place the 20[25]sts on st holder for rest of front on to working needle. Join yarn to inside edge, and cast on 15sts with A, for pocket lining.

Pocket lining and continuation of front: Working on these 35[40]sts, work 18 rows in Dogtooth patt, starting at RS row 9[1], thus ending on row 6[8] of patt.

Next row: Cast off 15sts for pocket lining, slip the st remaining after casting off on to LH needle, and break yarn.

A black/lilac colourway.

With RS facing, place 15sts from st holder for outer side of pocket on to LH needle, join yarn to start of row and patt across all 35[40]sts by working row 7[9] of Dogtooth-patt chart.

Work in patt until piece measures 18[19]cm/7[7½]in from beg, ending with a RS row, so that front length matches back length to start of sleeve shaping.

Shape sleeve lower edge (WS facing): Keeping continuity of patt correct, cast on 10sts at beg of next and every foll alt row until there are 125[130]sts. Cont straight until front matches back to start of sleeve upper-edge and shoulder shaping, ending with a RS row.

Shape sleeve upper edge and shoulder: Cast off 10sts at beg of next and every foll alt row, 8 times in total. Cast off 20sts at beg of foll alt row, and work 1 row. Cast off rem 25[30]sts.

Left front

Using the larger needles and A, cast on 35[40]sts. Join in B, and work 8[10] rows in Dogtooth patt, starting at row 1 of chart, working a half patt rep (for smaller size only) at end of all RS knit rows and beg of all WS purl rows.

Divide for pocket (RS facing): Patt 20[25]sts, turn, and leave rem 15sts on st holder for outer side of pocket.

Pocket lining and continuation of front: Cast on 15sts for pocket lining, and, working on these 35[40]sts, cont in patt for 16 rows, starting at row 10[2], thus ending on row 5[7] of patt. Cast off 15sts at beg of next row, patt to end, and leave these 20[25]sts on a st holder for rest of front. Place 15sts on st holder for outer side of pocket on to working needle. With RS facing, join yarn to inside edge of these sts, and work 18 rows in Dogtooth patt, starting at RS row 9[1], thus ending on row 6[8] of patt. Break yarn.

Next row (RS facing): Place 20[25]sts from st holder for rest of front on to LH needle that is already holding the 15sts for outer side of pocket, join yarn to start of row and patt across all 35[40]sts, starting from row 7[9] of Dogtooth-patt chart.

Work in patt until piece measures 18[19]cm/7[7½]in from beg, ending with a WS row, so that front length matches back length to start of sleeve shaping.

Shape sleeve and shoulder: Starting with RS facing, complete sleeve and shoulder shaping to mirror that of right front.

Pocket bands

Using the smaller needles and A, with RS facing, pick up and knit 18sts along front edge of first pocket opening. Work 7 rows in k1, p1 rib, and cast off loosely in rib.

Oversew short ends of pocket band securely to front. Rep for second pocket opening.

Collar and front bands

These are knitted sideways as two halves, worked in k1, p1 rib throughout, and later seamed together and to the garment body.

Left half
With A and the smaller needles, cast on 141[145]sts.
Rows 1–2: Starting with k1, rib 20sts, turn, sl1, rib to end.
Rows 3–4: Rib 24sts, turn, sl1, rib to end.
Rows 5–6: Rib 28sts, turn, sl1, rib to end.
Rows 7–8: Rib 32sts, turn, sl1, rib to end.
Rows 9–10: Rib 36sts, turn, sl1, rib to end.
Rows 11–12: Rib 3sts, * (p1, k1, p1) into next st, rib 5sts; rep from * 5 times, rib 1 st, turn, sl1, rib to end. (153[157]sts)
Rows 13–14: Rib 56sts, turn, sl1, rib to end.
Cont in same way, working 4 sts more on each alt row until the row worked as 'rib 96[100], turn, sl1, rib to end' is completed. **
Rib 10 rows across all sts. Cast off loosely in rib.

Right half
With A and the smaller needles, cast on 141[145]sts, and work 1 row of k1, p1 rib, starting with k1.
Work as for left half to ** but start row 1 with p1 and work the increases on row 11 as (k1, p1, k1) into next st.
Rib 9 rows across all sts. Cast off loosely in rib.

Making up and finishing

Sew side and sleeve lower-edge seams using backstitch.

Waistband

Using the smaller needles and A, with RS facing, pick up and knit 148[166]sts in total (32[36]sts from each front and 84[94]sts from back) around lower body. Work 9cm/3½in of k1, p1 rib. Cast off loosely in rib.

Assembly and seams

Using backstitch, sew shoulder and sleeve upper-edge seams. Steam press seams but do not press main pieces. Neatly oversew centre-back seam of collar. Pin collar and front bands into position, with cast-on edges to the inside, to later be sewn into the seam, and cast-off edges to the outside, taking care to match centre back of jacket to centre back of collar, and arrange fullness evenly around collar. Oversew collar and fronts in place from WS.

On left-front band, mark position of 3 buttons at 2.5cm/1in, 14cm/5½in and 23cm/9in from lower edge of garment. Sew on buttons. Using a medium-size crochet hook and A, fasten yarn securely to WS of right-front band, and work 3 button loops of 12 chains each at RS of right-front band to correspond with positions of buttons, so that the loops lay along the outer edge of the front band, and fasten off securely for each button loop.

Turn in each cuff by 1.5cm/½in, slip stitch edge into position on WS, and slip stitch cast-on and cast-off edges of both pocket linings into position securely.

Dogtooth Sweater

For tension and notes on working the pattern, *see* the Dogtooth-jacket instructions.

Sizes and measurements

Two sizes to fit up to a 89[97]cm/35[38]in bust/chest circumference

Knitted measurements
Width at underarms: 54[56.5]cm/21½[22½]in
Length: 58.5[61]cm/23[24]in
Sleeve length: 49.5cm/19½in

Materials

Yarn
Knitted in a mohair–wool-blend yarn with approx 75-per-cent-mohair content and 100m/50g (for example, Wool and the Gang's Take Care Mohair) in 2 colours:
Main colour (A): 6 × 30g balls
Contrast colour (B): 5 × 30g balls

Recommended needles and accessories
Two pairs of needles are required: one pair of the size to give the correct tension, for patterned st-st parts, and one pair of two sizes smaller, for ribbing.
1 pair 6mm (US 10, UK 4) needles for patterned st-st parts
1 pair 5mm (US 8, UK 6) needles for ribbing
Stitch holder

The original 1980s image of the Dogtooth jacket and sweater in which the classic dog-tooth check is teamed with spots for a pattern clash that works. (Photo: David McIntyre)

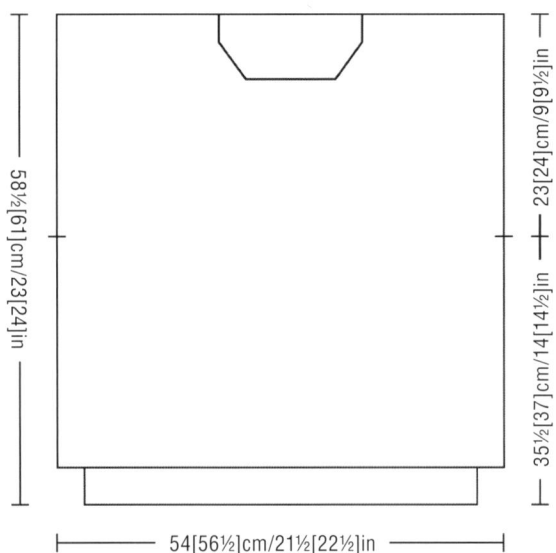
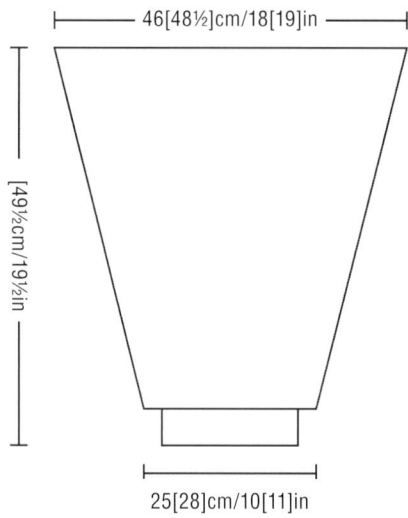

Dogtooth-sweater measurement diagram.

Abbreviation and special stitch

p b&f = purl back and front: purl into back loop of next stitch on LH needle, purl into front loop of same stitch and then allow purled-into st to slip off LH needle

Pattern

Additional notes on working the pattern
For notes on working the colourwork Dogtooth patt, *see* the Dogtooth-jacket instructions.

Ribs
All ribs are worked in k2, p2 twisted rib (that is, k2, p2 rib with every knit st being worked into the back loop of the stitch of the previous row).

Sizes
The instructions for the first and second sizes are set out separately for back and front.

Back

Using the smaller needles and A, cast on 68[76]sts, and work in k2, p2 twisted rib for 6.5cm/2½in, ending with a RS row.

Change to the larger needles.
Inc row (WS): Purl across and, *at the same time*, inc by p b&f into 6th[1st] st and every foll alt[3rd] st to last 6sts[to end]. (97[102]sts) *

First size only: Join in B, and work as folls:
Row 1 (RS): Knit 1A, 2B, 2A, 1B, (5A, 2B, 2A, 1B) to last st, 1A.
Row 2 (WS): Purl 1A, (2B, 2A, 1B, 5A) to last 6sts, 2B, 2A, 1B, 1A.

Second size only: Join in B, and work as folls:
Row 1 (RS): Knit 1B, (5A, 2B, 2A, 1B) to last st, 1A.
Row 2 (WS): Purl 1A, (2B, 2A, 1B, 5A) to last st, 1B.

Both sizes: Cont straight in patt as set, foll Dogtooth-patt chart, until work measures 58.5[61]cm/23[24]in from beg, but placing markers for underarms of armholes at each side after 35.5[37]cm/14[14½]in have been worked. Knit 1 row with B. Cast off loosely, placing markers on 32nd[34th] and 65th[68th] sts for sides of neck.

Front

Work as for back to *. Work Dogtooth patt as folls:

First size only: Join in B, and work as folls:
Row 1: Knit 1B, (5A, 2B, 2A, 1B) to last 6sts, 5A, 1B.
Row 2: Purl 1B, 5A, (2B, 2A, 1B, 5A) to last st, 1B.

Second size only: Set out patt as for back second size.

Both sizes: Cont straight in patt as set, foll Dogtooth-patt chart until work measures 51[52]cm/20[20½]in from beg, ending with a WS row.

Shape neck (RS): Patt 40[42]sts, turn, and place rem 57[60]sts on a st holder; cont on these 40[42]sts in patt as set, and, *at the same time*, dec 1 st at inner edge, for left side of neck, of next 8 rows. Work straight until front length matches back length. Cast off loosely. Place sts from st holder back on to needle. With RS facing, join yarn to inside edge, cast off 17[18]sts for centre and start of neckline, and patt rem 40[42]sts. Cont in patt as set, and, *at the same time*, dec 1 st at inner edge, for right side of neck, of next 8 rows. Complete shaping to mirror that of left side of neck.

Sleeves

Both sleeves are worked alike.
Using the smaller needles and A, cast on 32[36]sts, and work in k2, p2 twisted rib for 5cm/2in, ending with a RS row. Change to the larger needles.
Inc row (WS): Purl across and, *at the same time*, inc by p b&f into 5th and every foll alt st to last 3[5]sts, purl to end. (45[50]sts)

Work Dogtooth patt as folls:
Row 1 (RS): First size only – first knit 2B, 2A, 1B; then both sizes – knit (5A, 2B, 2A, 1B) to end.
Row 2 (WS): Both sizes – purl (2B, 2A, 1B, 5A) 4[5] times; then first size only – knit (2B, 2A, 1B).

Shape sleeves: Cont in patt as set, and, *at the same time*, inc 1 st at each end of 5th and every foll 4th row to 83[88] sts, incorporating the new sts into Dogtooth patt. Cont straight in patt until work measures 49.5cm/19½in. Cast off.

Neckband

Using side-of-neck markers as a guide, sew left shoulder seam using backstitch. With A and smaller needles, with RS facing, evenly pick up and knit 34sts across back neck and 46sts around front neckline edge (80sts). Work in k2, p2, twisted rib for 7.5cm/3in. Cast off loosely in rib.

A dark-mauve/pale-pink colourway.

A blue/red colourway.

Making up and finishing

Do not press pieces. Darn in all loose ends.
Using side-of-neck markers as a guide, sew right shoulder seam using backstitch. Sew side and sleeve seams. Set in sleeves to armholes, using the underarm markers as a guide. Fold neckband in half around its circumference, turn it to the inside of the garment, and slip stitch the cast-off edge loosely in place, taking care that the neckband will fit over the intended wearer's head.

Triangles Sweater

The ridged yoke gives structure and swagger to the Triangles design. (Photo: Jo Teasdale)

This sweater is knitted in a mohair-blend yarn in the stocking-stitch Triangles pattern, and it has a ridged yoke, knitted separately and later sewn to the rest of the garment body, and a double-thickness stand-up collar. The greatest enjoyment in knitting this pattern comes from using the colours entirely at random. Each small triangle is knitted with a separate ball of yarn so beware – for the body, there are seventeen or nineteen little balls used across each row. This version uses ten colours, but many different colour palettes can be chosen, for example, including tonal shades of blues and greens. The design also works well with fewer colours overall, but a minimum of seven is suggested, to ensure plenty of colour choice. This is a very good design to use up your remnants of yarn colours from other projects!

Sizes and measurements

Two sizes to fit up to a 89(97)cm/35(38)in bust circumference

Knitted measurements
Width at underarms: 48[53.5]cm/19[21]in
Length: 56[61]cm/22[24]in
Sleeve length: 46cm/18in

Materials

Yarn
Knitted in a mohair–wool-blend yarn with approx 75-per-cent-mohair content and 100m/50g in 10 colours as folls:
The sample garment is knitted in Wool and the Gang's Take Care Mohair, with Black as the main colour and Punk Pink, Misty Mauve, Lipstick Red, Deep Grey, Tangerine Dream, Powder Green, Cinnamon Dust, Blue Steel and Midnight Blue as contrast colours.
Many different colour combinations can be devised – if fewer colours are used then more of each colour will be needed.
Main colour (MC): 5 × 50g balls
Contrast colours (C): 1 × 50g ball each of 9 colours, for colourwork triangles

Recommended needles and accessories
Two pairs of needles are required: one pair of the size to give the correct tension, for main parts, and one pair of one size smaller, for ribbing.
1 pair 5mm (UK 6, US 8) needles for main parts
1 pair 4.5mm (UK 7, US 7) needles for ribbing
2 stitch holders
For making ridges, use one of the 4.5mm (smaller) needles or an even smaller size, as preferred

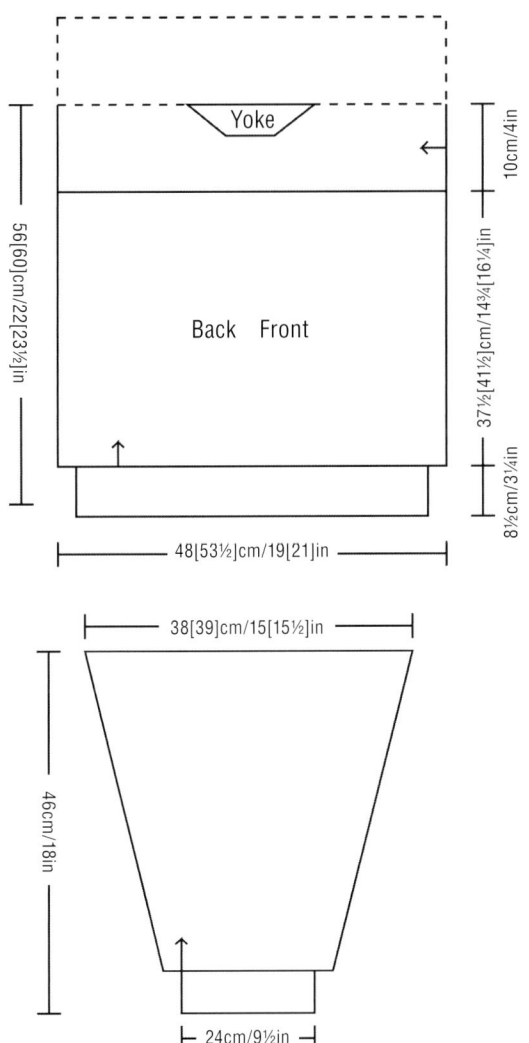

Measurement diagram.

Tension

17sts and 24 rows to 10cm/4in, measured over Triangles patt, using 5mm (UK 6, US 9) needles or the size required to give the correct tension and therefore measurements.

To avoid disappointment, it is essential to check your tension carefully before commencing the knitting of the garment and to use the needles that give you the correct tension. These needles may not be of the needle size quoted in the standard tension information, as each knitter knits differently.

How to check tension
This step is also an opportunity for test knitting of the pattern, which is easily learnt. Using the recommended needles and MC, cast on 25sts. Using any 6 cols, A, B, C, D, E and F, work as folls in st st, starting with a knit row:
Row 1: Knit 1A, 9B, 1C, 9D, 1E, 4F.
Row 2: Purl 4F, 1E, 9D, 1C, 9B, 1A.
Row 3: Knit 2A, 7B, 3C, 7D, 3E, 3F.
Row 4: Purl 3F, 3E, 7D, 3C, 7B, 2A.
Row 5: Knit 3A, 5B, 5C, 5D, 5E, 2F.
Row 6: Purl 2F, 5E, 5D, 5C, 5B, 3A.
Row 7: Knit 4A, 3B, 7C, 3D, 7E, 1F.
Row 8: Purl 1F, 7E, 3D, 7C, 3B, 4A.
Row 9: Knit 5A, 1B, 9C, 1D, 9E.
Row 10: Purl 9E, 1D, 9C, 1B, 5A.

These written instructions correspond to the first 25sts of rows 1–10 of the Triangles-patt chart. Work from the chart, first working rows 11–20 and then rep rows 1–10, using col for each triangle at random. (30 rows completed.)

Pin the knitted swatch square down flat, without stretching the fabric. Place a pin between 2sts near the left side of the swatch, count 17sts across to the right, and place another pin between the 17th and 18th sts. Mark out 24 rows in the same manner, starting from 2sts near the top of the swatch. Measure the distance between each pair of pins. The measurements should both be 10cm/4in. If a measurement is less than 10cm/4in, your knitting is too tight – try using needles of one size larger to reknit the swatch, and again check the tension. If a measurement is more than 10cm/4in, your knitting is too loose – try using needles of one size smaller to reknit the swatch, and again check the tension. Repeat the process until the correct tension is achieved. Do not be afraid to go up or down by more than one size from the recommended needles to achieve the required tension. Adjust the needle size of the smaller pair of needles for the ribbing accordingly.

Abbreviation and special stitch

p b&f = purl back and front: purl into back loop of next stitch on LH needle, purl into front loop of same stitch and then allow purled-into st to slip off LH needle

Pattern

Notes on working the pattern
- One square of the chart represents one knitted stitch. Odd-numbered rows (RS) are read from right to left and the corresponding stitches are to be knitted; even-numbered rows (WS) are read from left to right and the corresponding stitches are to be purled.
- For the written instructions, C = contrast colour. All colours are to be used at random, so C does not refer to any specific colour and also includes the main colour (MC).

Triangles pattern
Each triangle is 9sts at the base, decreasing by 1 st at each side on every alt row to an apex of 1 st. Make small butterfly twists (*see* below) or wind bobbins of all colours, and use these at random, leaving ends of about 7.5cm/3in for finishing off at beg and end of each triangle. Always cross yarns by picking up the new yarn from under the previous one when changing yarn colours, to link the colours and prevent holes appearing in the knitting.

Butterfly twists
Measure off yarn in lengths of approx 135cm/53in. Leaving an end of yarn in palm of hand, wind yarn in a figure-of-eight path around thumb and little finger, and fasten the wound yarn by wrapping yarn end around the centre a few times and securing this end with a half hitch. Work from loose yarn end left at start of butterfly twist – the yarn of a butterfly twist does not then unravel during knitting and so minimizes annoying tangling! *See also* Chapter 4.

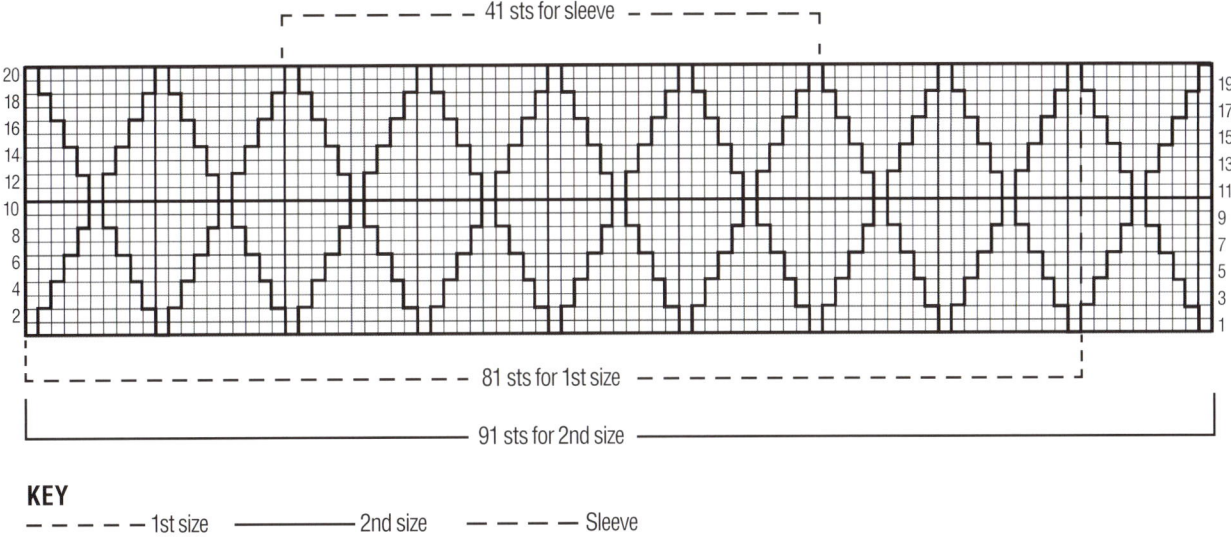

Triangles-pattern chart.

Back

Using the smaller needles and MC, cast on 65[74]sts.
Row 1 (WS): K2, (p1, k2) to end.
Row 2 (RS): P2, (k1, p2) to end.
Working in p2, k1 rib as set, cont rib as folls, joining in C as necessary: (4 rows MC, 2 rows C) twice, 6 rows MC, thus ending with a RS row. *

Inc row (WS): Purl across and, *at the same time*, inc by p b&f into 3rd[7th] st and every foll 4th st. (81[91]sts)

Change to the larger needles. Work colourwork patt by foll Triangles-patt chart and joining in 17[19] twists or bobbins of C in random order, including MC, as folls:
Row 1 (RS): Knit 1 st with first C, knit 9sts with second C, knit 1 st with third C, knit 9sts with fourth C, knit 1 st with fifth C, and so on, to end of row.
Row 2 and all WS rows: Purl each st with the same col (C) as used for prev row.
Row 3: Knit 2sts with first C, knit 7sts with second C, knit 3sts with third C, knit 7sts with fourth C, knit 3sts with fifth C, knit 7sts with sixth C, and so on, to end of row. **

Detail of the Triangles pattern.

An example of an alternative colourway using neutrals with dark greens.

Cont working in patt as set from row 4 of Triangles-patt chart until rows 1–10 are completed (= first band of triangles). Break off all cols. Join in 17[19] cols, ensuring that any col used in the first band of triangles appears in a different position in the triangle sequence of the next row, and work rows 11–20 of chart. Rep rows 1–20 of Triangles-patt chart, joining in a new col sequence every 10 rows, until 90[100] rows, that is, 9[10] bands of triangles, are completed, ending with a WS row.

Make ridge: Using MC, work 6 rows in st st, ending with a WS row. Using one of the smaller needles, pick up one loop from each st of first row of st st in MC from the WS on to this needle. With RS facing and holding smaller needle behind LH needle, knit 1 st from LH needle tog with corresponding st from smaller needle (that is, for this pair of sts, k2tog) to end of row.
Purl 1 row.
Cast off.

Front

Work as for back, using the same or a different col arrangement, as preferred.

Sleeves

Using the smaller needles and MC, cast on 32sts. Work rib as for back to * but using different cols.
Inc row (WS): Purl across and, *at the same time*, inc by p b&f into 6th st and every foll 3rd st. (41sts)

Change to the larger needles, and work as given for back from change to larger needles to ** but by using 9 cols instead of 17[19] over 41sts as indicated by the Triangles-patt chart. Cont in Triangles patt, and, *at the same time*, inc 1 st at each end of every 6th[5th] row, incorporating new sts into patt, until there are 65[67]sts. Work straight until 9 bands of triangles have been completed (90 rows). Cast off by using all cols used in prev row in turn.
Work the second sleeve in the same way, using the same or a different col arrangement, as preferred.

Yoke

Using the larger needles and MC, cast on 34sts, and work 8 rows in st st, starting with a RS knit row. Make first ridge by picking up one loop for each st of 2nd row of st st in MC from the WS on to a smaller needle, then cont to make ridge as given for back. * Join in any C and work 5 rows in st st, then break off C. Using MC, work 6 rows in st st, and again make ridge as set. Rep from * 4[5] times, using a different C each time (6[7] ridges in MC).

Divide for neck: With next C, purl 17sts, and leave these sts on a st holder, for front neck. Cont straight in ridge patt as set on rem 17sts, for back neck, until a further 5 ridges and 6 col stripes have been worked, then leave these 17sts on a st holder. With RS facing, place 17sts on front-neck st holder on to LH needle, and join yarn to inside edge.

Shape front neck: Cast off 4sts at beg of next row, and cont in ridge patt, and, *at the same time*, dec 1 st at neck edge on 3rd, 4th and 5th rows of first-C stripe and 2nd, 3rd and 4th rows of next C stripe (7sts rem). Cont straight in ridge patt as set until fourth ridge after dividing for neck is completed. Cont in patt, and, *at the same time*, inc 1 st at neck edge on 2nd, 3rd and 4th rows of next C stripe and 1st, 2nd and 3rd rows of foll C stripe. Cast on 4sts at neck edge on next row, and complete rest of front yoke to match rest of back neck (17sts). Break yarn. Place 17sts on back-neck st holder on to LH needle, to join back and front of yoke. To complete yoke, cont straight in ridge patt as set until 6[7] more ridges have been completed (17[19] ridges from beg). Cast off.

Collar

Note that it is important not to cast on and cast off too tightly for this snug-fitting collar.
Using the smaller needles and MC, loosely cast on 77sts, and work in p2, k1 rib, as for back, as folls, joining in C as necessary: rib (4 rows MC, 1 row C) 4 times, 6 rows MC, (1 row C, 4 rows MC) 4 times. Rib 1 row C, and cast off loosely. Oversew cast-off and cast-on edges of collar together loosely, ensuring collar can still stretch.

The original 1980s photograph, showing a classic timelessness. (Photo: David McIntyre)

Making up and finishing

Do not press pieces. Darn in all loose ends carefully, closing up any gaps between areas of different colours *at the same time*.
Taking care to preserve ridges at seams and using backstitch, join yoke to front and back. Join sleeves to straight edges of body and yoke, taking care to match centre of sleeves to centre of yoke. Sew side and sleeve seams.
With oversewn edge to neckline edge and RS together, pin collar into position all round neckline, taking care to position the opening at exactly centre front. Oversew collar in place, and oversew open short ends of collar. Take care that opening will fit over the intended wearer's head.

Bobbly Grid Cardigan

The Bobbly Grid cardigan is highly versatile: the base colour and contrast colours are easily changed for a different effect. (Photo: Jo Teasdale)

The original Bobbly Grid cardigan, here dressed up for a smarter look. (Photo: David McIntyre)

Sizes and measurements

Two sizes to fit up to a 91[97]cm/36[38]in bust circumference

Knitted measurements

All-round circumference at underarms, including front bands: 99[104]cm/39[41]in
Length: 56[57]cm/22[22½]in
Sleeve length: 57[58.5]cm/22½[23]in

Materials

Yarn

Knitted in a mohair–wool-blend yarn with approx 75-per-cent-mohair content and 100m/50g, for example, Wool and the Gang's Take Care Mohair, in 9 colours:

Main colour (MC): 9 × 50g balls
Contrast colours (C): 1 small ball (approx 20g), or oddments, in each of 8 (or more/fewer) colours

Recommended needles and accessories

Two pairs of needles are required: one pair of the size to give the correct tension, for main parts, and one pair of three sizes smaller, for ribbing.
1 pair 5.5mm (UK 5, US 9) needles for main parts
1 pair 4mm (UK 8, US 6) needles for ribbing
Stitch holder or spare needle
6 buttons

This versatile cardigan is knitted in mohair-rich yarn in stocking stitch, with contrast-colour bobbles knitted into the fabric in a grid formation. It can be worn in either casual or smarter style, as shown in the photographs. There are two front pockets, and the collar and front bands are knitted in one piece in k1, p1 rib. It is suggested here to use eight contrast colours, but this can of course be varied as you wish. Have fun with the colours – these are picked at random and are great for using up some of your yarn oddments!

Tension

16sts and 20 rows to 10cm/4in, measured over st st, using 5.5mm (UK 5, US 9) needles or the size required to give the correct tension and therefore measurements.

A grid 'square' measures 10cm/4in wide by 7.5cm/3in deep from centre to centre of bobble lines.

To avoid disappointment, it is essential to check your tension carefully before commencing the knitting of the garment and to use the needles that give you the correct tension. These needles may not be of the needle size quoted in the standard tension information, as each knitter knits differently.

How to check tension

Using the recommended needles and a light colour, cast on 24sts, and work in st st for 30 rows. Cast off. Pin the knitted swatch square down flat, without stretching the fabric. Place a pin between 2sts near the left side of the swatch, count 16sts across to the right, and place another pin between the 16th and 17th sts. Mark out 20 rows in the same manner, starting from 2sts near the top of the swatch. Measure the distance between each pair of pins. The measurements should both be 10cm/4in. If a measurement is less than 10cm/4in, your knitting is too tight – try using needles of one size larger to reknit the swatch, and again check the tension. If a measurement is more than 10cm/4in, your knitting is too loose – try using needles of one size smaller to reknit the swatch, and again check the tension. Repeat the process until the correct tension is achieved. Do not be afraid to go up or down by more than one size of the recommended needles to achieve the required tension. Adjust the size of the smaller pair of needles for the ribbing accordingly.

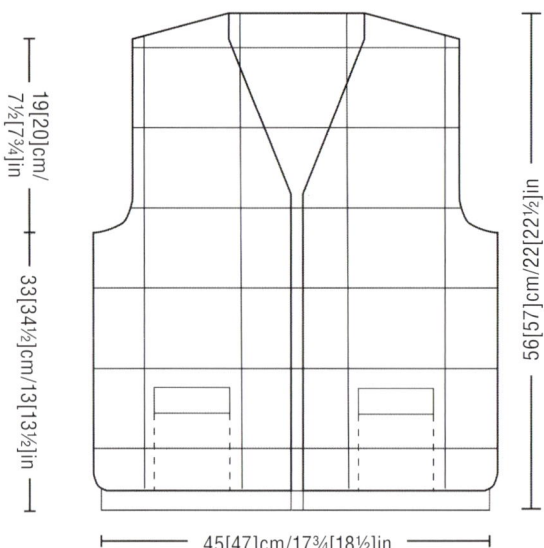
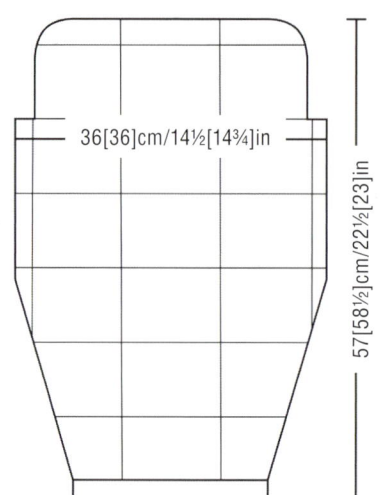
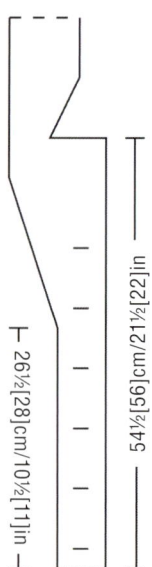

Measurement diagram.

Abbreviations and special stitches

mb = make bobble (*see* Bobbles in 'Notes on working the pattern)
sl1k = slip 1 st knitwise from LH needle to RH needle
yrn = yarn round needle

Pattern

Notes on working the pattern

- **Bobbles**
  Bobbles are made on knit rows only as folls: Using C, knit into front and back of next st (2sts). Turn, k2, turn, p2, and pass the 2nd C st, furthest from the point of the RH needle, over the 1st C st, closest to the point of the RH needle. Slip rem C st on to the LH needle and knit this st with MC. This process is abbreviated 'mb', for 'make bobble', within the written instructions).

- **Bobbly Grid pattern**
  Bobbles are made on all RS (knit) rows, on alt sts for horizontal lines and alt rows for vertical lines. There are 6 bobbles (13sts) between vertical bobble lines and 7 bobbles (15 rows) between horizontal bobble lines. Therefore, the grid pattern repeats over 14sts and 16 rows. Each new bobble is of a different col to that used for the adjacent bobble, whether beside or below the new bobble to be made, by using all 8 contrast cols (C) randomly. Break yarn after each bobble is completed, leaving ends of approx 5cm/2in for later fastening off the yarn. It is recommended to prepare short lengths of all contrast cols before starting to knit the garment, then to use these lengths at random, thus avoiding balls of yarn entangling.

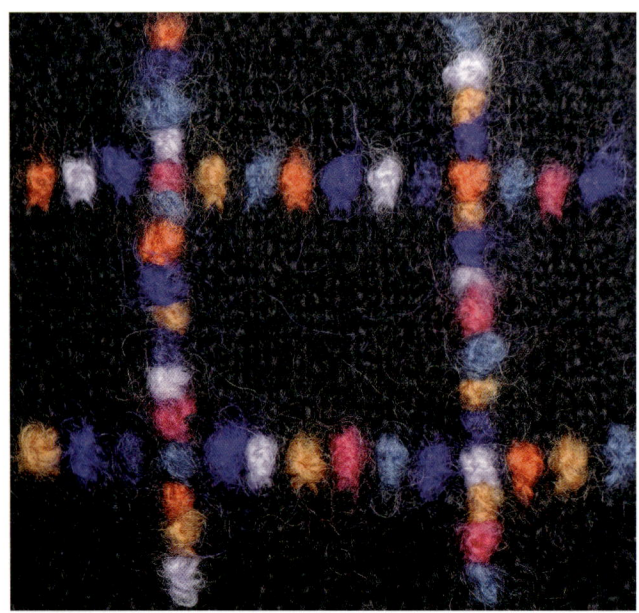

Detail of the Bobbly Grid pattern on a black base.

Back

Using the smaller needles and MC, cast on 69[73]sts, and work in k1, p1 rib for 2.5cm/1in.

Change to the larger needles. Purl 1 row, and, *at the same time*, inc 1 st at beg and end of row. (71[75]sts)

Beg Bobbly Grid patt with 4[6] vertical lines of bobbles as folls:
Row 1 (RS): K14[2] MC, mb, (k13 MC, mb) 3[5] times, k14[2] MC.
Row 2 and all WS rows: Purl in MC.
Rep rows 1–2 6 times (7 bobbles in vertical lines).

Cont Bobbly Grid patt with first horizontal line of bobbles as folls:
Row 15: K2 MC, mb, (k1 MC, mb) 33[35] times, k2 MC.
Row 16: Purl in MC.
Rows 1–16 form Bobbly Grid patt. Cont straight in patt until work measures 33[34.5]cm/13[13½]in from beg.

Shape armholes: Cast off 3sts at beg of next 4 rows. Dec 1 st at beg of next 6 rows (53[57]sts). Cont in patt without shaping until back measures 52[54]cm/20½[21¼]in from beg.

Shape shoulders: Cast off 4sts at beg of next 6[4] rows and 5sts at beg of next 2[4] rows. Cast off rem 19[21]sts.

Pocket linings

Both pocket linings are worked alike and are to be used doubled. Using the larger needles and MC, cast on 13sts and work in st st for 23cm/9in, and leave these 13sts on a st holder or spare needle.

Right front

Using the smaller needles and MC, cast on 33[35]sts, and work in k1, p1 rib for 2.5cm/1in. Change to the larger needles. Purl 1 row, and, *at the same time*, inc 1 st at beg and end of row (35[37]sts). *
Beg working Bobbly Grid patt as folls:
Row 1 (RS): K8 MC, mb, k13 MC, mb, k12[14] MC.
Row 2: Purl in MC.
Rep rows 1–2 6 times.

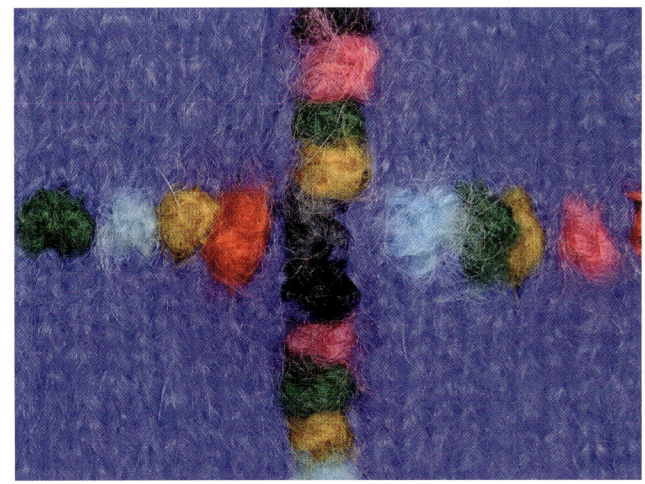

A blue colourway.

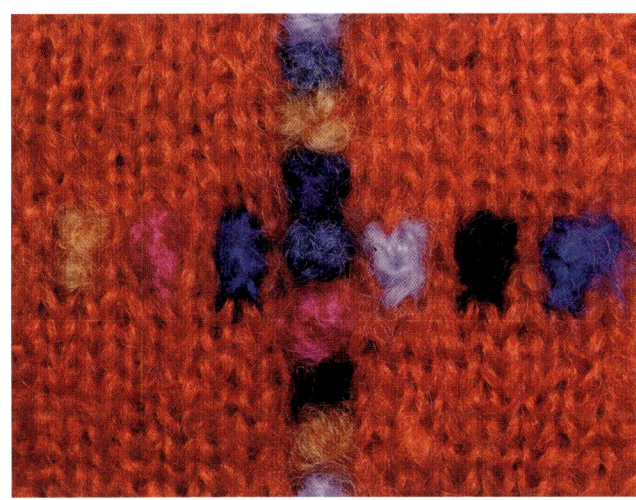

A red colourway.

A grey colourway.

Row 15: K2 MC, (mb, k1 MC) 16[17] times, k1 MC.
Row 16: Purl in MC.
Rep rows 1–2 of patt, then work pocket band as folls:
Row 19: K8 MC, mb, rib 13sts MC, mb, k12[14] MC.
Row 20: P13[15] MC, rib 13sts MC, p9 MC.
Rep rows 19–20 twice.

Divide for pocket: K8 MC, mb, with MC cast off next 13sts in rib, sl last st worked on to LH needle, and break yarn. Place 13sts from pocket-lining st holder on to LH needle. With RS facing, join MC and k13 (pocket-lining sts), mb, k12[14] MC.
Cont straight in patt until front length matches back-to-underarm length, ending with a RS row.

Shape armhole: Keeping continuity of patt correct, cast off 3sts at beg of next row and 2sts at beg of foll alt row.
Dec 1 st at armhole edge of foll 2 alt rows (28[30]sts).
Patt 2 rows.
Shape neck: Dec 1 st at centre-front edge of next and every foll alt row until 17[18]sts rem. Cont straight until armhole length matches that of back armhole, that is, to start of shoulder shaping, ending with a RS row.
Shape shoulder: Cast off 4sts at beg of next and foll 2[1] alt rows. Cast off 5sts at beg of foll 1[2] alt rows.
Cast of rem sts.

Left front

Work as for right front to *.
Beg Bobbly Grid patt as folls:
Row 1 (RS): K12[14] MC, mb, k13 MC, mb, k8 MC.
Row 2: Purl in MC.
Cont in patt as set, placing the right-front pocket at the mirror-image position of that for the left-front pocket, and ending with a WS row before beg armhole shaping. Complete armhole, neckline and shoulder shaping by reversing right-front shaping. Cast of rem sts.

Sleeves

Both sleeves are worked alike.
Using the smaller needles and MC, cast on 39[41]sts, and work in k1, p1 rib for 2.5cm/1in. Change to the larger needles, and purl 1 row.
Beg Bobbly Grid patt as folls:
Row 1 (RS): K12[13] MC, mb, k13 MC, mb, k12[13] MC.
Row 2: Purl in MC.
Row 3: Inc in 1st st, k11[12] MC, mb, k13 MC, mb, k11[12]MC, inc in last st. (41[43]sts)
Cont in patt as set, with 2 vertical bobble lines only up centre of sleeve, and, *at the same time*, inc 1 st at each end of RS (knit) rows until there are 7 bobbles vertically, ending with a WS row. (51[53]sts)
Row 15: (K1 MC, mb) 25(26) times, k1 MC.
Row 16: Purl in MC.
Rows 1–16 form Bobbly Grid patt for sleeves. Cont in patt as set, and, *at the same time*, inc 1 st at each side of every 12th row to 57[59]sts, working additional bobbles into the horizontal bobble lines of Bobbly Grid patt as necessary. Work straight until sleeve measures 39.5[40.5]cm/15½[16]in from beg. (Adjust sleeve length at this point, if desired.)

Shape sleeve top: Cast off 3sts at beg of next 2 rows. Cont straight in patt until sleeve measures 52[53.5]cm/20½[21]in from beg. Dec 1 st at each end of every foll row until 29[31]sts rem. Sleeve as written should measure 57[58.5] cm/22½[23]in. Cast off.

Fronts edging and collar

Knitted throughout in k1, p1 rib by using the smaller needles and MC and worked in one piece, starting at bottom edge of right front.
Cast on 12sts, and work as folls:
Row 1 (RS): Sl1k, p1, (k1, p1) 5 times.
Row 2 (WS): (K1, p1) 6 times.
Rep these rows 1–2 once. Make first buttonhole as folls:
Next row (RS): Sl1k, p1, k1, p2tog, yrn to create buttonhole, rib to end.
Next row: (K1, p1) 6 times, working into the yrn loop for buttonhole of prev row.
Cont straight in rib, slipping first st of all RS rows (outer edge of front edging) as set and making 5 more buttonholes at intervals of 7cm/2¾in. *At the same time*, when work measures 26.5[28]cm/10½[11]in, shape inside edge only for collar by inc 1 st on next and every foll 3rd row until there are 25sts. With a coloured thread or other marker, mark inside edge of this row of front edging with 25sts.
Cont straight in rib until work measures 54.5[56]cm/21½[22]in, ending with a WS row (at outer edge of front edging).

A diagonal-lines bobble-pattern variation on a dark-green base.

The Bobbly Grid cardigan in red – great fun!

Shape lapel and back collar: Cast off 13sts at beg of next row (outer edge). Work 1 row. Inc 1 st at beg of next and every foll alt row until there are 18sts. Cont straight until work measures 70[71]cm/27½[28]in from beg, ending with a WS row.
Now, cont to shape second half of front edging as reverse of first side, starting as folls:
Dec 1 st at beg of next and every foll alt row until 12sts rem, ending with a WS row. Cast on 13sts at beg of next row, and cont straight until work measures same as first side to coloured thread. Complete second half of front edging to mirror first side but omitting buttonholes.

Making up and finishing

Do not press pieces. Darn in all loose ends, or securely tie off C bobble ends, on inside of work.
Using backstitch, sew shoulder, side and sleeve seams. Set in sleeves to armholes, easing fullness to the top of each sleeve. Pin front band around front and neck edges, aligning points of collar to shoulder seams. Oversew front band into position from the inside of the garment. Sew on buttons.
Stitch lower edge of each pocket lining to WS of base of pocket band to form the pocket bag, and backstitch together each side of each folded pocket lining.

FURTHER GRAPHIC DESIGNS

The Sandy Black mohair range included many variations on the graphic theme, using all-over geometric patterns such as rectangles or hexagons (as in the Stained Glass sweater) or, alternatively, utilized scattered geometric motifs, such as for the Curves cardigan. These two designs are featured here with the original 1980s styled photographs and may provide further inspiration for your own ideas. In contrast, the graphic theme also extended to summer cotton garments, as illustrated by the Matisse-inspired dress and top.

A stained-glass-inspired geometric-patterned cardigan and sweater. The dark, contrasting outlines unify the colours and are either embroidered on to or knitted into the fabric. The sweater has intarsia-knitted hexagons embroidered with chain stitch outlining the borders; the diamond-patterned cardigan is intarsia knitted with contrast-colour travelling cables – see also Chapter 2. (Photo: David McIntyre)

LEFT: The Curves cardigan features a lively abstract motif that is intarsia knitted from a chart and varied in colour and size over the entire piece. (Photo: David McIntyre)

ABOVE: A tribute to the colour and unique shapes developed by the artist Matisse featuring in the bold Sandy Black Cotton Fizz summer dress, worked with machine-knitted intarsia. (Photo: David McIntyre)

LEFT: A much-simplified Matisse-inspired top from the Sandy Black cotton-kits range. (Photo: Barbara Bellingham)

CHAPTER 8

FLORAL

Throughout the history of textiles, both naturalistic and stylized floral designs have been a continuous feature – especially in printed and woven designs. Hand-knitted floral designs are harder to find in this history, with the exception of several seventeenth-century knitted floral-patterned jackets that are held in several museums[1] (*see* Chapters 1 and 2). A new wave of designer knitters of the 1980s[2] embraced colour, texture and pattern in knitting as never before to create floral and decorative patterns, often inspired by printed and woven textiles.

In my own work, flowers have been a constant inspiration, at all stages of their life, including as they wilt and die. Having mostly lived in homes without a proper garden, I love to have vases of flowers, both fresh and dried, indoors. Amongst my favourites are gladioli, anemones, tulips, iris and roses – all have featured in my knitwear designs, and some were translated into knitting-pattern kits.

This chapter includes three different floral designs from the Sandy Black ranges, two in a more naturalistic vein, knitted in mohair yarns to give a softened effect, and one

OPPOSITE PAGE: The Posy Trellis cardigan, knitted in Sandy Black textured cotton, with embroidered flowers. Made and styled in true 1980s fashion, with mini shoulder pads for silhouette emphasis. (Photo: Barbara Bellingham)

more stylized, worked in wool. The Trailing Roses sweater embeds a simplified rose motif in an all-over, dense pattern of leaves, and three different colour combinations are used throughout the repeating pattern to give variety. In contrast, the batwing Iris-sweater design takes advantage of the large area and simple shape of this garment style to feature two bold sprays of iris flowers, which I drew from life and translated into knitted stitches. However, the colours do not have to be completely naturalistic, so experiment with your own ideas. A smaller-scale version of this iris motif was also used on the front and back of a short jacket, as shown, and this was always a popular kit design. The third pattern in this chapter, the Persian Flower tunic, was inspired by historical decorative frieze patterns. I researched these from museum objects and reference books, reinterpreting elements to create the decorative border, and added texture to some of the floral motifs with small bobbles. The leaf design used in the collar and cuffs is a typical border pattern found in many decorative arts.

Here, photographs of some of my other floral-inspired designs also are presented. The Posy Trellis cardigan is similar in concept to that of the Trailing Roses sweater, with an all-over diamond-trellis pattern on which a series of posies are positioned. In this design, only the leaves of the posy are knitted in; the flowers are embroidered on after the knitting is completed, giving an additional

The Tapestry Flower tunic, with stylized-flower motifs, knitted in a wool yarn, with angora-yarn flower petals. (Photo: David McIntyre)

dimension to the fabric and design. The Tapestry Flower tunic is another design to feature a repeated flower motif. The idea of scaling up the motif is one that I exploited fully in the Vase of Flowers coat – one of my bestselling ready-to-wear designs, which became a true classic, selling season after season. Here, the ornate vase of anemones fills the entire back of the coat design and spills over on to the sleeves. This design was also featured on the cover of Suzy Menkes' book *The Knitwear Revolution*, published in 1983 (*see* Chapter 1).

Trailing Roses Sweater

The Trailing Roses sweater, worn in a relaxed manner in this original 1980s photograph. (Photo: David McIntyre)

This casual sweater is designed to be loose fitting, comfortable and lightweight and is knitted in mohair-rich yarn. The all-over repeating design of leaves and flowers is knitted in stocking stitch from charts, mainly in two-colour stranded-colourwork (Fair Isle) knitting, with individual roses being knitted by using two contrast colours each, in three different colour combinations. The original version is shown in naturalistic colours of green leaves on a light grey ground with roses in pink, red and plum, but you can have fun with many different colour combinations. The chart shows pink, red and orange flowers, and the colourway photographs show alternative suggestions. The design works well in both naturalistic colourings and more unusual combinations.

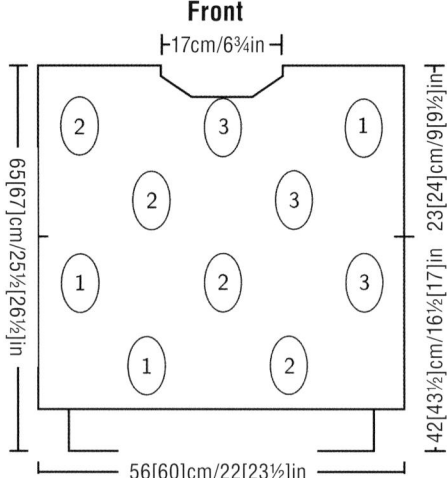

Sizes and measurements

Two generous sizes to fit up to a 91(97)cm/36(38)in bust circumference

Knitted measurements
Width at underarms: 56[60]cm/22[23½]in
Length: 65[67.5]cm/25½[26½]in
Sleeve length: 49.5cm/19½in

Materials

Yarn
Knitted in a mohair–wool-blend yarn with approx 75-per-cent-mohair content and 100m/50g, for example, Wool and the Gang's Take Care Mohair, in 5 colours as folls:
Main colour (MC): 7[8] × 50g balls
Contrast colours:
Main contrast (G): 5[5] × 50g balls
Other contrast colours (A, B and C): 1 ball, or approx 20g, each of 3 flower colours

Recommended needles and accessories
Two pairs of needles are required: one pair of the size to give the correct tension, for main patterned parts, and one pair of two sizes smaller, for ribbing.
1 pair 6mm (UK 4, US 10) needles for main patterned parts
1 pair 5mm (UK 6, US 8) needles for ribbing
1 circular needle or set of double-pointed needles in the smaller size
Stitch holder

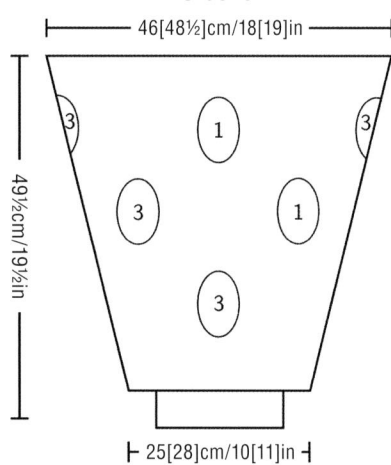

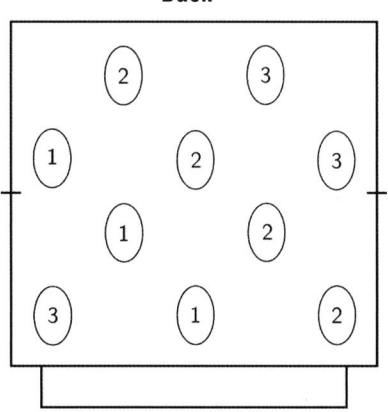

Measurement and pattern-positioning diagram.

Flower colourway	1	2	3
Outer colour	A (red)	B (pink)	C (plum or orange)
Inner colour	B (pink)	C (plum or orange)	A (red)

Flower-colourway table.

Tension

18sts and 18 rows to 10cm/4in, measured over stranded-colourwork patt, using 6mm (UK 4, US 10) needles or the size required to give the correct tension and therefore measurements.

To avoid disappointment, it is essential to check your tension carefully before commencing the knitting by the garment and to use the needles that give you the correct tension. These needles may not be of the needle size quoted in the standard tension information, as each knitter knits differently.

How to check tension

Using the recommended needles and MC, cast on 30sts, and work a tension swatch from the back chart, starting with a knit row at row 1 and working sts 1–30. Work in st st until row 30 is completed, then cast off loosely. Pin the knitted swatch square down flat, without stretching the fabric. Place a pin between 2sts near the left side of the swatch, count 18sts across to the right, and place another pin between the 18th and 19th sts. Mark out 18 rows in the same manner, starting from 2sts near the top of the swatch. Measure the distance between each pair of pins. The measurements should both be 10cm/4in. If a measurement is less than 10cm/4in, your knitting is too tight – try using needles of one size larger to reknit the swatch, and again check the tension. If a measurement is more than 10cm/4in, your knitting is too loose – try using needles of one size smaller to reknit the swatch, and again check the tension. Repeat the process until the correct tension is achieved. Do not be afraid to go up or down by more than one size from the recommended needles to achieve the required tension. Adjust the size of the smaller pair of needles for the ribbing accordingly.

Abbreviation and special stitch

p b&f = purl back and front: purl into back loop of next stitch on LH needle, purl into front loop of same stitch and then allow purled-into st to slip off LH needle

Pattern

Notes on working the pattern

- One square of the chart represents one knitted stitch. Odd-numbered rows (RS) are read from right to left and the corresponding stitches are to be knitted; even-numbered rows (WS) are read from left to right and the corresponding stitches are to be purled.
- Use one ball of MC and one ball of G across the width of the knitting, as specified by the charts, and weave in the colour not in use loosely every 4th st at the back of the knitting; use separate lengths of yarn for the flower colours, and weave in MC and G behind the flowers, taking care not to pull the yarn strands too tightly.
- All flowers are not the same: they are knitted in 3 different colour combinations using two of the three colours A, B and C in each flower, arranged in diagonal lines as shown in the pattern diagram.

Back

Using the smaller needles and MC, cast on 68[80]sts, and work in k2, p2 twisted rib (that is, k2, p2 rib, with every knit st being worked into the back loop of the st of the previous row) for 6.5[7.5]cm/2½[3]in, ending with a RS row.

Inc row (WS): Change to the larger needles, purl across and, *at the same time*, inc by p b&f into 4th[1st] st and every foll alt[3rd] st to last 4[1]sts, purl to end. (99[107]sts) *
Join in G, and beg working from back chart at row 1 with a knit row, and work 8 rows of Trailing Roses patt (leaves),

KEY
☐ Background colour ■ Green ■ Red ■ Cinnamon ■ Pink -- 1st size front

Chart for front.

KEY
☐ Background colour ■ Green ■ Red ■ Cinnamon ■ Pink – – 1st size back – – 1st size sleeve — 2nd size sleeve

Chart for back and sleeves.

FLORAL 157

then join in flower cols (for flower colourways 2, 1 and 3) on row 9 as indicated on the chart and pattern diagram. Cont working straight in patt from chart, placing markers for armholes at 42[43]cm/16½[17]in from beg. Cont in patt without shaping until row 105[109] of chart is completed. Cast off loosely, placing markers on 34th[38th] st and 66th[70th] st for neck opening.

Front

Work as for back to *. Join in G, and beg working from front chart at row 1 with a knit row, joining in flower cols on row 9 as indicated on chart and patt diagram, and cont straight in patt until row 96[98] is completed.

Shape neck (row 97[99]): Patt 41[45]sts, turn, and leave rem 58[62]sts on a st holder. Cont working on these 41[45] sts for first side of neck, and, *at the same time*, dec 1 st at neck edge of next 7 rows. Work straight until row 105[109] is completed. Cast off loosely.

Place sts from st holder on to LH needle. With RS facing, join yarn to inside edge, cast off next 17sts for neck, and patt to end. Cont working on these 41[45]sts for second side of neck, and, *at the same time*, dec 1 st at neck edge of next 7 rows. Work straight until row 105[109] is completed. Cast off loosely.

Detail of the design, in a naturalistic colourway.

A colourway of green with lilac leaves.

A colourway of blue with lilac leaves.

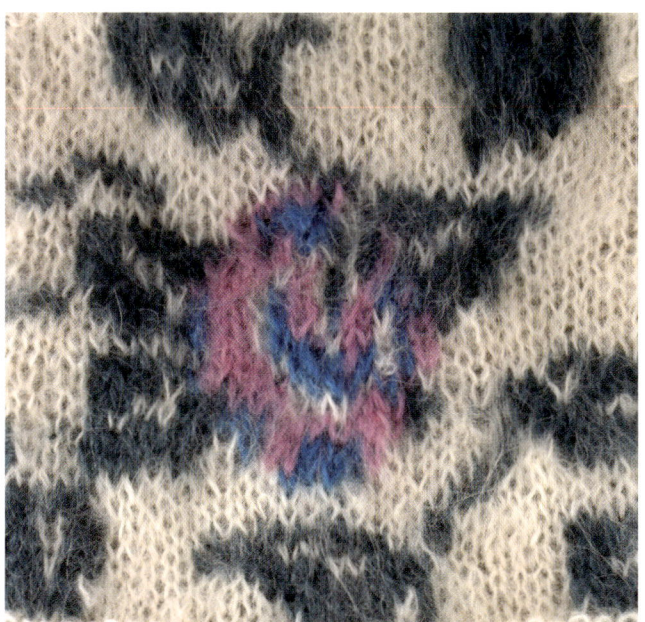

A colourway of white with green leaves, worked in a finer mohair yarn.

A version using an alternative light-aran-weight wool yarn for the background, with mohair-yarn leaves and flowers.

Sleeves

Both sleeves are worked alike.
Using the smaller needles and MC, cast on 32[36]sts, and work in k2, p2 twisted rib as before for 5cm/2in, ending with a RS row. Change to the larger needles.

Inc row (WS): Purl across and, *at the same time*, inc by p b&f into 5th and every foll alt st to last 3sts, p3. (45[51]sts) Join in G, and beg working from sleeve chart at row 1 with a knit row, to work 5 rows straight.

Shape sleeve: Foll appropriate size outline on chart (for first size, indicated by a black dashed line, or second size, corresponding to the solid black line), cont in patt, and, *at the same time*, inc 1 st at each end of row 6 and every foll 4th row to 81[88]sts, incorporating new sts into patt. Cont straight until row 80 is completed or work measures 49.5cm/19½in. Cast off loosely.

Collars

Knitted-on collar

Using backstitch, sew both shoulder seams. Using MC and the circular needle, with RS facing, pick up and knit 80[84]sts around neck edge, starting and finishing at the centre front as folls: 23[24]sts from right front, 34[36]sts from back neck, 23[24]sts from left front. Work 4 rounds in k2, p2 twisted rib, then divide at centre front and work in rows of rib back and forth, until collar measures 10cm/4in. Cast off loosely in rib.

Knitted-separately collar

With the smaller pair of needles, work the collar separately by casting on 80[84]sts. Work k2, p2 twisted rib in rows until collar measures 10cm/4in. Cast off loosely in rib.

Making up and finishing

Do not press pieces. Darn in all loose ends.
For a knitted-separately collar, oversew collar to neck edge, with the opening positioned at centre front, and neatly sew left and right sides of first 4 rows of collar together at centre front. Using backstitch, sew sleeves into armholes, using the underarm markers as a guide. Using backstitch, sew side and sleeve seams. Lightly steam press the seams only.

Iris Sweater

The batwing Iris sweater incorporates bold but elegant floral sprays on the front and is knitted in one main piece, from cuff to cuff. (Photo: Jo Teasdale)

This elegant batwing sweater is knitted in a mix of fine lace-weight wool and mohair yarns used together. It is worked in stocking stitch in one main piece, with two iris sprays knitted into the front, worked from a chart. The main piece is knitted from cuff to cuff, so the floral design is actually knitted sideways, the back is plain and waist ribbing is added at the end. For a plain version of this design, simply omit the flowers from the front.

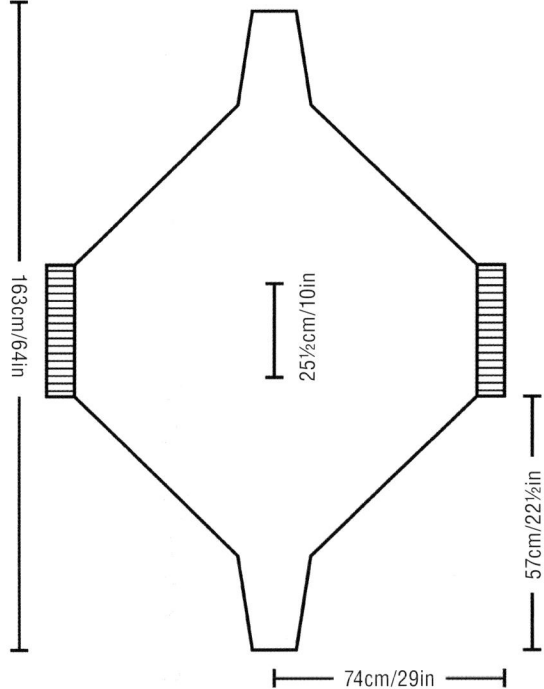

Measurement diagram.

Tension

16sts and 20 rows to 10cm/4in, measured over st st, using 5.5mm (UK 5, US 9) needles or the size required to give the correct tension and therefore measurements.

To avoid disappointment, it is essential to check your tension carefully before commencing the knitting of the garment and to use the needles that give you the correct tension. These needles may not be of the needle size quoted in the standard tension information, as each knitter knits differently.

Size and measurements

One generous size to fit up to a 97cm/38in bust circumference

Knitted measurements
Cuff-to-cuff width: 163cm/64in
Length: 74cm/29in (*see accompanying measurement diagram*)
Sleeve length: 57cm/22½in (*see accompanying measurement diagram*)

Materials

Yarn
The main, background fabric is knitted with two yarns being used together as one (collectively referred to as 'MC' in the following instructions): a combination of a lace-weight wool-blend yarn and a mohair–silk-blend yarn. The iris flowers are also knitted with the mohair–silk-blend yarn, in several contrast colours; note that the mohair-blend yarn of each colour for the flowers is used doubled. The featured garment was knitted with Rowan Fine Lace and Rowan Kidsilk Haze.

Main colour (MC):
3 × 50g balls of Rowan Fine Lace alpaca–wool yarn
6 × 25g balls of Rowan Kidsilk Haze mohair–silk yarn, in a colour to match that of the Fine Lace
The MC yarn colours used in the sample are Fine Lace 933 Aged and Kidsilk Haze 582 Trance.

Contrast colours: 1 × 25g ball each of Rowan Kidsilk Haze in 4 contrast colours: A (blue), B (mulberry), C (rose) and D (hot pink).
The contrast colours used in the sample are Kidsilk Haze 675 Bluebird (A), 679 Mulberry (B), 583 Blushes (C) and 606 Candy Girl (D).

Recommended needles and accessories
Two pairs of needles are required: one pair of the size to give the correct tension, for main parts, and one pair of two sizes smaller, for ribbing.
1 pair 5.5mm (UK 5, US 9) needles for main parts
1 pair 4.5mm (UK 7, US 7) needles for ribbing
Stitch holder
Medium crochet hook

How to check tension

Using the recommended needles and one strand of the alpaca–wool yarn and one strand of the mohair-blend yarn held together as one, cast on 28sts, and work in st st for 15cm/6in. Cast off. Pin the knitted swatch square down flat, without stretching the fabric. Place a pin between 2sts near the left side of the swatch, count 16sts across to the right, and place another pin between the 16th and 17th sts. Mark out 20 rows in the same manner, starting from 2sts near the top of the swatch. Measure the distance between each pair of pins. The

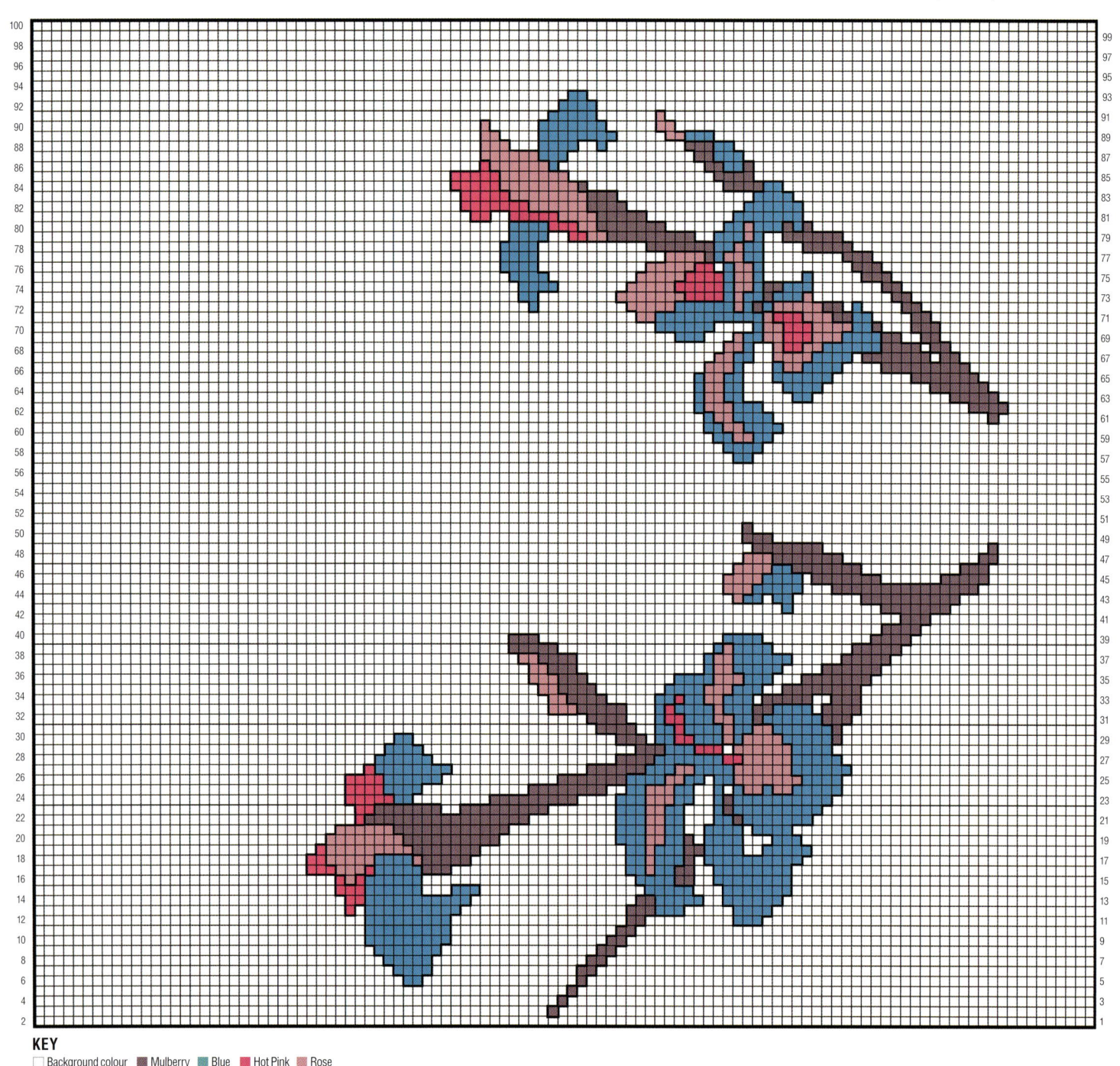

KEY
☐ Background colour ■ Mulberry ■ Blue ■ Hot Pink ■ Rose

Iris-flower pattern chart. All stitches are to be knitted in the appropriate yarn colour as indicated on the chart.

162 FLORAL

measurements should both be 10cm/4in. If a measurement is less than 10cm/4in, your knitting is too tight – try using needles of one size larger to reknit the swatch, and again check the tension. If a measurement is more than 10cm/4in, your knitting is too loose – try using needles of one size smaller to reknit the swatch, and again check the tension. Repeat the process until the correct tension is achieved. Do not be afraid to go up or down by more than one size from the recommended needles to achieve the required tension. Adjust the size of the smaller pair of needles for the ribbing accordingly.

Pattern

Notes on working the pattern

- One square of the chart represents one knitted stitch. Odd-numbered rows (RS) are read from right to left and the corresponding stitches are to be knitted; even-numbered rows (WS) are read from left to right and the corresponding stitches are to be purled.
- For working the iris flowers, to minimize tangling of colours, wind small bobbins (which can be made from card) or butterfly twists of each yarn colour: allow these to hang close to the needle, and unravel just a small amount at a time as required (*see* Chapter 4). Use a separate bobbin, twist or length of yarn for each area of colour, and cross the yarns when changing colours, to link them and prevent holes appearing in the knitting. Note that each contrast colour is formed of two strands of yarn, by doubling the yarn.

Main piece

Using the larger needles and MC, cast on 40sts. Working in st st throughout, proceed as folls:
Starting with a knit row, inc 1 st at each end of every 4th row until there are 60sts. Work 3 rows straight, then inc 1 st at each end of every row until there are 198sts.
Cast on 10sts at beg of next 2 rows; RS of work should be facing for next row (218sts). Now, introduce Iris-flower patt on right half of piece (front), by working these sts from chart and beg at row 1, as folls (note that chart sts are presented in brackets):
Row 1 (RS): Knit (109sts MC), 109sts MC.
Row 2: Purl 109MC, (54MC, 1B, 49MC).
Row 3: Knit (48MC, 1B, 55MC), 109MC.
Row 4: Purl 109MC, (56MC, 1B, 47MC).
Row 5: Knit (46MC, 1B, 16MC, 2A, 39MC), 109MC.
Cont in patt as set until row 24 of chart has been worked, ending with RS facing.

Divide for neck (RS): Work 109sts from row 25 of chart and turn, leaving rem sts on a st holder, or spare needle, for back. Cont working from chart on these 109sts only, for front, until row 75 is completed. Break yarn, and return to sts on st holder for back. Work 51 rows of st st in MC on this second set of sts only, ending with a RS knit row.
Next row (WS): Purl 109sts, patt 109sts from row 76 of chart. (218 sts)
Cont in patt across all sts as before, by working chart rows 77–100.
Cast off 10sts at beg of next 2 rows (198sts). Dec 1 st at each end of every row until there are 60sts. Work 3 rows straight. Now, dec 1 st at each end of next and every foll 4th row until 40sts rem. Work 3 rows straight. Cast off.

Note: For a plain sweater, work entirely in MC; disregard the instructions for using specific colours.

Detail of knitted iris sprays, worked sideways, using four contrast colours.

The original Iris cardigan from 1982, knitted in mohair yarns. (Photo: Barbara Bellingham)

Waistband

The back and front sections of the waistband are knitted separately.

Using the smaller needles and MC, with RS facing, pick up and knit 66sts evenly from straight edge of back. Work in k1, p1 rib for 7.5cm/3in. Cast off loosely in rib.

For front section of waistband, pick up and knit 66sts evenly from straight edge of front as above, and complete waistband as for back section.

Finishing

Do not press pieces. Using backstitch, sew side seams, excluding waistband ribbing. Neatly oversew left sides of waistband together and right sides of waistband together. With MC, work a row of double crochet around each cuff to neaten its edge, but allow the neck edges to roll naturally inwards, without further finishing.

A luxurious 100-per-cent-angora version of the Iris cardigan. (Photo: Barbara Bellingham)

Persian Flower Tunic

The Persian Flower tunic features a deep V-neck offsetting a stylized-flower border, with some flowers in relief over the border, body and sleeves. (Photo: Jo Teasdale)

Inspired by Persian decorative arts, the dramatic border patterning of this long-line sweater is offset by small flowers scattered over the body. The knitting is all in stocking stitch, enhanced with stitch details of cable twists and bobbles in the flower motifs. The design is finished with a two-colour leaf motif on the neckline and cuff edgings.

Sizes and measurements

One generous size to fit up to a 102cm/40in bust circumference

Knitted measurements
All-round circumference at underarms: 127cm/50in
Length: 75cm/29½in
Sleeve length: 49cm/19½in

Materials

Yarn
Knitted using a light-aran- or textured DK-weight 100-per-cent-wool yarn with approx 200m/100g.

The sample was knitted in the 100-per-cent-wool double-knitting yarn Winterburn dk by baa ram ewe.

Main colour (A): 6 × 100g hank in grey (shade Aire)
Contrast colours:
B: 1 × 100g hank in claret (shade Bantam)
C: 2 × 100g hanks in light green (shade Bramley Baths)
D: 1 × 100g hank in purple (shade Bishopthorpe)
E: 1 × 100g hank (or 50g ball) in rose (shade Rose Window)
F: 1 × 100g hank in lilac or pink (shade Heathcliff)
G: an oddment in blue (shade Lotherton)

Recommended needles and accessories
Three pairs of needles are required: one pair for the border pattern, one pair for the main body and sleeves and one pair for the rib and inner edgings.
1 pair 4.5mm (UK 7, US 7) for border pattern
1 pair 4mm (UK 8, US 6) needles for main body and sleeves
1 pair 3.5mm (UK 9, US 4) needles for rib and inner edgings
Cable needle
Large-eyed yarn needle

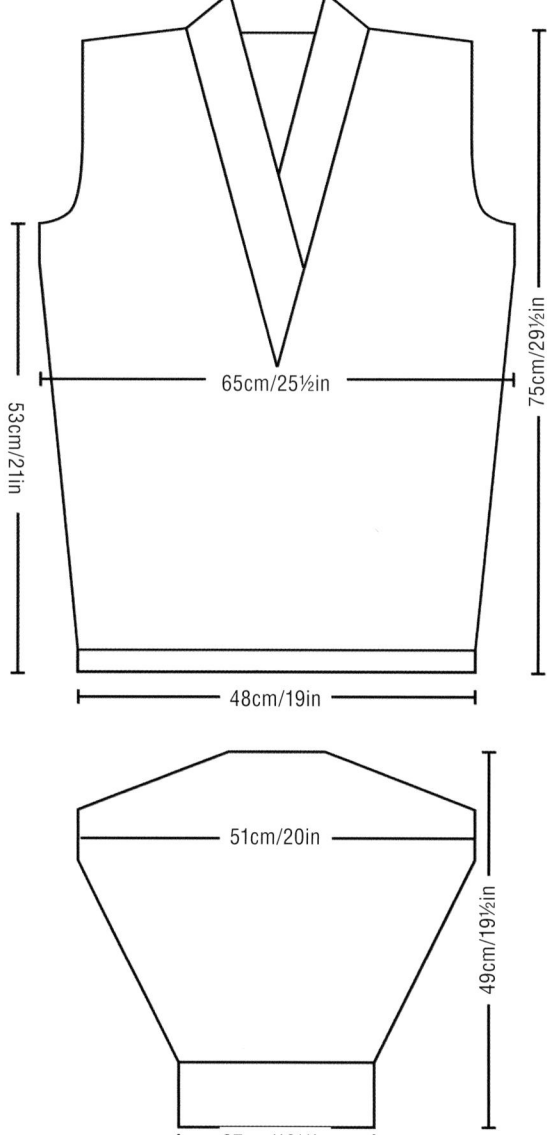

Measurement diagram.

Tension

22sts and 28 rows to 10cm/4in, measured over st st, using 4mm (UK 7, US 6) needles or the size required to give the correct tension and therefore measurements.

To avoid disappointment, it is essential to check your tension carefully before commencing the knitting of the garment and to use the needles that give you the correct tension. These needles may not be of the needle size quoted in the standard tension information, as each knitter knits differently.

How to check tension

Using the recommended needles and main colour (A), cast on 36sts, and work in st st for 40 rows. Cast off. Pin the knitted swatch square down flat, without stretching the fabric. Place a pin between 2sts near the left side of the swatch, count 22sts across to the right, and place another pin between the 22nd and 23rd sts. Mark out 28 rows in the same manner, starting from 2sts near the top of the swatch. Measure the distance between each pair of pins. The measurements should both be 10cm/4in. If a measurement is less than 10cm/4in, your knitting is too tight – try using needles of one size larger to reknit the swatch, and again check the tension. If the measurement is more than 10cm/4in, your knitting is too loose – try using needles of one size smaller to reknit the swatch, and again check the tension. Repeat the process until the correct tension is achieved. Do not be afraid to go up or down by more than one size from the recommended needles to achieve the required tension. Adjust the size of the two other pairs of needles accordingly. If you cannot achieve both stitch and row tension, work to the correct stitch tension and lengths as given.

Abbreviations and special stitches

c2b = cable 2sts back: keeping continuity of cols in cable crossing by working each st in appropriate colour, slip next st purlwise on to cable needle and leave it at back of work, k1, then k1 from cable needle

c2f = cable 2sts front: keeping continuity of cols in cable crossing by working each st in appropriate colour, slip next st purlwise on to cable needle and leave it at front of work, k1, then k1 from cable needle

central double increase = knit into back then front of next st, with LH needle pick up vertical strand just formed between 2sts just knitted (on RH needle), then knit into back of this strand (2 new sts, 3sts total)

k2tog-tbl = knit next 2sts together through the back loops

mb = make bobble: with contrast col, knit into front, back, front and back of next st (4sts on RH needle). Pass 2nd, 3rd and 4th sts, furthest from RH-needle point, over 1st st, closest to RH-needle point, and knit into back loop of rem st with MC. Note: when working bobbles on WS rows, work in the same way, but purl rem st with MC and push finished bobble through to RS of work

Pattern

Notes on working the pattern

- The majority of this design is worked in st st, including the colourwork patterns presented as charts. One square of the chart represents one knitted stitch. Odd-numbered rows (RS) are read from right to left and the corresponding stitches are to be knitted; even-numbered rows (WS) are read from left to right and the corresponding stitches are to be purled.
- When working the Persian Flower border, take the contrast colours C (for the border background) and D across the whole row, as for the stranded-colourwork technique. Loosely strand the yarns not in use across the back of the work, over no more than 5sts; when more that 5sts need to be spanned, the colour not in use should be woven in at the back of the work (*see* Chapter 4). For each border flower, use separate small lengths or bobbins of the other contrast-colour yarns, as for the intarsia technique, crossing the yarns when changing colours, to link them and prevent holes appearing in the knitting. Note that the narrow flowers in the lower part of the border are worked with bobbles.
- The cuffs and neckband are worked in two-colour stranded-colourwork knitting; again, strand the yarn not in use loosely across back of the work over not more than 5sts, as described earlier.

Flower motif

Each flower is worked over 7sts and 8 rows, and, during its working, 2sts are increased and then decreased. The stem is knitted in one contrast colour, and a cable needle is used when working the upper parts of each stem, to keep the continuity of colours for the stem and background. The flower head is a bobble that is worked in a second contrast colour. Each flower motif starts on a WS row (note: WS rows are odd numbers on the flower motif chart), positioned according to the back-and-front chart and sleeves flower motif placement charts. Choose the contrast colours for each flower randomly, and use a different pair of colours for adjacent flowers.

Using just a short length of each colour, work a practice flower as folls over 7sts on a st-st ground:

Row 1 (WS): P3, p1 using contrast col for stem (to place flower), p3.

Row 2: K3, central double increase in stem colour, k3.

Row 3: P3, p3 in stem colour, p3.

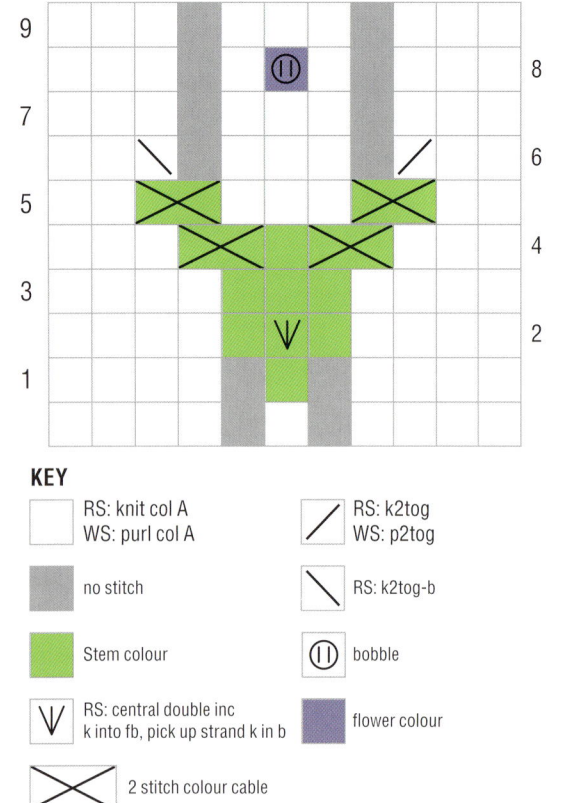

KEY

- RS: knit col A / WS: purl col A
- no stitch
- Stem colour
- RS: central double inc k into fb, pick up strand k in b
- 2 stitch colour cable
- RS: k2tog / WS: p2tog
- RS: k2tog-b
- bobble
- flower colour

Flower-motif chart.

Flower-motif detail.

Three scattered Flower motifs.

Row 4: K2, c2b, k1 in stem colour, c2f, k2.
Row 5: P1, c2f, p3, c2b, p1, and break off stem colour.
Row 6: K2tog, k5, k2tog-tbl.
Row 7: Purl.
Row 8: K3, mb (using contrast col for flower), k3.
Row 9: Purl.

Back

Edging: Using 3.5mm needles and B, cast on 108sts, and work diagonal rib as folls:
Row 1 (WS): (K3, p3) to end.
Row 2: (K2, p3, k1) to end.
Row 3: (P2, k3, p1) to end.
Row 4: (P3, k3) to end.
Row 5: (K1, p3, k2) to end.
Row 6: (p1, k3, p2) to end.
Rows 1–6 form diagonal-rib patt. Rep rows 1–6 once, then work row 1 again, and, *at the same time*, inc 4sts across the row at 15th, 40th, 65th and 90th sts. (112sts)
Border: Change to using 4.5mm needles. Start working the Persian Flower border from row 1 of the chart, starting with a knit (RS) row, joining in cols as needed and, *at the same time*, inc 1 st at each end of 9th and then every foll 8th row, to 124sts (50 rows of border chart are completed).

KEY
☐ Background colour ■ Purple ■ Rose ■ Blue ■ Lilac ◆ Bobble ■ Grey ■ Claret

Persian Flower border chart.

Body: Change to using 4mm needles and st st for body, and cont working with A, shaping sides as noted and working scattered flowers, positioned according to back-and-front chart, which starts at row 51 (RS row). Note that each Flower motif starts on a WS row with a contrast col chosen at random and that the first row of flowers starts on row 60, with one flower each being placed at the 24th, 48th, 73rd and 98th sts. Shape sides as shown on back-and-front chart by inc on 6th and every foll 9th row until there are 140sts. Cont straight until row 136 is completed and work measures 53cm/21in from beg.
Shape armholes: Cast off 5sts at beg of next 2 rows and then dec 1 st at beg of every row until 106sts rem.
Cont straight until row 194 is completed.
Shape shoulders and neckline: Cast off 10sts, k23 and turn, leaving rem sts on a st holder for second side of neckline and shoulder. Cont as folls:
Next row: P2tog, p to end.
Next row: Cast off 10sts, k to last 2sts, k2tog.
Next row: P2tog, p to end.
Cast off rem 11sts.
Return to sts on st holder for right side of neckline and shoulder, and, with RS facing, join yarn to inside edge. Cast off 38sts for back neck, k to end.
Complete right side of neckline and shoulder to mirror the left side, by reversing the shaping.

Detail of the knitted Persian Flower border, showing intarsia-knitted flowers and flowers made with bobbles.

Front

Work edging and border as for back.
For body, work as for back, using 4mm needles, and cont working in st st with A, working scattered flowers, positioned according to back-and-front main chart and, *at the same time*, inc at sides as before until row 100 is completed and work measures 42cm/16½in. Place marker between centre sts.
Divide for neck: With RS facing, patt to 2sts from centre marker, p2tog and turn, leaving rem sts on holder for right side of body. Cont in patt for three rows straight, then dec

FLORAL 169

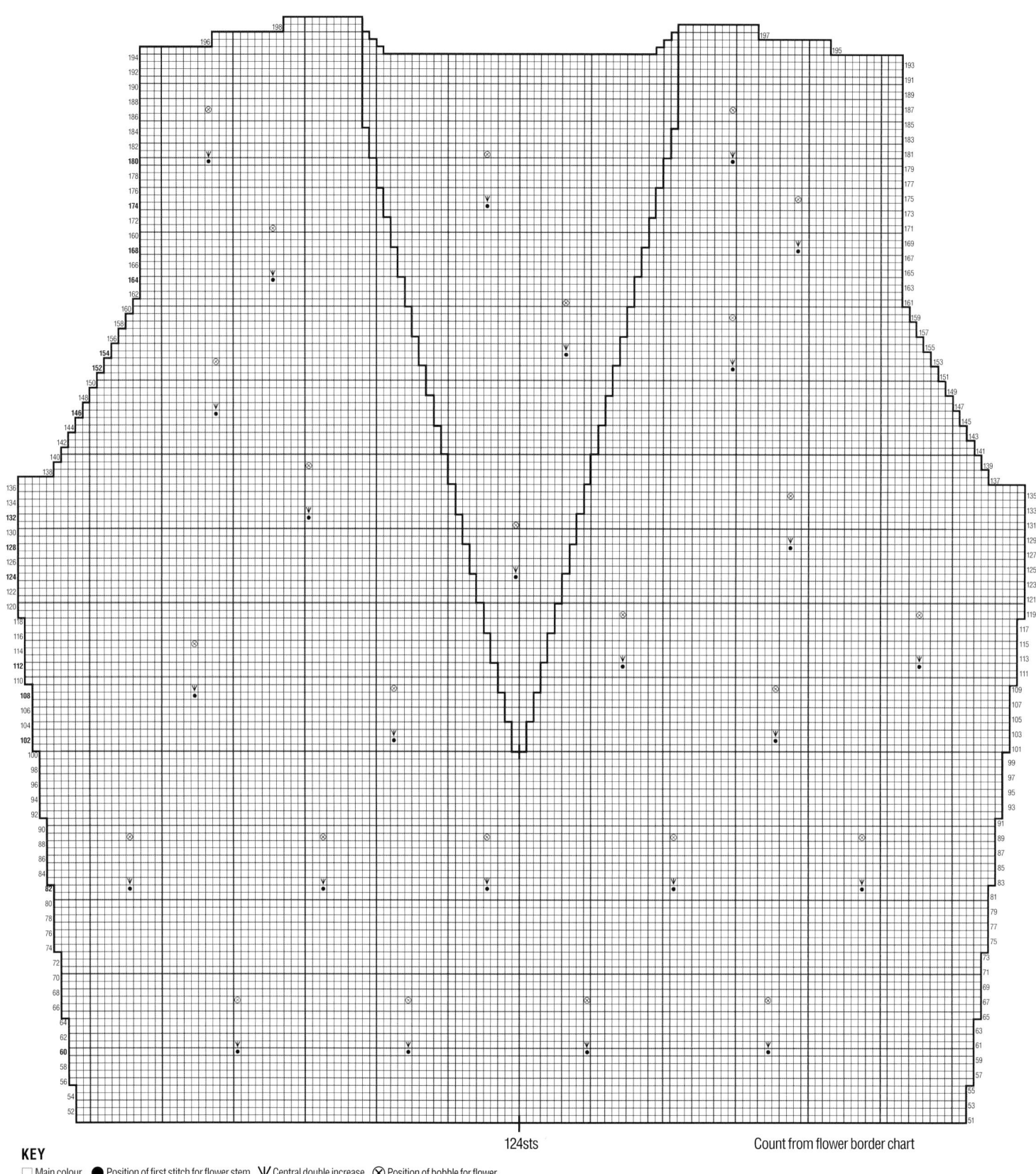

124sts   Count from flower border chart

KEY
☐ Main colour   ● Position of first stitch for flower stem   V Central double increase   ⊗ Position of bobble for flower

Back and front chart and Flower-motif placement diagram.

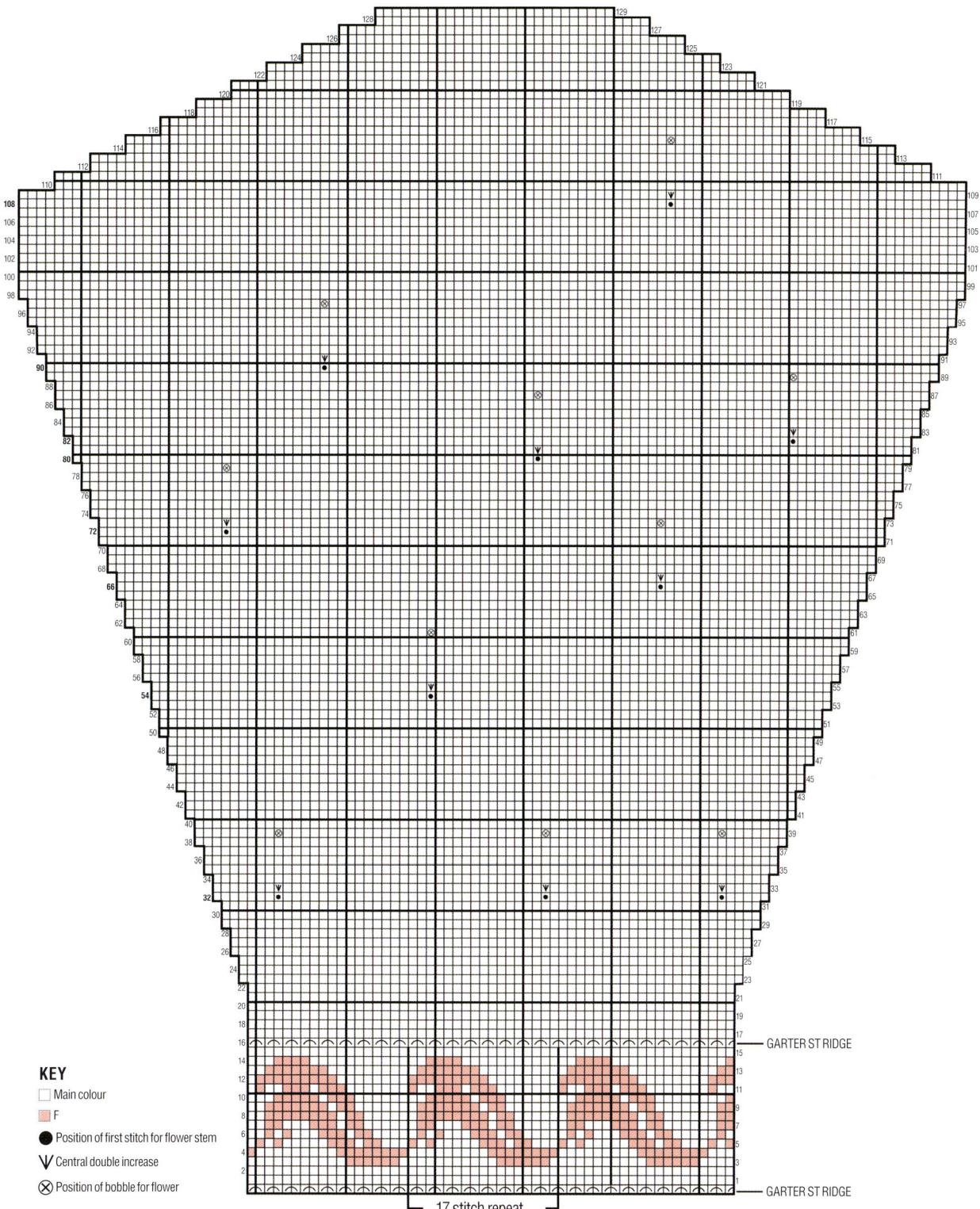

Sleeve chart, Flower-motif placement diagram and embedded leaf-edging chart.

1 st at neck edge on next and every foll 4th row, and, *at the same time*, cont to inc at side edge every 9th row and cont in flower patt as set until 8sts have been increased at side edge. Now, work straight at side edge but cont shaping neck edge as set, until row 136 is completed and work measures 53cm/21in from beg, ending with a RS row.

Shape armhole: Cont to dec at neck edge every 4th row, cast off 5sts at beg of next row and then dec 1 st at beg of every foll alt row 12 times, to 37sts. Now, cont straight at armhole edge, but cont to dec every 4th row at neck edge, until there are 31sts. Cont straight until row 194 is completed, ending with a RS row.

Shape shoulder: Cast off 10sts at beg of next row and follow alt row.
Work 1 row, and cast off rem 11sts.

With WS facing, return to sts on st holder for right side of body, join yarn to inside edge, p2tog and patt to end. Cont to place flowers where indicated by back-and-front main chart and complete right-side shaping of body, for neckline, armhole and shoulder, to mirror that of left side.

Sleeves

Both sleeves are worked alike.
Using 3.5mm needles and B, cast on 55sts, and work 17 rows in st st, starting with a knit (RS) row. Knit 1 row, to make ridge.
Change to using 4mm needles and A, and start working from the sleeve chart from row 1, with leaf edging patt in st st, joining in contrast-col F for edging pattern (3 patt reps plus 2 edge sts each side), and work to row 15.
Next row: Knit 1 row in B, to make ridge.
Shape sleeve: Cont in A and, *at the same time*, position scattered flowers over sleeve according to sleeve chart (starting on row 32), work 3 rows in st st and then inc 1 st at each end of next and every foll 3rd row to 107sts, then cont straight until row 108 is completed and sleeve measures 42cm/16½in from ridge in centre of cuff.
Shape top of sleeve: Cont with last Flower motif, cast off 4sts at beg of next and every foll row until 31sts rem.
Cast off.

Neckband

Worked in 2 pieces.
Using backstitch, sew shoulder seams.
Using 4mm needles and A, with RS facing, pick up and knit 104sts from centre of back neck to centre front.
Knit 1 row, to make ridge. Join in C, and work leaf edging patt as for sleeve cuff (6 patt reps + 2 edge sts), ending with a WS row.
Knit 1 row, to make ridge. Change to using 3.5mm needles and A, work 17 rows in st st. Cast off.
Complete second side of neckband to match the first side.

Making up and finishing

Lightly steam press the pieces under a damp cloth, avoiding areas of diagonal rib.

The Persian Flower tunic, here in its original 1980s version. (Photo: Paul Dennison)

Using backstitch, set in sleeves, and sew side and sleeve seams. Sew together centre back of neckband. Sew side seams of cuffs, turn cuff facings to inside of garment and slip stitch edges into position.

Overlap front neckband ends at centre front, and neatly sew both ends into position.

Give a final press to seams and edgings.

FURTHER FLORAL DESIGNS

In other interpretations of the Floral design theme, the scale of different motifs is varied, from the all-over repeat of the Posy Trellis design to the whole-body scale of the Vase of Flowers coat. In the Tapestry Flower tunic, featured at the beginning of this chapter, a stylized floral motif is scattered over a plain background, creating dramatic visual interest, which is surprisingly flattering. The Rose jacket features similar bold motifs: a naturalistic full-blown rose and a graphic scribble.

The Vase of Flowers 100-per-cent-angora coat. (Photo: David McIntyre)

The Posy Trellis cardigan, knitted in white textured cotton. (Photo: courtesy of Rowan Yarns)

The Rose jacket, knitted in mohair yarns, combining a naturalistic rose with an abstract motif. (Photo: David McIntyre)

CHAPTER 9

HERALDIC

This group of designs, inspired by the rich iconography of heraldry and its fantastical beasts – lion, unicorn, griffin and eagle, utilize all the graphic elements, in bold and sometimes highly intricate arrangements. The ready-to-wear collection also included the dramatic Coat of Arms design, featured at the start of this chapter, incorporating a large shield upheld by two lions rampant and complete with plumes and a mock ermine edging made with 100-per-cent-angora yarn. It was lined in sumptuous purple satin for ultimate luxury. This range of heraldic designs for oversized sweaters and cardigans received a Design Council award in 1984 and continued to be popular for a number of years, as both ready-to-wear knitwear and as knitting kits. The two hand-knitting patterns included in this chapter are worked from detailed colour charts and were both also available as Sandy Black for Rowan knitting kits.

The Shield sweater and cardigan feature a bold shield motif on the sweater front or cardigan back that is relatively simple to knit. The colour-block intarsia technique is used

The Sandy Black for Rowan Shield sweater pattern. (Photo: David McIntyre)

The Sandy Black for Rowan Lion and Unicorn sweater pattern. (Photo: David McIntyre)

OPPOSITE PAGE: *The Coat of Arms coat, a showpiece of the ready-to-wear Heraldic collection, 1984, worked with machine-knitted intarsia in wool yarn with angora-yarn details and lined with satin. (Photo: David McIntyre)*

The Fleur de Lys sweater, with a slash neck, in a pale colourway. (Photo: David McIntyre)

The Small Shields sweaters, knitted in two different base colours, grey and ecru. (Photo: David McIntyre)

for both the main shield and the small embedded shields of the designs. The Lion and Unicorn sweater is the *pièce de résistance* of the hand-knitting group of designs, with eight animal motifs positioned around a central shield, creating an intense, but highly rewarding, knitting experience. I was intrigued to see on Ravelry that one knitter bought this design as one of my knitting kits in 1987, and, three children later, finally finished it in 2010 – I really admire her perseverance!

Two other simpler designs in the original Sandy Black Heraldic collection are shown in the featured photos – the Fleur de Lys sweater, with an all-over repeating pattern reminiscent of ornate floor tiles, and the Small Shields sweater, with plain and patterned shields, also reminiscent of flags. The photos also illustrate the effect of using two different colour palettes for these boldly patterned designs: one intensely bright against neutral backgrounds and the other in paler pastel or tonal colours. The effect of different background colours is also illustrated.

Shield Sweater and Cardigan

The Shield sweater and cardigan, both ecru with bright colours. The sweater was knitted to the smaller size by using needles that are one size smaller than those used to obtain the stated tension. (Photo: David McIntyre)

These generously sized garments are knitted with pure-wool yarns and include stocking-stitch motifs on a reverse-stocking-stitch background. Two variations of the sweater are included, with different lengths and necklines – either shorter with a wide slash neckline and a large cabled collar or longer with a crew neck, longer sleeves and a smaller cabled collar (shown worn by a man in the featured photographs). Both the sweater and the cardigan are knitted from the same charts: the sweater with the large shield motif placed on the front, and the cardigan with it on the back. Small textural shield motifs are worked in stocking stitch on the reverse-stocking-stitch background, scattered over the sleeves, sweater back, cardigan fronts and around the large shield. An embroidered motto is added to the scroll beneath the large shield after the knitting is completed. As can be seen, a completely different effect is achieved by using either bright contrasts or pastel colours for the motifs. These pieces were originally knitted in Rowan's Sandy Black Wool Twist yarn, a light-aran-weight 100-per-cent-wool yarn. The Shield cardigan is also shown knitted from the same pattern in mohair-rich yarns, with a mohair content of approx 60–75 per cent, worked at a similar tension to that for the wool yarns.

A mohair version of the Shield cardigan, knitted to the same tension as the wool version. (Photo: David McIntyre)

Sizes and measurements

The pattern is written for one large size to fit up to a 102cm/40in bust/chest. However, a smaller-sized sweater of up to 10cm/4in smaller all round can be created by a change in tension by using a smaller needle size.

Knitted measurements

Full-size sweater and cardigan
Slash-neck-sweater length: 61cm/24in; sleeve length: 43cm/17in
Crew-neck-sweater length: 67cm/26½in; sleeve length: 48cm/19in
Underarm width of both sweater versions and cardigan: 76cm/30in
Cardigan length: 66cm/26in; sleeve length: 43cm/17in
Smaller-size sweater
Slash-neck-sweater length: 57cm/22½in
Crew-neck-sweater length: 63cm/25in
Underarm width: 71cm/28in

Materials

Yarn
Knitted in an aran-weight 100-per-cent-wool or wool-rich-blend yarn (with a wool content of approx 75 per cent) and with 90–100m/50g (or, 180–200m/100g) in 6 colours.

Main colour (MC):
Sweater (both versions): 750g total (15 × 50g balls or 8 × 100g balls)
Cardigan: 900g total (18 × 50g balls or 9 × 100g balls)

Contrast colours:
Both garments: 1 × 50g ball in each of 5 contrast colours to form one colourway:
Brights colourway: Gold (Gd), Blue (Bl), Purple (Pp), Red (Rd), Emerald (Em)
Pastels colourway: Eau de Nil (N), Lilac (L), Rose (Rs), Mid Grey (Mg), Purple (Pp)

Recommended needles and accessories
Two pairs of needles are required: one pair of the size to give the correct tension, for main parts, and one pair of four sizes smaller, for edgings.
1 pair 5.5mm (UK 5, US 9) needles for main parts
1 pair 3.75mm (UK 9, US 5) needles for edgings
Cable needle
Stitch holders: 1 for crew-neck sweater and 2 for cardigan
7 buttons, for cardigan only

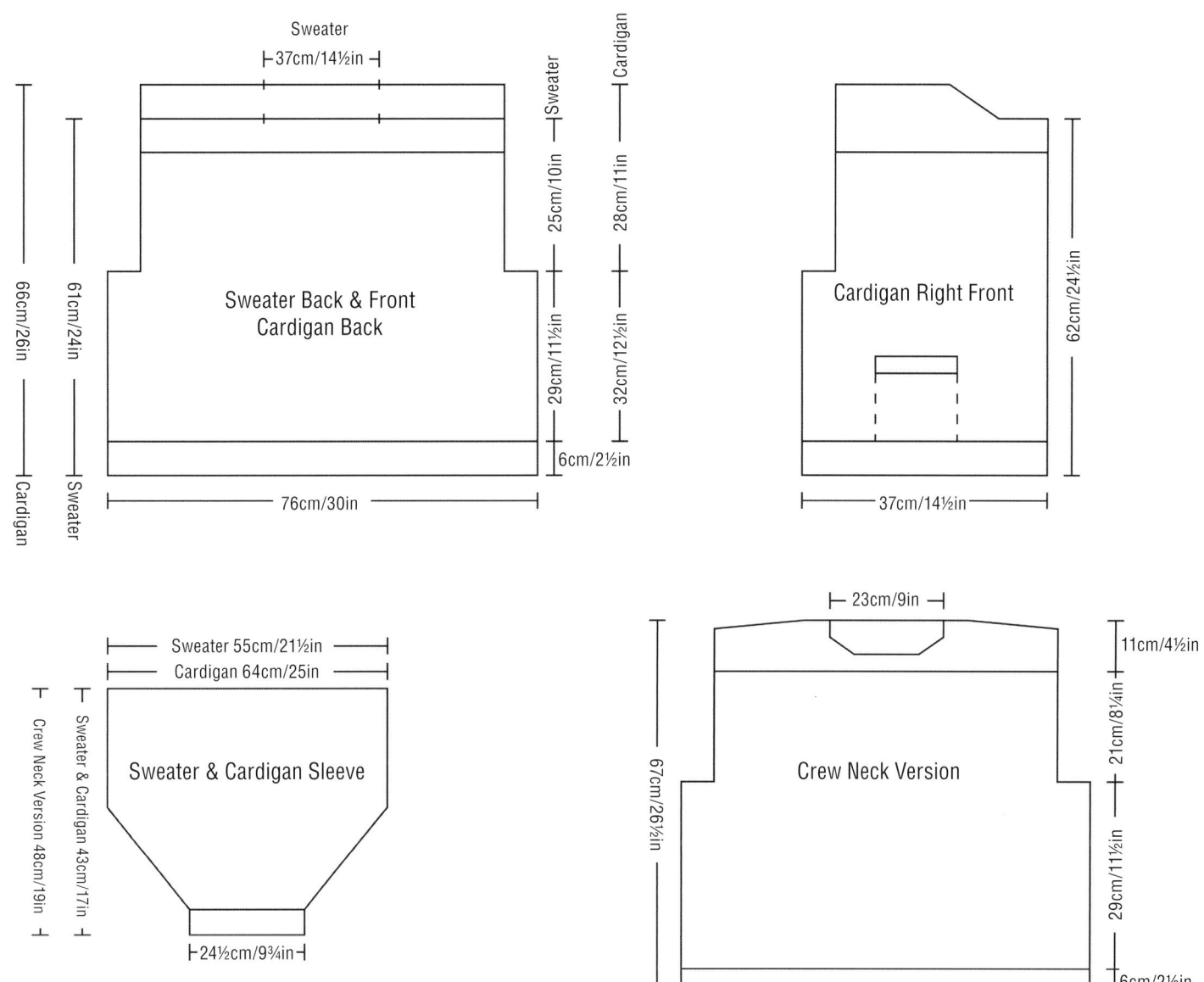

Sweater and cardigan measurement diagrams.

Tension

18sts and 24 rows to 10cm/4in, measured over rev st st, using 5.5mm (UK 5, US 9) needles or the size required to give the correct tension and therefore measurements.

To avoid disappointment, it is essential to check your tension carefully before commencing the knitting of the garment and to use the needles that give you the correct tension. These needles may not be of the needle size quoted in the standard tension information, as each knitter knits differently.

How to check tension

Using the recommended needles and MC, cast on 30sts, and work in rev st st for 8 rows (starting with a purl row as RS), then work a textural small shield as folls:

Row 9 (RS): P15, k1, p14.
Row 10: K13, p3, k to end.
Row 11: P13, k5, p to end.
Row 12: K11, p7, k to end.
Row 13: P11, k9, p to end.
Row 14: K9, p11, k to end.

Row 15: P10, k11, p to end.
Rows 16–21: Rep rows 14–15 three times.
Row 22: As row 14.
Row 23: K to end.
Cont in rev st st for 10 rows. Cast off loosely. Lightly steam press the fabric with a steam iron or under a damp cloth. Pin the knitted swatch square down flat, without stretching the fabric. Place a pin between 2sts near the left side of the swatch, count 18sts across to the right, and place another pin between the 18th and 19th sts. Mark out 24 rows in the same manner, starting from 2sts near the top of the swatch. Measure the distance between each pair of pins. The measurements should both be 10cm/4in. If a measurement is less than 10cm/4in, your knitting is too tight – try using needles of one size larger to reknit the swatch, and again check the tension; if a measurement is more than 10cm/4in, your knitting is too loose – try using needles of one size smaller to reknit the swatch, and again check the tension. Repeat the process until the correct tension is achieved. Do not be afraid to go up or down by more than one size from the recommended needles to achieve the required tension. Adjust the size of the smaller pair of needles for the edgings accordingly.

Size note: A smaller-sized sweater can be simply knitted from the same pattern by determining the needle size for the correct tension as above and then adjusting both pairs of needles to be of one size smaller: use these smaller needles as necessary throughout the working of the pattern. This should result in a garment that is approx 10cm/4in smaller all round and approx 4cm/1½in shorter. For reference, in the photographs, the grey sweater worn by the man is the full-sized, crew-neck version, the brights sweater on the beach is the slash-neck sweater in this smaller size and the pastels sweater is the slash-neck version at full size.

The Shield sweater and cardigan: the man is wearing the longer, crew-neck version of the sweater. (Photo: David McIntyre)

Abbreviations and special stitches

c4b = cable 4sts back: slip next 2sts purlwise on to cable needle and leave it at back of work, k2, then k2 from cable needle

tw2 = twist 2sts: knit into front of 2nd st on LH needle, knit into front of 1st st on LH needle, then allow both knitted-into sts to slip off LH needle together

A pastels colourway of the Shield sweater and an eau-de-nil colourway of the Fleur de Lys sweater. (Photo: David McIntyre)

Pattern

Notes on working the pattern

- One square of the chart represents one knitted stitch. Odd-numbered rows (RS) are read from right to left; even-numbered rows (WS) are read from left to right. Each chart square corresponds to a knit or purl stitch as follows: all outlined pattern areas are worked in st st (odd-numbered rows are knit; even-numbered rows are purled). All background areas are worked in rev st st

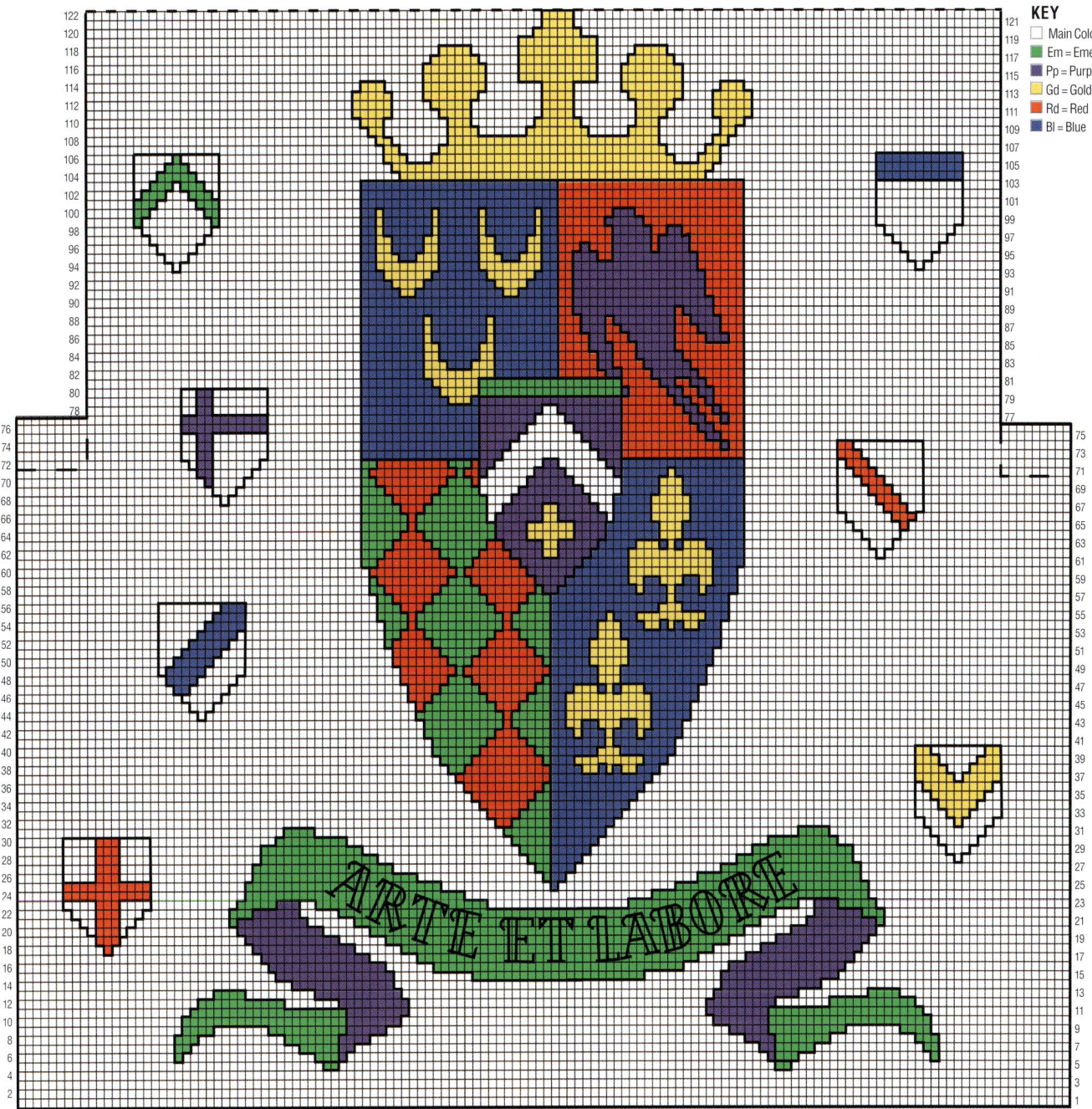

Chart A for sweater front and cardigan back – brights colourway.

(odd-numbered rows are purled; even-numbered rows are knitted). The main shield and scroll are worked in st st in the colours indicated by chart A, either the brights version or the pastels version. The small shields are worked in st st mainly in MC and with motif details worked with a contrast colour, as indicated by chart B.

- Use separate balls or butterfly twists of yarn (*see* Chapter 4) for each area of colour, and avoid stranding colours across the back of the work. Cross yarns by picking up the new yarn from under the previous one when changing yarn colours, to link the colours and prevent holes appearing in the knitting. Use a separate ball of background colour at each side of the main shield.

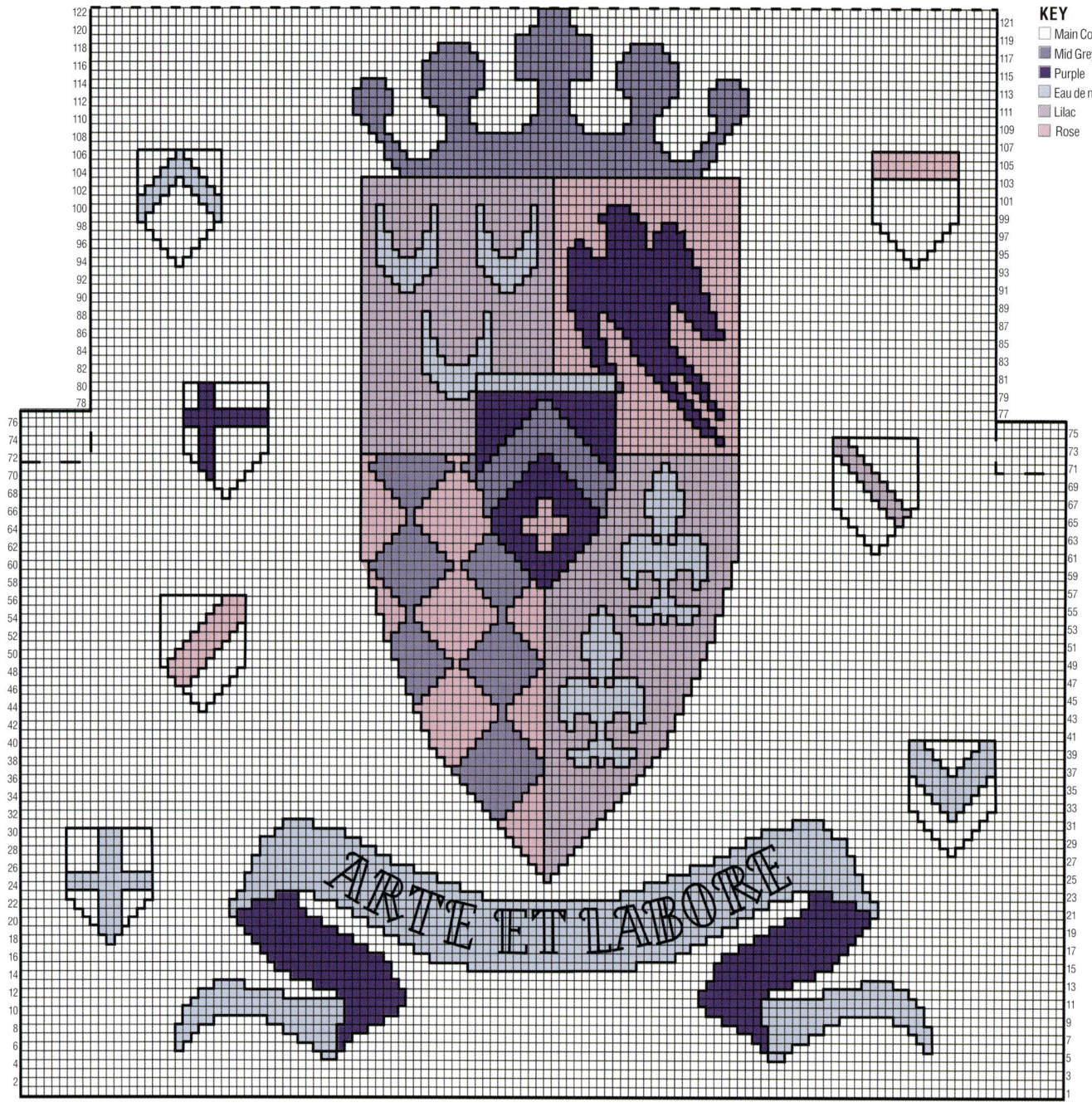

Chart A for sweater front and cardigan back – pastels colourway.

Note: To give neat outlines around coloured areas, when changing back to the MC at the top of a coloured shape, work only these coloured stitches in stocking stitch instead of rev st st. This applies in particular around the scroll and crown shapes.

Sweater front and cardigan back

The slash-neck and crew-neck sweater fronts and cardigan back are worked from the same chart, chart A, with adjustments made to the length of the cabled yoke as given. Using the smaller needles and MC, cast on 134sts, and work in twisted-rib patt as folls:
Row 1 (RS): P2, (k2, p2) to end.
Row 2 (WS): K2, (p2, k2) to end.
Rows 3–4: Rep rows 1–2.
Row 5: P2, (tw2, p2) to end.
Row 6: As row 2.
Rep rows 1–6 until work measures 6cm/2½in, and, *at the same time*, inc 1 st on last row, ending with a WS row (135sts). *

Change to the larger needles and beg working from chart A at bottom right with a purl row for rev st st. Work from chart with background in rev st st and scroll and shield in st st, joining in contrast cols (here presented for the brights colourway) as required as folls:
Row 1 (RS): Purl to end.
Row 2 (WS): Knit to end.
Rows 3–4: As rows 1–2.
Row 5: P36 MC, k2 Pp, p56 MC, k2 Pp, p to end in MC.
Row 6: K20 MC, p1 Em, k17 MC, p3 Em, p1 Pp, k54 MC, p1 Pp, p3 Em, k17 MC, p1 Em, k to end in MC.

Cont working from chart in this manner, and beg working small shields in st st on even-numbered (WS) rows as shown on chart. Cont until row 70 (sweater) or row 76 (cardigan) is completed.

Shape armholes: Keeping continuity of patt correct, cast off 9sts at beg of next 2 rows (117sts). Cont working from chart A until row 120 (sweater) or row 122 (cardigan) is completed.

Beg cabled yoke: Work in cable-rib patt as folls:
Row 1: P3, (k4, p2) to end.
Row 2: K2, (p4, k2) to last st, k1.
Rows 3–4: Rep rows 1–2.
Row 5: P3, (c4b, p2) to end.
Row 6: As row 2.
Rep rows 1–6 for cable-rib patt. Cont in cable-rib patt as set until work measures 61cm/24in (sweater) ** or 66cm/26in (cardigan) from beg.

Cardigan: Cast off loosely in rib.
Slash-neck sweater: Cast off loosely in rib, placing markers for neck opening at 25th and 92nd sts.
Crew-neck sweater: Do not cast off, but cont working in cable-rib patt and, *at the same time*, shape neckline as folls, beg with RS facing:
Shape front neck: Patt 48sts and turn, placing rem 69sts on a st holder for right side of body.
Cont working on these 48sts as set, for left side of body, and, *at the same time*, dec 1 st at neck edge of next 10 rows. Work 1 more row so that RS of work is facing. (38sts)
Shape shoulder: Cast off 9sts at beg of next and foll alt row, then work 1 row. Cast off 10sts at beg of next and foll alt row.
Place sts from st holder for right side of body on to LH needle. With RS facing, join yarn to inside edge, and cast off 21sts for centre and start of neckline. Complete neckline and shoulder shaping to mirror that of left side.

Sweater back

Work as given for front to *. Change to the larger needles, and beg working from chart B at bottom right with a purl row. Beg each shield motif on an even-numbered (WS) row, joining in contrast cols (presented on the chart for the brights colourway) as required, until row 120 is completed. Now, work cable-rib-patt yoke as given for front until work matches front length to **.

Slash-neck sweater: Cast off loosely in rib, placing markers for neck opening as for front at 25th and 92nd sts.
Crew-neck sweater: Do not cast off, but work a further 12 rows in cable-rib patt.

Detail of the large Shield pattern, featuring a darker variation of tones instead of all brights.

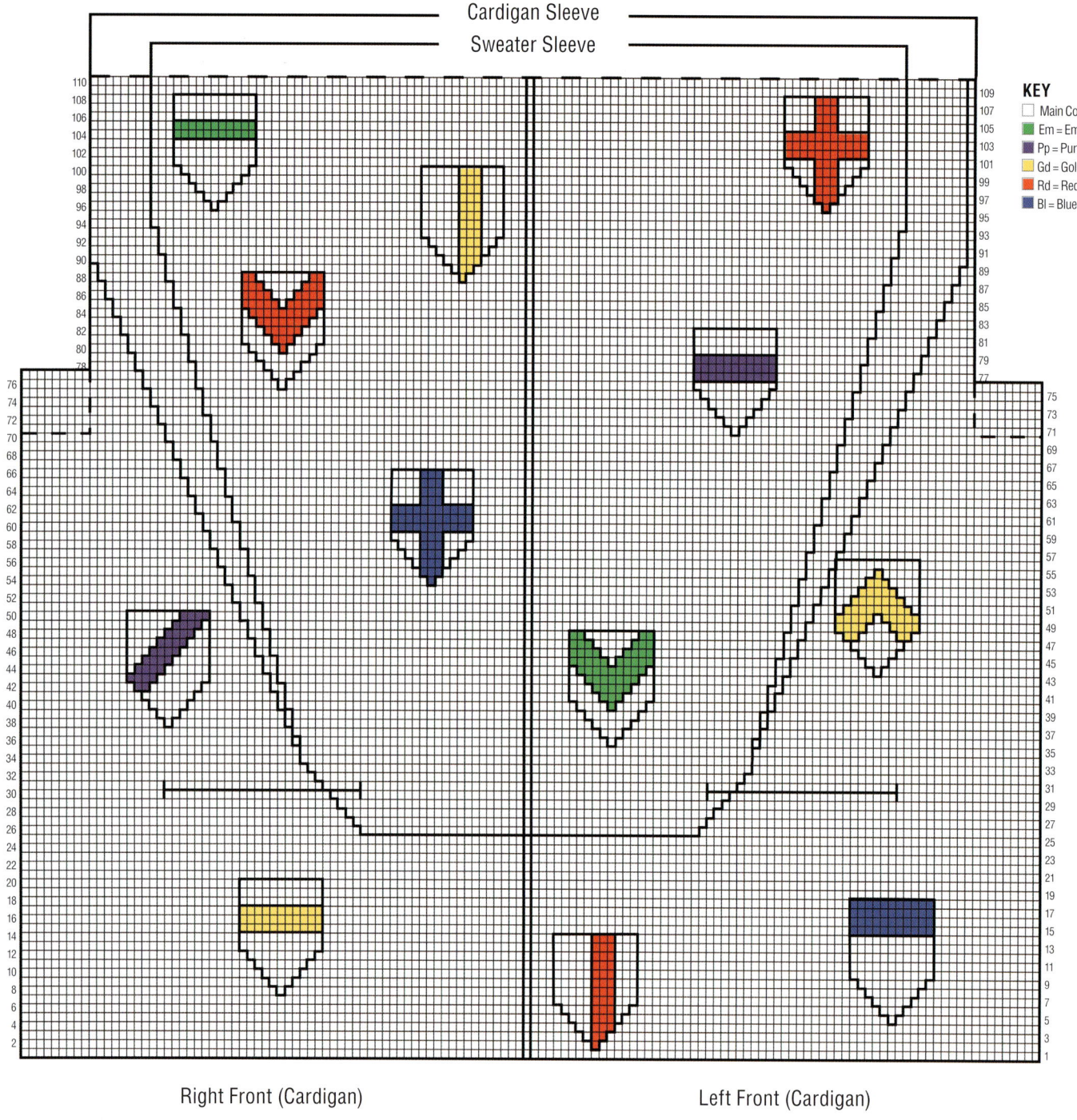

Right Front (Cardigan)   Left Front (Cardigan)

Chart B for sweater back, cardigan fronts, sweater sleeves and cardigan sleeves – brights colourway. If using the pastels colourway, substitute the contrast colours listed in the key as follows: for Em, use N; for Pp, use Pp; for Bl, use Rs; for Gd, use Mg, and for Rd, use L. Alternatively, use the five contrast colours of the pastels colourway as desired to complete the contrast-colour details of the small-shields motifs.

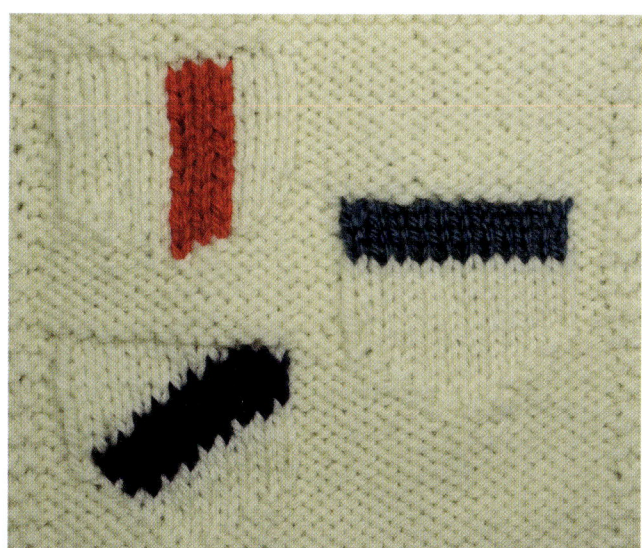

Detail of the textural small shields. These can be worked in two contrast colours, rather than one, as in the Small Shields design featured earlier.

Detail of a grey version of the Shields sweater, showing knitted motifs on a purl ground.

Shape shoulders: Cast off 9sts at beg of next 4 rows, then cast off 10sts at beg of foll 4 rows. Cast off rem 41sts.

Cardigan fronts and pockets

Pocket lining
Using the larger needles and MC, cast on 26sts, and work 13cm/5¼in in rev st st, ending, with a knit row. Make a second pocket lining to match first, and leave sts of both pocket linings on a st holder or spare needle.

Cardigan front
Work through these instructions twice, once for the left front and once for the right front.

Using the smaller needles and MC, cast on 66sts, and work in twisted-rib patt as set out for back for 6cm/2½in, and, *at the same time*, inc 1 st on last row, ending with a WS row (67sts). Change to the larger needles and rev st st, and beg working from appropriate half of chart B, for left or right front, starting at row 1, at bottom right. Cont working from chart, and beg each shield on an even-numbered (WS) row as shown, until row 30 is completed.
Place pocket: P19 (for left front) or p22 (for right front), place next 26sts on to st holder for pocket edging, p 26sts from st holder for one pocket lining, p to end.
Cont in patt from chart B until row 76 (for left front) or row 77 (for right front) is completed.
Shape armhole: Cast off 9sts, patt to end (58sts).
Cont working straight until row 110 of chart is completed. Work 12 rows in rev st st.

Beg cabled yoke: Work in cable-rib patt as folls:
Row 1: P3, (k4, p2) to last st, p1.
Row 2: K3, (p4, k2) to last st, k1.
Rows 3–4: Rep rows 1–2.
Row 5: P3, (c4b, p2) to last st, p1.
Row 6: As row 2.
Rep rows 1–6 for cable-rib patt. Cont in cable-rib patt as set until work measures 62cm/24½in, ending at centre front.
Shape neck: Cast off 11sts, patt to end. Keeping continuity of cable-rib patt correct, dec 1 st at neck edge of every row until 38sts rem. Cast off loosely in rib.

Pocket edgings
Place one set of 26sts from pocket-edging st holder on to the smaller needles and, using MC and with RS facing, work in twisted rib for 4cm/1½in as set out for back. Cast off in rib. Rep for second set of pocket-edging sts on st holder.

Cardigan front bands

Left front: Using MC and the smaller needles, with RS facing, pick up and knit 122sts along front edge, and work 26 rows (6cm/2½in) in twisted-rib patt as set for back. Cast off loosely in rib.
Right front: Work as for left-front band for 6 rows. Make first set of buttonholes as folls:
1st buttonhole row: Patt 4sts, (cast off 4sts, patt 14sts) 6 times, cast off 4sts, patt 6sts.
2nd buttonhole row: Work in patt, casting on 4sts over each set of cast-off sts of prev row.
Work 10 rows more, then rep buttonhole rows 1–2 as given above. Work 6 rows. Cast off loosely in rib.

Sweater and cardigan sleeves

Both sleeves are worked alike.
Using the smaller needles and MC, cast on 42sts, and work in twisted-rib patt as set for back for 5cm/2in, ending with a WS row, and, *at the same time*, inc 1 st at beg and end of last row. (44sts)
Change to the larger needles and rev st st, and beg working sweater or cardigan sleeve, as appropriate, from chart B, starting at row 1, at bottom right, with a purl row. Shape the sleeve by inc 1 st at each end of every foll row 8 times to 60sts. Cont in patt from the sleeve chart, shaping as folls:

Cardigan only: Inc 1 st each end of every foll alt row to 116sts.
Sweaters only: Inc 1 st at each end of every foll 3rd row to 100sts.
Cardigan and slash-neck sweater: Cont working straight until chart is completed, then cont in rev st st until sleeve measures 43cm/17in. Cast off loosely.
Crew-neck sweater: Cont working straight until chart is completed, then cont in rev st st until sleeve measures 48cm/19in. Cast off loosely.

Collars for slash-neck sweater and cardigan

Note that the collar is knitted using the smaller needles for the cardigan but the larger needles for the slash-neck sweater.

Knitted-flat collar
Using MC, cast on 162sts.
Row 1 (RS): (P1, k4, p1) to end.
Row 2 (WS): (K1, p4, k1) to end.
Rows 3–4: Rep rows 1–2.
Row 5: (P1, c4b, p1) to end.
Row 6: As row 2.
Rep rows 1–6 5 times or until collar measures 13cm/5¼in. Cast off loosely in rib.

Closed cowl collar
Alternatively, to work this collar variation, work the collar in the round by using a circular needle.

Using MC, cast on 162sts, and arrange cast-on sts and needle points to work in the round, taking care not to twist the sts. All rounds are RS rounds.

Rounds 1–4: (P1, k4, p1) to end.
Round 5: (P1, c4b, p1) to end.
Round 6: As round 1.
Rep rounds 1–6 5 times or until collar measures 13cm/5¼in. Cast off loosely in rib.

Collar for crew-neck sweater

Using the larger needles and MC, cast on 114sts.
Rep rows 1–6 of cable patt as given for knitted-flat collar until collar measures 11.5cm/4½in. Cast off loosely.

Making up and finishing

Embroidery
Using chart A as a guide, draw the given motto, or words of your own choice, on to vanishing muslin or a similar thin fabric or interlining. Securely pin your fabric lettering guide on to the knitting, positioning the lettering centrally on the scroll below the main shield. Using a contrast col, stitch over the outlined letters and through the knitted fabric, using a large backstitch and following the outlines as drawn. When completed, tear off the fabric guide carefully to leave the stitching intact.

Assembly and seams
Darn in all loose ends, working up and down, not across, the back of the work, to avoid the ends later pulling out. Lightly steam press pieces under a damp cloth or using a steam iron, avoiding the cabled edgings and yoke.
With RS together and using backstitch, sew shoulder seams. Using backstitch, join straight upper edge of each sleeve to one side of body along straight edge of armhole between the cast-off sts at each side of armhole, so that each sleeve fits squarely into the corners of the armhole. Then, on each side separately, join each set of cast-off sts at underarm to uppermost part of adjacent sleeve side, to form first part of sleeve seam . Join rest of sleeve together as normal to complete sleeve seam. Join side seams.

Slash-neck sweater: Using a flat oversewn seam, join collar into a circle (if knitted flat). With WS of collar to RS of neckline, pin collar into position, and join to body with a flat edge-to-edge seam.

Crew-neck sweater: Placing open ends of collar to centre front and with WS of collar to RS of neckline, pin collar into position, and join to body with a flat edge-to-edge seam.

Cardigan: Fold front bands in half along long edge, turn outer edge to the inside of the garment, and slip stitch band edge in place to WS. For right front only, sew around each buttonhole to join the two sides of the band together at each buttonhole, and sew on buttons to the left-front band to correspond to the positions of the buttonholes. Fold each pocket edging in half along long edge, turn outer edge to the inside of the pocket, and slip stitch band edge in place.

The Shield cardigan and Shield sweater say farewell. (Photo David McIntyre)

Slip stitch the pocket lining into position on WS of garment for each front. With WS of collar to RS of neck edge, pin collar into position so that the collar edges start and finish halfway across top of front bands. Using a flat oversewn seam, join collar to body.

Lion and Unicorn Sweater

Back view of the Lion and Unicorn sweater. (Photo: Jo Teasdale)

This generously sized sweater is worked in a light-aran- to medium-weight 100-per-cent-wool yarn, in stocking stitch, working from the chart and knitting in blocks of colour by using separate balls of yarn (known as the intarsia technique). The intricate design features four fabulous heraldic creatures – lion, eagle, griffin and unicorn – around a central shield, and the sweater body is identical on front and back. The sleeve features a trefoil design created from bobbles, and the edgings and collar are worked in cabled rib.

Size and measurements

One large size to loosely fit up to a 102cm/40in bust circumference

Knitted measurements
Width at underarms: 67cm/26½in
Length: 63cm/25in
Sleeve length: 46cm/18in

Materials

Yarn
Knitted with a light-aran or medium-weight 100-per-cent-wool yarn with approx 200–230m/100g in 7 colours.
The featured sample was knitted in the 100-per-cent-wool double-knitting yarn Winterburn dk by baa ram ewe in the colours Bishopthorpe (purple, MC), Brass Band (gold), Bantam (claret), Wesley Bob (red), Eccup (blue), Chevin (green) and Yorkstone (light grey).
Main colour (MC): 4 × 100g hanks/balls, for edgings, sleeves and collar – purple is used here but also suggested is gold, claret or dark grey
Contrast colours: 1 × 100g hank/ball each in gold, claret, red, blue, purple and green (note that the selected MC may also be a colourwork-pattern colour)
1 × 50g ball in light grey

Recommended needles and accessories
Two pairs of needles are required: one pair of the size to give the correct tension, for main parts, and one pair of two sizes smaller, for edgings.
1 pair 5mm (US 8, UK 6) needles for main parts
1 pair 4mm (US 6, UK 8) needles for edgings
Cable needle
Large-eyed yarn needle
Optional: Crochet hook for completing bobble motifs

Front view of the Lion and Unicorn sweater – the back and front are the same. (Photo: Jo Teasdale)

The original 1980s image of two colourways of the Lion and Unicorn sweater – dark grey and gold. (Photo: David McIntyre)

HERALDIC 189

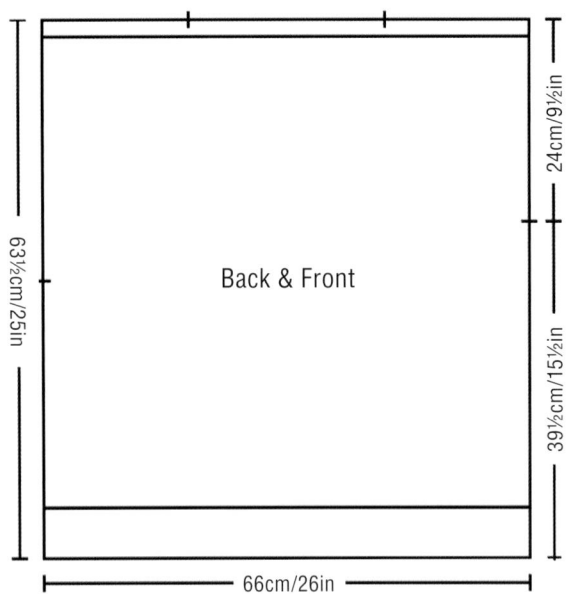
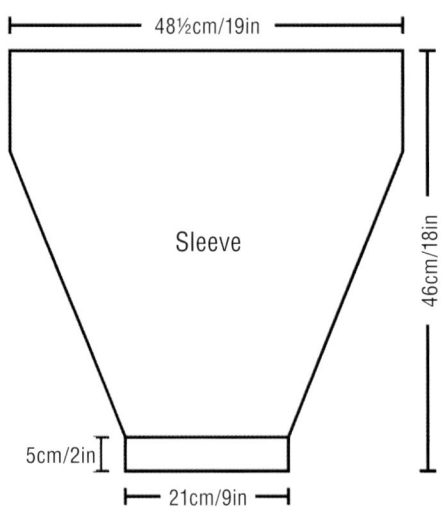

Measurement diagram.

Tension

19sts and 25 rows to 10cm/4in, measured over st-st colourwork patt, using 5mm (US 8, UK 6) needles or the size required to give the correct tension and therefore measurements.

To avoid disappointment, it is essential to check your tension carefully before commencing the knitting of the garment and to use the needles that give you the correct tension. These needles may not be of the needle size quoted in the standard tension information, as each knitter knits differently.

How to check tension
Using 5mm needles and MC, cast on 30sts, and, joining in contrast cols as required, work a section from the chart as folls (*see* 'Notes on working the pattern'):

Starting from row 1 with a knit row, work from the 1st st to the 30th st on knit rows and the 30th st to the 1st st on purl rows, until row 35 is completed. Cast of loosely. Lightly steam press the swatch with a steam iron or under a damp cloth. Pin the knitted swatch square down flat, without stretching the fabric. Place a pin between 2sts near the left side of the swatch, count 19sts across to the right, and place another pin between the 19th and 20th sts. Mark out 25 rows in the same manner, starting from 2sts near the top of the swatch. Measure the distance between each pair of pins. The measurements should both be 10cm/4in. If a measurement is less than 10cm/4in, your knitting is too tight – try using needles of one size larger to reknit the swatch, and again check the tension; if a measurement is more than 10cm/4in, your knitting is too loose – try using needles of one size smaller to reknit the swatch, and again check the tension. Repeat the process until the correct tension is achieved. Do not be afraid to go up or down by more than one size from the recommended needles to achieve the required tension. Adjust the size of the smaller pair of needles for the edgings accordingly.

Abbreviations and special stitches

c4b = cable 4sts back: slip next 2sts purlwise on to cable needle and leave it at back of work, k2, then k2 from cable needle

inc 1 k = knit into front loop of next st on LH needle, knit into back loop of same st and then allow knitted-into st to slip off LH needle

mb = make bobble: with contrast col, knit into front, back, front, back and front of next st (5 contrast-col sts on RH needle). Pass 2nd, 3rd, 4th and 5th sts, furthest from point of RH needle, over 1st st, closest to point of RH needle, place rem contrast-col st on to LH needle, and knit this st with MC

tw2 = twist 2sts: knit into front of 2nd st on LH needle, knit into front of 1st st on LH needle, then allow both knitted-into sts to slip off LH needle together

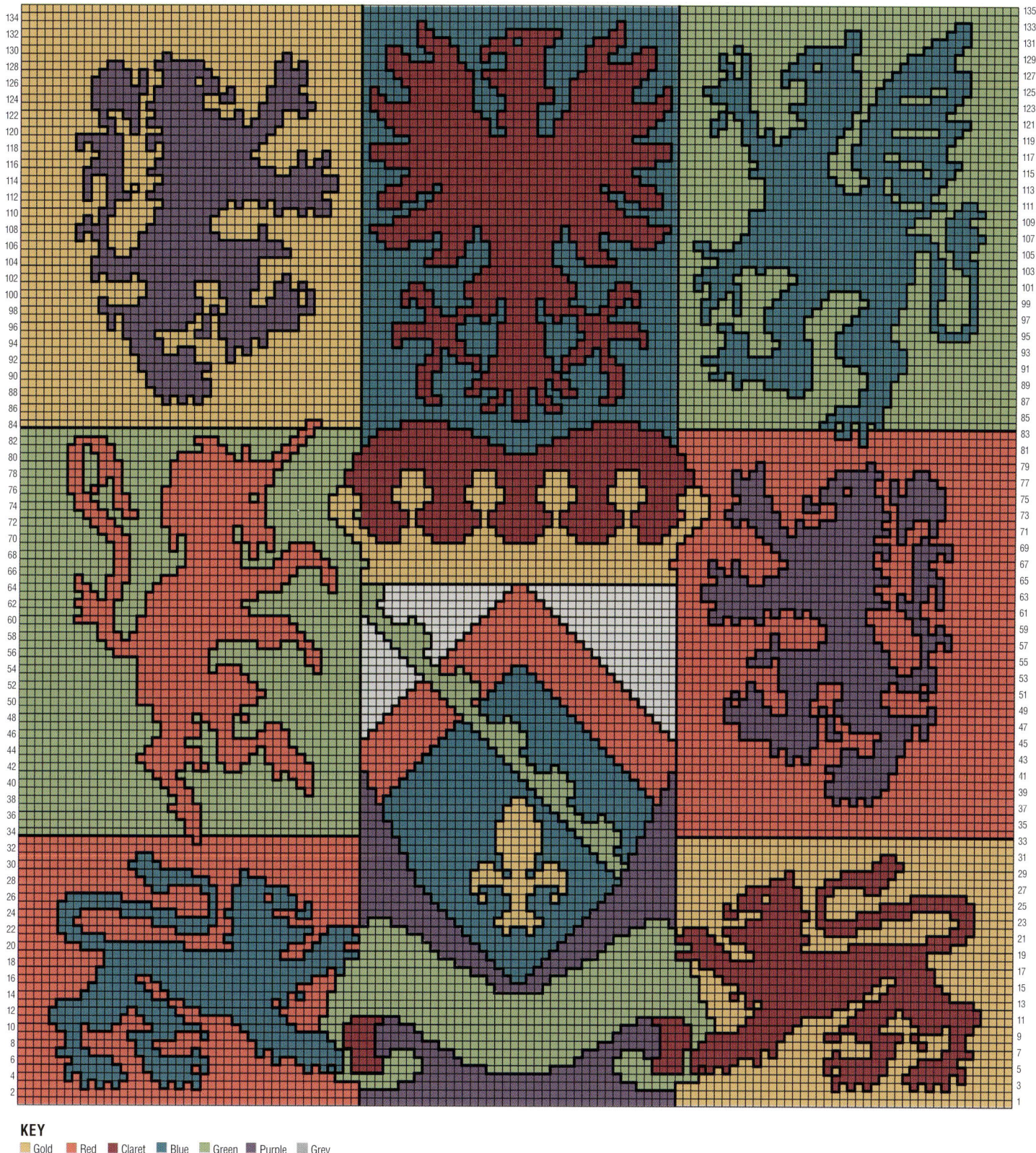

KEY
Gold Red Claret Blue Green Purple Grey

Back and front chart.

HERALDIC 191

Bobble motifs

Each motif consists of 3 bobbles: two bobbles worked on one knit row and the third bobble worked on the foll knit row between the first two bobbles. Each 3-bobble motif is worked with a separate length of contrast-col yarn. Leave the yarn ends for each bobble motif 6cm/2½in long, and push these ends through to the RS of the fabric, for decoration. Each bobble is made where indicated by the abbreviation 'mb' in the written instructions.

Pattern

Notes on working the pattern

- One square of the chart represents one knitted stitch. Odd-numbered rows (RS) are read from right to left and the corresponding stitches are to be knitted; even-numbered rows (WS) are read from left to right and the corresponding stitches are to be purled.
- Use a separate ball, butterfly twist or length of yarn for each main area of colour, including the background MC yarn at each side of a motif, and avoid stranding yarns across the back of the work, except for working some small details. Cross yarns when changing yarn colours, to link the colours and prevent holes appearing in the knitting, but take care not to pull the yarns too tight, as too-tight strands and links will distort the knitting. For more details on handling yarn colours, *see* Chapter 4.

Front detail of the Lion and Unicorn sweater.

Back and front

Using the smaller needles and MC, cast on 126sts, and work in twisted rib as folls:

Row 1 (RS): P2,(k2, p2) to end.
Row 2 (WS): K2, (p2, k2) to end.
Rows 3–4: As rows 1–2.
Row 5: P2, (tw2, p2) to end.
Row 6: As row 2.

Rep rows 1–6 until work measures 6cm/2½in, ending with a WS row.

Change to the larger needles, and beg working from chart at row 1 with a knit row, joining in cols as required. Place markers for underarms of armholes at each end of row 82. Cont straight in patt by working from chart until row 135 is completed. Change to using MC only, and work 6 rows of collar cable-rib patt (given below). Cast off loosely in rib, placing markers at 43rd and 84th sts for neck opening.

Sleeves

Both sleeves are worked alike.
The sleeves are worked in st st with bobble motifs worked in one of the contrast-col yarns and placed irregularly, according to the instructions below.

Beg sleeves: Using the smaller needles and MC, cast on 42sts, and work in twisted-rib patt as set for back for 5cm/2in, ending on a WS row. Change to the larger needles, and cont in st st, shaping sleeve by inc 1 st at each end of the next 9 rows (60sts). Purl 1 row, and place first bobble motif (using contrast col) on next row as folls:

Row 11: K40, mb, k1, mb, k17.
Row 12 and all WS rows: Purl.
Row 13: Inc 1 k in 1st st, k40, mb, k17, inc 1 k in last st (first bobble motif completed).
Row 15: K14, mb (to start next bobble motif on 15th st), k1, mb, k to end.
Row 17: Inc 1 k in 1st st, k14, mb, k to last st, inc 1 k in last st (second bobble motif completed). (64sts)

Cont in st st, shaping sleeve as set by inc 1 st at each end of every 4th (RS) row to 92sts (73 rows completed) then cont without shaping, and, *at the same time*, place bobble motifs irregularly, starting on the stitches stated as folls (or, alternatively, position bobble motifs as you wish over the sleeve):

Row 23: 39th st.

Detail showing the sleeve textural trefoil motifs.

Row 31: 33rd st.
Row 37: 14th st.
Row 41: 53rd st.
Row 49: 34th st.
Row 57: 48th st.
Row 61: 18th st.
Row 71: 65th st.
Row 81: 32nd st.
Row 87: 39th st.
Row 91: 72nd st.
Row 95: 12th st.

Cont in st st until sleeve measures 46cm/18in. Cast off loosely.

Collars

Knitted-flat collar
Using the larger needles and MC, cast on 162sts, and work in cable-rib patt as folls:
Row 1 (RS): (P1, k4, p1) to end.
Row 2 (WS): (K1, p4, k1) to end.
Rows 3–4: As rows 1–2.
Row 5: (P1, c4b, p1) to end.
Row 6: As row 2.
Rep rows 1–6 5 times or until collar measures 14cm/5½in. Cast off loosely in rib.

Closed cowl collar
Alternatively, to work this collar variation, work the collar in the round by using a circular needle.

The inside of the Lion and Unicorn sweater, with finished yarn ends.

Using the larger needles and MC, cast on 162sts, and arrange cast-on sts and needle points to work in the round, taking care not to twist the sts. All rounds are RS rounds.
Rounds 1–4: (P1, k4, p1) to end.
Round 5: (P1, c4b, p1) to end.
Round 6: As round 1.
Rep rounds 1–6 5 times or until collar measures 14cm/5½in. Cast off loosely in rib.

Making up and finishing

Darn in all loose ends carefully (except for bobble motifs on sleeves), closing all gaps in the knitted fabric and working up and down and not across the work to avoid the ends pulling out. For bobble motifs, using a knitting needle or crochet hook, bring all tail ends of contrast-col yarns to front of work. Lightly steam press pieces to block them to size, avoiding all cabled sections.

Using backstitch, sew shoulder seams. Using underarm markers as a guide, using backstitch, join sleeves to body, and sew side and sleeve seams. For knitted-flat collar, oversew short ends of collar to make a closed circle, or leave collar open at the side, if preferred. For knitted-flat and closed cowl collars, with WS of collar to RS of neckline and using a flat seam, oversew collar from inside of neckline with collar seam (if present) at centre back.

CHAPTER 10

ORNAMENTAL

The three designs featured in this chapter include ornate and intricate patterns that are cleverly worked to minimize the knitting difficulty. Some of my original collections featured larger pieces including coats created by using a patchwork technique to simplify the knitting involved. This method of working allows quite complex patterning to be created from small sections of knitting that are then pieced together. The designs featured either a repeated motif with edgings that interlock together, as in the Tapestry Flower coat and Lotus Flower jacket illustrated, or an all-over tile pattern that creates a larger motif when the tiles are used in different orientations. I have long been fascinated with the basic mathematics of repeating designs and enjoyed studying the ornamental tile patterns found on my travels in wonderfully ornate historic palaces and civic buildings.

The Azulejos tunic and jacket feature the patchwork-tile technique, and the complex-looking pattern is made up of only two basic tiles, one the reverse of the other and that are put together in different orientations to form the overall pattern. With the patchwork technique, the knitting becomes portable and more manageable, although the making up is a little more time-consuming. A similar technique is also used in

OPPOSITE PAGE: *The tile design of the Azulejos tunic chimes with the style of an ornate seafront bandstand. (Photo: Jo Teasdale)*

The Tapestry Flower coat, knitted in wool and angora yarns, is constructed from a patchwork of identical tile modules, with a stylized-flower and asymmetric-border design. (Photo: David McIntyre)

The Lotus Flower jacket, knitted in wool and chenille yarns, is based on the same construction as the Tapestry Flower coat but using a different motif and leaf border worked in two colours and with a shorter length. (Photo: David McIntyre)

The Medieval Tile sweaters are constructed from one main tile used in different orientations to create a new visual pattern of diamond motifs. Designed to be knitted in light and dark colourways and as a shorter and longer version, with the longer version including one more row of tiles. (Photo: Paul Dennison)

A rich, dark colourway of the Tapestry Flower coat, with ermine-effect edging – perfect for a night at the theatre! (Photo: David McIntyre)

the Medieval Tile sweater shown in the featured photograph in two colourways. This design uses only one basic tile, pieced together in different orientations. A further example of the patchwork-tile technique is shown for the Scroll gilet in Chapter 5.

The Rosette tunic appears complex, but the design is built up from just one simple circle motif repeated all over – it is the colouring of the circles that creates the decorative pattern, entailing the management of different balls of colours across the width of the knitting for a combination of stranded-colourwork and intarsia techniques. In this pattern, the chart is used as a guide to the colour and shape layout of the circles, as the circle pattern is easily learnt. Many interesting variations can be achieved by using contrasting yarn weights and textures, as shown.

The final pattern is the *trompe l'œil* Shawl cardigan – it was designed to give the impression of a shawl with a paisley border being worn over a cabled sweater and was great fun to create. Whilst having strong visual impact, the knitting is not too demanding, as only a section of each row is knitted from the charted design, and many features are embroidered after the knitting is completed. This cardigan was the last of several designs produced for BBC television when I was resident knitwear designer for their series *Bazaar* from 1988 to 1990.

Azulejos Tunic and Jacket

The Azulejos tunic is an aran-weight garment of double thickness that is ideal for outdoor wear and for making an impact. (Photo: Jo Teasdale)

The original Azulejos tunic, knitted in two shades of grey with cream. (Photo: Paul Dennison)

This original cardigan version of the Azulejos design is simply left open at the front and edged with the border pattern. (Photo: Paul Dennison)

Sizes and measurements

One generous size to fit up to a 102cm/40in bust circumference

Knitted measurements

All-round circumference at underarms (when made up): 129.5cm/51in (tunic) or 140cm/55in (jacket)
Length: 79cm/31in
Sleeve length: 47cm/18½in

Materials

Yarn

Knitted in an aran-weight pure-wool yarn with approx 160m/100g. The featured sample is knitted in Erika Knight for John Lewis Aran 100-per-cent-wool yarn in colours as described in the following sections. Erika Knight Vintage Wool Aran is an alternative yarn.

Tunic

Main colour (MC): 8 × 100g balls in ecru (N)
Contrast colours:
5 × 100g balls in dark grey (G), as first contrast colour
3 × 100g balls in maroon (M), as second contrast colour

Jacket

Main colour (MC): 9 × 100g balls in natural (N)
Contrast colours:
5 × 100g balls in dark grey (G), as first contrast colour
3 × 100g balls in maroon (M), as second contrast colour

Recommended needles and accessories

Three pairs of needles are required: one pair of the size to give the correct tension, for main parts (tiles), and one pair of one size smaller and one pair of two sizes smaller than the larger needles, for both sleeve panels and edgings. For further details, *see* the tension section.
1 pair 5mm (UK 6, US 8) needles for main parts (tiles)
1 pair 4.5mm (UK 7, US 7) needles for sleeve panels and edgings
1 pair 4mm (UK 8, US 6) needles for sleeve panels and edgings
1 circular 4.5mm (UK 7, US 7) needle for jacket edgings
Large-eyed yarn needle

This design was inspired by ancient decorative tiles, called 'azulejos' in Portuguese. There are two garment versions – a tunic and a jacket. Both are identical in construction except that the front is left open for the jacket and the edgings are knitted on differently. The design is constructed from individually knitted tiles, worked in three colours from a small chart, that are later sewn together in patchwork fashion to make a larger motif. Four special tiles create the neck shaping. The two-colour patterned edgings and textured sleeve panels are knitted on after the tiles have been assembled. The trade-off here is for more manageable knitting and the fun of seeing the pattern take shape but additional making up! Several stages of the knitting and making-up process are illustrated as work in progress in the accompanying photographs.

Tension

One tile as worked from the chart should measure 17cm/6¾in in each direction when using 5mm (UK 6, US 7) needles or the size required to give the correct tension and therefore measurements.

How to check tension

Work one tile from either chart A or B, using the recommended needles. Lightly steam the fabric, and lay the tile down flat as a square, without stretching the fabric. Measure the tile from side to side and top to bottom. If a measurement is less than 17cm/6¾in in either direction (say, by

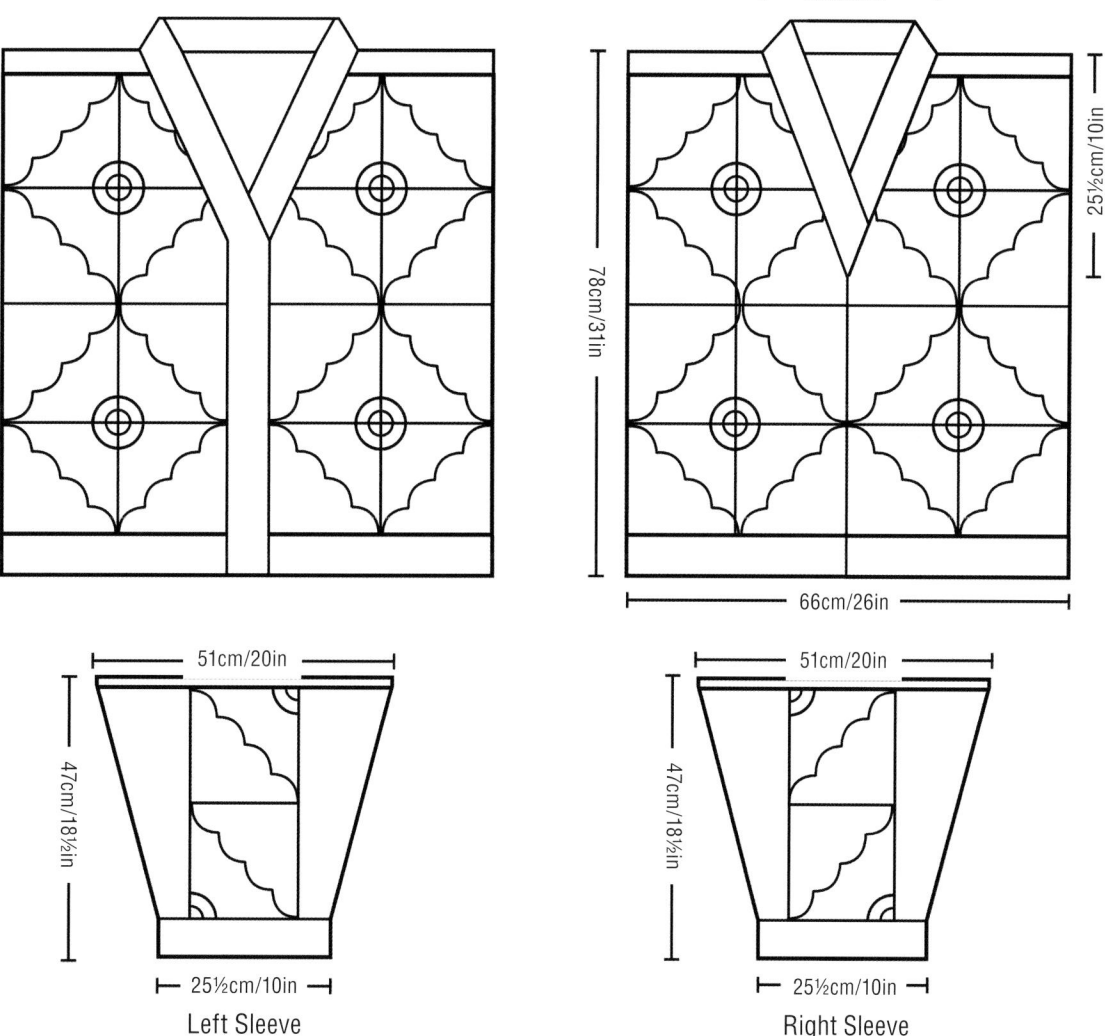

Tunic and jacket measurement diagram.

approx 1cm/½in), your knitting is too tight, and the garment will be too narrow and too short – try using needles of one size larger to reknit the tile, and again check the tension. If a measurement is more than 17cm/6¾in in either direction, your knitting is too loose, and the garment will be larger and longer – try using needles of one size smaller to reknit the tile, and again check the tension. Repeat the process until the correct tension is achieved. If your tension is correct, this is one of your finished tiles!

Do not be afraid to go up or down by more than one size from the recommended needles to achieve the required tension, if necessary. Adjust the size of all the other needles to be used accordingly. Care taken at this stage will avoid disappointment later.

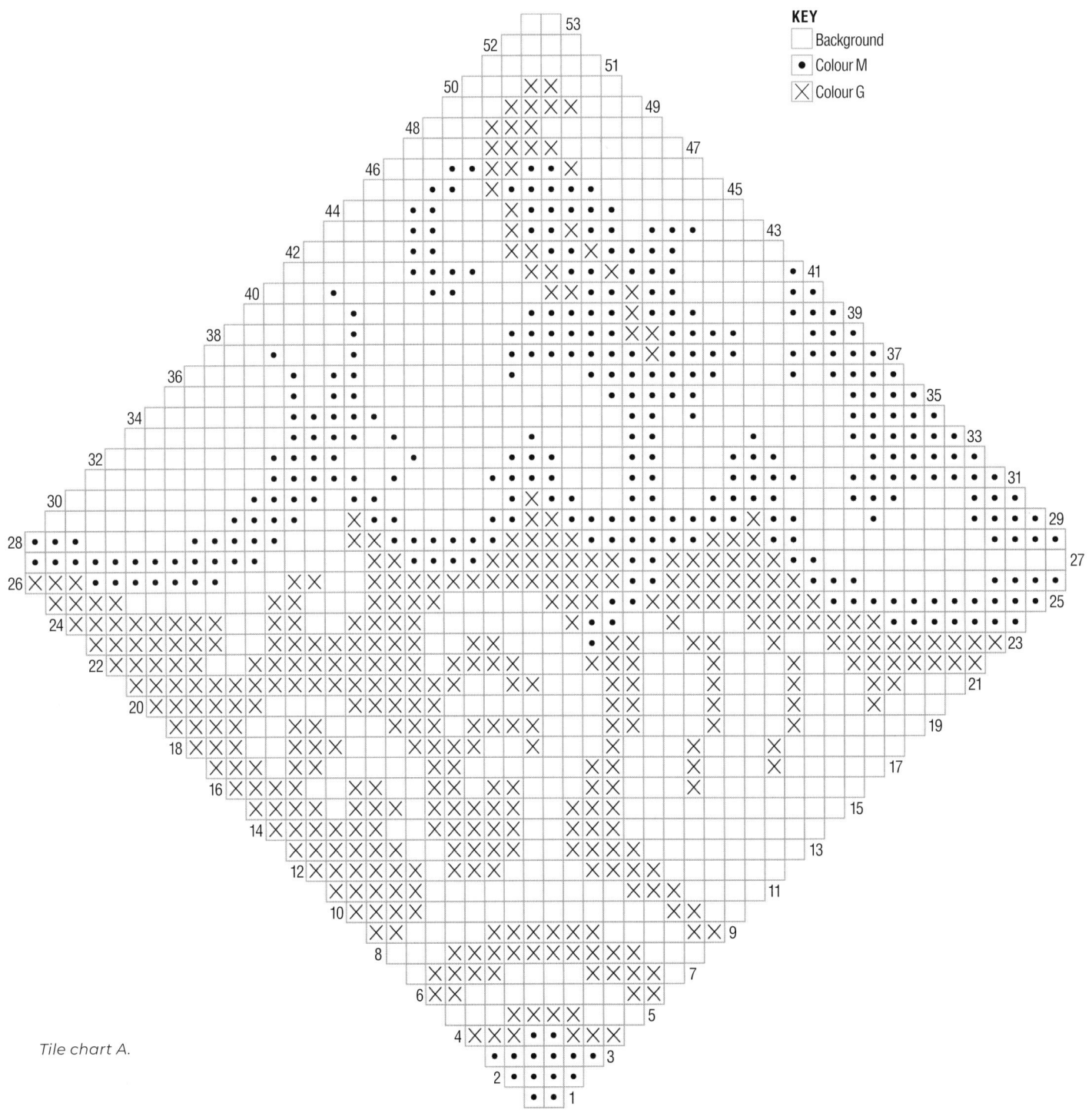

Tile chart A.

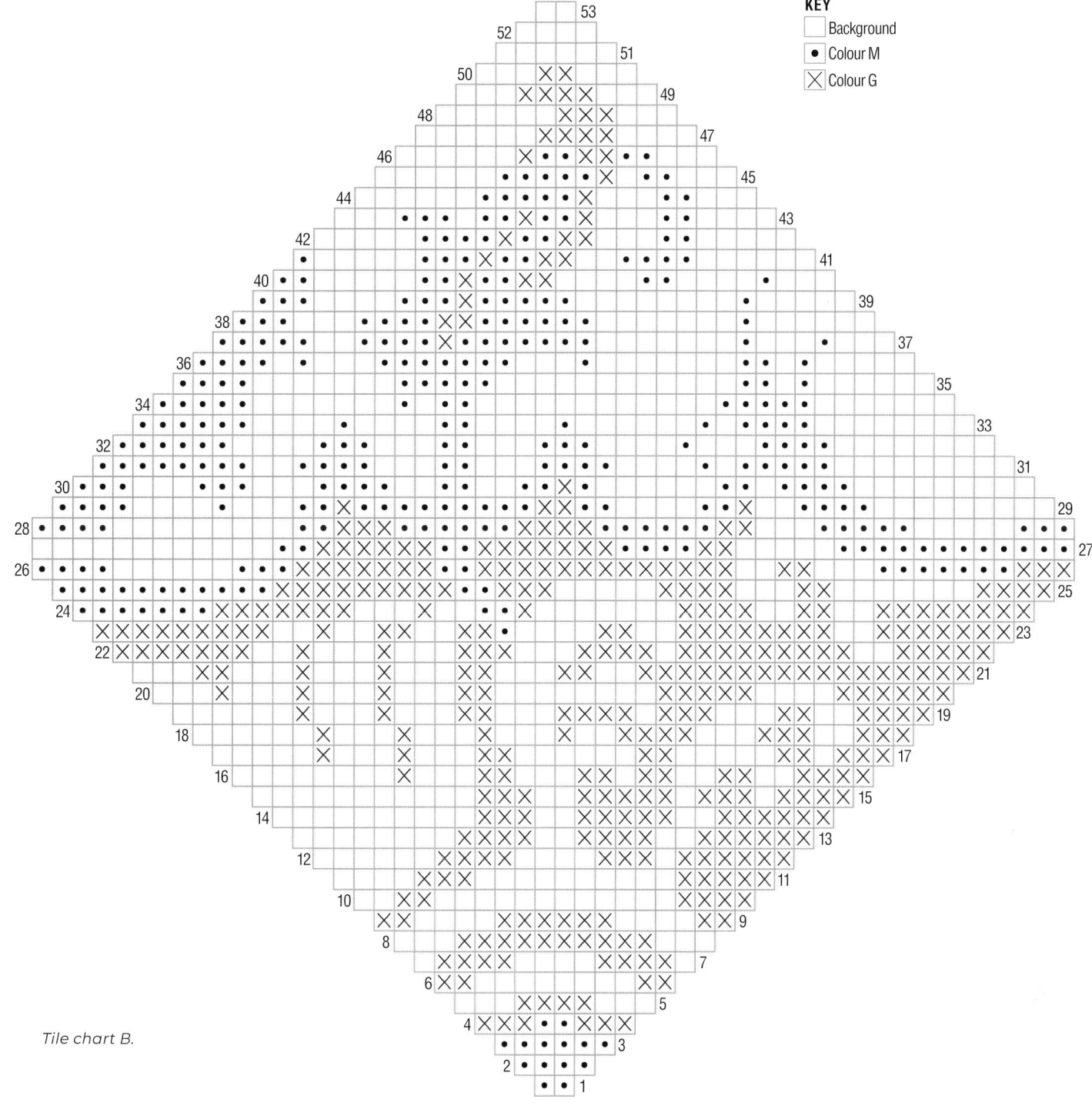

Tile chart B.

ORNAMENTAL 201

Knitted tiles A and B – one is the mirror image of the other.

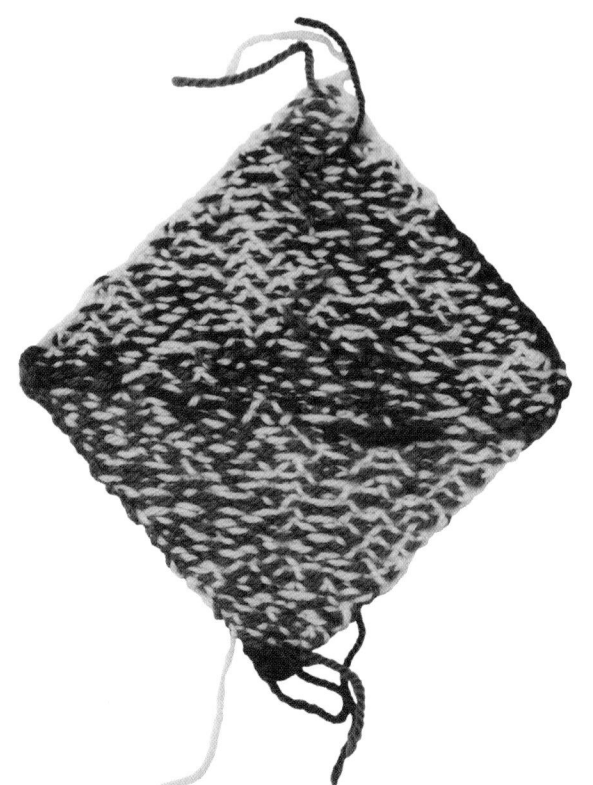

Back view of a knitted tile, illustrating yarn stranding, weaving in of yarn, and the double thickness of the fabric.

Pattern

Notes on working the pattern
- One square of the chart represents one knitted stitch. Odd-numbered rows (RS) are read from right to left and the corresponding stitches are to be knitted; even-numbered rows (WS) are read from left to right and the corresponding stitches are to be purled.
- There are two basic tile types that make up this design: the main tiles and the special tiles. Both are worked in stocking stitch from a chart A or B, which are the reverse of each other. Each tile starts with 2sts, and 1 st is increased at each end of every row to row 25 (52sts), 3 rows are worked straight, and then 1 st is decreased at each end of every row to 2sts (53 rows completed).
- The tiles are worked mainly with two-colour stranded-colourwork knitting, using N, the background colour (MC), and G, the first contrast colour, in the lower half of each tile, and N and M, the second contrast colour, in the top part, with sections in the centre and top worked as three-colour stranded-colourwork knitting. Within each tile area, strand the yarns across the back loosely, weaving colours in on the back of the work every 3rd

st. In the top leaf motif, the third colour can be brought in only where needed, using just a length of yarn. The tile should have a double thickness throughout, formed from the stranded yarns – if the tiles were not of double thickness then the pieces may be distorted and not square. When joining in or breaking off colours, always leave sufficient lengths for the yarns ends to allow sewing of the tile seams later with matching colours.

Tunic and jacket back and front

Using 5mm needles (or the size to give the correct tension), make 32 main tiles and 4 special tiles as follows:
For the back, 8 each worked from chart A and chart B
For the front, 6 each worked from chart A and chart B, plus one each of the 4 special tiles for the neck shaping, worked from charts B1 to A4)
For the sleeves, 2 each worked from chart A and chart B.

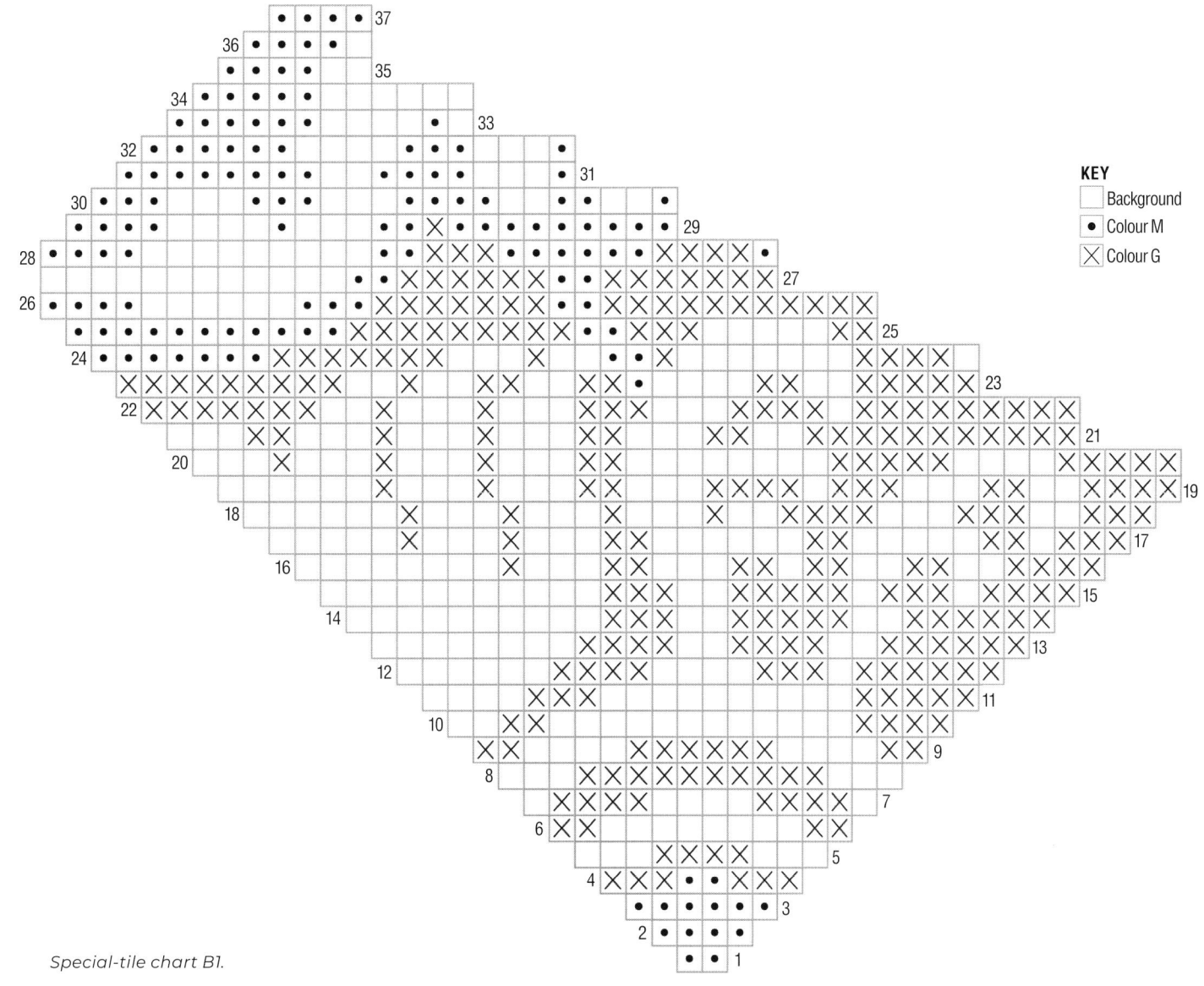

Special-tile chart B1.

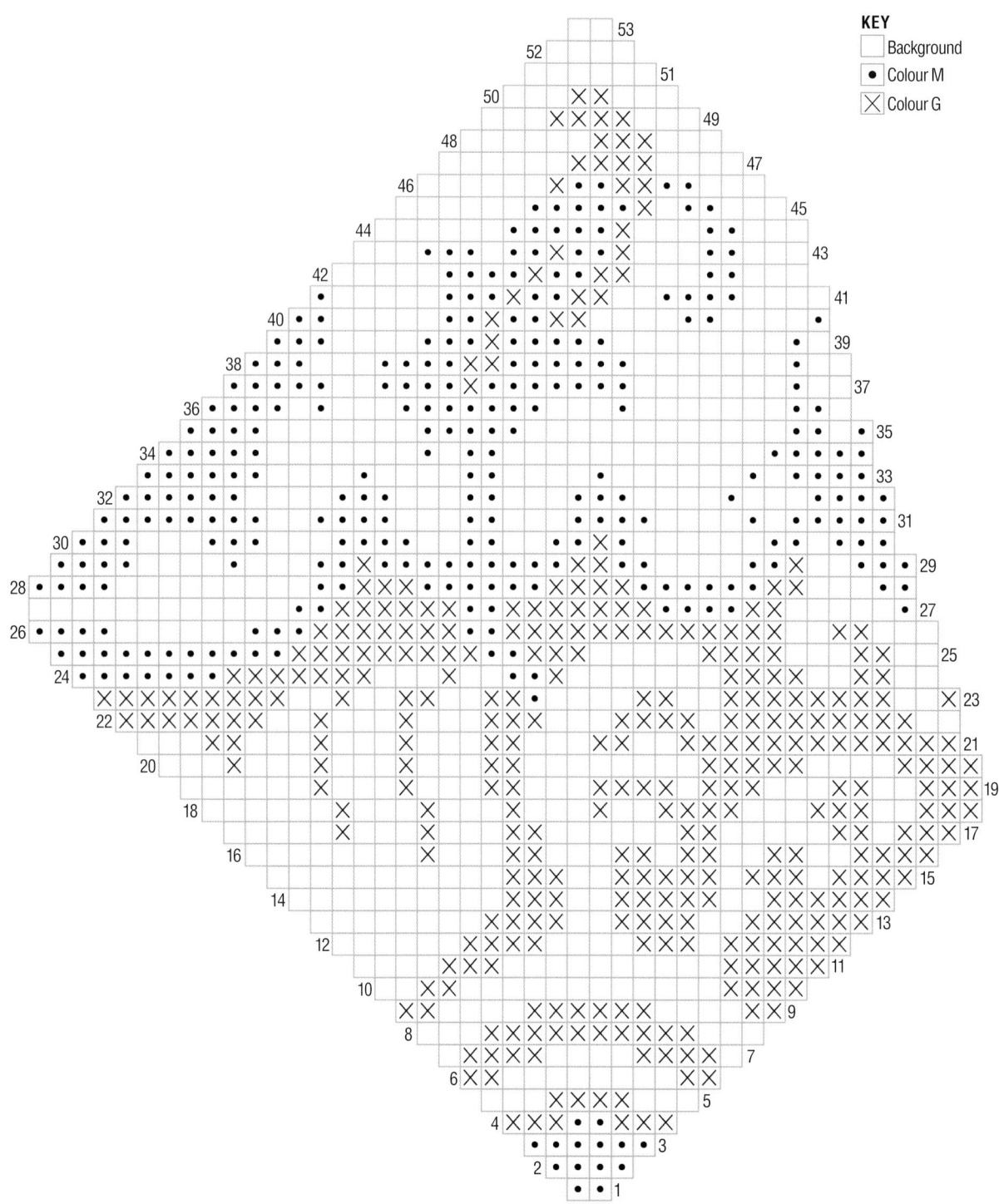

Special-tile chart B2.

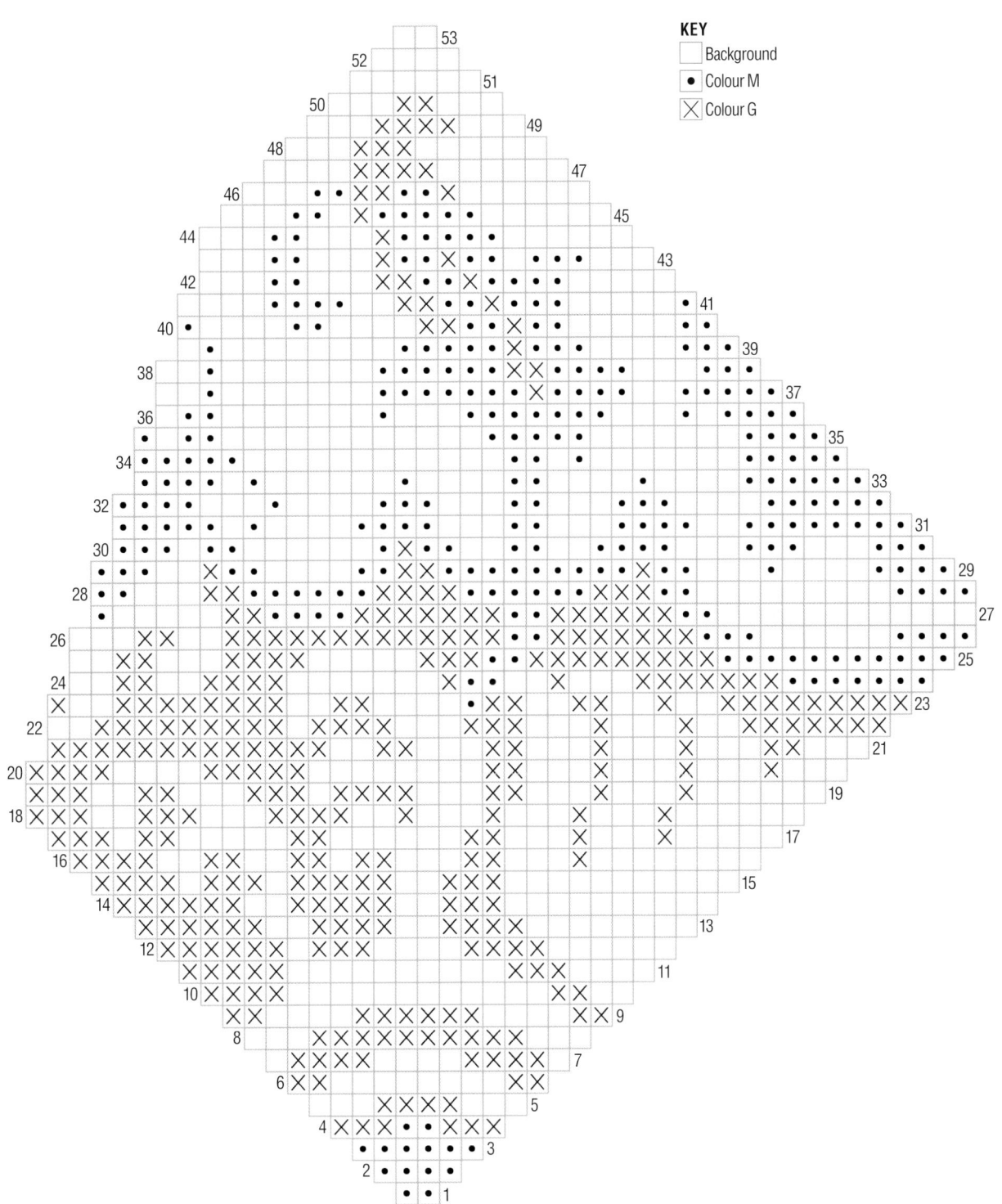

Special-tile chart A3.

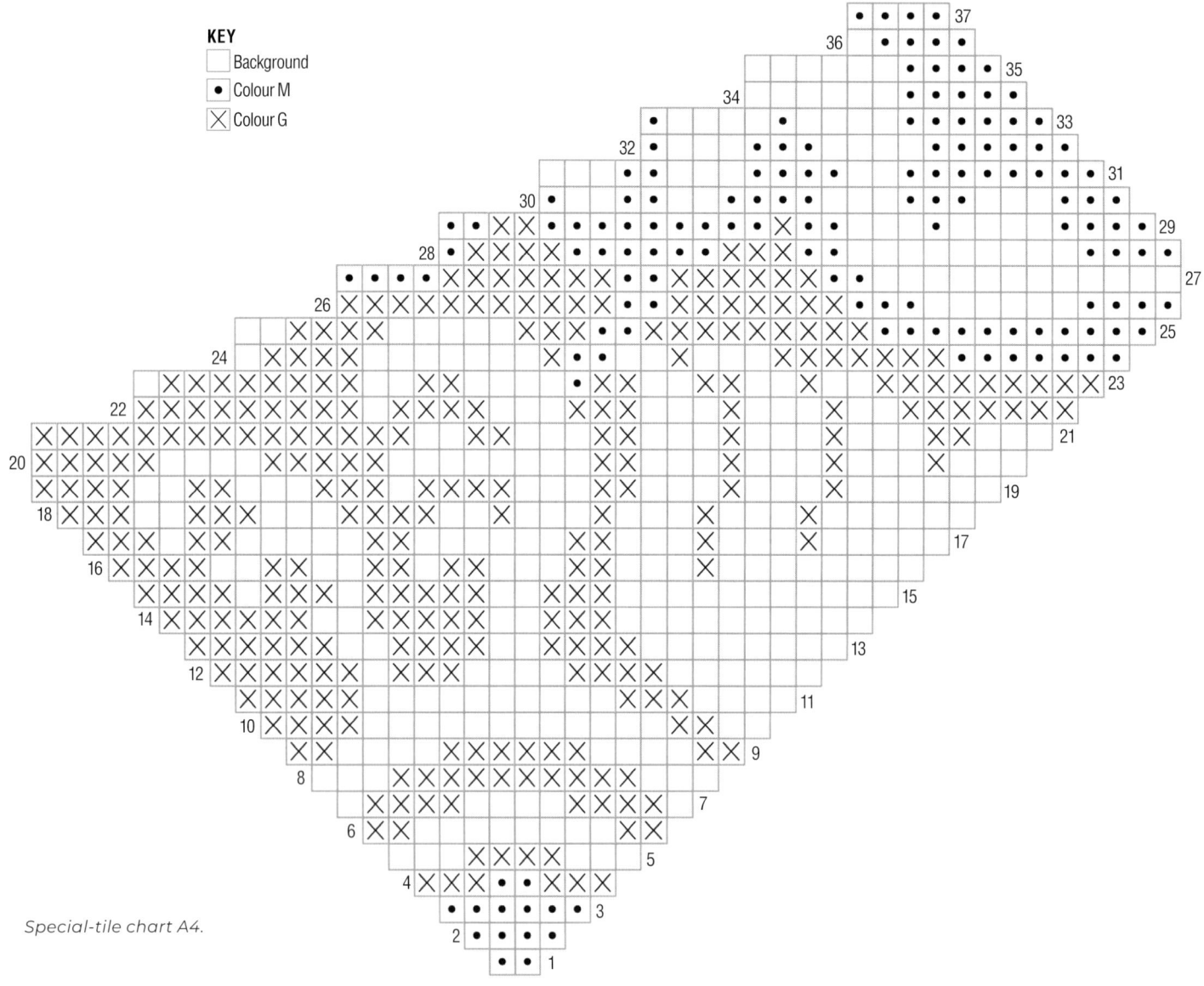

Special-tile chart A4.

Tunic assembly

For the back, arrange the tiles as shown in the layout diagram for the back, ensuring that the tiles are oriented in the direction of the knitting as indicated by the direction of the arrows on the diagram, so that the tiles tessellate to form larger pattern units of four squares, with four larger units making the back as shown.

For the front, the assembly is similar to that of the back, but with the four special tiles forming the V-neck; again ensuring that the tiles are oriented correctly, arrange the tiles as shown in the layout diagram for the front.

Working from the RS of the work, using mattress or ladder stitch, carefully join all of the pieces in the correct layout, taking care to match the patterns across the adjacent tiles. Use the appropriate yarn ends (left from when the ends were cut during the knitting of the tiles) to match the colour of each section of the colourwork pattern to the yarn end used for seaming, to create an almost invisible join between the tiles.

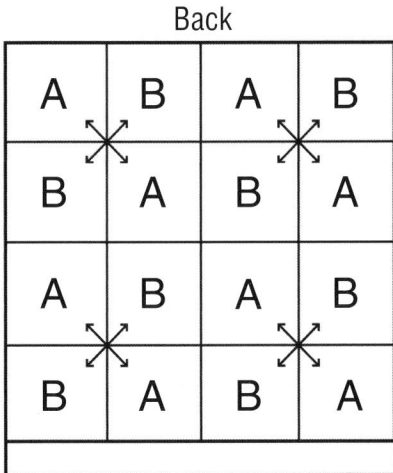

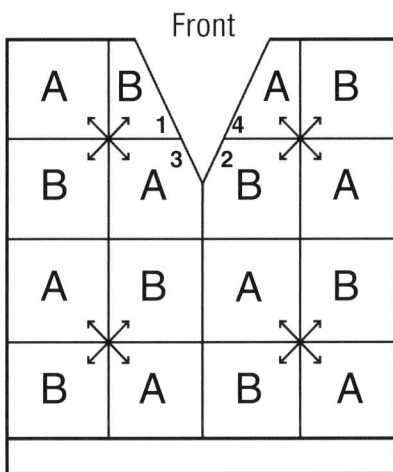

Layout diagram for tunic and jacket front and back. For the cardigan, to create the opening between the right and left cardigan fronts, do not join the three adjoining central pairs of tiles (A3 and B2, B and A, and A and B, from top to bottom).

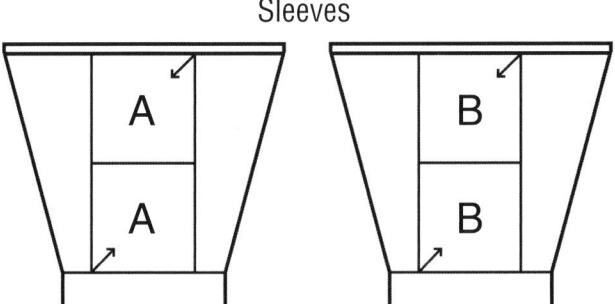

Layout diagram for sleeves.

Four Azulejos-design main tiles, positioned to create a large symmetric motif.

Four Azulejos-design main tiles sewn together.

ORNAMENTAL 207

Four Azulejos-design special tiles to form the V-neck; those for the right-front neckline are already joined, and one of those for the left-front neckline is still in progress and will later be seamed to the other left-front special tile.

Jacket assembly

Follow instructions as for tunic assembly, but leave the front open as two halves as shown on the measurement and layout diagrams.

Jacket and tunic sleeve

The sleeves are constructed from a centre panel, composed of tiles, and two sleeve side panels.

Centre-panel assembly
For each sleeve, join 2 A or B tiles together in the orientations shown in the sleeve layout diagram, to form the sleeve centre panel.

Side panels
Using 4mm needles and N, pick up and knit sts from each side of A-tile-sleeve centre panel as folls:
With RS facing, pick up and knit 66sts (33sts from each tile), and work 6 rows in g st. Purl 1 row, then start working in textured-diamond patt as folls:
Row 1 (RS): K1, (k4, p1, k3) to last st, k1.
Row 2: P1, (p2, k1, p1, k1, p3) to last st, p1.
Row 3: K1, (k2, p1, k3, p1, k1) to last st, k1.
Row 4: P1, (k1, p5, k1, p1) to last st, p1.
Row 5: K1, (p1, k7) to last st, k1.
Row 6: As row 4.
Row 7: As row 3.
Row 8: As row 2.
Rows 1–8 form textured-diamond patt. Cont in patt without shaping for 12 rows, then start to shape sleeve by casting off 4sts at beg of next and every foll alt row until 10sts rem. Cast off. Work the second side as above, but reverse shaping by working one extra row straight before starting shaping.

Sleeve top edge: Using 4.5mm needles and N, with RS facing, pick up and knit approx 115sts across top edge of sleeve, and work 6 rows in g st. Cast off loosely.

Complete B-tile sleeve as for A-tile sleeve.

A side panel of an Azulejos-design sleeve in progress.

The border of an Azulejos-design sleeve in progress.

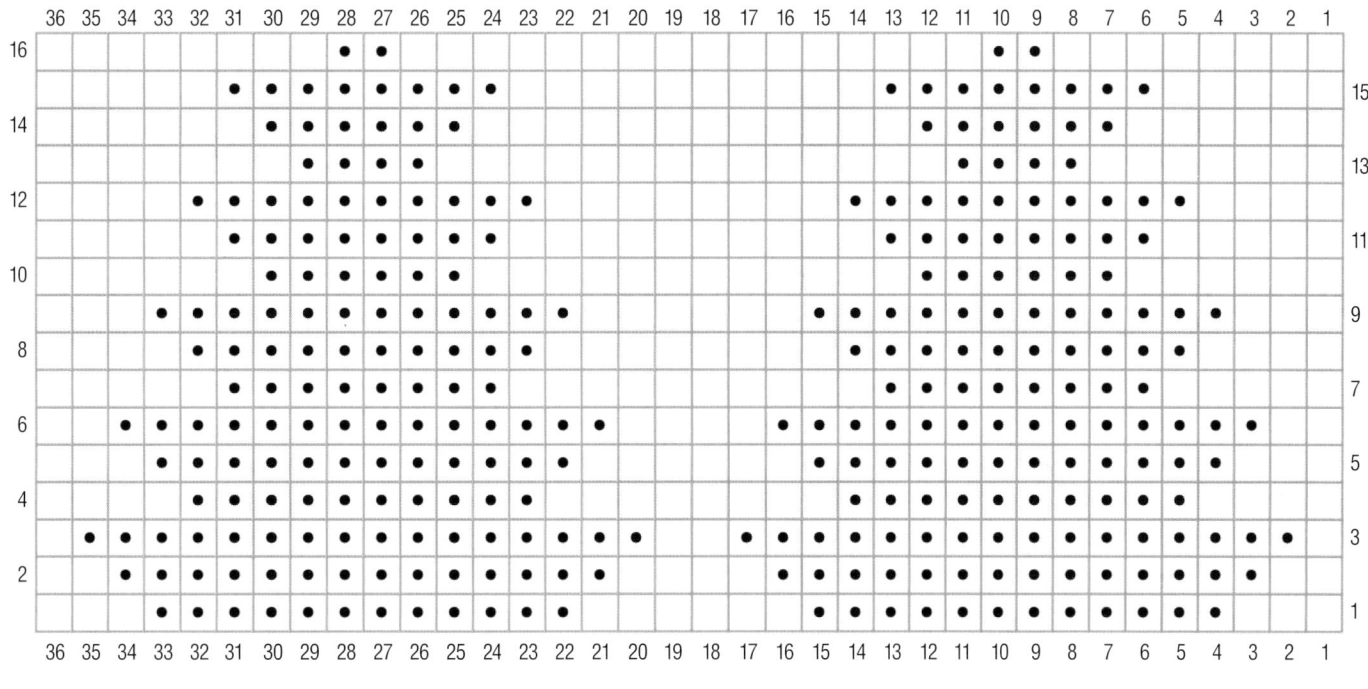

Azulejos border chart.

Tunic patterned edgings

Lower edging

Work for back and front alike.
Using 4.5mm needles and N, with RS facing, pick up and knit 110sts along lower edge of back or front. Change to G, and knit 1 row, to make ridge.
Using N and G as necessary, work two-colour patt from edging chart, starting with a knit row, working as folls:
1 edge st, 6 patt reps, 1 edge st, and, *at the same time*, weave in yarn not in use loosely at the back of the work. Cont until all 16 rows of edging chart are completed.
Using G, purl 1 row, then knit 1 row, to make ridge. Change to 4mm needles, and cont in st st, starting with a knit row, for 17 rows, to make inside of double edging. Cast off loosely.

Cuffs

Using 4.5mm needles and N, with RS facing, pick up and knit 56sts from sleeve bottom edge. Change to G, and knit 1 row, to make ridge, then complete as for lower edging, but working as folls: 1 edge st, 3 patt reps, 1 edge st.

Shoulders: For each front shoulder, using 4mm needles and N, with RS facing, pick up and knit 43sts, and work 6 rows in g st. Cast off.
Using backstitch, join front shoulder to back shoulder.

Neckband

Worked in 2 sections.
Using 4.5mm needles and N, with RS facing, pick up and knit 83sts along left-side garment edge between centre back and centre front. Complete edging as for lower edging, but work as folls: 1 edge st, 4.5 patt reps (with half patt rep positioned at centre back), 1 edge st.

Complete second half of edging as for first half, but pick up and knit 83sts along right-side garment edge between centre back and centre front. Ensure that edging patt will match at centre back, to create a complete patt rep once neckband pieces are seamed.

An alternative colourway, with mid-blue as the highlight colour.

Jacket patterned edgings

Work back lower edging and cuffs as for tunic.

Front lower edgings
Using 4.5mm needles and N, with RS facing, pick up and knit 56sts from each lower front edge, and complete as for lower back edging, but work as folls: 1 edge st, 3 patt reps, 1 edge st.

Shoulders: Work g-st edgings on front shoulders and join shoulders as for tunic.

Front-opening edgings
Worked in 2 sections.
Using 4.5mm circular needle and N, with RS facing, pick up and knit 182sts along left-side garment edge between centre of back neck and ridge at centre of front lower edging. Complete edging as for back lower edging, but work as folls: 1 edge st, 10 patt reps + 1 edge st).

Complete second half of edging as for first half, but pick up and knit 182sts along right-side garment edge between centre of back neck and ridge at centre of front lower edging.

Making up and finishing

Press all pieces, avoiding g-st sections. Darn in all loose ends into seams.
Place a marker in centre of each sleeve top, and position sleeves at shoulders. Using backstitch, join sleeves to body, and sew sleeve seams. Using mattress stitch and with RS facing, sew side seams. Using backstitch, sew all edging seams.
For lower edgings and cuffs, fold plain half to inside of garment and slip st edge into position on WS.
For tunic neckband, overlap ends at centre front, and neatly sew both ends into position.
For jacket front edgings, slip st lower ends together along edges.
Give a final press to seams and edgings, again avoiding g-st sections.

The Azulejos tunic featured in Cosmopolitan *magazine in January 1990 as a Sandy Black knitting kit.*

A light colourway of the Medieval Tile design, with one each of the four half motifs present on the tile sides.

An alternative dark colourway of the Medieval Tile design.

Design Variation

The Medieval Tile sweater design was created in a similar manner to that of the Azulejos design, by using just one main tile in different orientations in order to match the motifs across tiles. It is featured here in two colourways: dark and light.

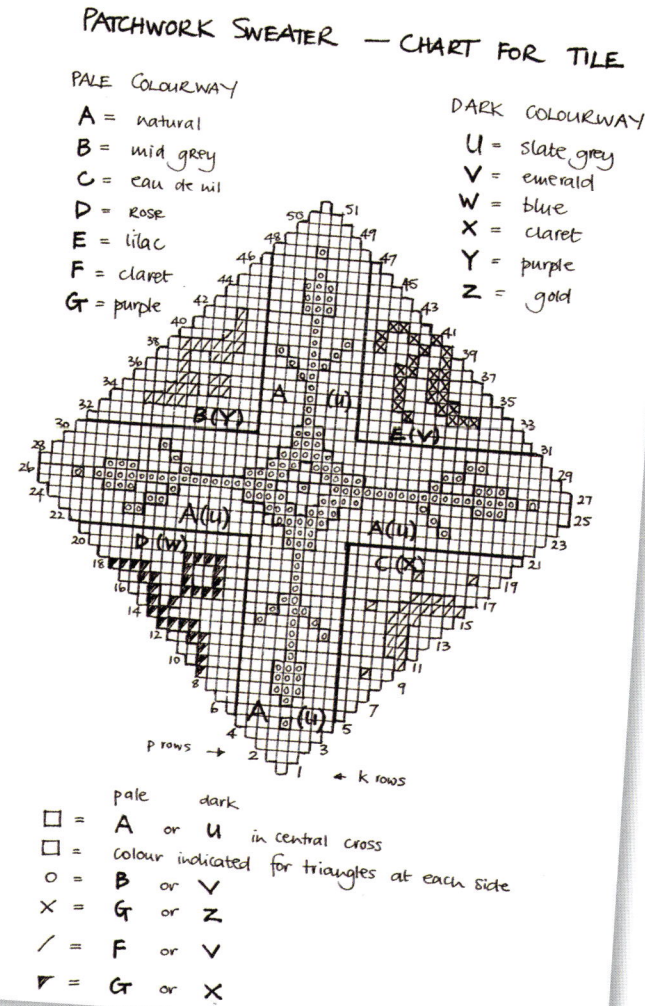

The original hand-drawn chart for the Medieval Tile design.

ORNAMENTAL 211

Rosette Tunic

The Rosette tunic, reknitted in contemporary yarns in a range of soft colours of wool and mohair-blend yarns. (Photo: Jo Teasdale)

The original Rosette sweater, knitted in subdued but rich colours in wool and in angora contrast-colour yarns, with additional colour highlights Swiss darned into the rosette circles. (Photo: David McIntyre)

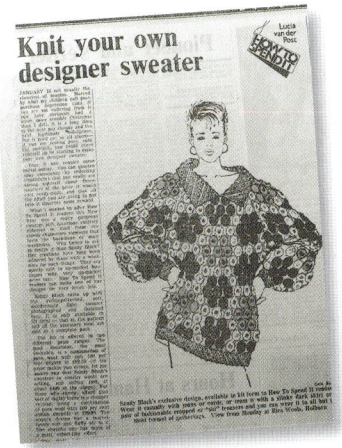

A press cutting from the Financial Times 'How To Spend It' section in January 1986, with an exclusive Rosette-sweater knitting-kit special offer.

A promotional photograph romantically styled for the Design Studio Autumn/Winter 1985 brochure, featuring work from a group of British fashion and knitwear designers showing our collections at the British Designers Show fashion trade fair in London. (Photo: Michael Woolley)

This generously sized, long-line tunic is knitted in stocking stitch and combines two yarn types: one plain, for the background, and one more textured, for the colourwork pattern. To complement the patterning, the collar and edgings are knitted in diagonal rib with main yarn. The sleeve styling is unusual, creating a rounded, full shape. The all-over pattern of identical small circles is coloured to form hexagonal rosettes, each surrounded by circles of the main contrast colour. The circles pattern is easy to learn, so the focus can be on working the colour arrangement. Have fun mixing your own colours and yarns, or, if preferred, the design can be knitted with just one contrast yarn and colour, for a bold effect and simpler knitting.

This original version of the design was featured in a January 1986 issue of the *Financial Times* in the 'How to Spend It' section (which is still going strong today) and was knitted in either wool and angora yarns or wool and chenille yarns. This version is knitted in lighter-weight wool and mohair yarns, giving more drape and a longer-line silhouette.

Size and measurements

One size to fit up to a 102cm/40in bust circumference

Knitted measurements

All-round circumference at underarms: 108cm/42½in
Length: 79cm/31in
Sleeve length: 66cm/26in

Materials

Yarn

Several yarn combinations can be used, such as a light-aran-weight-wool or tweed yarn for the background and a mohair or other textured yarn for the circles pattern. This example was knitted in Rowan Kid Classic, a blend of wool, mohair and nylon, for the main yarn, together with Rowan Kidsilk Haze, a mohair–silk-blend yarn, used double throughout, for the circles pattern, in colours as folls:

Main colour (MC): 11 × 50g balls of Rowan Kid Classic in grey green (890 Cement)

Contrast colours:

Main contrast: 5 × 25g balls of Rowan Kidsilk Haze in mulberry (679 Mulberry)

Other **contrast colours:** 2 × 25g balls each of Rowan Kidsilk Haze in pink, rose, lilac and green (606 Candy Girl, 583 Blushes, 600 Dewberry and 582 Trance, respectively)

Recommended needles and accessories

Two pairs of needles are required: one pair of the size to give the correct tension, for main parts, and one pair of three sizes smaller, for edgings.
1 pair 5mm (UK 6, US 8) needles for main parts
1 pair 3.5mm (UK 9, US 4) needles for edgings
Stitch holder

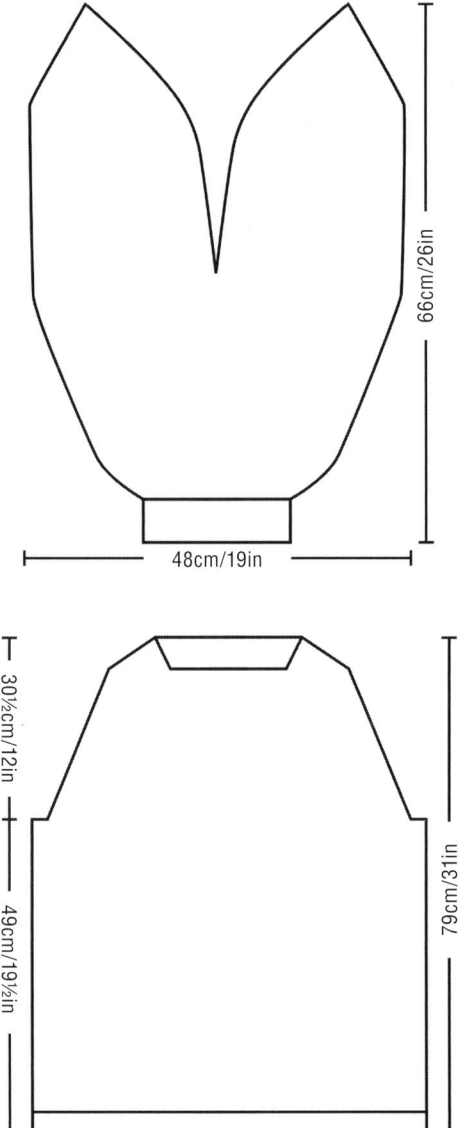

Measurement diagram.

Tension

24sts and 22 rows to 10cm/4in, measured over circles patt, using 5mm (UK 6, US 8) needles or the size required to give the correct tension and therefore measurements.

To avoid disappointment, it is essential to check your tension carefully before commencing the knitting of the garment and to use the needles that give you the correct tension. These needles may not be of the needle size quoted in the standard tension information, as each knitter knits differently.

How to check tension

Read the notes on working the pattern. Using the recommended needles and MC, cast on 28sts, and, joining in colours as required, work a section from chart for back as folls:

Starting from row 1 with a knit row, work from the 1st st to the 32nd st on knit rows and the 32nd st to the 1st st on purl rows, until row 28 is completed. Cast off loosely. Pin the knitted swatch square down flat, without stretching the fabric. Place a pin between 2sts near the left side of the swatch, count

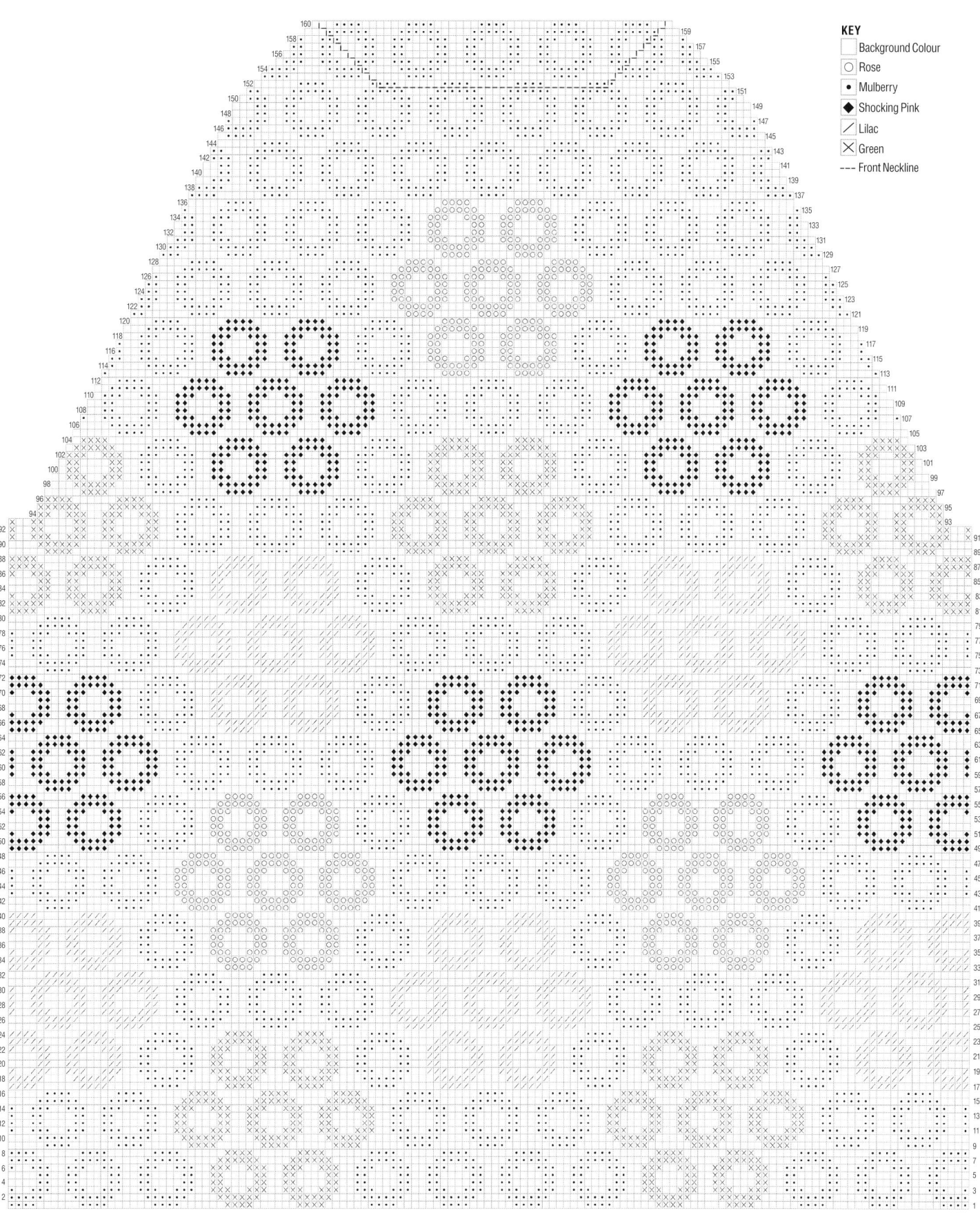

ORNAMENTAL 215

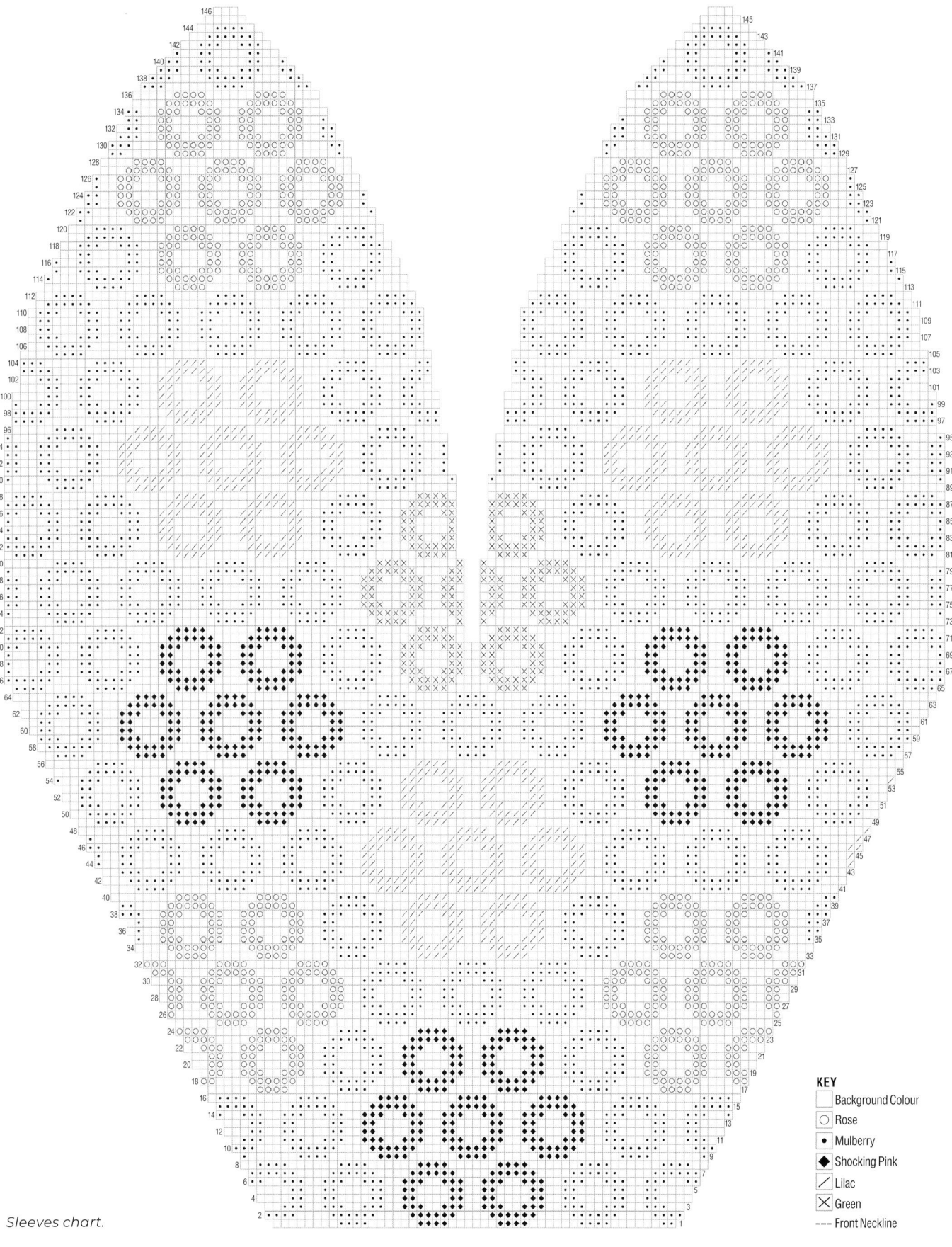

Sleeves chart.

216 ORNAMENTAL

24sts across to the right, and place another pin between the 24th and 25th sts. Mark out 22 rows in the same manner, starting from 2sts near the top of the swatch. Measure the distance between each pair of pins. The measurements should both be 10cm/4in. If a measurement is less than 10cm/4in, your knitting is too tight – try using needles of one size larger size to reknit the swatch, and again check the tension. If a measurement is more than 10cm/4in, your knitting is too loose – try using needles of one size smaller to reknit the swatch, and again check the tension. Repeat the process until the correct tension is achieved. Do not be afraid to go up or down by more than one size from the recommended needles to achieve the required tension. Adjust the size of the smaller pair of needles for edgings accordingly.

Pattern

Notes on working the pattern

- One square of the chart represents one knitted stitch. Odd-numbered rows (RS) are read from right to left and the corresponding stitches are to be knitted; even-numbered rows (WS) are read from left to right and the corresponding stitches are to be purled.
- Use 1 ball of background (MC) yarn across each row, but use separate balls of contrast-colour yarns for each coloured rosette of 7 circles and also for the circles of main-contrast-colour yarn between rosettes. Do not strand the background yarn across more than 4sts, and do not strand contrast-colour yarns between the rosettes.
- Cross yarns by picking up the new yarn from under the previous one when changing yarn colours, to link the colours and prevent holes appearing in the knitting. Take care not to pull the yarn strands at the back of the work too tight, as too-tight strands will distort the knitting. To minimize tangling, wind bobbins (made from card) for contrast-colour yarns, and allow these to hang close to the needle, and unravel just a short amount at a time as required.

Back

Using the smaller needles and MC, cast on 126sts, and work in diagonal rib as folls:
Row 1: (K3, p3) to end.
Row 2: (K2, p3, k1) to end.

Close-up of the colour pattern for the sleeves.

Row 3: (P2, k3, p1) to end.
Row 4: (P3, k3) to end.
Row 5: (K1, p3, k2) to end.
Row 6: (P1, k3, p2) to end.
Rep rows 1–6 twice or work until edging measures 5cm/2in, ending with a WS row, and, *at the same time*, inc 8sts across final row by working into front and back of 1st st and every foll 18th st (6 ribs) to last st, then inc 1 st. (134sts)
Change to the larger needles, and beg working circles patt from chart for back at row 1, starting with a knit row, and joining in contrast cols as required. Work straight until row 92 of chart is completed.

Shape raglan: Keeping continuity of patt correct, cast off 4sts beg next 2 rows, then work 1 row. Dec 1 st at each end of next and every foll 2nd row until there are 72sts (row 148 completed). *
Work 1 row. Dec at each end of next and every foll row until 50sts rem. Cast off loosely.

Front

Work as for back to * (ending with WS row). Work 1 row. Dec 1 st at each end of next row. (70sts)

Divide for neck (row 151, RS facing): K2tog and patt 18sts, leaving rem sts on st holder.
Turn, cont in patt, and, *at the same time*, dec 1 st at each end of every foll row until 1 st rem. Fasten off this last st. With RS facing, place sts on st holder on to LH needle. Join yarn to inside edge, cast off 30sts for front neck, patt to last 2sts, then k2tog. Turn, and complete shaping to mirror that of first side.

Sleeves

Using smaller needles and MC, cast on 46sts, and work in diagonal rib as for back, and, *at the same time*, inc 4sts evenly across the last row to 50sts. Change to the larger needles, and beg working circles patt from chart for sleeves, starting from row 1 of chart with a knit row, joining in contrast cols as required, and, *at the same time*, shape sleeve by inc 1 st at each side of next and every foll 2nd row until there are 116sts. Work 4 rows straight (70 rows of chart completed).

Divide for sleeve top: Work 56sts in patt, k2tog and turn, leaving rem 58sts on a st holder. Cont shaping centre edge of sleeve top by dec 1 st at beg of foll 10th row twice more (55sts). Patt 4 rows straight, then start to shape both centre and outer edges of sleeve top.
Dec 1 st at each end of next and every foll 5th row three times until there are 47sts (row 111 completed).
Now, cont shaping by dec 1st at each end of every foll 2nd row until row 136 is completed (23sts). Then, dec 1 st at each end of every row until 3sts rem. Cast off.

Return to 58sts on st holder, join yarn to inside edge, and, cont to follow chart for sleeves, complete second side of sleeve top to mirror first side.

Collar

Using the smaller needles and MC, cast on 132sts, and work collar in diagonal rib as for back. Work straight until collar measures 14cm/5½in. Cast off loosely in rib.

Finishing

Darn in all loose ends carefully, closing up any gaps in the fabric *at the same time*. Lightly steam each piece to shape, avoiding edgings. Using backstitch, sew centre sleeve seams then raglan seams. Sew side and sleeve seams. Using a flat oversewn seam, working from WS, join collar to neck, with opening at centre front.

Colour and Yarn Variations

Many variations of this garment can be created through the choice of yarn textures and colours, giving distinctive results, as shown in the swatches and original photograph of the alternative purple colourway. A simper knitting option would be to knit in two colours and fill in the centres of the circles with highlight colours as desired after the knitting is completed.

An alternative colourway in reds and oranges, knitted using Rowan Kid Classic for the background and Wool and the Gang Take Care Mohair yarn for the colourwork pattern, giving a firmer fabric.

The Rosette-tunic circles pattern worked with two colours, knitted using Rowan Hemp Tweed for the background and Rowan Kid Classic for the circles.

The Rosette-tunic circles pattern worked with two colours, knitted using Rowan Felted Tweed Aran for the background (dark grey) and Rowan Kid Classic for the circles (light grey).

The Rosette-tunic circles pattern worked with two colours, knitted using Rowan Felted Tweed Aran for the background (dark grey) and Wool and the Gang Take Care Mohair for the circles (orange).

An original alternative Rosette-sweater colourway, with a purple tweed-wool yarn for the background, fuchsia angora yarn as the main contrast and dark rosettes highlighted with Swiss-darned bright colours. (Photo: David McIntyre)

Shawl Cardigan

*The trompe l'œil Shawl cardigan is both great fun to knit, combining colourwork knitting with simple cables, and fun to wear, complete with its tassels.
(Photo: Jo Teasdale)*

RIGHT: All of the scattered flowers and some details of the Shawl border are embroidered after the knitting is completed, to streamline the knitting process. (Photo: Jo Teasdale)

This unusual cardigan is designed to give the *trompe l'œil* effect of a large shawl with a decorative border, complete with tassels for added emphasis, being worn over a sweater, and it is great fun to wear. Although twelve colours are used, the knitting is not as difficult as it may seem, because some of the detail giving extra richness to the finished design is embroidered after the knitting is completed.

The lower half of the cardigan is worked in a simple cabled rib, which gradually changes to the flower border pattern, and this in turn blends into the shawl itself, which is simply knitted in plain stocking stitch – all of the scattered flowers are embroidered later. The flower border is the most intricate part of the knitting, but this is worked from a clear colour chart that gives a picture of the work as it progresses. Importantly, the colourwork knitting never forms more than a section of each row at any stage. To streamline the making up, the garter-stitch front bands and collar are knitted together with the front panels of the cardigan.

Size and measurements

One generous size to comfortably fit up to a 102cm/40in bust circumference

Knitted measurements
All-round circumference at underarms: 127cm/50in
Length: 71cm/28in
Sleeve length: 48cm/19in

Materials

Yarn
The following colours are suggestions – other colours can be substituted as desired, for example, for the flowers. The original yarns used were Rowan Designer Double Knitting pure-wool yarn and Rowan Fleck wool–cotton-blend yarn, in a combination of 12 colours. Current Rowan double-knitting wool and alpaca yarn equivalents range from 125m–200m/50g and include Felted Tweed DK and Alpaca Soft DK. A variety of double-knitting yarns are also available that would be compatible to use together. The flower border is also an opportunity to use up some oddments of different yarn colours.

Knitted in 100-per-cent-wool double-knitting yarn in 12 colours as folls:
9 × 50g balls in stone (lower cable panels)
6 × 50g balls in dark grey or navy (shawl)
3 × 50g balls in maroon (border background)
1 × 50g ball each in red, lilac, teal, light blue, purple, gold, blue/green, olive and light olive (paisley and flower border)

Recommended needles and accessories
Two pairs of needles are required: one pair of the size to give the correct tension, for main parts, and one pair of three sizes smaller, for ribbing.
1 pair 4mm (UK 8, US 6) needles for main parts (lower cable panels, border and upper shawl)
1 pair 3.25mm (UK 10, US 3) needles for ribbing
Stitch holder or spare needle
Large-eyed wool needle
6 buttons

ORNAMENTAL 221

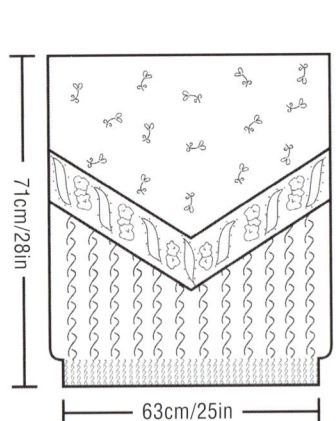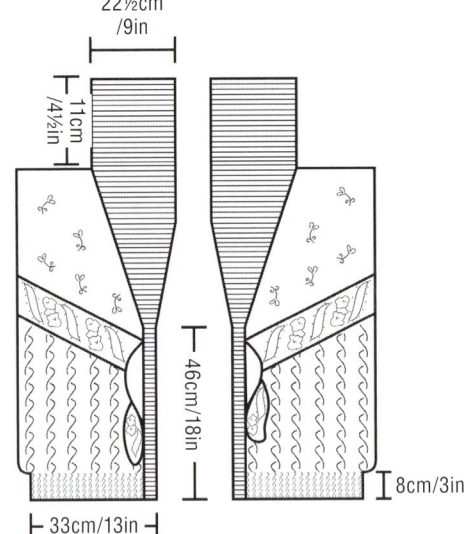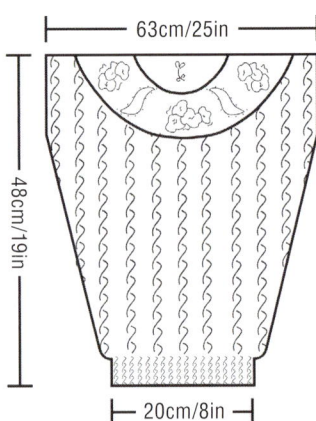

Measurement diagram.

A detail of the overall design, showing the lower cables, border of paisley and flower motifs, and upper embroidered flowers.

Tension

26sts and 28 rows to 10cm/4in, measured over cable patt, using 4mm (UK 8, US 5) needles or the size required to give the correct tension and therefore measurements.

24sts and 32 rows to 10cm/4in, measured over st st, using 4mm (UK 8, US 5) needles or those of the size required to give the correct tension and therefore measurements.

To avoid disappointment, it is essential to check your tension carefully before commencing the knitting of the garment and to use the needles that give you the correct tension. These needles may not be of the needle size quoted in the standard tension information, as each knitter knits differently.

How to check tension

Using 4mm needles and stone, cast on 32sts, and work as folls:
Row 1 (RS): P8, (k4, p8) to end.
Row 2 and all WS rows: K8, (p4, k8) to end.
Row 3: As row 1.
Row 5: P8, (c4b, p8) to end.
Rep rows 1–6 until work measures 15cm/6in, ending with WS row 2. Cast off. Pin the knitted swatch square down flat, without stretching the fabric. Place a pin between 2sts near the left side of the swatch, count 26 sts across to the right, and place another pin between the 24th and 25th sts. Mark out 28 rows in the same manner, starting from 2sts near the top of the swatch. Measure the distance between each pair of pins. The measurements should both be 10cm/4in. If a measurement is less than 10cm/4in, your knitting is

too tight – try using needles of one size larger to reknit the swatch, and again check the tension; if a measurement is more than 10cm/4in, your knitting is too loose – try using needles of one size smaller to reknit the swatch, and again check the tension. Repeat this process until the correct tension is achieved. Do not be afraid to go up or down by more than one size from the recommended needles to achieve the required tension. Adjust the size of the smaller pair of needles for edgings accordingly.

Abbreviations and special stitches

c4b = cable 4sts back: slip next 2sts on to cable needle and leave it at back of work, k2, then k2 from cable needle.
k2tog-tbl = knit next 2sts together through the back loops
m1 = make 1 st: pick up strand of yarn running between st closest to LH-needle point and st closest to RH-needle point so that the yarn passes over LH-needle point from front to back and then knit into back of strand.
p2tog-tbl = purl next 2sts together through the back loops
tw2 = twist 2sts: knit into front of 2nd st on LH needle, knit into front of 1st st on LH needle, then allow both knitted-into sts to slip off LH needle together.

Pattern

Notes on working the pattern
- One square of the chart represents one knitted stitch. When working the charts for the back, fronts and right sleeve, odd-numbered rows are read from right to left and the corresponding stitches are to be knitted; even-numbered rows are read from left to right and the corresponding stitches are to be purled. When working the chart for the left sleeve only, the chart is reversed as folls: odd-numbered rows are to be knitted but read from left to right; even-numbered rows are to be purled but read from right to left.
- When starting to work the Shawl border pattern, use separate balls of stone and maroon for each area of colour, and cross yarns by picking up the new yarn from under the previous one when changing yarn colours, to link the colours and prevent holes appearing in the knitting.
- Maintain the continuity of the cable pattern throughout.
- When working the Shawl border pattern, use smaller lengths of contrast-colour yarns for the paisley, flower and leaf motifs, but strand the maroon yarn for the border background loosely across back of the knitting over no more than 5sts; where 5sts or more need to be spanned, weave in the yarn not in use on the back of the work.
- Use two separate lengths of dark-grey yarn for each side of the paisley-motif outline, crossing the yarns when changing colours as above. Knit the main areas of colour within the motifs, but leaving the smaller details such as the dotted paisley outlines and the centres of the flowers to be Swiss darned on to the knitting during making up.
- For the Shawl border motifs, use short lengths of yarn, rather than balls or bobbins: yarn of about 60cm/23½in long should be enough to knit a flower, 75cm/29½in should be enough to knit the centre of a paisley motif, and smaller lengths of 12cm/4¾in should be enough to knit a leaf motif. Using these short lengths of yarn will avoid excessive tangling of yarns when knitting the Shawl border, as short lengths can be pulled free from any other yarn lengths, leaving larger balls of only stone, maroon and dark-grey yarn to manage. Whenever starting or ending an area of colour, always leave a long enough yarn end to sew in during making up.
- Try working a practice swatch by knitting a small area of the back chart that has some cable pattern and border pattern, and remember that the techniques involved are much easier than they might sound!

Back

Using the smaller needles and stone, cast on 146 sts, and work in twisted rib as folls:
Row 1 (RS): P2, (tw2, p2) to end.
Row 2: K2, (p2, k2) to end.
Row 3: P2, (k2, p2) to end.
Row 4: As row 2.
Rep rows 1–4 5 times, and, *at the same time*, inc 1 st at each end of last row. (148sts)

Change to the larger needles, and work in cable patt as folls:
Row 1 (RS): P6, (k4, p8) to last 10 sts, k4, p5.
Row 2 and all WS rows: K5, (p4, k8) to last 10sts, p4, k6.
Row 3: P6, (c4b, p8) to last 10sts, c4b, p6.
Row 5: As row 1.
Row 6: As row 2.
Rep rows 1–6 until work measures 22.5cm/9in, ending with a WS row.

Back chart.

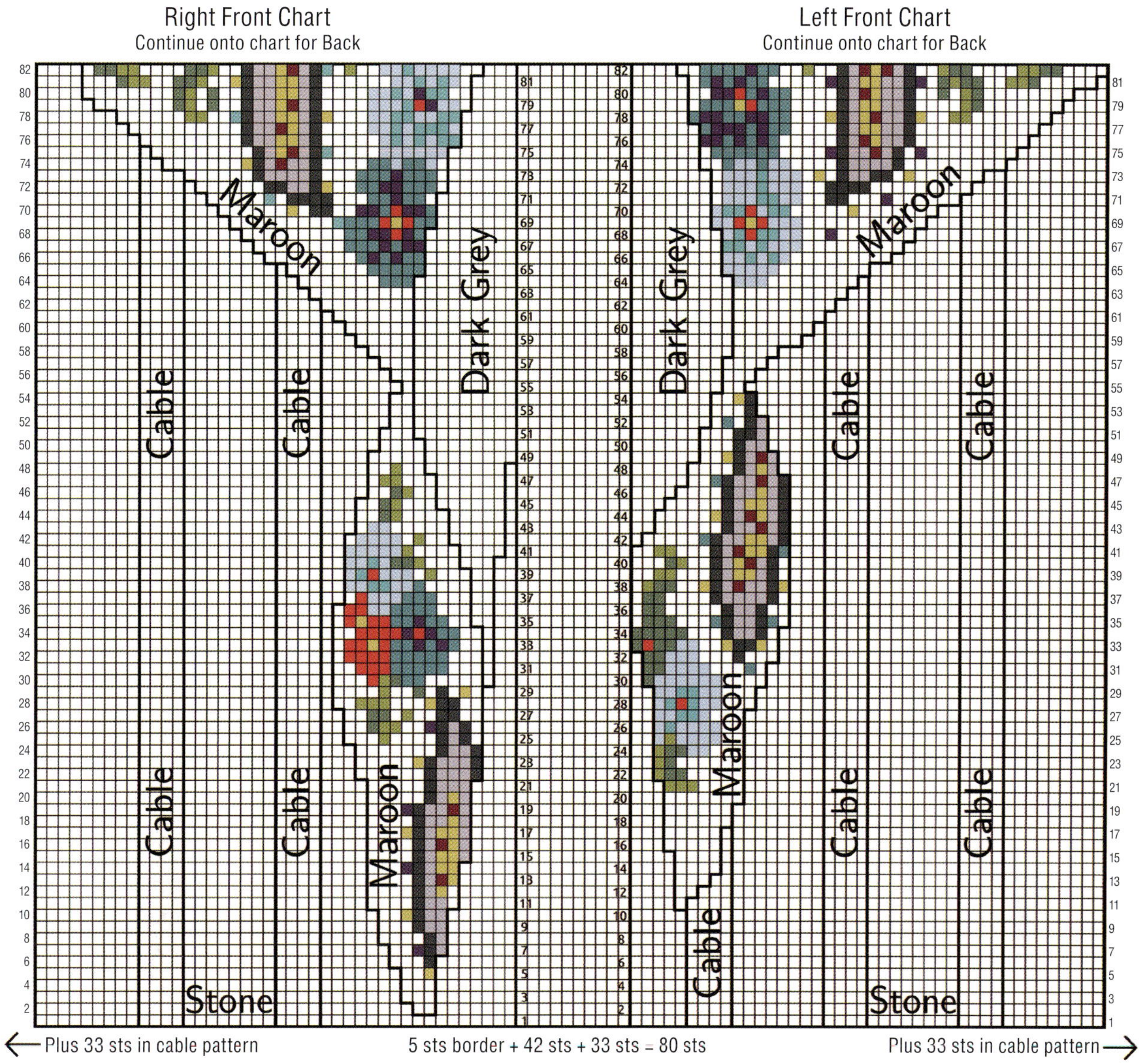

Fronts chart.

KEY

- ☐ Background Colour
- ■ Red
- ■ Gold
- ■ Light Olive
- ■ Olive
- ■ Lilac
- ■ Light Blue
- ■ Purple
- ■ Blue/Green
- ■ Maroon
- ■ Dark Grey
- ■ Teal

Key for colours.

Now, beg working from back chart at row 1, starting with a RS row, as folls:

Rows 1–2: Work these rows as a continuation of cable patt.

Row 3: Patt 74sts as continuation of cable patt, join in maroon and k1, join in another ball of stone, and work 73sts in cable patt.

Row 4: Patt 71sts in cable patt, p5 using maroon, patt 72sts in cable patt.

Joining in cols for border and main upper part of shawl as required, cont working from back chart, keeping cable patt correct at each side of border until row 73 and cable patt is

ORNAMENTAL 225

completed. Cont in colourwork patt until row 111 and Shawl border is completed. Cont in st st using dark grey only until work measures 71cm/28in, ending with a WS row.

Shape shoulders: Cast off 51sts at beg of next 2 rows. Cast off rem 46sts.

Right front

Using the smaller needles and stone, cast on 79sts. Work in twisted rib as folls, noting that the g-st front buttonhole band of 5sts is worked *at the same time*.
Row 1 (RS): K5, p2, (tw2, p2) to end.
Row 2: (K2, p2) to last 7sts, k7.
Row 3: K2, cast off 2sts, k1, p2, (k2, p2) to end.
Row 4: As row 2, but cast on 2sts to cover the gap where 2sts were cast off on row 3, to complete 1st buttonhole.
Rep rows 1–4 5 times but omitting buttonholes, then work rows 1–2 rows again. Rep working buttonhole rows 3–4, for 2nd buttonhole, and, *at the same time*, inc 1 st at beg of last row (80sts).
Change to the larger needles, and work in cable patt as folls:
Row 1 (RS): K5, p5, (k4, p8) to last 10sts, k4, p6.
Row 2 and all WS rows: K6, (p4, k8) to last 14sts, p4, k10.
Row 3: K5, p5, (c4b, p8) to last 10sts, c4b, p6.
Row 5: As row 1.
Row 6: As row 2.
Work 4 rows more in cable patt as set, ending with a WS row. Now, beg working from right-front chart at row 1, starting with a RS row and joining in contrast cols as required. Note that chart shows only the first 42sts of the right front: work the rem 33sts in cable patt as set. Cont in patt, keeping g-st border correct, and, *at the same time*, work 2-row buttonholes as previously on every foll 23rd and 24th rows, counting from 1st row worked with the larger needles (so that 3rd buttonhole is worked over rows 13–14 of right-front chart), until 6 buttonholes have been worked in total, and, note, at row 48 of right-front chart, change colour of g-st border to dark grey to match background col with that of upper shawl. Cont in patt until row 82 is completed.
Keeping continuity of border patt as set, now cont working patt from left half of back chart, beg with row 37.
Cont in patt until row 60 of back chart is completed and 6 buttonholes have been worked.

Shape collar and neckline: Work as folls:
Row 1 (RS): K1, m1, k4, m1, k1, k2tog-tbl, patt to end.
Row 2: Patt to last 7sts, k7.
Row 3: K7, patt to end.
Row 4: Patt to last 10sts, p2tog-tbl, p1, m1, k6, m1, k1.
Row 5: K9, patt to end.
Row 6: Patt to last 9sts, k9.
Row 7: k1, m1, k8, m1, k1, k2tog-tbl, patt to end.
Row 8: Patt to last 11 sts, k11.
Row 9: K11, patt to end.
Row 10: Patt to last 14sts, p2tog-tbl, p1, m1, k10, m1, k1.
Row 11: K13, patt to end.
Cont in this way, keeping continuity of patt correct, dec for neckline every 3rd row and, *at the same time*, inc to shape collar as set until Shawl border patt is completed. Cont using dark grey only, shaping collar until there are 47sts in g-st collar. Now, keeping collar edge straight, cont to dec front edge on every 3rd row at inside edge of collar until 51sts rem in st st, with 98sts in total.

Cont straight until work measures same as back to shoulder length (noting that there will be fewer rows worked in dark grey), ending with a RS row (However, note, for left front, work one extra row here, to end with WS row). Cast off 51sts at beg of next row (47sts rem).
Work 11cm/4½in in g st on rem 47sts for back of collar. Leave these sts on a st holder or spare needle.

Left front

Using the smaller needles and stone, cast on 79sts. Work in twisted rib as folls:
Row 1 (RS): P2, (tw2, p2) to last 5sts, k5.
Row 2: K7, (p2, k2) to end.
Row 3: P2, (k2, p2) to last 5sts, k5.
Row 4: As row 2.

Rep rows 1–4 6 times, and, *at the same time*, inc 1 st at end of last row (80sts).
Change to the larger needles, and work in cable patt as folls:
Row 1 (RS): P6, (k4, p8) to last 14sts, k4, p5, k5.
Row 2 and all WS rows: K10, (p4, k8) to last 10sts, p4, k6.
Row 3: P6, (c4b, p8) to last 14sts, c4b, p5, k5.
Row 5: As row 1.
Row 6: As row 2.

Work 4 rows more in cable patt.

Now, work as given for right front, but by foll left-front chart and omitting all buttonholes. When row 82 of left-front chart is completed, cont working patt from right half of back chart, beg with row 37, until row 60 is completed.

Shape collar and neckline: Work as folls:
Row 1 (RS): Patt to last 8sts, k2tog, k1, m1, k4, m1, k1.
Row 2: K7, patt to end.
Row 3: Patt to last 7sts, k7.
Row 4: K1, m1, k6, m1, p1, p2tog, patt to end.
Row 5: Patt to last 9sts, k9.
Row 6: K9, patt to end.
Complete as for right front, shaping collar as set and note that 1 extra row is worked at the end, before casting off for shoulder.

Sleeves

Note that in order to match both front and back borders, which finish at slightly different levels, the sleeve patterning is not symmetrical, so right and left sleeves are mirror images of each other. This is achieved by following the same chart, but reversing the usual direction of reading each row for the left sleeve only, so RS rows are read left to right and WS rows read right to left.

Right sleeve

Using the smaller needles and stone, cast on 58sts.
Work rows 1–4 of twisted rib as given for back 7 times, and, *at the same time*, inc 1 st at each end of last row. (60sts)
Change to the larger needles, and work in cable patt as folls:
Row 1 (RS): P4, (k4, p8) to last 8sts, k4, p4.
Row 2: K4, (p4, k8) to last 8sts, p4, k4.
Row 3: Inc 1 st in first purl st, p3, (c4b, p8) to last 8sts, c4b, p3, inc 1 st in last purl st. (62sts)
Cont in patt as now set, cabling every foll 6th row, and, *at the same time*, inc 1 st at each end of every foll 3rd row until there are 116sts. **
Beg working from sleeve chart at row 1, starting with a RS row, and, *at the same time*, cont to inc at each end of every 3rd row until there are 136sts. Cont working from chart until row 42 is completed. Cast off.

Left sleeve

Work as for right sleeve to **.
Beg working from sleeve chart at row 1, starting with a RS row, but reverse patt by reading all RS rows from left to right and WS rows from right to left.

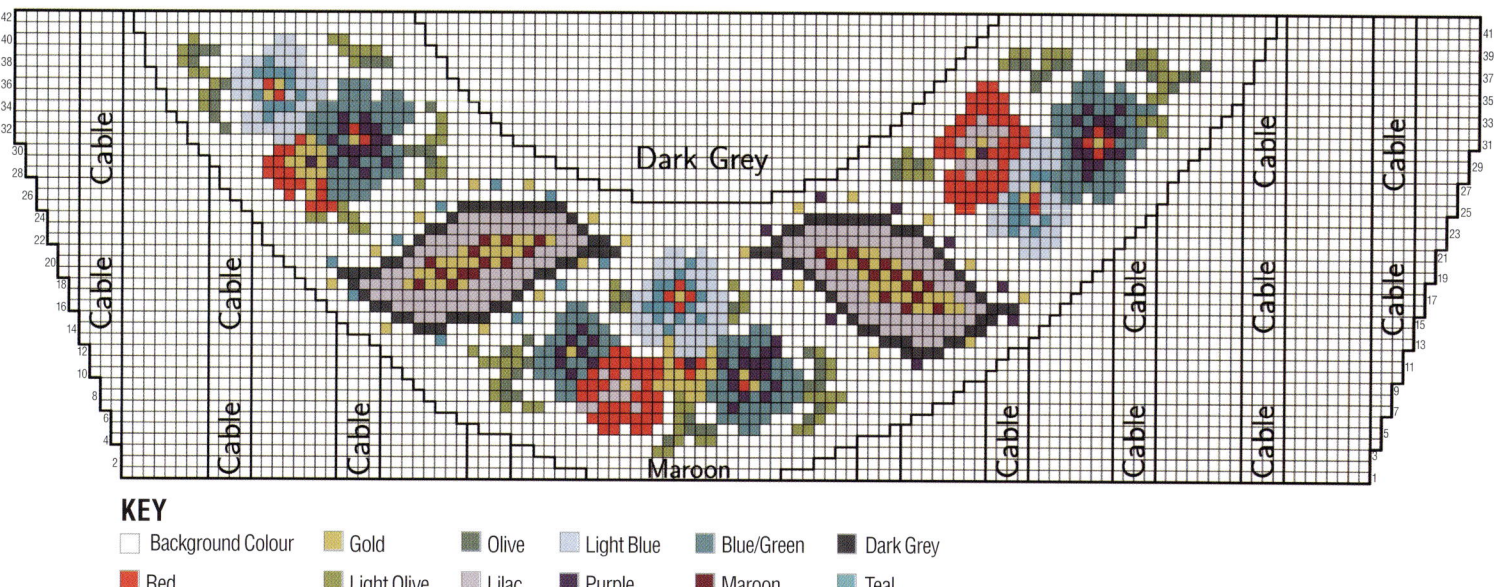

Sleeves chart. The chart is presented to be worked for the right sleeve; for the left sleeve, work this chart in reverse, as described in the section 'Notes on working the pattern'.

Embroidery

Flower border

Using the technique of Swiss darning (*see* the diagrams in Chapter 3), embroider the centres of the flowers in the contrast cols as shown on relevant chart. Embroider the single stitches around the outer edge of the paisley shapes using gold and blue/green alternately with gold and purple. Using dark-grey yarn and loose backstitches, embroider an outline around the entire lower edge of border, between the maroon- and stone-coloured stitches.

Scattered flowers on shawl

Using the embroidered-flower diagram as a guide, work flowers over the dark-grey sections of the cardigan, scattered randomly in different directions – *see* the back chart for suggested positioning. Use light olive for the stems and half of the leaves, working in stem stitch and straight stitches.

A single embroidered-flower motif.

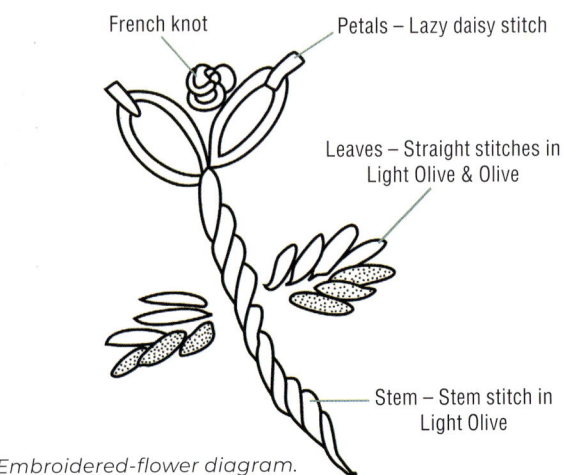

Embroidered-flower diagram.

Back view of the Shawl border and scattered flowers.

Fill in the lower half of the leaves in olive. The flower petals (2 or 3 petals, as desired) are worked in lazy-daisy stitch, with each flower centre worked with a French knot (for the featured flowers, the yarn was loosely wound 3 times around the needle before pulling the needle through). Flowers are worked in three suggested colour combinations: maroon with a red centre, teal with a light-blue centre and blue/green with a teal centre, but do try other combinations.

Making up and finishing

With each RS facing, cast off both sets of collar sts together, by picking up 1st st from left-front collar and placing it on to LH needle beside 1st st of right-front-collar sts, and knit these 2sts together. Next, work k2tog with next st of left front and next st of right front, then cast off the first st resulting from the k2tog. Cont by working k2tog with next st of left front and next st of right front, then cast off st resulting from the previously made k2tog, to end of row.
Using backstitch, sew shoulder seams, and oversew collar to back-neck edge.
Using backstitch, attach sleeves to body, ensuring that patt matches across joins.
Using backstitch, sew side and sleeve seams, except, for twisted-rib edging, use mattress stitch, to achieve a flat seam. Lightly steam press all seams.

RIGHT: This original shot of the Shawl cardigan, taken on the beach, illustrates its casual versatility. (Photo: Paul Dennison)

FAR RIGHT: Directly inspired by Chinese porcelain ware of the same name, the Cloisonné cardigan includes a delicate all-over pattern repeat that complements an intensely coloured yoke and border. (Photo: Paul Dennison)

Tassels

Using maroon and dark-grey yarns held together, wind strands around a 5cm/2in piece of stiff card 5 or 6 times, cut strands to the same length, and fold the strands over to form a tassel and secure the strands and tassel top. Make 29 tassels in total, and attach them to the lower edge of paisley and flower border all around cardigan: position 9 tassels on back and 5 on each sleeve and front.

Further Ornamental Designs

A favourite source of ideas is fairgrounds, in particular the traditional carousel rides featuring wonderful decorative horses and other creatures. The Merrygoround sweater (and coat) was one of the more intricate Sandy Black mohair knitting-kit designs, featuring a riot of knitting techniques used together – cables, bobbles, Fair Isle, colour-block knitting, embroidery, flowers and tassels! The asymmetry of the design also owes something to the traditional design of playing cards, which I have always loved since meticulously making a painting of them at school, never imagining I would one day translate these into knitwear. The Cloisonné cardigan was inspired by the colours and decoration of Chinese porcelain ware in Brighton Museum.

The intricate Merrygoround sweater combined my interest in both fairground imagery and the kings and queens from traditional playing cards. Many techniques are combined, and the garment is finished with chain-stitch embroidery. An angora coat and cardigan were also included in the range. (Photo: Barbara Bellingham)

ORNAMENTAL 229

CHAPTER 11

ACCESSORIES

Many people learn to knit by starting with a scarf, then perhaps a hat, so knitting accessories is also a good way to practise and learn new techniques such as knitting from charts. Accessories also make excellent gifts, without too many problems of fit! The patterns in this section are all knitted in mohair-rich yarn on medium-sized needles and are fun to knit and fun to wear. The simple beret and mittens can be knitted in random stripes to help use up your stash of yarns or simply be made plain in one colour, and all of the designs can be adapted to work with other yarns with a little experimentation.

I like to inject a little humour into my designs, and, when asked to create a piece for the wonderful book *Wild Knitting* (published in 1979), I decided to make a wrap in the form of an armadillo!

This was the start of designing a series of animal scarves, including a snake, but the key accessory was a leopard scarf, which accompanied an entire outfit of sweater, pencil skirt, scarf and mittens, topped off with a pillbox hat and clutch bag. I was delighted to be able to recreate this outfit almost entirely when taking the photos for this book, after a colleague contacted me about her charity-shop find of one of the original sweaters and a scarf. The leopard-skin pattern has been one of the most enduring visual images, through many eras of fashion to the present day.

The Leopard scarf was first made in Courtelle acrylic yarn for a promotional feature, but I quickly adapted it to fluffy angora-blend, mohair and finally 100-per-cent-angora yarn for an increasingly luxurious effect. Two other cat designs

The Armadillo wrap as featured in Wild Knitting, *1979, knitted in wool in a drop-stitch pattern with textured head and legs, completed with claws and a pink rayon lining.*

OPPOSITE PAGE: *The Leopard, Tiger and Siamese Cat scarves with matching mittens are evidently great fun to wear. (Photo: Jo Teasdale)*

A slinky Snake scarf, machine knitted in a slip-stitch honeycomb pattern in green lurex and fine brown wool, lined with lilac rayon.

The original 1980s Leopard outfit – sweater, scarf, mittens, pillbox hat and clutch bag – there was also a pencil skirt to complete the top-to-toe leopard dressing!

followed – the Siamese Cat and Tiger scarves, and all three are included here, together with matching mittens for the Tiger and Leopard designs, all knitted in stocking stitch. For all three cats, the patterning and shaping for the head is followed carefully from the chart, and the head is finished with embroidered details for the eyes. The ears are knitted separately and sewn into position. The Siamese Cat scarf is of course the easiest to knit, as the body is plain, and is a good introduction to colourwork knitting from a chart, as the number of stitches to work is small. I hope you enjoy knitting them!

Notes on working the scarf patterns
- One square of the chart represents one knitted stitch, to be worked in the colour as indicated on the chart. Odd-numbered rows are read from right to left and the corresponding stitches are to be knitted. Even-numbered rows are read from left to right and the corresponding stitches are to be purled.
- Shaping is followed from the outline of the chart. Where the line moves out or in horizontally over more than one square, these sts are cast on or off at the beg of that row.
- Steps of single squares represent ordinary increasing by working twice into the first stitch at the beginning of and/or into the last stitch at the end of a row, or decreasing by working 2sts together (for example, with a k2tog or p2tog decrease).
- When working the colourwork patterns, where appropriate, strand the yarn colour not in use loosely across the back of the work over not more than 4sts; when more then 4sts need to be spanned, the colour not in use should be woven in at the back of the work (*see* Chapter 4). For the face, use separate balls of background colour at each side of the central face panel, and use separate lengths of yarn for each eye.

The first incarnation of the Leopard scarf was knitted in Courtelle yarns and featured in the 'Knit Hits' supplement of the fashion magazine Over 21 in 1979.

The Leopard scarf, knitted in angora–wool-blend yarns, features on a cover of Elle magazine from December 1980.

The cover of the pattern booklet for the cat scarves offered as knitting kits with 100-per-cent-angora yarn.

Sketches of the three cat scarves from the original pattern booklet.

ACCESSORIES 233

Siamese Cat Scarf

The Siamese Cat scarf is simple to knit, with just a small amount of colourwork knitting required from the chart. (Photo: Jo Teasdale)

Size and measurements
One size

Knitted measurements
Length: 138cm/54in
Width: 16.5cm/6½in

Materials

Yarn
Knitted in a mohair–wool-blend yarn with approx 75-per-cent-mohair content and 100m/50g (for example, Wool and the Gang Take Care Mohair) in 2 main colours plus oddments of colours for details:

Main colour (MC): 4 × 50g balls
Contrast colours:
Main contrast (A): 1 × 50g ball
Other **contrast colours:** Oddments in B (pink, for nose) and C (pale blue, for eyes)

The example shown is knitted in Wool and the Gang Take Care Mohair in the colours MC = Misty Mauve, A = Space Black, B = Bubblegum Pink and C = Icy Morn. Other suggested colour combinations:
1. MC = mushroom, A = chocolate, B = pink, C = blue
2. MC = black, A = grey, B = pink, C = mustard or khaki
3. MC = grey, A = black, B = pink, C = mustard or khaki
4. MC = fox, A = chocolate, B = pink, C = green

Recommended needles and accessories
1 pair 5mm (US 8, UK 6) needles
Medium-sized crochet hook
Large-eyed yarn needle

This simple cat scarf is knitted in stocking stitch from the chart for the head and the written instructions for a plain body.

Tension

18sts and 22 rows to 10cm/4in, measured over st st, using 5mm (US 8, UK 6) needles or the size required to give the correct tension and therefore measurements.

How to check tension
Using the recommended needles, cast on 28sts, and work 15cm/6in in st st. Pin the knitted swatch square down flat,

Close-up of the Siamese Cat scarf.

without stretching the fabric. Place a pin between 2sts near the left side of the swatch, count 18sts across to the right, and place another pin between the 18th and 19th sts. Mark out 22 rows in the same manner, starting from 2sts near the top of the swatch. Measure the distance between each pair of pins. The measurements should both be 10cm/4in. If a measurement is less than 10cm/4in, your tension is too tight – try using needles of one size larger to reknit the swatch, and again check the tension. If a measurement is more than 10cm/4in, your tension is too loose – try using needles of one size smaller to reknit the swatch, and again check the tension. Repeat the process until the correct tension is achieved. Do not be afraid to go up or down by more than one size from the recommended needles to achieve the required tension. If your tension does not correspond to the pattern tension for both stitches and rows then ensure that your stitch tension is correct, and work to the lengths given in the pattern.

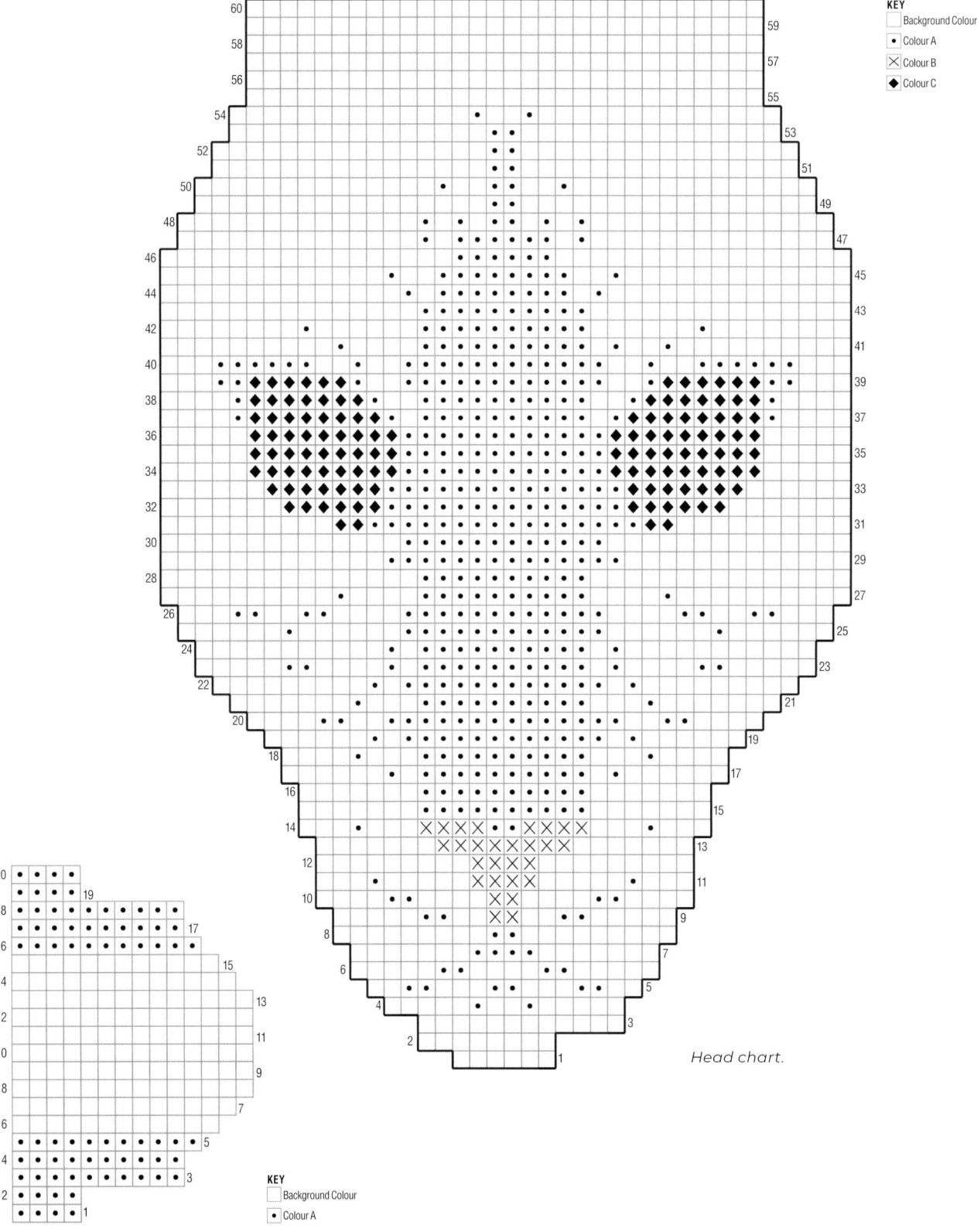

Head chart.

Ear chart.

236 ACCESSORIES

Pattern

See 'Notes on working the scarf patterns'.

Underside

This is worked in st st in MC with highlights in A, foll shaping only from chart for head (not the colourwork patt for upper head).
With A, cast on 6sts, and inc sts where indicated on chart until row 6 is completed. Change to MC, and cont working from chart until head shaping is completed (30sts). *

Cont straight in st st for a further 61cm/24in.

Shape tail: Dec 1 st at each end of next and every foll 5th row 4 times. Then, dec 1 st at each end of every 3rd row until 14sts rem. Dec 1 st at each end of every 15th row to 6sts, and, *at the same time*, when 8sts are left, change background colour (MC) to A. Work 4 rows straight, and cast off.

Upper side

Using MC, cast on 6sts, and start working from chart for head, foll shaping from chart and joining in cols A, B and C as required (*see also* 'Notes on working the scarf patterns'). Cont until row 60 is completed (30sts). Complete as for underside, by cont to work from *.

Ears

Inner ears
Both inner ears are worked alike.
These are knitted sideways in st st in MC and A from ear chart. Using A, cast on 4sts, and, changing col where shown, follow shaping of chart, casting on and casting off a group of 6sts on row 3 and row 19, respectively, then cast off last 4sts.

Outer ears
Both outer ears are worked alike.
These are knitted only in MC, exactly as for inner ears but without any changes of col.

Using MC, cast on 4sts, and follow shaping of ear chart to end. Cast off last 4sts.

Making up and finishing

Do not press pieces. Sew in all loose yarn ends.

Embroidery

With A, embroider pupils of eyes (*see* eye-embroidery diagram). Add in another col highlight (blue or yellow) in centre of eyes between embroidered areas, if desired.

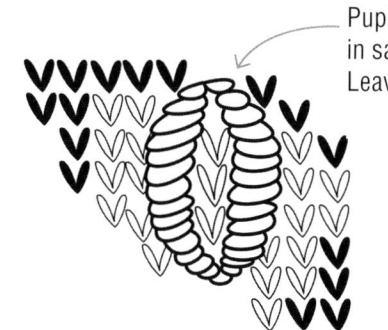

Pupil of eye embroidered in satin stitch. Leave a gap in the centre

Eye-embroidery diagram.

Seaming and assembly

Ears: Placing knit side of outer ear to purl side of inner ear, work a row of double crochet round outside edge by using A to join the 2 pieces together, leaving the ear base open. Sew one ear on to each side of head with a curved shape, making a small pleat in inner ear.

Head and body: With RS of pieces together, join upper side and underside by using backstitch, leaving a section of head seam open. Turn scarf the right way out, and oversew rest of head seam. If desired, pad nose section lightly before completing head seam, to give extra dimension to head.

Leopard Scarf and Mittens

The Leopard scarf and mittens set. (Photo: Jo Teasdale)

Leopard Scarf

This scarf is knitted in stocking stitch from the charts, using the two- or three-colour stranded-colourwork knitting (Fair Isle) technique for two different patterns, one for the upper side and one for the underside. You can choose to knit the upper side by working with all three colours of the leopard spot pattern or, to simplify the knitting, by working in two colours only and the third colour being added afterwards by using a simplified Swiss-darning technique.

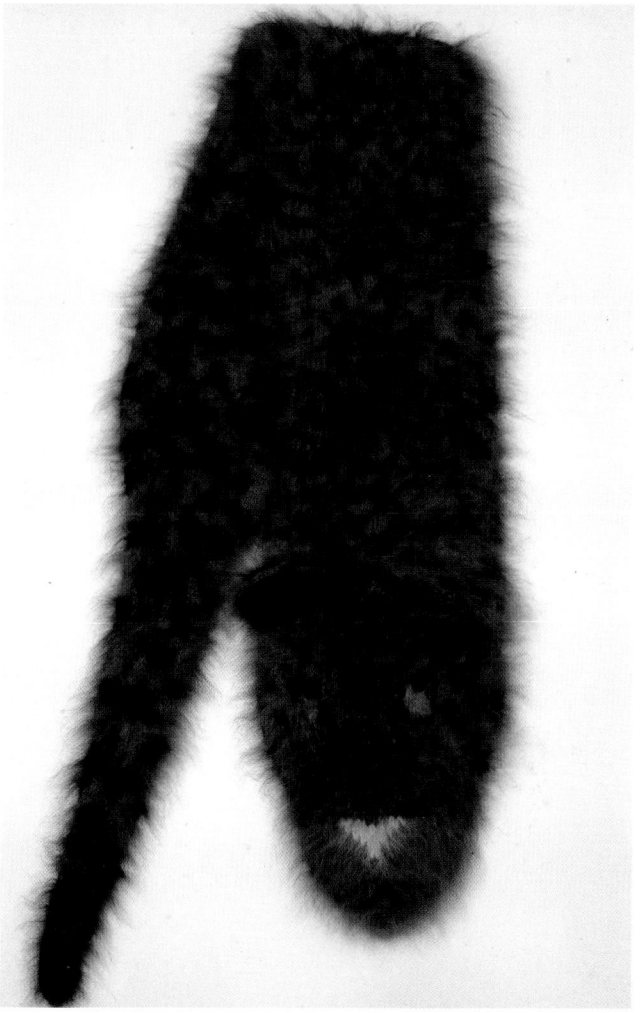

The original 100-per-cent-angora Leopard scarf, knitted in a burgundy/black/grey colourway.

Size and measurements
One size

Knitted measurements
Length: 146cm/57½in
Width: 17cm/6¾in

Materials

Yarn
Knitted in a mohair–wool-blend yarn with approx 75-per-cent-mohair content and 100m/50g (for example, Wool and the Gang Take Care Mohair) in 4 main colours plus oddments of 2 additional colours for details of the eyes and nose:

Main colour (MC): 3 × 50g balls for background
Contrast colours:
Main contrast A: 2 × 50g balls for leopard-pattern base colour
Main contrast B: 1 × 50g ball for face panel and tail
Other contrast colours:
C: 1 × 50g ball for leopard-pattern upper-side spot centres
D: Oddments in green or blue for eyes, ears and tail
E: Oddments in pink for nose

The example shown is knitted in Wool and the Gang Take Care Mohair in the colours MC = Winter White, A = Deep Grey, B = Cinnamon Dust, C = Lazy Latte, D = Steel Blue and E = Bubblegum Pink.
Other suggested colour combinations:
1. MC = white, A = grey, B = rust or khaki, C= mushroom, D = green, E = pink
2. MC = burgundy. A = black, B and C = grey, D = green, E = pink
3. MC = mushroom, A = chocolate, B and C = khaki, D = fox, E = pink

Recommended needles and accessories
1 pair 4.5mm (US 7, UK 7) needles
Large-eyed yarn-darning or embroidery needle

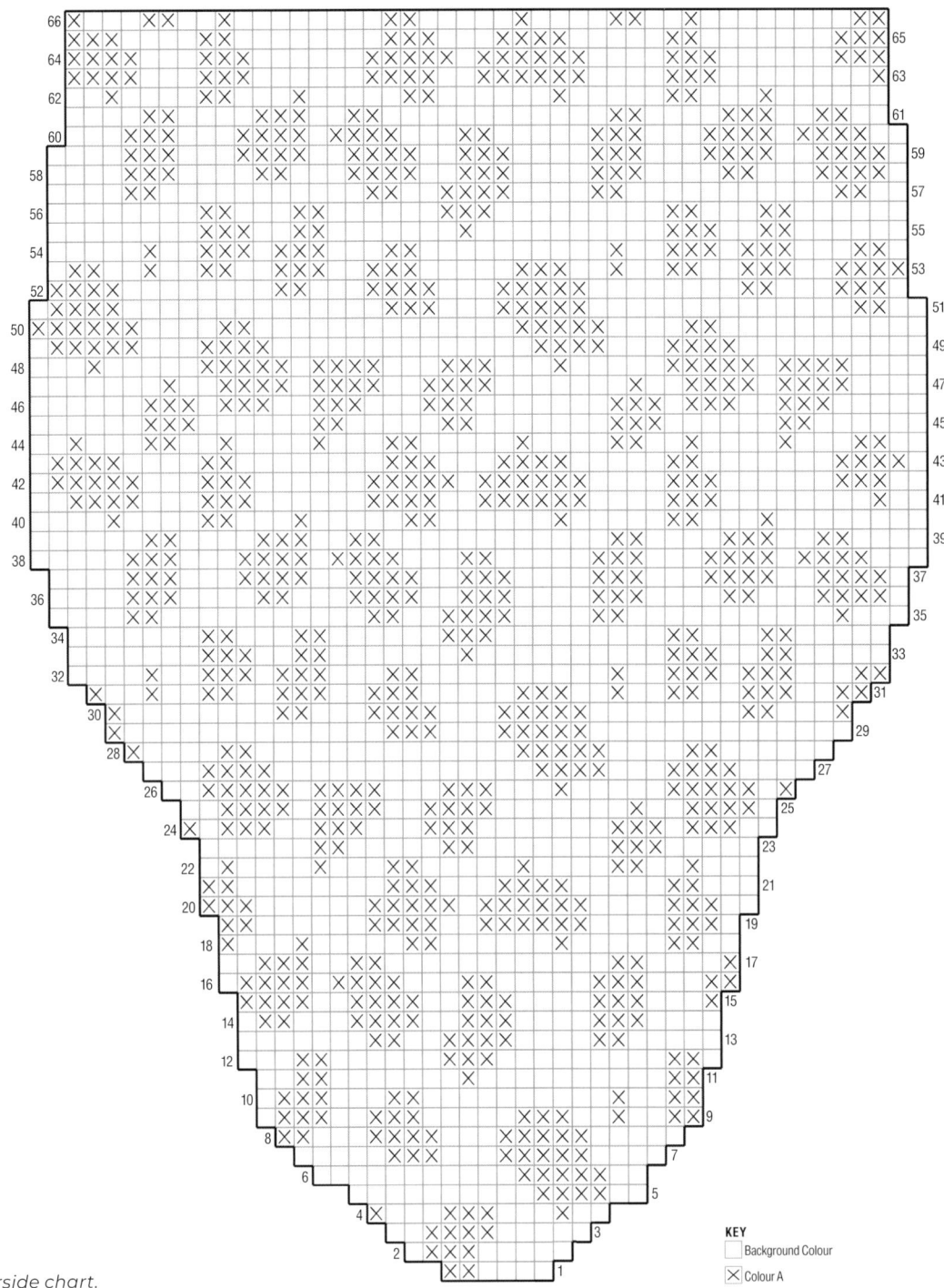

Head-underside chart.

Tension

24sts and 24 rows to 10cm/4in, measured over underside patt, using 4.5mm (US 7, UK 7) needles or the size required to give the correct tension and therefore measurements.

To avoid disappointment, it is essential to check your tension carefully before commencing the knitting of the pattern pieces and to use the needles that give you the correct tension. These needles may not be of the needle size quoted in the standard tension information, as each knitter knits differently.

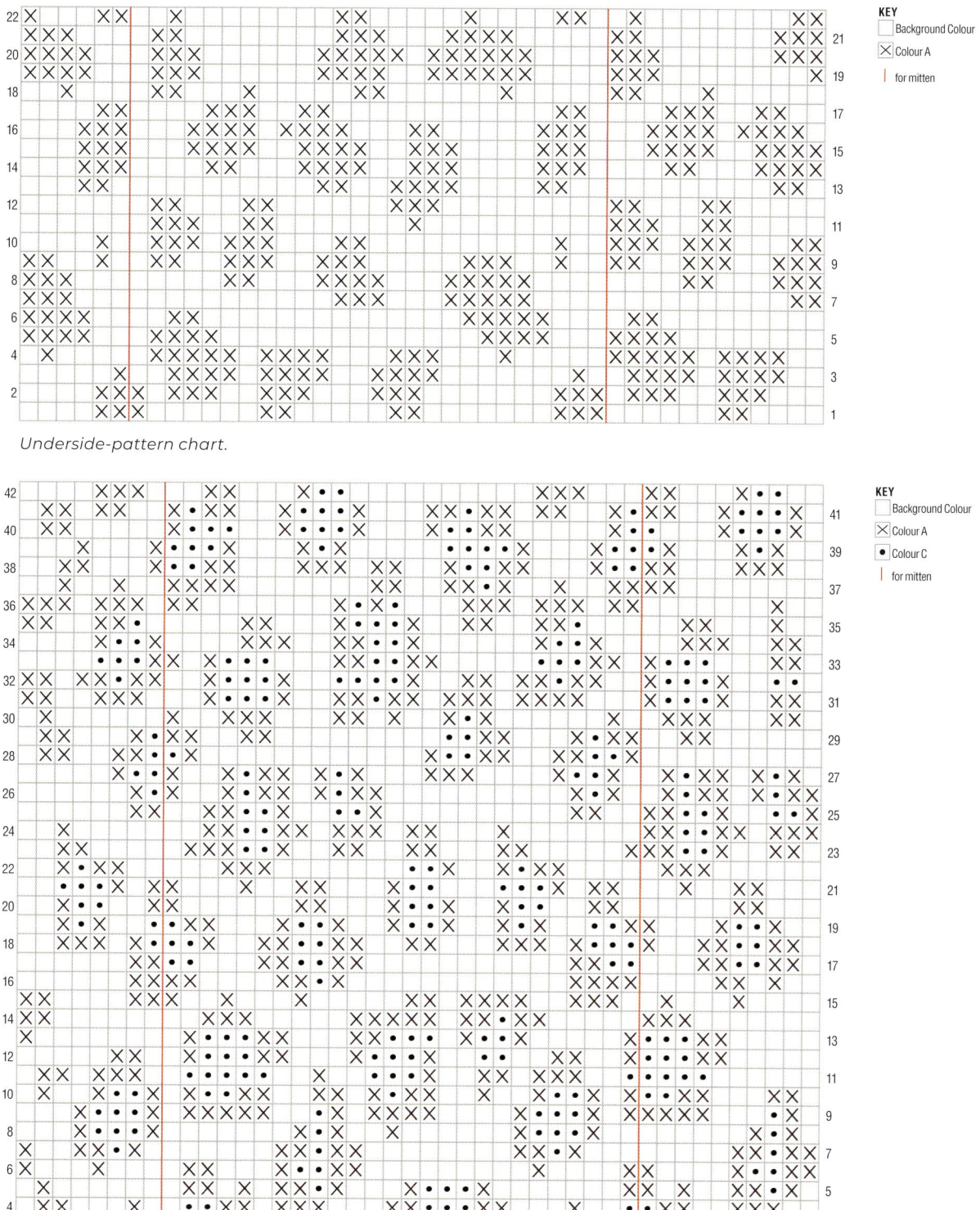

Underside-pattern chart.

Upper-side-pattern chart.

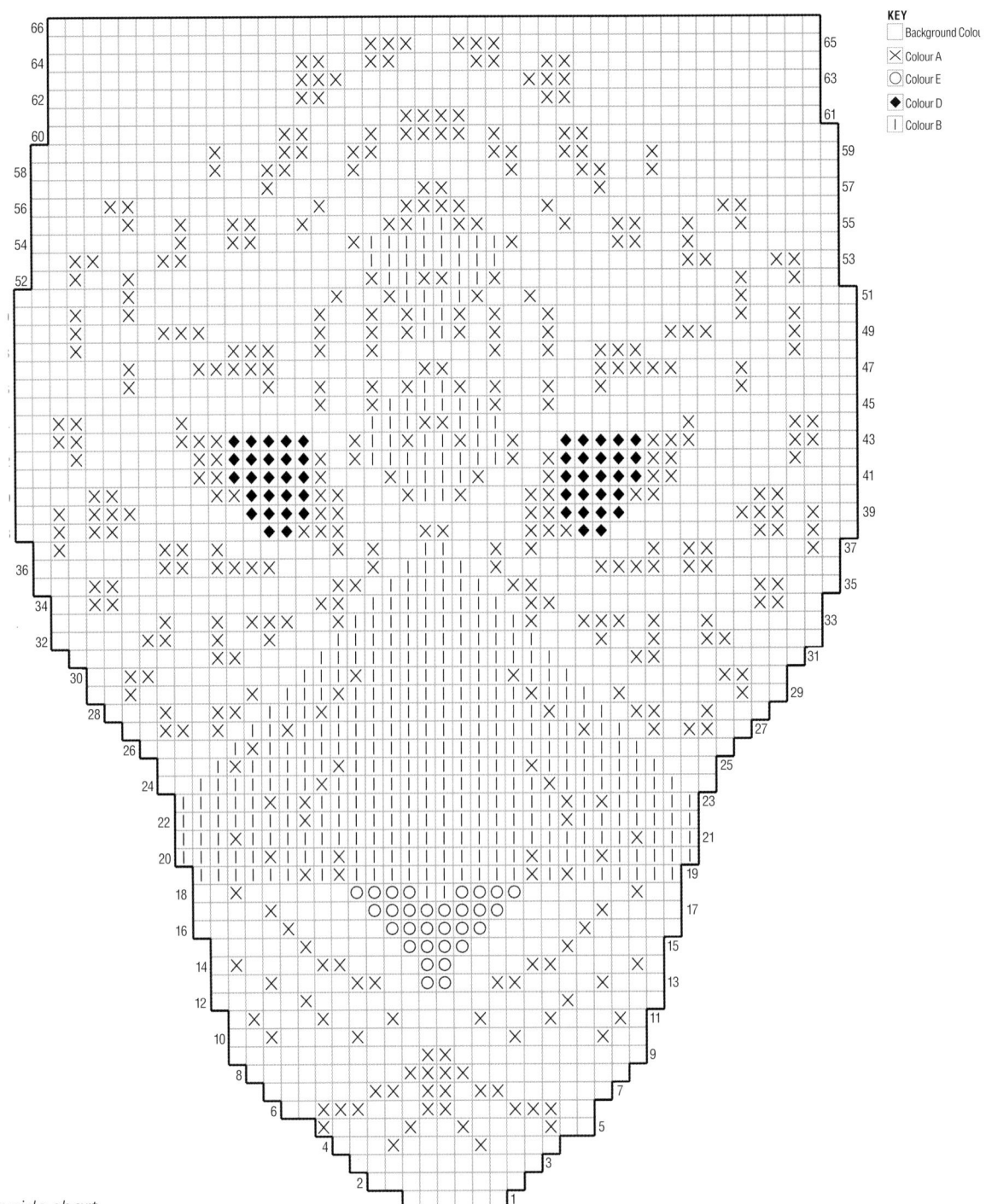

Head-upper-side chart.

How to check tension

Using the recommended needles and MC, cast on 30sts, and, joining in A as required, work a section from the underside chart as folls:

Starting from row 1 with a knit row, work from the 1st st to the 30th st on knit rows and the 30th st to the 1st st on purl rows in patt for rows 1–22, then repeat rows 1–8 (30 rows). Cast off loosely. Pin the knitted swatch square down flat, without stretching the fabric. Place a pin between 2sts near the left side of the swatch, count 24sts across to the right, and place another pin between the 24th and 25th sts. Mark out 24 rows in the same manner, starting from 2sts near the top of the swatch. Measure the distance between each pair of pins. The measurements should both be 10cm/4in. If a measurement is less than 10cm/4in, your tension is too tight – try using needles of one size larger to reknit the swatch, and again check the tension. If a measurement is more than 10cm/4in, your tension is too loose – try using needles of one size smaller to reknit the swatch, and again check the tension. Repeat the process until the correct tension is achieved. Do not be afraid to go up or down by more than one size from the recommended needles to achieve the required tension.

If your tension does not correspond to the pattern tension for both stitches and rows then ensure that your stitch tension is correct, and work to the lengths given in the pattern.

Pattern

See 'Notes on working the scarf patterns'.

Underside

This is worked in st st in MC and A with the two-colour stranded-colourwork technique.
With MC, cast on 6sts, and work from chart for underside of head, foll shaping until row 66 is completed (44sts). Next, work from chart for underside patt, starting from row 1 and rep rows 1–22 throughout, for 72cm/28½ in.

Shape tail: Keeping continuity of underside patt correct, dec 1 st at each end of next and every foll 3rd row 5 times. Dec 1 st at each end of every foll 2nd row until there are 20sts. Dec 1 st at each end of every foll 10th row until 8sts rem. Change background colour (MC on chart) to B, cont in underside patt, and, *at the same time*, dec on foll 10th row to 6sts. Change background colour (MC on chart) to D, and work straight in underside patt for 15 rows. Cast off.

Upper side

Using MC, cast on 6sts, and work from chart for upper side of head, foll shaping from chart and joining in A, B, D and E as required (*see also* 'Notes on working the scarf patterns'). Cont until row 66 is completed (44sts). Next, work from chart for upper-side patt by using MC and A, and C if desired, starting from row 1 and rep rows 1–42 throughout, for 72cm/28½in. Note: The upper side can be knitted in three cols as indicated or, alternatively, in two cols only, by

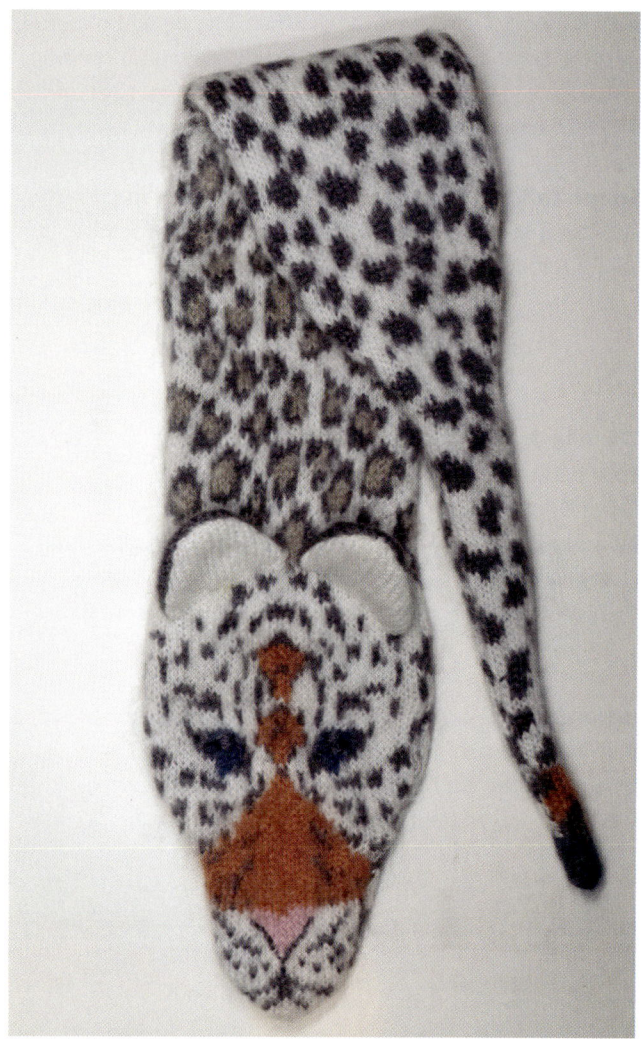

Details of the Leopard scarf.

Detail of the Leopard upper-side pattern, knitted with the three-colour stranded-colourwork technique.

ACCESSORIES 243

substituting MC or A for C. C can then later be embroidered over the areas indicated on the chart by using a simplified Swiss-darning technique (*see* the accompanying diagram and the section 'Swiss darning' in Chapter 3).

Shape tail: Keeping continuity of upper-side patt correct and using MC and A, shape tail and change cols as given for tail for underside of scarf.

Ears

Outer ears
Both outer ears are worked alike.
Using D, cast on 20sts, join in A, and work in underside patt by using 20-st section of underside-patt chart and by using D as MC. Dec 1 st at each end of every 3rd row 4 times, then dec 1 st at each end of every row to 6sts. Cast off.

Inner ears
Both inner ears are worked alike.
Using MC, cast on 20sts, and work in st st. Shape as given for outer ears, without underside patt.

Making up and finishing

Do not press pieces. Sew in all loose yarn ends.

Embroidery

With A, embroider pupils of eyes (*see* eye-embroidery diagram), and outline nose with a few backstitches for added emphasis. If required, with C, embroider the centres of the leopard spots of the upper-side patt, using the elongated Swiss-darning technique (*see* the accompanying diagram and example) covering areas marked as C on upper-side chart, by filling in each area with two or three elongated stitches.

Seaming and assembly

Ears: Placing knit side of outer ear to purl side of inner ear, using backstitch, join the two pieces together, leaving the ear base open. Turn each ear to RS, and sew one ear on to each side of the head with a curved shape, making a small pleat in inner ear.

Head and body: With RS of pieces together, pin upper-side and underside pieces together, matching shapings. Join upper side and underside by using backstitch, leaving a section of the head seam open around the jaw. Turn scarf the right way out, and oversew rest of head seam. If desired, insert slight padding into the jaw area before completing head seam, to give extra dimension to head.

Diagram for the elongated Swiss-darning technique, to add the third colour to the Leopard upper-side spot pattern.

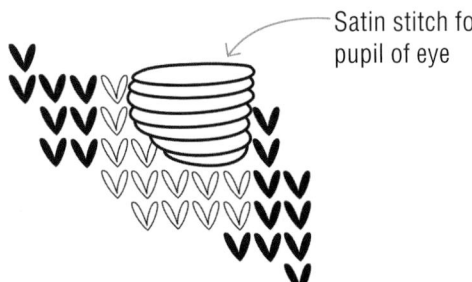

Eye-embroidery diagram.

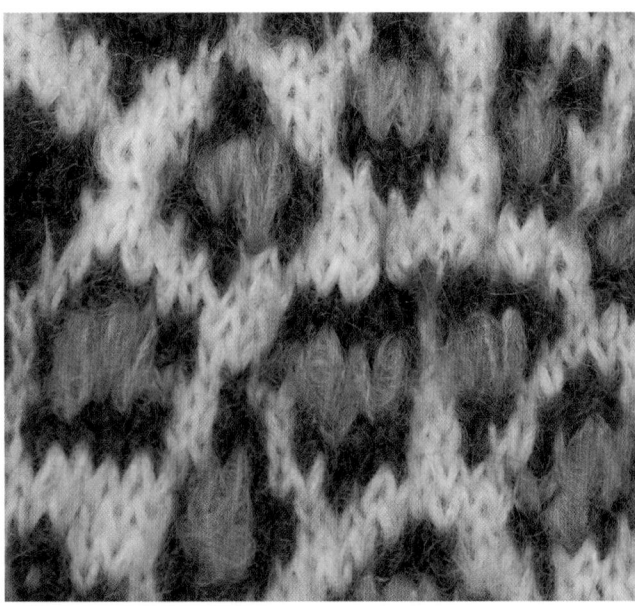

Close-up of the Leopard upper-side pattern, showing the Swiss-darned third colour, as in the mittens.

Leopard Mittens

The mittens are knitted flat in one piece, with the thumb knitted into the centre of this piece and the 'paw' being shaped at the top. There is one side seam. They are worked in the two leopard spot patterns of the Leopard scarf, to make a matching set: on the back of the hand, the three-colour upper-side pattern is used (with the third colour being knitted in or Swiss darned); on the palm side, the two-colour underside pattern is used.

The Leopard mittens with 'paws'.

Tension

24sts and 24 rows to 10cm/4in, measured over Leopard underside patt, using 4.5mm needles (UK 7, US 7) or the size required to give the correct tension and therefore measurements.

To avoid disappointment, it is essential to check your tension carefully before commencing the knitting of the pattern and to use the needles that give you the correct tension. These needles may not be of the needle size quoted in the standard tension information, as each knitter knits differently.

Size and measurements

One size, to fit average adult hands

Knitted measurements
Length: 23cm/9in, but length can be varied
Width: 11.5cm/4½in

Materials

Yarn
Knitted in a mohair–wool-blend yarn with approx 75-per-cent-mohair content and 100m/50g (for example, Wool and the Gang Take Care Mohair) in 3 colours (see Leopard scarf for suggested colour combinations):

Main colour (MC): 1 × 50g ball for background
Contrast colours:
Main contrast A: 1 × 50g ball for Leopard-pattern base colour
Main contrast C: 1 × 50g ball for Leopard-pattern upper-side spot centres

The sample is knitted in Wool and the Gang Take Care Mohair in the colours MC = Winter White, A = Deep Grey and B = Lazy Latte.

Recommended needles and accessories
Two pairs of needles are required: one pair of the size to give the correct tension, for main parts, and one pair of two sizes smaller, for ribbing.
1 pair 4.5mm (UK 7, US 7) needles for main parts
1 pair 3.75mm (UK 9, US 5) needles for ribbing
Stitch holder
Large-eyed yarn-darning or embroidery needle

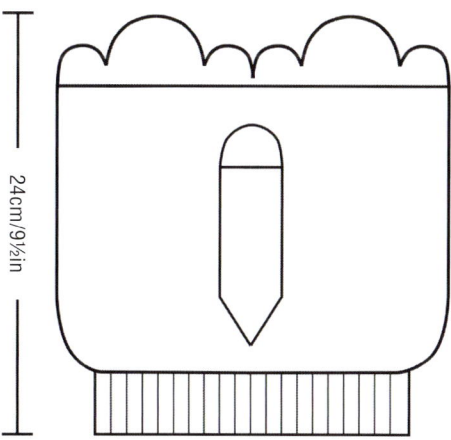

Measurement diagram.

Abbreviations and special stitches

k b&f = knit back and front: knit into back loop of next stitch on LH needle, knit into front loop of same stitch and then allow knitted-into st to slip off LH needle

pk1 = make 1 st (m1): pick up strand of yarn running between st closest to LH-needle point and st closest to RH-needle point so that the yarn passes over LH-needle point from front to back and then knit into back of strand

Pattern

Left hand

* Using the smaller needles and MC, cast on 40sts.
Work 4cm/1½in of k2, p2 rib in stripes of 2 rows MC, 2 rows A, ending with a WS row.
Inc row (RS): Using MC, knit 4sts, inc in next st by k b&f and then inc by k b&f in every foll 3rd st to end. (52sts)

Change to the larger needles, and purl 1 row. * Beg working colourwork patt in st st by foll relevant chart sections marked in red from the Leopard-scarf patt, beg with knit rows, as folls: k 26sts from underside chart, k 26sts from the upper-side chart. Work 6 rows from the charts as set.
Gusset: Keeping Leopard patts correct, work gusset for thumb as folls, working the gusset in st st with A:
Next row: K 25sts in underside patt, pk1 using A, k 1 st A, pk1 A, k 26sts in upper-side patt.
Next and every WS row: P 26sts in upper-side patt, p gusset sts in A, p 25sts in underside patt.
Next RS row: K 25sts in underside patt, pk1 A, k 3sts A, pk1 A, k 26sts in upper-side patt.
Next RS row: K 25sts in underside patt, pk1 A, k 5sts A, pk1 A, k 26sts in upper-side patt.
Next RS row: K 25sts in underside patt, pk1 A, k 7sts A, pk1 A, k 26sts in upper-side patt.
Next RS row: K 25sts in underside patt, pk1 A, k 9sts A, pk1 A, k 26sts in upper-side patt.
Next RS row: K 25sts in underside patt, pk1 A, k 11sts A, pk1 A, k 26sts in upper-side patt. (64sts)
Next row: P in patt and with A as set.
Divide for thumb: K 38sts in patt and with A as set, place rem 26sts on to st holder (for back of hand) and turn.

Next row: P13 with A and turn, leaving rem 25sts (for palm) on needle.
Thumb: Work in st st with A on these 13sts for the thumb until thumb measures 2.5cm/1in, change to MC and work 4 rows more in st st, ending with a WS purl row.
Shape top of thumb: K1, (k2tog) to end.
Next row: P2tog to end. (7sts)
Cut yarn, leaving a long yarn end, thread end on to yarn-darning or embroidery needle and run yarn end through rem sts. Using the yarn end, tightly close and secure top of thumb and sew thumb seam.

Upper hand: With RS facing, place 26sts from st holder for back of hand on to LH needle, join yarn to inside edge, pick up and knit 3sts from base of thumb with RH needle that is holding the 25sts for palm and knit in upper-side patt to end (54sts).
Cont in patt for back of hand and palm as set (incorporating the additional 2sts over base of thumb in the centre of mitten into patt) until work measures 20cm/8in from beg, ending on a WS row. Extra length may be added here if required.

Shape mitten top: Cont in st st in MC only, divide sts into two groups of 27sts, for palm and back of hand, and shape top of mittens as 'paws' as folls:
Next row (RS): K2tog, k23, k2tog and turn, leaving rem sts for back-of-hand side on st holder.
Next row (WS): P2tog, p21, p2tog.
Next row: K2tog, k19, k2tog.
Next row: Cast of 5sts purlwise, p to last 2sts, p2tog.
Next row: Cast off 5sts knitwise, k to last 2sts, k2tog.
Next row: P2tog, p5, p2tog.
Next row: K2tog, k3, k2tog.
Cast off rem 5sts.

Return to the second set of 27sts for back-of-hand side, place these 27sts on to LH needle, join MC yarn to inside edge with RS facing and shape top of mitten as given above for palm side.

Right hand

Work as for left hand from * to *. Beg working colourwork patt in st st by foll relevant charts from the Leopard-scarf patt, beg with knit rows, and reversing the patts as folls: k 26sts from upper-side chart, k 26sts from underside chart. Work 6 rows from the charts as set.

Gusset: Keeping the Leopard patts correct, work gusset for thumb as folls, working the gusset in st st with A:

Next row: K 26sts in upper-side patt, pk1 A, k 1 st A, pk1 A, k 25sts in underside patt.

Next and every WS row: P 25sts in underside patt, p gusset sts in A, p 26sts in upper-side patt.

Next row (RS): K 26sts in upper-side patt, pk1 A, k 3sts A, pk1 A, k 25sts in patt.

Cont to inc for thumb gusset as set until the row 'k 26sts in upper-side patt, pk1 A, k 11sts A, pk1 A, k 25sts in underside patt' has been worked. (64sts)

Next row: Purl in patt and with A as set.

Divide for thumb: K 39sts in patt and with A as set, place rem 25sts on to st holder (for palm) and turn.

Next row: P13 with A and turn, leaving rem 26sts (for back of hand) on needle.

Complete thumb to match that of left hand by foll earlier 'Thumb' instructions.

Upper hand: With RS facing, place 25sts from st holder for palm on to LH needle, join yarn to inside edge, pick up and knit 3sts from base of thumb with RH needle that is holding the 26sts for back of hand and knit in underside patt to end (54sts).

Cont in patt for palm and back of hand as set (incorporating the additional 2sts over base of thumb in the centre of mitt into patt) until work measures 20cm/8in from beg, ending on a WS row. If extra length was added here for left mitten, work to the same length for right mitten.

Shape mitten top: Work as given for left mitten, but noting that the sts for the back-of-hand side are worked first, followed by the palm-side sts.

Making up and finishing

Embroidery
Using the elongated Swiss-darning technique (*see* the accompanying diagram and the example for the Leopard scarf), cover the centres of the leopard spots of the upper-side patt with C.

Seaming
Sew in all loose yarn ends carefully. With RS together, sew top and side seams using backstitch.

Tiger Scarf & Mittens

The Tiger scarf and mittens set. (Photo: Jo Teasdale)

Tiger Scarf

This scarf is knitted in stocking stitch from the charts, using the two-colour stranded-colourwork knitting (Fair Isle) technique for two different patterns, one for the upper side and one for the underside.

Size and measurements

One size

Knitted measurements
Length: 150cm/59in
Width: 20cm/8in

Materials

Yarn
Knitted in a mohair–wool-blend yarn with approx 75-per-cent-mohair content and 100m/50g (for example, Wool and the Gang Take Care Mohair) in 3 main colours plus oddments of 2 additional colours for details of the eyes and nose:
Main colour (MC): 2 × 50g balls in fox or red for background
Contrast colours:
Main contrast A: 2 × 50g balls in grey or chocolate
Main contrast B: 2 × 50g balls in white
Other contrast colours: Oddments in C (cedar green for eyes) and D (pink for nose).
The example shown is knitted in Wool and the Gang Take Care Mohair in the colours MC = Lipstick Red, A = Misty Mauve, B = Winter White, C = Powder Green and D = Bubblegum Pink.

Recommended needles and accessories
Two pairs of needles are required: one pair of the size to give the correct tension, for the upper side, and one pair of one size smaller, for the underside.
1 pair 4.5mm (US 7, UK 7) needles for upper side
1 pair 4mm (US 6, UK 8) needles for underside
Large-eyed yarn-darning or embroidery needle

Detail of the Tiger head and upper-side pattern.

Tension

20sts and 26 rows to 10cm/4in, measured over Tiger upper-side stripe patt, using 4.5mm (UK 7, US 7) needles or the size required to give the correct tension and therefore measurements.

To avoid disappointment, it is essential to check your tension carefully before commencing the knitting of the pattern and to use the needles that give you the correct tension. These needles may not be of the needle size quoted in the standard tension information, as each knitter knits differently.

ACCESSORIES 249

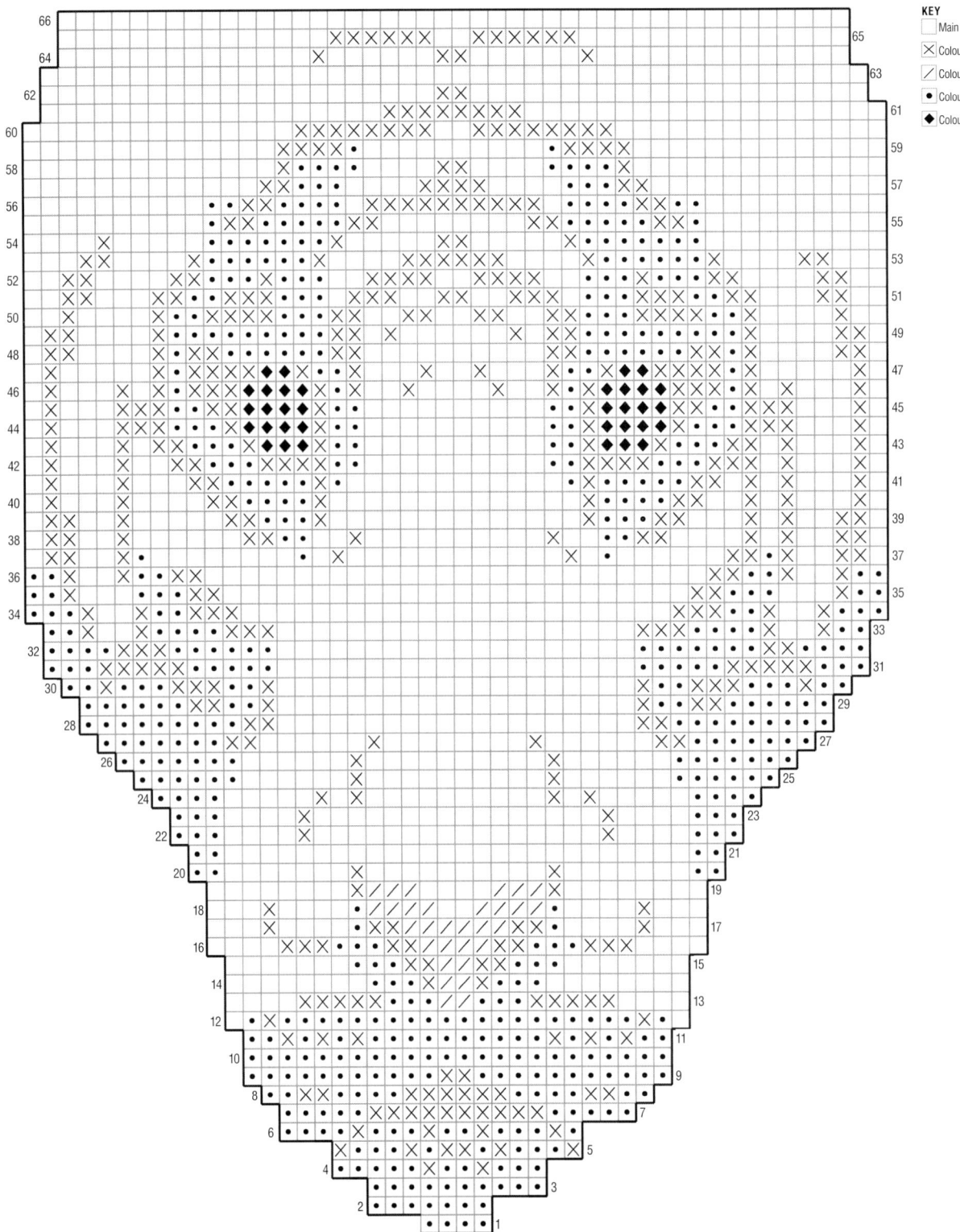

Head chart.

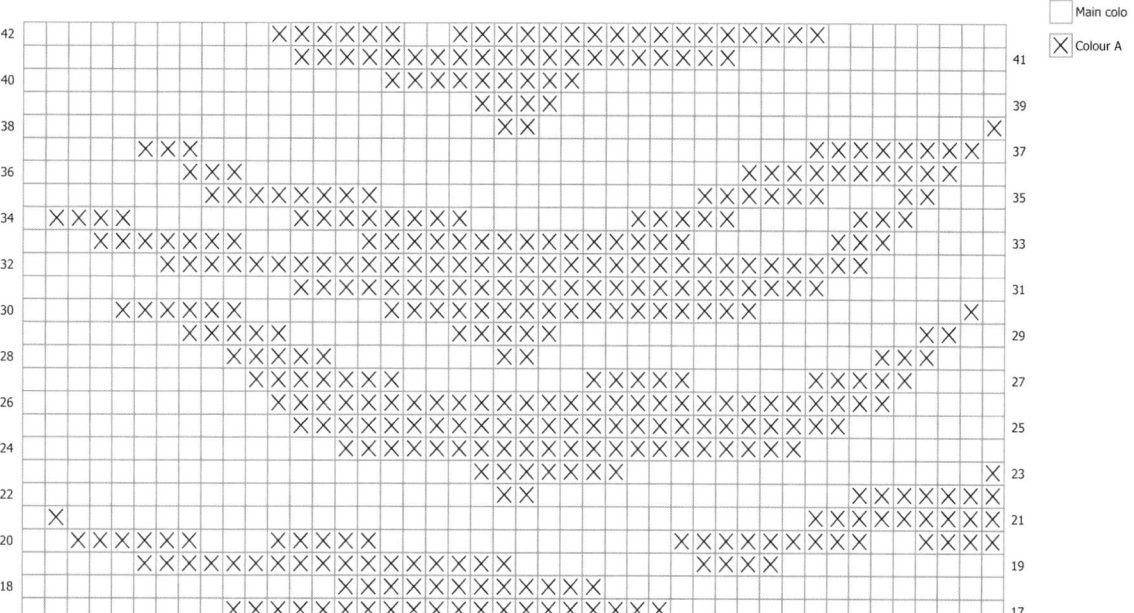

Upper-side-pattern chart.

How to check tension

Using the recommended needles and MC, cast on 26sts. Join in A as required, and work a section from the Tiger upper-side stripe-patt chart as folls:

Starting from row 1 with a knit row, work from the 1st st to the 26th st on knit rows and the 26th st to the 1st st on purl rows in patt for rows 1–34. Cast off loosely. Pin the knitted swatch square down flat, without stretching the fabric. Place a pin between 2sts near the left side of the swatch, count 20sts across to the right, and place another pin between the 20th and 21st sts. Mark out 26 rows in the same manner, starting from 2sts near the top of the swatch. Measure the distance between each pair of pins. The measurements should both be 10cm/4in. If a measurement is less than 10cm/4in, your tension is too tight – try using needles of one size larger to reknit the swatch, and again check the tension. If a measurement is more than 10cm/4in, your tension is too loose – try using needles of one size smaller to reknit the swatch, and again check the tension. Repeat the process until the correct tension is achieved. Do not be afraid to go up or down by more than one size from the recommended needles to achieve the required tension. If your tension does not correspond to the pattern tension for both stitches and rows then ensure that your stitch tension is correct, and work to the lengths given in the pattern.

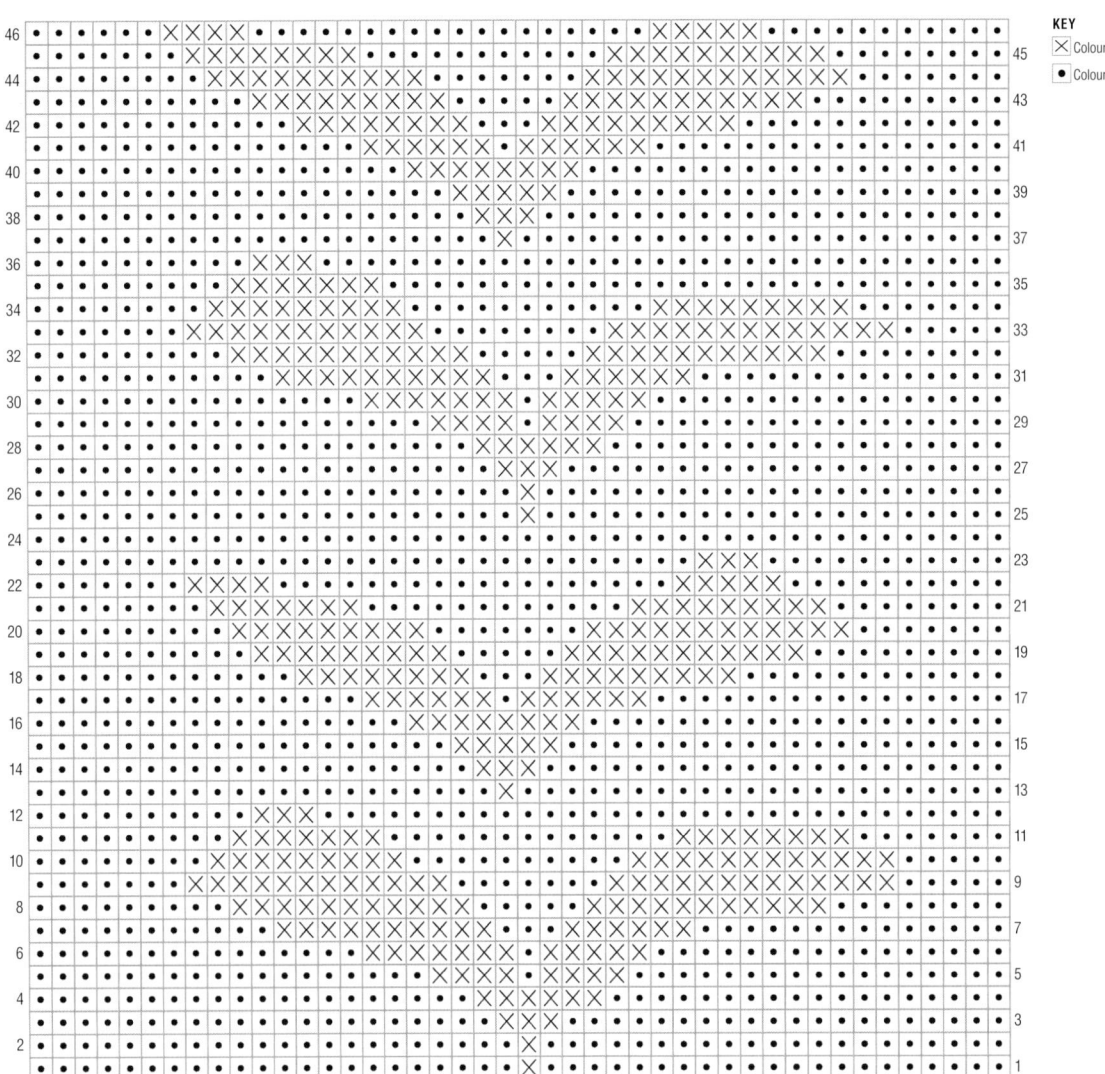

Under-side-pattern chart.

Pattern

Additional note on working the pattern
- Use separate balls of B, C and D for each side of face.
  See also 'Notes on working the scarf patterns'.

Underside

Using the smaller needles, the underside of the head is worked in B only in st st, then the body and tail are worked with two-colour stranded-colourwork knitting with A and B. With B, cast on 4sts, and work from chart for head but foll shaping only (not the colourwork patt for upper head) until row 66 is completed (44sts). Join in A, and work from chart for underside patt, starting from row 1, and rep rows 1–46, for a further 76cm/30in.

Shape tail: Keeping continuity of underside patt correct, dec 1 st at each end of next and every foll 5th row 4 times. Then, dec 1 st at each end of every foll 3rd row until 20sts rem. Dec 1 st at each end of every foll 10th row until 8sts rem. Cont in st-st stripes of varying widths using A and B alternately, and, *at the same time*, dec 1 st at each end of foll 10th row, then work 15 rows more. Cast off.

Upper side

Using the larger needles and B, cast on 4sts, and work from chart for head, foll shaping and joining in cols MC, A, C and D as necessary. Cont until row 66 is completed (44sts). Next, work from chart for upper-side patt by using MC and A, starting from row 1, and rep rows 1–42 throughout, working straight for a further 76cm/30in.

Shape tail: Keeping continuity of upper-side patt correct and using MC and A, shape as given for tail for underside of scarf, changing to stripes at end of tail to correspond to those of tail underside.

Ears

Both ears are worked alike.

Outer ears
Using the larger needles and MC, cast on 20sts. Work in st st, and dec 1 st at each end of every 3rd row 4 times, then dec 1 st at each end of every row to 6sts. Cast off.

Inner ears
Worked exactly as for outer ears but using the smaller needles and A.

Making up and finishing

Do not press pieces. Sew in all loose yarns ends.

Embroidery

With A, embroider pupils of eyes using straight satin stitches (*see* eye-embroidery diagram).

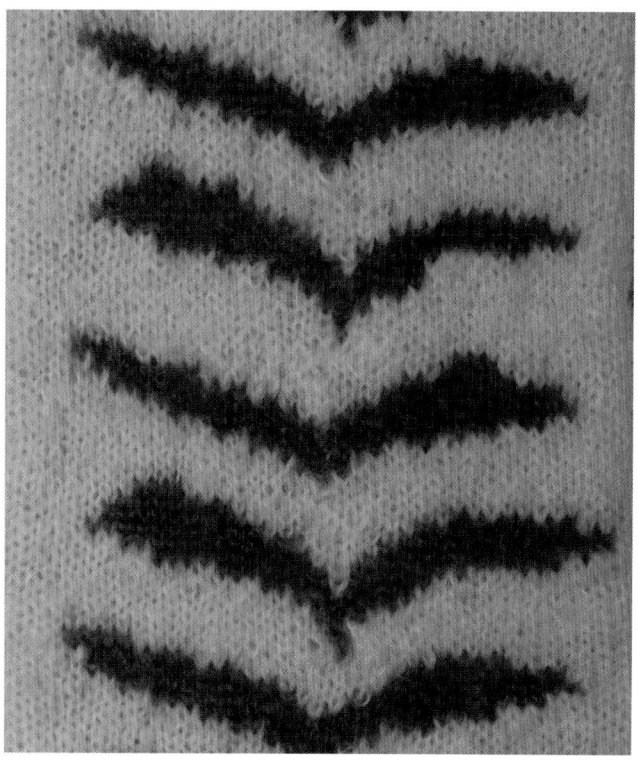

Detail of the Tiger underside pattern.

Seaming and assembly

Ears: Placing knit side of outer ear to purl side of inner ear, oversew the two pieces together, leaving the ear base open. Turn each ear to RS, and sew one ear on to each side of head with a curved shape, making a small pleat in inner ear.
Head and body: With RS of pieces together, pin upper-side and underside pieces together, matching shapings. Join upper side and underside by using backstitch, leaving a section of the head seam open around the jaw. Turn scarf the right way out, and oversew rest of head seam. If desired, insert slight padding into the jaw area before completing head seam, to give extra dimension to head.

Eye-embroidery diagram.

Tiger Mittens

The mittens are knitted flat in one piece, with the thumb knitted into the centre of this piece and the 'paw' being shaped at the top. There is one side seam. They are worked in the two-colour Tiger upper-side stripe pattern, to make a matching set with the Tiger scarf.

The Tiger mittens with 'paws'.

Tension

20sts and 26 rows to 10cm/4in, measured over Tiger upper-side stripe patt, using 4.5mm needles (US 7, UK 7) or those of the size to give the correct tension and therefore measurements.

To avoid disappointment, it is essential to check your tension carefully before commencing the knitting of the pattern and to use the needles that give you the correct tension. These needles may not be of the needle size quoted in the standard tension information, as each knitter knits differently.

Abbreviations and special stitches

k b&f = knit back and front: knit into back loop of next stitch on LH needle, knit into front loop of same stitch and then allow knitted-into st to slip off LH needle

Size and measurements

One size, to fit average adult hands

Knitted measurements

Length: 23cm/9in, but length can be varied
Width: 11.5cm/4½in

Materials

Yarn

Knitted in a mohair–wool-blend yarn with approx 75-per-cent-mohair content and 100m/50g (for example, Wool and the Gang Take Care Mohair) in 3 colours, although only 20g of the third colour is required:

Main colour (MC): 1 × 50g ball in red or fox
Contrast colours:
Main contrast (A): 1 × 50g ball in chocolate, grey or purple
Second contrast (B): 1 × 50g ball in white, for paws and thumb tip

The sample is knitted in Wool and the Gang Take Care Mohair in the colours MC = Lipstick Red, A = Misty Mauve and B = Winter White.

Recommended needles and accessories

Two pairs of needles are required: one pair of the size to give the correct tension, for main parts, and one pair of two sizes smaller, for ribbing
1 pair 4.5mm (US 7, UK 7) needles for main parts
1 pair 3.75mm (UK 9, US 5) needles for ribbing
Stitch holder
Large-eyed yarn-darning needle

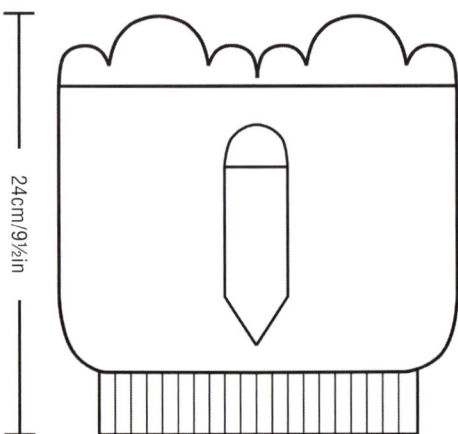

Measurement diagram.

pk1 = make 1 st (m1): pick up strand of yarn running between st closest to LH-needle point and st closest to RH-needle point so that the yarn passes over LH-needle point from front to back and then knit into back of strand

Pattern

Left hand

* Using the smaller needles and MC, cast on 36sts. Work 4cm/1½in of k2, p2 rib in MC, ending with a WS row.
Inc row (RS): Using MC, knit 3sts, inc in next st by k b&f and then inc by k b&f in every foll 6th st to end (44sts)

Change to the larger needles, and purl 1 row. * Beg working colourwork patt in st st by foll upper-side chart, beg with a knit row, as folls: work rows 1–6 from chart.
Gusset: Keeping patt correct, work gusset for thumb as folls, working the gusset in st st with A:
Next row: K 21sts in patt, pk1 using A, k 1 st A, pk1 A, k 22sts in patt.
Next and every WS row: P 22sts in patt, p gusset sts in A, p 21sts in patt.
Next RS row: K 21sts in patt, pk1 A, k 3sts A, pk1 A, k 22sts in patt.
Next RS row: K 21sts in patt, pk1 A, k 5sts A, pk1 A, k 22sts in patt.
Next RS row: K 21sts in patt, pk1 A, k 7sts A, pk1 A, k 22sts in patt.
Next RS row: K 21sts in patt, pk1 A, k 9sts A, pk1 A, k 22sts in patt.
Next RS row: K 21sts in patt, pk1 A, k 11sts A, pk1 A, k 22sts in patt. (56sts)
Next row: Purl in patt and with A as set.
Divide for thumb: K 34sts in patt and with A as set, place rem 22sts on to st holder (for back of hand) and turn.
Next row: P13 with A and turn, leaving rem 21sts (for palm) on needle.
Thumb: Work in st st with A on these 13sts for the thumb until thumb measures 2.5cm/1in, change to B and work 4 rows more in st st, ending with a WS purl row.
Shape top of thumb: K1, (k2tog) to end.
Next row: P2tog to end. (7sts)
Cut yarn, leaving a long yarn end, thread end into yarn-darning or embroidery needle and run yarn end through rem sts. Using the yarn end, tightly close and secure top of thumb and sew thumb seam.

Upper hand: With RS facing, place 22sts from st holder for back of hand on to LH needle, join yarn to inside edge, pick up and knit 3sts from base of thumb with RH needle that is holding the 21sts for palm and knit in upper-side stripe patt to end (46sts).
Cont in upper-side stripe patt as set (incorporating the additional 2sts over the base of thumb in the centre of mitten into patt) until work measures 20cm/8in from beg, ending on a WS row. Extra length may be added here if required.

Shape mitten top: Cont in st st in B only, divide sts into two groups of 23sts, for palm and back of hand, and shape top of mittens as 'paws' as folls:
k 23sts and turn, leaving rem sts on st holder. Purl 1 row.
Next row (RS): K2tog, k19, k2tog.
Next row (WS): P2tog, p17, p2tog.
Next row: K2tog, k15, k2tog.
Next row: Cast of 3sts purlwise, p to last 2sts, p2tog.
Next row: Cast off 3sts knitwise, k to last 2sts, k2tog.
Next row: P2tog, p5, p2tog.
Next row: K2tog, p3, k2tog.
Cast off rem 5sts.

Return to the second set of 23sts for back-of-hand side, place these 23sts on to LH needle, join B to inside edge with RS facing and shape top of mitten as given above for palm side.

Right hand

Work as for left hand from * to *. Beg working colourwork patt in st st by foll upper-side stripe-patt chart, beg with a knit row as folls: work rows 1–6 from chart.
Gusset: Keeping patt correct, work gusset for thumb as folls, working the gusset in st st with A:
Next row: K 22sts in patt, pk1 A, k 1 st A, pk1 A, k 21sts in patt.
Next and every WS row: P 21sts in patt, p gusset sts in A, p 22sts in patt.
Next RS row: K 22sts in patt, pk1 A, k 3sts A, pk1 A, k 21sts in patt.
Cont to inc for thumb gusset as set until the row 'k 22sts in patt, pk1 A, k 11sts A, pk1 A, k 21sts in patt' has been worked. (56sts)

Next row: Purl in patt and with A as set.
Divide for thumb: K 35sts in patt and with A as set, place rem 21sts on to st holder (for palm) and turn.
Next row: P13 A and turn, leaving rem 22sts (for back of hand) on needle.
Complete thumb to match left hand by foll earlier 'Thumb' instructions.

Upper hand: With RS facing, place 21sts from st holder for palm on to LH needle, join yarn to inside edge, pick up and knit 3sts from base of thumb with RH needle that is holding the 22sts for back of hand and knit in underside patt to end (46sts).
Cont in patt for palm and back of hand as set (incorporating the additional 2sts over base of thumb in the centre of mitt into patt) until work measures 20cm/8in from beg, ending on a WS row. If extra length was added here for left mitten, work to the same length for right mitten.

Shape mitten top: Work as given for left mitten, but noting that the sts for the back-of-hand side are worked first, followed by the palm-side sts.

Finishing

Sew in all loose yarn ends carefully. With RS together, sew top and side seams using backstitch.

STRIPED DESIGNS

The Striped beret and mittens are great for using up leftover yarns. (Photo: Jo Teasdale)

The beret and mittens are knitted in mohair-rich yarn and worked in the round in stocking stitch in stripes of randomly chosen colours and varying widths throughout, to use up your leftover yarn. Or, these designs can simply be knitted in one colour! They can be worked on double-pointed needles or a circular needle: if using a circular needle, use the magic-loop technique[1] to knit the mittens and to finish the crown of the beret as the number of stitches decreases.

Striped Beret

Size and measurements
One size, to fit an average adult head

Knitted measurements
Circumference at ribbing: 40.5cm/16in
Diameter of laid-flat beret: 29cm/11½in

Materials
Yarn
Knitted in a mohair–wool-blend yarn with approx 75-per-cent-mohair content and 100m/50g (for example, Wool and the Gang Take Care Mohair): 60g total in assorted colours

Recommended needles and accessories
Two circular needles, or two sets of equivalently sized double-pointed needles, are required: one of the size to give the correct tension, for main parts, and one of three sizes smaller, for ribbing.
1 circular 5.5mm (UK 5, US 9) needle for main parts
1 circular 4mm (UK 8, US 6) needle for ribbing
Large-eyed yarn needle

Tension

16sts and 20 rows to 10cm/4in, measured over st st, using a 5.5mm (UK 5, US 9) needle or the size to give the correct tension.

Pattern

Using the smaller needle, cast on 100sts. Arrange cast-on sts and needle points to work in the round, taking care not to twist the sts. All rounds are RS rounds.
Work in k1, p1 rib for 5cm/2in, changing col for stripes as desired throughout.

Change to the larger needle, and work as folls:
Next round: (K9, inc 1 st) to end. (110sts)
Next round: Knit, without shaping.
Next round: (K10, inc 1 st) to end. (120sts)
Work 19 rows straight in st st.
Next shaping round: K2tog, (k7, k2tog) to last st, k1. (106sts)
Next and every alt round: Knit, without shaping.
Next shaping round: (K6, k2tog) to last 2sts, k2. (93sts)
Next shaping round: (K5, k2tog) to last 2sts, k2. (80sts)
Next shaping round: (K4, k2tog) to last 2sts, k2. (67sts)
Next shaping round: (K3, k2tog) to last 2sts, k2. (54sts)
Next shaping round: (K2, k2tog) to last 2sts, k2. (41sts)
Next shaping round: (K1, k2tog) to last 2sts, k2. (28sts)
Next shaping round: (K2tog) to end. (14sts)
Next shaping round: (K1, k2tog) to last 2sts, k2. (10sts)
Cut yarn, leaving a long yarn end, thread end on to yarn needle and run yarn end through rem sts. Using the yarn end, tightly close and secure top of beret crown.

Finishing

Do not press fabric. Sew in all loose yarn ends.

Striped Mittens

Size and measurements
One size, to fit average adult hands

Knitted measurements
Length: 23cm/9in, but length can be varied
Width: 11.5cm/4½in

Materials

Yarn
Knitted in a mohair–wool-blend yarn with approx 75-per-cent-mohair content and 100m/50g (for example, Wool and the Gang Take Care Mohair): 45g total in assorted colours

Recommended needles and accessories
Two short circular needles, or two sets of equivalently sized double-pointed needles, are required: one of the size to give the correct tension, for st-st parts, and one of four sizes smaller, for ribbing.
1 circular 6mm (UK 4, US 10) needle for st-st parts
1 circular 4mm (UK 8, US 6) needle for ribbing
Stitch holder

Details of the Striped beret and mittens, knitted in the round.

Tension

14sts and 18 rows to 10cm/4in, measured over st st, using a 6mm (UK 4, US 10) needle or the size to give the correct tension.

Abbreviation and special stitch

pk1 = make 1 st (m1): pick up strand of yarn running between st closest to LH-needle point and st closest to RH-needle point so that the yarn passes over LH-needle point from front to back and then knit into back of strand

Pattern

Left hand

* Using the smaller needles, cast on 32sts. Arrange cast-on sts and needle points to work in the round, taking care not to twist the sts. All rounds are RS rounds. Place a marker for beg of round.
Work in k2, p2 rib for 3cm/1¼in, changing cols for stripes as desired throughout.

Change to the larger needles, and work 6 rounds in st st. *
Gusset: Work gusset for thumb as folls:
Next round: K14, pk1, k1, pk1, k17.
Next and every alt round: Knit, without shaping.

Next shaping round: K14, pk1, k3, pk1, k17.
Next shaping round: K14, pk1, k5, pk1, k17.
Next shaping round: K14, pk1, k7, pk1, k17.
Next shaping round: K14, pk1, k9, pk1, k17. (42sts)
Next round: Knit, without shaping.
Divide for thumb: K25, place rem 17sts on to st holder (for back of hand) and turn.
Next row: P11 and turn, leaving rem 14sts (for palm) on needle.

Thumb: Work straight in st st in rows on only these 11sts for the thumb for 5cm/2in, ending with a WS purl row.

Top of thumb: K1, (k2tog) to end. (6sts)
Next row: Purl.
Next row: K2tog to end. (3sts)

Cut yarn, leaving a long yarn end, thread end on to yarn needle and run yarn end through rem sts. Using the yarn end, tightly close and secure top of thumb and sew thumb seam.

Upper hand: With RS facing, place 17sts from st holder for back of hand on to LH-needle point (or double-pointed needle), join yarn to inside edge, pick up and knit 3sts from base of thumb with RH-needle point (or double-pointed needle) that is holding the 14sts for palm, and knit to end. (34sts)
Cont in rounds of st st in stripes until work measures 20cm/8in from beg. Extra length may be added here if required.

Shape mitten top: K2, k2tog, k8, k2tog, k4, k2tog, k8, k2tog, k2, k2tog.
Next and every alt round: Knit, without shaping.
Next shaping round: K2, k2tog, k6, k2tog, k4, k2tog, k6, k2tog, k1, k2tog.
Next shaping round: K2, k2tog, k4, k2tog, k4, k2tog, k4, k2tog, k2.
Next shaping round: K2, k2tog, k2, k2tog, k4, k2tog, k2, k2tog, k2. (16sts)
Next round: Knit.
Cast off.

Right hand

Work as for left hand from * to *.
Gusset: Work gusset for thumb as folls:
Next round: K17, pk1, k1, pk1, k14.
Next and every alt round: Knit, without shaping.
Cont to inc gusset as for left thumb until the row 'K17, pk1, k9, pk1, k14' has been worked. (42sts)
Next round: Knit, without shaping.
Divide for thumb: K28, place rem 14sts on to st holder (for palm) and turn.
Next row: P11 and turn, leaving rem 17sts (for back of hand) on needle.
Complete thumb to match that of left hand by foll earlier 'Thumb' instructions.

Upper hand: With RS facing, place 14sts from st holder for palm on to LH-needle point (or double-pointed needle), join yarn to inside edge, pick up and knit 3sts from base of thumb with RH-needle point (or double-pointed needle) that is holding the 17sts for back of hand, and knit to end (34sts).
Cont in rounds of st st in stripes until work measures 20cm/8in from beg. If extra length was added here for left mitten, work to same length for right mitten.

Shape mitten top: Work as given for left mitten. Cast off.

Finishing

Do not press fabric. Turn mitten inside out, sew together mitten-top cast-off edges using backstitch and sew in all loose yarn ends carefully.

APPENDIX

Further Reading

For more information about the history and culture of knitting, the following selected books give several different perspectives and comprehensive information, including bibliographies of further knitting literature. A selection of designer knitting-pattern books from the 1980s is also given. There are many books on knitting techniques, but the ones mentioned below are classics. In addition, there is a plethora of instructional knitting videos available online.

The History and Culture of Knitting

Black, S., *Knitwear in Fashion* (Thames & Hudson, 2002); published in paperback in 2005, with Japanese and German editions in 2003.

The first book to examine and celebrate twentieth-century knitwear design and innovation in relation to contemporary fashion and design around the world – and there are no knitting patterns! It includes sections on high-fashion knitwear and reinvented classics, innovation and experimentation in both arts education and industry, knitted accessories, and creative use of knitting in artworks, interiors and performance. The book is fully illustrated with images of key high-fashion knitwear designs, details of innovative fabrics and artworks.

Black, S., *Knitting: Fashion, Industry, Craft* (V&A Publishing, 2012).
This book surveys 1,700 years of the history of knitting as a craft, as an industry and in fashion, based on the extensive collection of knitted artefacts held in the Victoria and Albert Museum, London, plus other collections. These range from early knitted fragments, caps, stockings and virtuoso one-off

pieces, such as masterpiece carpets, to contemporary designer fashions. The book intertwines the history of technologies used in making knitting through time, the social context in which the items were made and the evolution of technology in the knitting industry and its links to fashions in historical and contemporary knitwear. A timeline maps out key developments in technology, and a comprehensive academic and popular knitting bibliography is included.

Black, S., *Original Knitting* (Unwin Hyman, 1987).
A book of thirty Sandy Black knitting patterns based around the design themes of Graphic, Floral, Heraldic and Ornamental. Some of these patterns have been revisited in the present book, Classic Knits of the 1980s.

Ben-Horin, K., de Meyere, G., and Merrill, J.,
The Sweater: A History (Schiffer Publishing, 2017).
From its humble beginnings as men's underwear, this book traces 300 years of the sweater's history as an aesthetic and craft object, telling the story of its materials and construction, national traditions, fads and fashions.

Dirix. E., *Unravel: Knitwear in Fashion*
(Lannoo Publishers, 2011).
A collection of short essays by curators, cultural theorists and historians on aspects of fashion knitwear, published to accompany the exhibition of the same name shown in the Netherlands in 2011. Topics include the twinset, the cardigan and masculinity, knitting for victory, and the void in knitting.

Fogg, M., *Vintage Fashion Knitwear: Collecting and Wearing Designer Classics* (Carlton, 2010).
A decade-by-decade survey of fashion knitwear through the twentieth century based on the fashion collection of Mark and Cleo Butterfield.

Gschwandtner, S., *KnitKnit: Profiles and Projects from Knitting's New Wave* (Stewart, Tabori and Chang, 2007).
This book brings together twenty-seven key examples of the new wave of experimental knitting practitioners, craftivists and artists working across the USA, Canada and the UK since the new millennium, capturing the new knitting zeitgeist.

Hemmings, J., *In the Loop: Knitting Now*
(Black Dog Publishing, 2010).
A collection of diverse essays on aspects of contemporary knitting practice, based on presentations given at the first academic conference dedicated to the subject of knitting in all its manifestations, In the Loop, that took place in 2008 in the UK. This echoed the resurgence of interest in knitting, particularly in the UK and US, and includes many contributions from knitting practitioners and artists.

Matthews, R., *The Mindfulness in Knitting* (Ivy Press, 2016).
A knitting artist and key instigator of knitting's new wave of craftivism at the turn of the millennium, Rachael Matthews' text casts fresh light on the often meditative craft of knitting and reveals how the simple repetition of plain and purl can in itself nurture well-being.

McDonald, A., *No Idle Hands: The Social History of American Knitting* (Ballantine, 1988).
A comprehensive historical account of the role of women and knitting in American social history from colonial times through to the late twentieth century, documenting changing roles for both women and knitting through times of both war and peace. Patriotism, fashion and family life are all entwined.

Rutt, R., *A History of Handknitting* (Batsford, 1987).
The first comprehensive history of hand knitting, with a particular focus on the British Isles, plus some information on the Americas and Eastern knitting. It includes a focus on techniques with some charted pattern motifs and is an excellent resource for the development of printed knitting patterns and publications. This book was republished by Interweave Press in the USA in 2003 and can be found in the lists of second-hand booksellers.

Rutter, E., *This Golden Fleece: A Journey through Britain's Knitted History* (Granta, 2019).
As indicated in the subtitle, Rutter knitted her way around Britain over a year, uncovering people and stories related to communities shaped by wool and knitting, whilst making some culturally iconic garments such as walking socks, a fisherman's gansey, a shawl and gloves, each chiming with their locations.

Sundbø, A., *Invisible Threads in Knitting*
(Torridal Tweed, 2007).
The third in a series of books telling stories of knitting culture and history in Norway, based on research starting with Sundbø's 1983 purchase of a Norwegian shoddy (recycled-wool) mill and the unfolding of its 'treasures from a ragpile'. The language of traditional knitting symbols is followed as one of many threads, with charts and patterns punctuating the narrative.

Turney, J., *The Culture of Knitting* (Berg, 2009).
An academic study of the culture(s) surrounding knitting, drawing on a range of sources and interviews connected with diverse practices including art, craft, design, fashion and performance. Knitting is also discussed as an everyday practice in the home and from psychological and political perspectives.

Twigger Holroyd, A., *Folk Fashion: Understanding Homemade Clothes* (I.B. Tauris, 2017).
Based on Twigger Holroyd's research for her PhD, and experience from her Keep and Share knitwear label, this academic yet accessible book explores and celebrates the craft of making, remaking and repair in everyday lives and communities, with a focus on knitting. It also introduces the notion of fashion as common land.

Visual Research

Gaimster, J., *Visual Research Methods in Fashion* (Bloomsbury, 2011).
Aimed at fashion students, this book provides some helpful strategies on undertaking systematic and productive visual research.

Murray, A., and Winteringham, G. *Patternity: A New Way of Seeing: The Inspirational Power of Pattern* (Conran Octopus, 2015).
The authors encourage everyone to look beyond the mundane to find inspiration and wonder in the hidden underlying patterns around us everywhere.

Knitting Techniques and Design

The classic resource books for knitting stitch patterns by Barbara Walker have been republished in more recent editions by the Schoolhouse Press since the 1990s and are still available. Montse Stanley is well known as a knitting author and collector and her classic handbook has been republished many times and with two further editions.

Ellen, A., *Hand Knitting: New Directions* (The Crowood Press, 2010).
Ellen, A., *Knitting: Colour, Structure and Design* (The Crowood Press, 2011).
Ellen, A., *Knitting: Stitch-Led Design* (The Crowood Press, 2015).

Stanley, M., *The Handknitter's Handbook* (David & Charles, 1986).
Walker, B., *A Treasury of Knitting Patterns* (Charles Scribner, 1968).
Walker, B., *A Second Treasury of Knitting Patterns* (Charles Scribner, 1970).
Walker, B., *Charted Knitting Designs: A Third Treasury of Knitting Patterns*. (Charles Scribner, 1972).
Walker, B., *A Fourth Treasury of Knitting Patterns* (Charles Scribner, 1975).

Selected Designer Knitting-pattern Books

Black, S., *Original Knitting* (Unwin Hyman, 1987).
Duckworth, S., *Knitting* (Ebury Press, 1988).
Fassett, K., *Glorious Knitting* (Century, 1985).
Fassett, K., *Kaffe Fassett's Pattern Library* (Ebury Press, 2001).
Garton, J. (ed.), *Wild Knitting* (Mitchell Beazley, 1979).
Kagan, S., *The Sasha Kagan Sweater Book* (Dorling Kindersley, 1984).
Kagan, S., *Country Inspiration* (Taunton Press, 2000).
Kagan, S., *The Classic Collection* (GMC Publications, 2011).
Keegan, V., *Designer Machine Knitting* (Pantheon, 1988).
Menkes, S., *The Knitwear Revolution* (Bell & Hyman, 1983).
Roberts, P., *Knitting Book* (W.H. Allen, 1981).
Roberts, P., *Second Knitting Book* (W.H. Allen, 1983).
Seaton, J. and Seaton, J., *The Seaton Collection* (Century, 1989).
Sheard, S. (ed.), *Summer & Winter Knitting: Rowan's Designer Collection* (Century Hutchinson, 1987).

Knitting-design Software

The following is a small selection of some popular software systems designed for hand knitters to produce charts for stitch- and colour-pattern designs, including lace. Costs vary, and others are free, but these paid-for software systems also have a free trial, so you can test them out to see whether their capabilities suit your needs. At the time of writing, only Stitchmastery supports both Macintosh and Windows platforms, but this may change. Support is available either direct from the company or from Ravelry-website groups. Many of the charts in this book were prepared with Stitchmastery software and others by using Adobe Illustrator.

Stitchmastery: www.stitchmastery.com
EnvisioKnit www.envisioknit.com
Knit Visualizer https://knitfoundry.com/knitvisualizer.html

Yarns and Suppliers

Generic Yarn Terms

Different terms are used in the UK and USA for describing yarn thickness – here is a useful table of widely used equivalent terms.

UK term	US term
2ply	0 lace
3ply	1 fingering
4ply	2 sport
double knitting	3 light worsted
aran	4 worsted/fisherman
chunky	5 bulky
super chunky	6 super bulky

The numbers represent the US Craft Yarn Council classification to standardize yarn weights by number as follows:
0 lace; 1 super fine; 2 fine; 3 light; 4 medium; 5 bulky; 6 super bulky (and also 7 jumbo).
For more information, see www.craftyarncouncil.com/standards/yarn-weight-system.

Substituting Yarns

The designs in this book were originally knitted in one of two aran-/medium-weight yarns:
Sandy Black Wool Twist by Rowan Yarns (100-per-cent wool), a light-aran-weight wool with a slightly wavy texture; length 95m (105yd)/50g.

Sandy Black Mohair (75-per-cent mohair, 15-per-cent wool, 10-per-cent nylon binder), a brushed mohair yarn with a fuzzy halo texture; length 98m (106yd)/50g.

For the reknitting of the original patterns for this book, many contemporary yarns have been tested that can be successfully substituted for the original yarns, as seen in the accompanying photos of completed garments and swatches. The designs are generally knitted using needles ranging from 4.5mm (US 7; UK 7) to 6.5mm (US 10.5; UK 3), to give different fabric qualities, and specific yarn guidance is given in each pattern.

Many pure-wool or wool-blend yarns are now available, but some manufacturers interpret 'aran-weight' differently. When selecting yarns for a design, always pay attention to the generic weight of the yarn on the ball band (for example, aran, double-knitting, worsted) and the metres/yards per 50g or 100g. However, an exact match of metres/yards is not absolutely essential, and, therefore, an approximation or range of metres/yards required is given in each pattern, to make finding a suitable yarn easier. It is essential, however, to knit a tension swatch or two and ensure that you can match the tension given for the pattern, particularly for the stitch tension, if not both the stitch tension and the row tension (see Chapter 3).

As for the mohair designs, the standard mohair yarn available in the 1980s was heavier than many of the lace-weight mohair yarns currently popular, but similar yarns are available, for example, Wool and the Gang's Take Care Mohair, which has been used in several designs in this book (see the Graphic, Floral and Accessories chapters). Other heavier mohairs, such as Rico Fashion Mohair or Katia Ingenua, can be found in online stores. Lace-weight mohair is used in two designs, either in combination with another yarn, as in the batwing Iris sweater, or used double, as in the Rosette tunic.

The following list is a small selection of yarn suppliers whose yarns have been utilized in one or more designs featured in this book, many of which use British wools. This is just indicative, and you will have your own favourites. There are now a great many small yarn businesses, some selling fleece and yarns online directly, and several online multiple-brand retailers such as LoveCrafts (www.lovecrafts.com), featuring both mainstream and specialist branded yarns, including from international suppliers. The Ravelry knitting-community website (www.ravelry.com) also has yarn listings and a filter to find local yarn shops in your area.

baa ram ewe
www.baaramewe.co.uk
Woollen yarns with excellent colour ranges using specific Yorkshire breeds of sheep including Masham. The Winterburn-dk colour range is used in both the Lion and Unicorn and Persian Flower designs.

Debbie Bliss Yarns
www.lovecrafts.com
Long-established natural-fibre yarns now available online from LoveCrafts, including Falkland Aran (suitable for knitting the Travelling Vine, Azulejos and Shield designs), Donegal Luxury Tweed Aran (suitable for knitting the Zig-Zag Cable and Rosette designs) and mohair Angel (suitable for knitting the Rosette and Iris designs).

Erika Knight Yarns
www.thehomeofcraft.co.uk
A considered and concise range of specialist wools, linen and cotton, available from the Home of Craft by Thomas Ramsden, and other online stores. The aran-weight yarn Erika Knight Vintage Wool can be used for the Azulejos designs.

Rowan Yarns
http://knitrowan.com
Celebrating over 40 years in business, based in Yorkshire, Rowan provides a wide range of natural-fibre yarns, in broad colour ranges, many developed with Kaffe Fassett, with stockists across the UK and internationally.

The Zig-Zag Cable sweater can be knitted using Rowan Tweed yarns and the Shawl design with a mix of Felted Tweed, Alpaca Soft and worsted double-knitting wools; the Rosette-tunic and Iris-sweater designs are knitted in Kid Classic with Kidsilk Haze, and many of the complementary designs featured were created for Rowan yarns, who also produced Sandy Black Wool Twist in the late 1980s.

West Yorkshire Spinners (WYS)
www.wyspinners.com
Manufacturers of British wool yarns and natural-fibre blends for over 20 years, based in Yorkshire, with a range of stockists across the UK and selling online.

The Travelling Vine design is knitted with WYS 100% Bluefaced Leicester Aran wool.

Wool and the Gang
www.woolandthegang.com
Arrived on the scene in 2008 with a new fun and fashionable take on knitting, specializing in helping new knitters. A broad range of wool, mohair and cotton yarns, with a sustainability agenda. Take Care Mohair has been used for most of the mohair designs in this book, including Fairisle Fun, Triangles, Trailing Roses, Bobbly Grid, Dogtooth and the accessories.

Needle-size Equivalents

The table below shows the generally accepted equivalents (where they exist, and agreement about equivalence isn't universal) between the metric system of needle sizes, the US system and the old-UK system. Note that not all metric sizes have equivalents in the US system, but a size above or below could be used and the tension checked as usual.

Metric	US	Old UK
2mm	0	14
2.25mm	1	13
2.5mm	1½	
2.75mm	2	12
3mm	2½	11
3.25mm	3	10
3.5mm	4	
3.75mm	5	9
4mm	6	8
4.5mm	7	7
5mm	8	6
5.5mm	9	5
6mm	10	4
6.5mm	10½	3
7mm		2
7.5mm		1
8mm	11	0
9mm	13	00
10mm	15	000

ENDNOTES

Preface

1. The teaching of adult numeracy was then in its infancy. With my co-author Diana Coben, I developed *The Numeracy Pack* workbooks for adults, first published in 1984 by the Adult Literacy and Basic Skills Unit and updated in four editions to 2006.
2. Black, S. *Knitwear in Fashion* (Thames & Hudson, 2002) and Black, S. *Knitting: Fashion, Industry, Craft* (V&A Publishing, 2012). These books integrate design, craft and technology through knitting and highlight knitting's social history.

Knitwear in Fashion, and the 1980s Knitwear Revolution

1. The earliest examples of seamless 'knitted' socks with a split toe, dated to the third to fifth centuries CE, were shown by Dorothy Burnham in 1972 to have been made by using a single-eyed sewing needle and short lengths of yarn, with the technique of *naalbinding*, or needle-looping, widely practised in Nordic countries. Samples of true knitting dated to the twelfth or thirteenth centuries exist in museums, together with many examples of later sixteenth-century items including Tudor caps and liturgical gloves. For more information, *see* Black, *Knitting: Fashion, Industry, Craft*, Chapter 1.
2. For further information, *see Knitting: Fashion, Industry, Craft*, pp.97–99.
3. 'Fashion Notes: The Brits' Knits', *The Washington Post* (17th September 1987). An article featuring the publication of *Summer and Winter Knitting*, a book of patterns by British designers, edited by Stephen Sheard of Rowan Yarns.
4. *The Knitwear Revue*, 1983, organized by The British Crafts Centre London, toured to eleven venues across the UK in 1983/84; *Knit One Purl One*, 1985, Victoria and Albert Museum, London, curated by Frances Hinchcliffe; and *Knitting a Common Art*, 1986, a joint Minories Galleries, Colchester, and Crafts Council exhibition, curated by June Freeman and touring to four UK venues.
5. In 1997, a major historical knitting exhibition, *Mils Anys de Disseny en Punt (1000 Years of Design in Knitwear)*, was mounted at the Textile Museum, Terrassa, Spain, based on its own collection, curated by knitting author Montse Stanley, with Eulàlia Morral and Silvia Carbonell. A catalogue was published by the museum.
6. *The New Knitting*, curated by Sandy Black, autumn 1998, first shown at The Knitting and Stitching Show in London, Harrogate, Dublin and Knutsford (Cheshire). Revised in 2000 and shown at the London College of Fashion, touring to The Harley Gallery, Nottinghamshire (2001) and Hawick Museum, Scotland (2002). *The New Knitting* catalogue was published by the London College of Fashion in 2000.
7. *Slipstitch+ New Concepts in Knitting*. Curated by John Allen and shown in 2000 at the Dutch Textile Museum, Tilburg, the Netherlands, with a catalogue published by the museum.
8. *Unravel: Knitwear in Fashion*, curated by Karen van Godtsenhoven and Emanuelle Dirix and shown in autumn 2011 at TwentseWelle Museum, Enchede, the Netherlands; *Breien!* (Knitting!), curated by Geineke Arnolli and shown in spring 2016 at the Fries Museum, Leeuwarden, the Netherlands.
9. *Visionary Knitwear*, curated by Sandy Black, shown at the Fashion and Textile Museum in London in autumn 2014,

alongside *Knitwear: Chanel to Westwood*, a major survey of twentieth-century knitted fashions, curated by Denis Nothdruft, based on the collection of Mark and Cleo Butterfield.

2 Design and Inspiration

1. Mary Harris, an educationalist, devised a British Council exhibition, *Common Threads*, in 1988, to demonstrate the many mathematical principles involved in textiles including those made with knitting, weaving and basketmaking. She memorably discussed the concept of lagging a bent pipe and used babies' socks to demonstrate symmetry. The archive is now housed at the Constance Howard Textile Archive, Goldsmiths, University of London, London.
2. *The Complete Book of Needlecraft* (Marshall Cavendish Editions, 1978).
3. *See* the Patternity website at www.patternity.org.
4. *The Complete Book of Needlecraft* (Marshall Cavendish Editions, 1978).

3 Knitting-Pattern Fundamentals

1. For many examples and ideas, *see* Alison Ellen's books *Hand Knitting: New Directions* (The Crowood Press, 2010), *Knitting: Colour, Structure and Design* (The Crowood Press, 2011) and *Knitting: Stitch-Led Design* (The Crowood Press, 2015).
2. This stitch is explained in many online how-to articles and video tutorials – just search for 'mattress stitch'.

4 Working with Colour and Imagery

1. Sourced from a reputable manufacturer where the animals' welfare was assured, based in France.

5 Designing Knitwear

1. *Summer and Winter Knitting* (Century Hutchinson, 1987), edited by Stephen Sheard.

7 Graphic

1. For more information, *see* Black, *Knitting: Fashion, Industry, Craft*, pp.58–61.

8 Floral

1. For more historical information, *see* Black, *Knitting: Fashion, Industry, Craft*, Chapter 1.
2. For examples of designers' work, *see* Black, *Knitting: Fashion, Industry, Craft*, pp.173–183.

11 Accessories

1. This technique is explained in many online video tutorials – just search for 'magic loop'.

Image captions (Chapter 2)

1. *The World We Live In*, special edition for young readers (Collins, 1957).
2. *The World We Live In*, special edition for young readers (Collins, 1957).

ACKNOWLEDGEMENTS

Many people have sustained the journey of making this book, most importantly my husband Morris, whose unfailing support has made it possible – not least his photography of the knitting details and documents for the book. Thanks for support are also due to Linda, Rosie, Annie and the entire family – I look forward to seeing more of you all. Thanks to my friends Diana and Stephanie who were there in the 1980s and are always happy to talk and share memories. Sincere thanks also to Diana for reading drafts.

I would like to express my gratitude to the knitters who so wonderfully recreated my 1980s designs with great enthusiasm: Tom van Deijnen, Wendy Speller, Judy Wilmot, Ali Firth (and her mum), Sarah Elson, Gillian de la Motte, Annie Black, Jennie Cox and her team, and Joao Caldas.

Special thanks are due to Jo Teasdale for the fantastic new-knitwear photography and to the fabulous models Lili, Ioasia, Daisy and Sarah. Thanks too to Maria Price for her valuable advice and assistance. I must also acknowledge the original photographers Barbara Bellingham, David McIntyre and Paul Dennison, some of whose 1980s images are included.

During the preparation of the graphics for the book, I was ably assisted by Rachel Graham and Bianca Bott from the University of Brighton Fashion and Textiles department – thanks for your contributions, and to Caterina Radvan for connecting us.

Many thanks to the Crowood team for bringing the book to fruition.

I am delighted to bring these designs to a new audience and so must recognize here the work of the original knitters and the entire Sandy Black Original Knits team from the 1980s, especially my partner in the business, Kevin Bolger.

INDEX

Italic numbers indicate the page number of a photograph

A
abbreviations 91–3
aftercare 61
Arches tunic *114,* 115
Artwork by Jane and Patrick Gottelier 21, *22,* 23
Azulejos tunic and jacket 15, 197–210

B
blocking 60
bobbins 64
bobbles 91
Bobbly Grid cardigan 14, 15, 118, 142–7
British knitwear designers 7, 21–22
    Artwork by Jane and Patrick Gottelier 21, *22,* 23
    Carrie White 24
    Jamie and Jessie Seaton 21, 263
    Kaffe Fassett 21, *22,* 23, 24, 25, 68, 263
    Martin Kidman for Joseph 21, *22*
    Patricia Roberts 21, *22,* 24, 25, *26, 32,* 263
    Sandy Black 7, *9–11, 18,* 23–5, *26,* 117, 261–2, 266
    Sasha Kagan 21, *22,* 24, 32, 263
    Susan Duckworth 21, *22,* 24
    Susie Freeman 24
    Vanessa Keegan 21, *22, 24,* 263
    Warm and Wonderful 32
butterfly twists 64, 138

C
cables 90, 106
charting graphic designs 68–9, 75–7
charts 14, 53–6, 69
    colour charts 15, 53–4, 221
    stitch-pattern charts 55, 108–10
Chevron Rib cardigan *115*
circular knitting 15
Cloisonné cardigan *229*
Coat of Arms coat *174*
Cobweb mosaic sweater *37*
collecting 42–3
colour-block knitting (*see* intarsia) 63–4, 118, 175, 189
colourways 66–9
crochet 29
culture of knitting, reference 261–3
Curves cardigan 118, *149*

D

designer knitting books 263
designer knitwear 7, 21–4, 32
designing a garment process 73–83,
    example: Heraldic sweaters 74–7
    example: Scroll gilet design 77–83
    exercise: 10 design stages 83–5
Dogtooth designs 14, 15, 118
    Dogtooth jacket 129–33
    Dogtooth sweater 133–5
    Dogtooth sweater calculations 72–3
duplicate stitch (*see* Swiss darning) 58–60
Duckworth, Susan 21, *22*, 24

E

embroidery stitches 56–8
    French knot 56, *57*
    chain stitch 56, *57*
    lazy daisy stitch 56, *58*
    stem stitch 56, *58*

F

Fair Isle (*see* stranded colourwork) 50, 63, 65–6, 117
Fairisle Fun sweater 15, 117, 119–27
fashion 10–11, 20–27, 117, 261–3
Fassett, Kaffe 21, *22*, 23, 24, 25, 68, 263
finishing techniques 60
Fleur de Lys sweater *176*
fully fashioned 31, 50

G

garter stitch 90
gauge (tension) 51–2, 68, 69, 71, 82
Grape Vine pattern chart 109

H

hand knitting 19, 20, 24, 29, 32, 50
history of knitting and reference 19–23, 261–2

I

inspiration 32–43
intarsia technique 8, 63–4
    machine knitted *6*, 8, *22*, 26, 33–5, *36*, *62*, *149*, *174*
    hand knitted *22*, 38–9, 63–4, 73, 89, 118, *148*, 175, 189, 196
    in-the-round (seamless) knitting 14, 29–32, *43*, 50, 259

Iris batwing sweater 15, 160–4
    Iris cardigan *164*

K

Kagan, Sasha 21, *22*, 24, 32, 263
Keegan, Vanessa 21, *22*, 24, 263
Kidman, Martin 21, *22*
knitting exhibitions 23–7, 266
knitting in the round (seamless knitting) 14, 29–32, *43*, 50, 259
knitting kit(s) 7, *11*, 24, 117, 175
knitting techniques and stitch reference 263
knitwear revolution 11, 14, 19–23

L

landscape sweaters *6*, 8, 33–6, 39–40, *62*, *67*
Leopard mittens 245–7
Leopard scarf 15, *233*, 238–44
Lion and Unicorn sweater 14, 15, 188–93
    sweater design stages 74–7
Lotus Flower jacket *196*

M

machine knitting 8, 23, *31*
    domestic 19, 23, 33, 45
    industrial 19, 21, 23
    invention 19, 29, 31
Matisse-inspired designs 149
Medieval Tile sweater *73*, *83*, *196*, 211
Merrygoround sweater *229*
modular (patchwork-tile) knitting 77–83, 195–6, 197–211
moss stitch 90

N

needle-size equivalents 265

O

Oval Window motif chart 110

P

partial knitting 46
patchwork 'tile' (modular) designs 77–83, 195–6, 197–211
pattern calculations 71
    example: Dogtooth sweater pattern 72–3
Persian Flower tunic 15, 165–73
Posy Trellis cardigan *57*, *67*, *150*, 151, 173
proportional graph paper 68–9, 75–6

R

Rectangles sweater *69*
reverse stocking stitch (stockinette) 90
Roberts, Patricia 21, *22*, 24, 25, *26*, *32*, 263
Rose jacket *173*
Rosette tunic 15, 196, 212–9
Rowan Yarns 21, 68, 78, 89, 97, 98, 265

S

Sandy Black Original Knits 7, 10, 13, 23, 89, 97, *174*, *261*
Scroll cardigan *114*, 115
Scroll motif chart 108
Scroll gilet modular design process 65, 77–83
seaming 61
seamless knitting 29–31, 50
Seaton, Jamie and Jessie 21, 263
shaping 14, *29, 30,* 53, 56
Shawl cardigan 14, 15, 196, 220–9
Shield sweater and cardigan 14, 15, 74, 177–87
Siamese Cat scarf 15, 234–7
Small Shields sweater *176*
sock heel construction 30–31
software for knit design 67, 69, 84, 263
Stained Glass sweater 118, *148*
    cardigan *148*
stocking stitch (stockinette) 48–50, 90
stranded-colourwork (or Fair Isle) technique 65–6
Striped beret and mittens 15, 257–60
structure of knit fabric 49–50
Swiss darning (duplicate stitch) 58–60

T

Tapestry Flower patchwork jacket *70*
    patchwork coat *195*, 196
    tunic *152*
tension (gauge) 51–2, 71
Textural bolero *115*
The Knitwear Revolution book *18,* 19, 152
Tiger mittens 254–6
Tiger scarf 15, 248–53
toe socks 19
Trailing Roses sweater 15, 153–9
Travelling Vine tunic 15, 103–13
Triangles sweater 15, 52, 118, 136–41
twisted rib 91
twisted stitches 90

V

Vase of Flowers *18,* 23, 25, *26, 66,* 152, 173
visual research 40–42, 263

W

Wild Knitting book 9, 231

Y

yarns and suppliers 264

Z

Zig-Zag Cable sweater 14, 15, 96–102

RELATED TITLES FROM CROWOOD

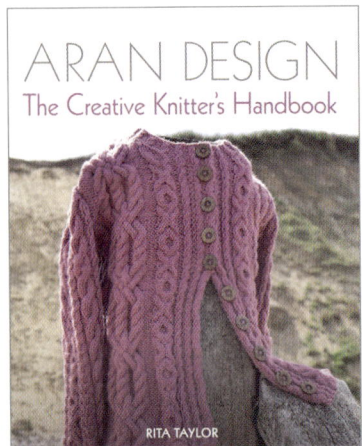

ISBN 978 1 78500 407 0

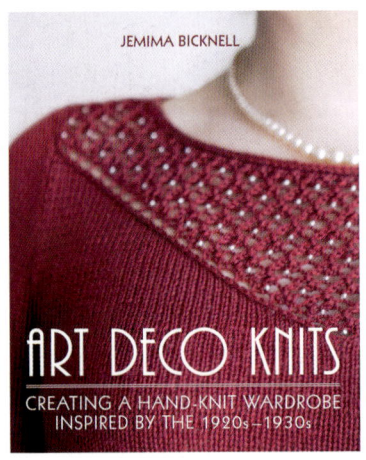

ISBN 978 1 78500 549 7

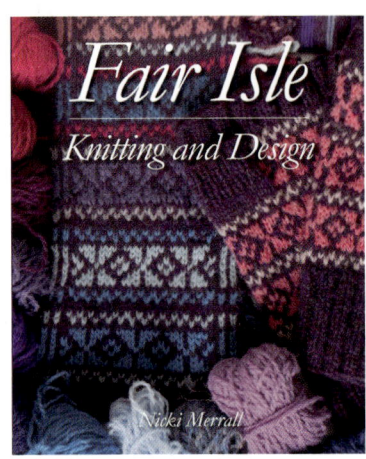

ISBN 978 1 78500 697 5

ISBN 978 1 78500 569 5

ISBN 978 1 78500 789 7

ISBN 978 1 78500 507 7

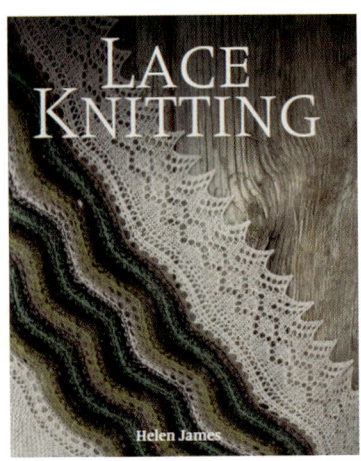

ISBN 978 178500 571 8

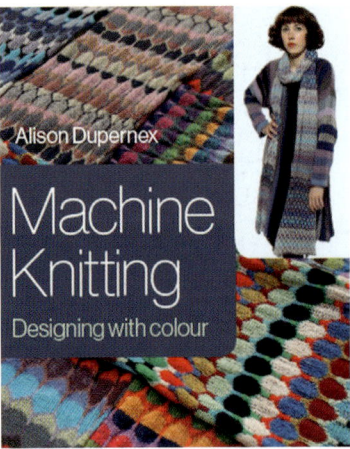

ISBN 978 1 78500 685 2

ISBN 978 1 78500 665 4